To Kevin,

Because he cares about good movies and the story behind them

Nate Swanson
October 25, 2019

Find "Download This Movie For a Reel Good Time" on the Internet

DOWNLOAD THIS MOVIE

For a Reel Good Time

Second Edition

BY

NATHAN SWANSON

Scott Faber

PHOTOGRAPHY STUDIO

scottfaber.com

Copyright © 2018 Go Fetch Publications.
Author contact: natswanson@me.com
Scott Faber, Author Photo
Carla Osborne, Book Design
Tim Osborne, Cover Photo
Jeanette BonDurant, Biographical Notes

All rights reserved. No part of this book may be reproduced, stored,
or transmitted by any means—whether auditory, graphic, mechanical,
or electronic—without written permission of the author, except in the
case of brief excerpts used in critical articles and reviews. Unauthorized
reproduction of any part of this work is illegal and is punishable by law.

Summary: *Download This Movie for a Reel Good Time* references the true-life facts of
what went on behind the camera during the production of 70 films, spanning the years
1933-1992. First published in 2010, the updated 2017 edition includes an additional
30 films with capsule recommendations, spanning the years 1927-2005. Readers can
discover what influenced the final version of the film, why specific actors or directors
were hired, which scenes were cut, and what cultural or political ideas were popular
at the time of production. Eavesdrop on creative discussions and outcomes and know
where the film placed in the careers of the principal cast and production crew, all of
which serves to heighten the interest and pleasures of viewing special and classic movies.

ISBN: 978-1-4834-7557-8 (sc)
ISBN: 978-1-4834-7558-5 (hc)
ISBN: 978-1-4834-7556-1 (e)

Because of the dynamic nature of the Internet, any web addresses or links contained in
this book may have changed since publication and may no longer be valid. The views
expressed in this work are solely those of the author and do not necessarily reflect the
views of the publisher, and the publisher hereby disclaims any responsibility for them.

Any people depicted in stock imagery provided by Thinkstock are models,
and such images are being used for illustrative purposes only.
Certain stock imagery © Thinkstock.

Rev. date: 2/12/2018

Contents

Dedication vi

Acknowledgements 1

Introduction 3

Download This Movie 11

Epilogue. 384

More Downloadable Movies. 385

Bibliographical Essay. 395

Glossary. 401

Dedication

This book is dedicated with appreciation to people, who, like myself, take their enjoyment of movies to another level. It's for those who seek reality in a profession devoted to make believe. They want to know what real things occurred when the film was being made. *Download This Movie for a Reel Good Time* is dedicated to people who find great satisfaction in knowing the story behind the story.

Acknowledgements

A special thank you goes to my mom, dad and grandmother. They understood and accepted my early and ongoing intense passion for film. My mother especially offered encouragement, once allowing me to stay home from school to watch a rarely broadcast classic film. A special note of appreciation goes to my cousin Jeanette Bondurant for writing the biographical notes.

Donna Martinez is a writer's best friend. She shortened copy, added detail to structure and proved to be a wonderful sounding board. Tim Clark and Carla Osborne came up with a beautifully creative book cover and design. The results are better than one could have imagined. Incidentally, the small toy film projector was a gift I received from Santa in 1970.

Scott Faber photographed models and actors in Hollywood before relocating to North Carolina. It was an honor to receive the same high degree of patience and expertise that he provided to celebrities whose greatest asset is their appearance.

I have been fortunate to meet and interview some great and gracious talent in the entertainment industry. The late great writer-actor Paul Mantee spoke to me from his home in Southern California to discuss his starring role in **Robinson Crusoe on Mars** (1964).

Actress Senta Berger offered a unique perspective on the Matt Helm series that starred Dean Martin. Her career continues to thrive in Europe and I treasure our years of corresponding across the Atlantic. Sue Ane Langdon, a featured player in **A Guide for the Married Man** (1967), also spoke at length on her experience in that hysterical film. Tina Louise (movie star Ginger Grant) and Russell Johnson (the professor) answer to my question "what did you do to find work after Gilligan's Island?" was inspirational. Actor and artist N. N. Williams Jr. (known in the movies as Aron Kincaid) was generous with insight through long distance correspondence.

Director Stanley Kramer spirited response to my inquiry

concerning **It's a Mad, Mad, Mad, Mad World** (1963) is framed and hangs on the wall in my den. Mitzi Gaynor, Tony Curtis, Debbie Reynolds, Andy Williams, Tab Hunter, Barbara Luna, Dennis Cole, Kathy Garver, Diane McBain, Julie Parrish, Andrew Prine, Caroline Munro, Jane Fonda, John Kerr, Grace Lee Whitney, Leslie Easterbrook, Patty Duke, Alice Faye, Margaret O'Brien, Jane Powell, Marsha Hunt and Liv Ullmann shared their personal experiences with me after their performance or public appearance.

Some of my most satisfying moments of all time have occurred when watching a movie theatre with friends and we witness the unfolding of a very good story. After the experience, there's a discussion over coffee or during the drive home. Some of the conversations I've had over the years with friends naturally seep its way to this work.

I thank everyone who has shared their friendship and time with me at the movies.

Introduction

Not too long ago, there were two ways to view a movie. We could travel to a local movie theatre, purchase a ticket and watch the story magically unfold on the big screen. The other choice was to watch a movie on television a few years after it had run its course in the theatres. Movie theatre owners or network executives determined what movie we were going to see and when we would see it. Going to the movies for many people was a regular event and a social occasion. People might have gone to see a different film each week. Their children might have attended a matinee each Saturday. Entire families would go to the local cinema or gather around the television set.

I remember this style of watching movies and television. Viewing **The Wizard of Oz** (1939) was a yearly event for me when I was growing up in the Midwest (not Kansas but Illinois!). It was almost an annual rite of passage. CBS aired this classic each spring. Millions of young people knew what time and channel to choose and we adjusted our lives accordingly. There was a buzz in the classroom, in the school yard or on the bus. My mom even bought my friends and siblings candy bars to enjoy with the spectacle viewed on our color television set.

The way we think about viewing movies is very different today. In addition to multi-screen theatres, we can enjoy movies on television through multiple cable channels or pay-per-view. We have vending machines that disperse movies like soda pop. We can have movies mailed to our residence or we can rent or purchase them from retailers. A copy of **The Wizard of Oz** now sits in my movie library.

Thanks to the internet, we have access to thousands of titles—all we have to do is select the movie, pick a convenient time and choose the place.

This can be any room in the house, in the entertainment center, on top of a desk, in our laps, on a cell phone, with a handheld device or in the backseat of an automobile. We have content on demand, when, where and how you want it. A scheduled appointment with your television set is no longer necessary.

Advances in accessing movies provide us with a significant amount of control. Dad may be in the den, mom may be in the bedroom, sis may be in the basement and brother may be in a tree house. But they are all able to watch a film of their choice when it's convenient for them. People have thousands of movie choices available to download on their home computer and TV system.

High definition and digital technology can also upgrade the picture and sound quality of movies produced 75 years ago. Our visual senses can detect a brighter, sharper image. We are able to hear a richer quality to the dialogue, music and sound effects through electronic manipulation.

Viewing a favorite film with higher definition and sound quality at your convenience is great news for people who enjoy the movie experience. When we decide to browse for an interesting title, this search is often time-consuming, perhaps overwhelming to find something worthwhile.

It becomes more complicated when your movie partners have different interests and there is great difficulty in finding common ground. I'm here to help. If anything, *Download This Movie for a Reel Good Time* saves vexation when there are many choices but little time. *Download This Movie* introduces you to some fine movies that you may not have thought about watching, but should.

Using download in the title is my strong recommendation to view the film. Not to be taken literally, *Download This Movie* urges one to view a specific movie available from many sources and not necessarily the internet. How one locates their selection may be far removed from downloading.

The subtitle *for a Reel Good Time* purposely blends old technology with the new. The reel that holds and spins the tape is now obsolete with digital and wireless applications.

I make recommendations on 70 films. They are my personal list. These films are salient to me, but not to me alone. Each recommendation represents a small microcosm of the film industry; each film chapter reflects parts of movie culture, history and reference.

Rating movie pleasure is complicated because interests, personal tastes, and experiences vary tremendously. Some may be bold and ask who is Nathan Swanson and what does he know about movies? What standards does Nathan use to justify this particular group? And why should we listen to Nathan?

Let me explain it this way. I'm not unlike the fellow who would approach a friendly face at a party while standing in front of the hors d'oeuvres and ask if she's seen this week's most popular movie playing on the big screen. Moreover, if she seems remotely interested and a long conversation follows, I may recite the complete movie list of the actor being discussed, biographical notes, and other lesser-known career facts that one might not be expecting to hear. You see, I really love movies. I mean I *really love movies*, especially when I know the stories behind them. In my lifetime I've spent countless hours in a dark theatre, in front of a television set or reading articles and books that report on the movie industry. Do you ever wonder what went on behind the camera or before the production began? Knowing the *story* behind the story offers a richer, more complete and multi-dimensional view of the work. This information makes the movie more interesting and pleasurable to watch.

My interest in film goes beyond passive viewing. I'm curious. I want to know more. I think it's interesting to know what Alfred Hitchcock was thinking when he hired Raymond Burr to play the villain in **Rear Window** (1954). Or what prompted Frank Sinatra to pull **The Manchurian Candidate** (1962) from public viewing for two decades. What audience reaction influenced the final outcome of **Sunset Boulevard** (1950), which actor was offered the role first or got fired, who played sexual politics, or what was happening in the world when the project was being made?

Where does the film fit in the body of work of the principal cast or director? Was somebody's career on a winning or waning streak? I approach each film looking at how actors, producers, screenwriters and the audience can yield a powerful influence over the reputation of a film. These nuggets and more are delivered in *Download This Movie*.

This collection includes films that are original, trend setting, action packed, thoughtful, suspenseful or even strange. The major players involved in the creation of these films are at the height of their creative powers. These films do fulfill their aspirations. More importantly, to be included in this group, strong emotions must be stimulated by the end of the film. My rule of thumb: if we're still thinking, feeling and experiencing some aspect of the film three days after viewing, it was worth your time and attention.

A movie also becomes special when all the bits and pieces of the artistry and engineering jell. These bits and pieces include the actors, actresses, costumes, screenplay, editing, cinematography, visual effects and music.

The actor or actress should wear the role played like a glove. They need appearance and ability to convince the audience that they are real. Their costumes should be an extension of this reality. The screenplay should be a rollercoaster of a ride from point A to point Z but not in any particular order. There should be diversions, unexpected twists and turns. The editing should keep this rollercoaster on task and moving forward toward a conclusion.

The cinematography should take advantage of as many possibilities that the mechanics of film offers. The visual effects should be what the advertising for **Superman** (1978) claimed: "You'll Believe a Man Can Fly!." The music should evoke the appropriate mood and heighten interest through sequencing and pace.

This collection of film ranges from 1933 (**Dinner at Eight**) to 1992 (**Defending your Life**). **Dinner at Eight** offers a view of life during the height of the depression in 1933. As the film unfolds, intimate and revealing social interactions take place over dinner. You may be surprised to learn that what is going on at this dinner party is as relevant today as it was in 1933.

Defending your Life is pretty radical. It's one definition of the meaning of life. It's about reincarnation. Against our will, we begin to think in unfamiliar ways. It's creative without being too cynical.

In between 1933 vintage and 1992 modern art, there's something for everyone.

The Graduate (1967) is scintillating because we have a villain, Mrs. Robinson, seducing a naïve young man in more ways than one. His seduction is one of the funniest moments on film.

The Loved One (1965) is an exposé on an unfunny subject—the funeral industry. It's one of the strangest movies ever made.

The screenplay for **Dirty Harry** (1971) deserves a closer analysis. Parts are inspired by the Zodiac killer, a real serial murderer that terrorized California in the late 60s. And wouldn't it be interesting to know what well decorated war hero was first asked to play this psychopath?

That Man from Rio (1964) is a French soufflé. It rises in the oven. This import has beautiful locations and young people experiencing the joy of life.

Attack of the 50 Foot Woman (1958) was written with some degree of seriousness during the beginning phase of space exploration. It's a "fun film" in today's more sophisticated world.

Robinson Crusoe on Mars (1964) is a remarkable science fiction film, a clever reworking of Daniel Defoe's classic novel.

Mogambo (1953) is a grand adventure tale filmed on location in Africa. It boasts three beautiful and exciting movie stars: Ava Gardner, Clark Gable and Grace Kelly.

Fasten your seatbelts for Bette Davis' best film **All About Eve** (1950). There's also Bruce Lee, Robert DeNiro, Lucille Ball and many more.

Just as the television and movie industries have changed through new technology, celebrity doesn't offer the same meaning that it once did. Today's actors don't have the glamour or longevity of stars from the past. Actors and actresses were once "manufactured" into movie stars as movie studios groomed these contracted employees before being paraded in front of an audience. An army of professionals were assigned to make actors and actresses appear larger than life. These efforts were very successful. However, this practice left us two generations ago. In another era, there might have been half a dozen new names in the movies each quarter.

Now we're lucky if we have one each year. Before, we would eagerly wait for a movie star's next project. Stars made one to three movies a year. We see less and less of this happening today. The last large grouping of "manufactured personalities" occurred in the late 50s and early 60s. Most of these folks are retired. But we know they left an incredible body of work waiting to be rediscovered. You may also be privileged to hear their thoughts on the DVD audio commentary. As the film plays they offer comments in real time as the action progresses. Their comments can be serious or entertaining. The discussion offers information that was not disclosed to audience members until now.

For example, **The Haunting** (1963) reunited Director Robert Wise, Writer Nelson Gidding and actors Claire Bloom, Julie Harris, Richard Johnson and Russ Tamblyn. The result was a more in-depth and fascinating analysis of the characters and actions, plus anecdotes on staging and special effects. I typically avoid engaging the commentary when watching a film for the first time. I want to make certain nothing detracts from what the filmmaker intended. If my enthusiasm contains curiosity, I return for a second viewing and allow the commentary to fill in the blanks.

Download This Movie will introduce you to those in an industry you may not be familiar with or have forgotten. If you like Bruce Willis, you'll certainly be thrilled by Lee Marvin. Annette Bening or Nicole Kidman fans may enjoy Ava Gardner. In addition to discovering or reacquainting ourselves with screen friends, *Download This Movie* allows us to visit exotic places, hear what interesting and sophisticated people say to each other and references significant cultural events. This collection of movies encourages us to think, laugh, cry, sit up straight, and maybe even be a better person. They move us to another level of pleasure.

A movie must fulfill a goal if it is to produce an emotional reaction or pleasure. If it's trying to be funny, then please let it be funny. If it's supposed to make us think or react strongly to some issue, then it should perform in an engaging and interesting manner. The film must have a clearly defined purpose, make an impact, strike an emotion and offer some sort of solution. It should take on a human quality and breathe. There should be a heart, a soul, a brain and eyes to the work. This is not an easy task to accomplish.

When it is accomplished, the subject is powerful enough to draw strangers together at parties. In fact, movie talk may be the perfect and safe opening line to spur conversation. Movies offer reference points to our lives. For example, a man remembers watching **A Guide to the Married Man** (1967) at the Avon Theatre in Decatur, Illinois during the blizzard of '67. After the movie, his assistance was accepted by a stranded woman and she later became his wife. The movie will always hold special significance for him, marking a turning point in his life. Movies can also be very helpful for two people going out on a first date. Seeing the same film and exchanging responses creates a bond that bring people together. Most movie "addicts" are familiar with John Wayne, Katharine Hepburn, Sean Connery and other stars with long and distinguished careers. They are actors that two strangers can talk about and proceed to discover commonalties. Films connect us and we all need to feel connected in some way.

Much has already been written about gold plated classics. While **Gone with the Wind** (1939) and **Citizen Kane** (1941) deserve to be in a collection such as this, they are not included. Everybody knows about them and to further examine their appeal would be redundant. They've already been downloaded quite a few times for sure. I could scratch for a twist, but to reveal that the actor who played Melanie's newborn in **Gone with the Wind** grew up and married Raquel Welch may not be pertinent to what is arguably the best film ever made.

However, included are a couple of films that would make nearly everyone's top 25. They are here only because I believe what I have written about them hasn't been discussed before. The purpose of this collection is to open our eyes to lesser-known objects of art that still glow or to gain a wider appreciation of something that's been around for quite some time and needs to be earmarked for viewing.

Listen, choose and enjoy.

Nathan Swanson

DOWNLOAD THIS MOVIE

1. **A Guide for the Married Man** (1967) *Protecting your loved ones is never easy, kid.*

2. **A Letter to Three Wives** (1949) *We're beginning to behave like a movie about a women's prison.*

3. **All About Eve** (1950) *Fasten your seatbelts. It's going to be a bumpy night.*

4. **A Night to Remember** (1958) *I don't think I'll ever feel sure about anything.*

5. **A Shock to the System** (1987) *I forgive you for failing.*

6. **Attack of the 50 Foot Woman** (1958) *Harry, I saw a satellite tonight!*

7. **The Bad Seed** (1955) *She knows what she wants and asks for it.*

8. **The Bank Dick** (1940) *We're making motion picture history here.*

9. **Beach Blanket Bingo** (1964) *Why me? Why me all the time?*

10. **Beat the Devil** (1954) *They're desperate characters—not one looked at my legs.*

11. **The Big Heat** (1953) *We're sisters under the mink.*

12. **The Blues Brothers** (1980) *We're on a mission from God!*

13. **Bob & Carol & Ted & Alice** (1969) *First, we'll have an orgy. Then we'll go see Tony Bennett.*

14. **Bye-Bye Birdie** (1963) *The next time I have a daughter, I hope it's a boy.*

15. **Charade** (1963) *I'm beginning to think women make the best spies.*

16. **Cool Hand Luke** (1967) *What we've got here is failure to communicate.*

17. **The Court Jester** (1956) *The king of jesters, the jesters of kings.*

18. **Defending your Life** (1992) *She's going to have a field day with this one.*

19. **Detour** (1948) *It was stupid for me to leave all that money on a dead man.*

20. **Dinner at Eight** (1933) *But everybody's broke, darling.*

21. **Dirty Harry** (1971) *Well, I'm all broken up about that man's rights.*

22. **Dr. Strangelove** (1964) *You can't fight in here, this is the war room!*

23. **$ (Dollars)** (1972) *Stick with it, Joe!*

24. **Eating Raoul** (1982) *He was a man. Now he's just a bag of garbage.*

25. **Enter the Dragon** (1973) *Never take your eyes off your opponent, even when you bow.*

26. **Emperor of the North** (1972) *Sounds like a ghost story to me.*

27. **Female on the Beach** (1955) *A woman's no good to a man unless she's a little afraid of him.*

28. **The Front** (1976) *So who can you sue?*

29. **The Graduate** (1967) *I'll see you later, Mrs. Robinson.*

30. **The Haunting** (1963) *Psychic phenomena is subject to certain laws.*

31. **It's a Mad, Mad, Mad, Mad World** (1963) *We're the ones with the Imperial and we're running last?*

32. **It Should Happen to You** (1954) *Would you come out and look at one sign?*

33. **Kiss Me, Stupid** (1964) *If you got what it takes, sooner or later somebody will take what you got.*

34. **The King of Comedy** (1982) *Is Mr. Langford expecting you?*

35. **Lolita** (1962) *How did we produce such a little beast?*

36. **The Long, Long Trailer** (1953) *Think of it as a train—40' of train.*

37. **Lonely are the Brave** (1962) *If it didn't take men to make babies …*

38. **Lord, Love a Duck** (1966) *Don't you realize these things are supposed to be dirty?*

39. **The Loved One** (1965) *Whispering Glades is a way of life.*

40. **The Love Bug** (1968) *Without a real car, I'm only half a man.*

41. **The Manchurian Candidate** (1962) *Raymond Shaw is the kindest, bravest, warmest, most wonderful human being I've ever known in my life.*

42. **Midnight Run** (1988) *I already know you all of two minutes and already I don't like you!*

43. **Mogambo** (1953) *Can't you get me a canoe, a truck or a pair of roller skates, anything to get me out of here?*

44. **Murder at the Gallop** (1963) *I shall have to investigate this myself.*

45. **Nashville** (1975) *This isn't Dallas! This is Nashville!*

46. **Network** (1976) *I'm mad as hell, and I'm not going to take it anymore!*

47. **One, Two, Three** (1961) *Is everybody in this world corrupt?*

48. **On Her Majesty's Secret Service** (1969) *This never happened to the other fella.*

49. **Ordinary People** (1980) *I would like to be in more control.*

50. **The Pajama Game** (1957) *My, but you're an impetuous girl.*

51. **The Pink Panther Strikes Again** (1976) *I thought you said your dog did not bite!*

52. **Point Blank** (1968) *We blew it.*

53. **The Rainmaker** (1956) *Can a woman take lessons in being a woman?*

54. **Raising Arizona** (1987) *You go right back up there and get me a toddler.*

55. **Rear Window** (1954) *What people ought to do is get outside their own house and look in for a change.*

56. **Reservoir Dogs** (1982) *All right ramblers, let's get rambling!*

57. **Robinson Crusoe on Mars** (1964) *A-Okay.*

58. **Roger & Me** (1987) *Well, the million tourists never came to Flint.*

59. **Ruthless People** (1985) *I've been kidnapped by Kmart!*

60. **The Silencers** (1965) *Why am I here? A guy could get killed doing this.*

61. **Slap Shot** (1977) *I got a good deal on those boys. The scout said they showed a lot of promise.*

62. **Sunset Blvd.** (1950) *I am big. It's the pictures that got small.*

63. **Superman** (1978) *We all have our little faults. Mine happens to be in California.*

64. **Sweet Charity** (1969) *I want very much to change my life.*

65. **That Man From Rio** (1964) *Whoa. Wait till Lebel hears about this.*

66. **Thelma and Louise** (1992) *Let's keep going.*

67. **This is Spinal Tap** (1987) *The sights, sounds, and smells of a hard working rock band.*

68. **Tiger Bay** (1959) *Don't let your emotions run your life.*

69. **Till The End of Time** (1946) *Are you all in one piece?*

70. **Who's Afraid of Virginia Woolf** (1966) *You can stand it. You married me for it.*

Chapter 1
A Guide for the Married Man

"Protecting your loved ones is never easy, kid."
—Ed Stander

A Guide for the Married Man is a very funny and creative movie from 1967. But it comes with a warning to wives: there are lots of plunging necklines and tight, short dresses to titillate husbands. It also broaches a subject that is not so funny—cheating on your spouse. In its defense, though, it approaches the subject with a degree of finesse not normally found in an era when antics outside the married bedroom could only be implied or heard about, and not actually seen in the movies. Director Gene Kelly handles the subject with a surprising degree of expertise, transforming what could have been just another tasteless (and innocuous) sex comedy from the 60s, into a very fun film with some very funny people.

Based on the novel by Frank Tarloff, the movie casts Walter Matthau as a happily married man who, with some coaxing from his friend, decides to cheat on his wife. It's not like he has a serious inclination to do it. He just decides to do it, because as guest star Jeffrey Hunter says, "it's there." Most would find this an odd reaction from someone who appears to have everything: a successful career, a beautiful wife and daughter, and a comfortable home in a nice California suburb (it looks as though The Brady Bunch could reside in the same subdivision).

This was Matthau's first starring role as a leading man. Though in films since the 50's Matthau spent years toiling as the guy next door. He even played a supporting role in the Elvis Presley movie **King Creole** (1958). He perfected Oscar Madison on Broadway in 1965 as one of **The Odd Couple** (1968), and then won a supporting actor academy award with **The Fortune Cookie** (1966), as a shyster bent on insurance fraud. Since he had just played an unethical character (and was quite good at it), he took friend Billy Wilder's advice and opted to play the nice guy this time around. Producers had sought him for the heel that Robert Morse eventually played. It was, in fact, very good professional advice since Matthau was able to essay a wide range of roles in a lengthy career.

As Paul Manning, Matthau has the respect of the community. Yet, he decides to risk it all to see what pleasure sex outside of marriage can provide him. He wants to taste other fruit, even if his own apples are very sweet and satisfying. Luscious Inger Stevens plays his perfect wife. She's warm, devoted, and easy on the eyes.

Cheating on the perfect wife makes the whole game beyond comprehension. Paul is confused. Perhaps it's because he's running with the wrong crowd. His best friend (Robert Morse) brags and boasts of his sexual prowess, outside of house and home. Impressionable, clumsy, and feeling a bit inadequate, Matthau decides to get involved in the swinging game, under Morse's professional supervision.

Morse's justification of cheating forms the core to the insane proceedings. He claims it's a natural thing for men to sample, that some 43 percent do it at some time in their marriage. However, he has the simple decency to do it well, to protect his loved ones from finding out and getting upset. He justifies his narcissistic impulses by claiming it's all in the best interest of his marriage. Not exactly Cary Grant, Morse makes his weasel role very funny when he attempts to convince us that he is capable of charming anything with a pair of legs.

Morse has a hatful of anecdotes and colorful examples in the art of cheating, as well as justification for this type of behavior. In retrospect, his advice is rather elementary in an imperfect world. He tells Matthau to never say you'll be where you can be found not to be, and never have an affair with someone who doesn't have as much to lose as you do. The highlights of the film belong to the big movie star names who demonstrate the practice and art of cheating in cameo appearances. Most did it as a favor to Kelly, who was widely respected in the industry. The credits appropriately list them as technical advisers.

Lucille Ball and Art Carney offer a bust up skit. Carney picks a fight with wife Ball, knowing she'll get upset and tell him to get out (he says he's tired of having chicken every night). Ball takes the bait, and Carney has an evening date with his buxom lady friend. The next morning he calls Ball from work and apologizes for his crazy temper. All is forgiven. The next scene has him skipping to work. We know he's had a very good time.

The most extreme and hilarious vignette uses a Hollywood insider joke. Carl Reiner plays a world famous movie star going to great lengths to hide a clandestine meeting with starlet Linda Harrison (Miss Stardust). Demonstrating that you can't be too careful, his smokescreen takes him halfway around the world to a Swiss chalet, only to get busted. Each segment is punctuated with clever details. Take special note of Miss Stardust's change of eyewear from each scene. The insider joke is that Harrison was reportedly dating 20th Century Fox's studio chief, Richard D. Zanuck, at the time. Though unknown to moviegoers and with only a few minutes of screen time, she had the clout to receive prominent billing. She later married Zanuck (for ten years), but not before finding small decorative roles in major 20th Century Fox productions, including playing Nova in the blockbuster **Planet of the Apes** (1968). You can find a contemporary, if brief view of her in the 2001 remake. She's the attractive middle-aged "human beast" in the cage.

Another episode would have been hilarious if not for an off-screen tragedy. The advice is to never bring a girl home, since she may lose something and your wife may find it. Illustrating this rule is Jayne Mansfield, whose measurements were 44-22-36. Miss Mansfield somehow loses her bra in the heat of passion. Terry Thomas goes crazy trying to find it, knowing all too well that the super-structured garment couldn't be mistaken for his wife's apparel. The sad fact is this was Miss Mansfield's last film appearance. She was killed during the summer of 1967 in a freakish car accident while enroute to a television interview.

There are many other amusing cameos. Wally Cox shows what can happens when a sexually frustrated husband loses control of his impulses. Polly Bergen offers a lesson to those who marry men with

Chapter 1

a history of cheating. Phil Silvers shows how one should react if an enemy catches you with your shapely girlfriend while on the way to a motel. And Jack Benny makes supreme use of his tightwad image when he disposes of a mistress who has worn out her usefulness.

Gene Kelly directed this vehicle with flair. Perhaps it was from the heady training he received during his Metro-Goldwyn-Mayer period. Kelly, along with director Stanley Donen, writers Adolph Green and Betty Comden, and producer Arthur Freed, were pioneers in incorporating a story line with music and dance. Prior to the late 40s, movie musicals used Broadway, summer stock, or some distant relative of staged entertainment to provide a backdrop (or excuse) for cast members to sing and dance. Then came Metro-Goldwyn-Mayer's **On the Town** (1949) and **Singin' in the Rain** (1950). Both had elements of singing and dancing, but they were seamlessly merged into the story. Their huge success brought forth some of the most innovative musicals of all time, making the 50s the peak period of the screen musical.

When the cycle ended, Kelly sought refuge in directing. His efforts included **Tunnel of Love** (1958), an innocuous Doris Day vehicle, and **Gigot** (1962), a serious, poignant vehicle for Jackie Gleason. For **A Guide for the Married Man**, Kelly cleverly inserts animation sequences, campy images, and quick one-line visuals—all items that could be jarring in the hands of someone less accomplished. Yet the film remains seamless and fluid, like a very good dance. Kelly's technological expertise and prior experience in the medium are clearly evident.

The featured cast includes many, many gorgeous women and lots of bosom and bottom shots, notably Sue Ane Langdon and Elaine Devry. Langdon's best view is from the rear when she has the opportunity to introduce the credits and title tune by *The Turtles*. Langdon fondly recalled that Kelly instructed her to walk with a big thump, thump, thump. She also had no idea her backside was going to be so prominent in the opening shot. The pop group was paid $10,000 for their song with the condition that it be released as a single. Somehow the record was lost in the shuffle. During the 70s, long after the group broke up and when this movie ran in perpetual reruns, fans were offered a glimpse of their superb if seldom heard work.

While the film purports to be a guide for men, wives and girl-friends should not be offended. In the face of equality, writer Frank Tarloff supervised the writing of a TV sequel in 1978. **A Guide for the Married Woman** offered a female perspective, but didn't begin to improve on the original premise.

Tarloff wrote for a wide variety of television shows, including *Make Room for Daddy, The Andy Griffith Show,* and *The Dick Van Dyke Show.* His career had several distinctions. Tarloff was black-listed during the McCarthy era for being an unfriendly witness to Congress. To continue writing, he adopted a "front" and wrote under the phony name of David Adler. However, just as sex and adultery had become common on the big screen by the late 60s, he was able to reacquire his original name and work without fear of repercussions. In fact, his work on **A Guide For the Married Man** was nominated for a Writer's Guild of America Screen Award as the Best Written American Comedy of 1967. He admitted that many of the anecdotes were inspired from locker room conversations with his buddies.

A Guide for a Married Man was a big hit in 1967, big enough for the studio to have confidence in Kelly and Matthau for the big screen version of **Hello, Dolly!** in 1969. Kelly was more of a referee between Matthau and costar Barbara Streisand. However, the film was very popular and ranks as one of the last peaks in screen musicals. This gift to movie fans might not have been possible without the success of **A Guide for a Married Man**.

Cast

Walter Matthau	*Paul Manning*
Inger Stevens	*Ruth Manning*
Sue Ane Langdon	*Mrs. Johnson*
Robert Morse	*Ed Stander*
Claire Kelly	*Harriet Stander*
Linda Harrison	*Miss Stardust*
Elaine Devry	*Jocelyn Montgomery*

Chapter 1

Virginia Wood	*Bubbles*
Jackie Joseph	*Janet Brody*
Lucille Ball	*Technical Adviser*
Jack Benny	*Technical Adviser*
Polly Bergen	*Technical Adviser*
Joey Bishop	*Technical Adviser*
Sid Caesar	*Technical Adviser*
Art Carney	*Technical Adviser*
Wally Cox	*Technical Adviser*
Jayne Mansfield	*Technical Adviser*
Hal March	*Technical Adviser*
Louis Nye	*Technical Adviser*
Carl Reiner	*Technical Adviser*
Phil Silvers	*Technical Adviser*
Terry-Thomas	*Technical Adviser*
Ben Blue	*Technical Adviser*
Ann Morgan Guilbert	*Technical Adviser*
Jeffrey Hunter	*Technical Adviser*
Marty Ingels	*Technical Adviser*
Sam Jaffe	*Technical Adviser*

Production

Gene Kelly	*Director*
Frank Tarloff	*Writer (also book)*
Frank McCarthy	*Producer*
John Williams	*Original Music – Title song sung by The Turtles*
Joseph MacDonald	*Cinematography*
20th Century Fox	*Production Company*
USA/89 minutes/1967	*Country/Runtime/Year Released*

Chapter 2
A Letter to Three Wives

*"We're beginning to behave like a
movie about a women's prison."*

—Deborah Bishop

Director, screenwriter, and producer Joseph Mankiewicz' trademark
was to punctuate his films with a sharp and sophisticated wit. At his
peak, his comedy is a scintillating commentary on human behavior,
warts and all. In 1949 and 1950, he delivered a one-two punch, with
A Letter to Three Wives and **All About Eve**. Both movies were
competitive at the Academy awards. On both occasions, he received
a well-deserved Oscar for his screenplay and direction.

A Letter to Three Wives takes place just after World War II.
Mankiewicz very artistically intertwines three couples, all with different agendas, but who are remarkably in sync with each other.
While they all subscribe to the same magazines and read the same
paper, they have differences as well as similarities. It is the common
interests that propel this story along. All three husbands have dallied
at some time or another with a female whose sexy voice the audience
can hear. She remains off camera so that the appearance to match her
magnetic personality is left to our imagination. From just her voice
(courtesy of Celeste Holm), though, she is a definite wow!

Besides admiring (or being envious of) the charms of the female
we never see, the three men and women shop at the same grocery
store, attend the same church, belong to the same country club, and
live within minutes of each other in a safe suburb away from the big
city. While they may not earn the same income, they all aspire to be
a part of the Great American Dream.

Ann Sothern and Kirk Douglas are couple number one. They

Chapter 2

21

both work hard at their jobs. She writes radio advertising. He teaches high school. She works in order to buy things at the store to impress her friends at social gatherings. He works hard, he says, to make things better for society. He thinks his wife should stay at home and take care of the kids, shades of 1949. She accuses him of seeing things as they should be and not as they are. Furthermore, he wears nice clothes to work because his wife has a job that pays for them. Their differences on work, money, and home have created a bit of friction.

Jeanne Crain and Jeffrey Lynn are couple number two. They are comfortable enough, economically speaking, but Ms. Crain has an inferiority complex. Despite her beauty, she becomes very nervous in social situations. It is her past that haunts her. She was a country girl plucked from the farm and has never learned the complicated rules of conduct in this tightly knit community. She gets tripped up on which dress to wear, what wine to order at dinner, and when to stop drinking. Her behavior has caused her ambitious husband great embarrassment.

Linda Darnell and Paul Douglas are couple number three. They appear to be the greatest mismatch, or at least the one whose marriage is most likely to fail. He is twice her age and is the richest man in town. She is gorgeous and from the wrong side of the tracks. In fact, in one of the funniest moments of the movie, we find out that her family lives very close to train tracks and their house violently shakes during certain hours of the day. He questions the sincerity of her intentions. She pretends to get tired of his questions at the most opportune time.

All three couples are ripe for a rotten tomato to drop into their laps and spoil everything. That vegetable (or fruit) is Addie Ross. In our imagination, she is the perfect woman, lover, mother, and friend. Apparently, she has a great understanding of the male animal. Addie sets the story into motion by writing all three wives a nifty letter, just as they are about to embark on a boat tour. You know something is up when, in the letter, she calls her three pals "her dearest friends." Her pursuit of easy wealth, by stealing a husband of a dear friend, cements the jokes.

In her letter, she says she has run off with one of their husbands. Each wife suspects it is her husband and has all day long on the boat to think about it. In flashbacks, each wife examines how she may have erred in judgment. All can reasonably see why their man would run off with someone as seemingly perfect as Addie Ross.

Take Sothern's predicament, for example. This is a comedy of manners, or appearance, as Kirk Douglas says in an argument with his wife. After another boring party ends on a crisis note, he's mad. He says the children have been made prisoners in their rooms, the furniture has to look like it hasn't been sat on, and everything must be full: the candy dish, cigarette holder, and the liquor cabinet. It is also important that dinner "be introduced." In a wonderful moment, unpretentious Thelma Ritter fouls that social rule by telling the high-brow guests that "Soup's on."

Going for the jugular, Douglas blames it all on the advertising trade, which is Sothern's gainful employer. He says their marketing schemes confuse people about what their appearance should be. Appearances are also of high order in Ms. Crain's marriage. She can't forget the time she wore an outdated, threadbare dress to the most important social event of the year and it literally fell apart on her. Addie apparently knows how to dress and when to undress.

Then there is the love/hate relationship between Darnell and Paul Douglas. They are newlyweds and still under the spell of mutual suspicion. While courting, Douglas had been able to buy what he wanted (or pay for it to go away). But Darnell was a challenge. That made her much more interesting to him, the unattainable goddess. He doesn't want her as wife, at first. When he asks her to sleep with him, she bares her claws and tells him she won't settle for anything less than her picture in a gold frame in his living room. So, to have sex with her, he marries her. Now that gold frame is the foundation of their marriage.

This a nice movie with some nice people. The master of appearances is Addie Ross, even though she never appears on screen. The most pleasant surprise is actress Ann Sothern. You have to hand it to her. She had been slugging it out in generally inferior movies for some

Chapter 2

20 years before landing this role of a lifetime. Severely underutilized by the industry, she was never out of a job, but most of her roles were rather forgettable and dependent on her vivacious personality. At age 40 and billed below the up-and-coming Crain and Darnell, she knew there was no place left for her in movies. Not long after this, she went to TV and did quite nicely as the *Private Secretary*. When she began to put on weight, character roles came her way. She finally received belated recognition with a best supporting actress nomination for **The Whales of August** (1987). The stars of this movie were Bette Davis and Lillian Gish. That she could hold her own against the talent of these two legends was a credit to her abilities.

When Jane Fonda, Lily Tomlin, and Dolly Parton scored a big hit in 1980 with **9 to 5**, there was industry talk of reuniting the trio for a remake of **A Letter to Three Wives**. Instead, it wound up on television in 1985 starring Loni Anderson, Stephanie Zimbalist, and Michelle Lee. Ann Sothern, then 76, appeared as Loni's mom, while Loni played the Linda Darnell role. Sothern's presence remains the sole distinction of the 80s version. She walks with a cane due to health problems, yet it is nice to see she still had the magic toward the end of her long career.

Crain, Darnell, and Kirk Douglas were all relatively fresh to the industry and very appealing. However, by the time Crain and Darnell had improved their acting, they had lost their freshness and the job offers dwindled. Crain, the mother of seven children, probably lost interest in a long career. Sadly, Darnell died at 44 in a house fire in 1965. Ironically, she was watching one of her old movies on TV the night of the fatal fire.

Douglas, at the beginning of his career, displayed an on-screen aggressiveness in this movie, something he was also known for off-camera. In 2012, at the age of 94, he participated in the Turner Classic Film Festival. The audience was shocked to see Douglas running to the stage to boast that he was the oldest person in the room.

In his mid-seventies, he wrote a book called *The Ragman's Son (1988)*, an autobiographical first novel that pleased many of his fans. That was followed by *My Stroke of Luck 2003)*, which chronicled his recovery from a stroke he had suffered in 1996 that impaired his ability to speak.

Classified as character actors, Paul Douglas and Thelma Ritter were so good at their craft that they rose out of featured roles and into starring parts. In light of the many terrific character actors in movies during their era, this was a rare occurrence, but a deserving one for these two scene-stealers. They were crowd pleasers throughout the 50s, with Ritter continuing into the 60s.

Director Mankiewicz followed this movie with **All About Eve** (1950), another moving film discussed in this book. Both films featured the work of the very fine actress Celeste Holm.

John Klempner's original novel offered five pairs of couples. The screen version subtracted two for the sake of brevity. Could his story be told today? Not really. Certainly these suspicious ladies would have carried cell phones full time to check on the whereabouts of their spouses.

Cast

Jeanne Crain	*Deborah Bishop*
Linda Darnell	*Lora Mae Hollingsway*
Ann Sothern	*Rita Phipps*
Kirk Douglas	*George Phipps*
Paul Douglas	*Porter Hollingsway*
Barbara Lawrence	*Babe*
Jeffrey Lynn	*Brad Bishop*
Connie Gilchrist	*Mrs. Finney*
Thelma Ritter	*Sadie*
Florence Bates	*Mrs. Manleigh*
Hobart Cavanaugh	*Mr. Manleigh*

Production

Joseph L. Mankiewicz	*Director*
John Klempner (novel), Vera Caspary,	
Joseph L. Mankiewicz, Sol C. Siegel	*Producer*
Alfred Newman	*Original Music*

Arthur C. Miller   *Cinematography*
20th Century Fox   *Production Company*
USA/103/1949   *Country/Runtime/Year Released*

Chapter 3
All About Eve

"Fasten your seat belts. It's going to be a bumpy night."

—Margo Channing

There are few actresses who can sustain a career of length and quality. It is easier for an actor to have a long-term relationship with his fans. There are a number of reasons for this. There are more roles in society for men, especially older men, and more writers are male than female, and writers write about what they know. Once a woman hits 40, they're too wise to play the ingénue. If their pride and bank account holds out until they're 60, they may be welcome in supporting roles like middling aunts and hip grandmothers. In between these years they are usually asked to play aging harlots, has-been actresses, monsters, or loyal support staff.

It takes stamina as well as talent to beat the odds. Perhaps the prime example of someone who defied the odds was Bette Davis. Her film career extended over half a century and her name was seldom below the title. She had peaks and valleys, but even in a downturn, she was usually more interesting than the flavors of the month. Even at her worst, when she hams and screams and bulges those eyes, she still has the style and verve to maintain your interest.

In interviews Davis came across as bright, witty, and direct. She transferred that persona to the screen in several dozen memorable characters. If you have a chance to view her 50 or so pictures before 1950, she revealed a very modern personality for the female animal. She defied protocol in a man's world. Her followers do this now and no one thinks anything of it. As she aged, her style became more mannered. She smoked like a chimney, stamped her feet, clipped

Chapter 3   27

her speech, and always had something wise to say to anyone who tried to stand in her way. Unlike most of her contemporaries, who couldn't find work after the early 50s, we welcomed her middle age because she was interesting, a piece of living art that had become larger than life.

In 1950 she played the perfect role in her career. Curiously, it was about reaching the top in the acting profession. Her Margo Channing in **All About Eve** is a brilliant portrait of an aging actress fearing the loss of her man, audience, and position in the theatre. Her worst enemy was a youthful, vibrant, and cunning member of her own sex.

All About Eve was based on *The Wisdom of Eve*, a short story and radio play by Mary Orr. Industry insiders said it was based on a true incident involving actress Elizabeth Bergner, who appeared on Broadway in *The Two Mrs. Carrolls* in 1943. Ms. Bergner was surprised when a cast member told her she was quitting her small part. That actress, Irene Worth, said she "wasn't good enough to be with you." Bergner talked her out of it and the two women developed a mutual admiration. However, unlike the female actresses in this movie, they remained friends.

There's more to the movie than just Davis. For the first time, it offered a backstage view of the theatre, warts and all. It becomes very exciting to us, despite never seeing the play she is supposed to be in. We are privy to theatre politics, the ugly side of writing, directing and casting, as well as the business aspect of publicity and ticket sales. There are a number of players in this arena, all with egos jockeying for position in the spotlight. This inward look at the underbelly of Hollywood was released at the same time as **Sunset Boulevard** (1950). Both are harsh portraits of an industry that puts a prize on youth, and they mark the beginning of a cynicism towards an industry that is more than just show and tell.

Along with Davis, the cast of **All About Eve** includes Ann Baxter, Gary Merrill, Hugh Marlowe, George Sanders, Celeste Holm, and Thelma Ritter. Also, in a small but showy role, Marilyn Monroe plays a graduate of the Copacabana School of Dramatic Art. She becomes a clever contrast to Ann Baxter's Eve, who uses carefully disguised guile to build her base of power. Monroe is an obvious carrot to the power brokers. She plays up the sexual aspects of her assets to focus attention on herself.

The film's dialogue is sharp and witty, with intelligent observations about human nature. The ensemble cast behaves with credible human strengths and weaknesses. Davis is high strung, flamboyant, and neurotic.

Director Joseph Mankiewicz supposedly based her character on the flamboyant stage actress Tallulah Bankhead. Perhaps so, but Davis is more flesh and blood without the histrionics. Male animals Merrill and Marlowe do not understand the scenario until they have been used. However, acid mouthed critic George Sanders understands the game dear old mom taught the girls, and plays it both ways. Perhaps Sanders and Baxter represent people without feeling for anybody but themselves. Holm is the warm friend to Davis whose good judgment and loyalty is tested. However, the straight shooter award goes to Thelma Ritter, who reacts early on to Baxter's tale of woe with "What a story! Everything but the bloodhounds snappin' at her rear end!"

Despite the varsity teamwork, it is Davis who dominates the movie. When her position is threatened, it permits her to have a complete range of tantrums and indictments. She does it from a sense of loneliness as someone who is about to lose her identity as friend, star, lover, and woman. Director Mankiewicz also wrote the screenplay. Some of the most poignant and revealing lines he crafted for Margo occurs when she knows the curtain is going up without her. She says "Funny business, a woman's career. The things you drop on your way up the ladder so you can move faster. You forget you'll need them again when you go back to being a woman. That's one career all females have in common, whether we like it or not: being a woman. Sooner or later we've got to work at it, no matter what other careers we've had or wanted. And in the last analysis, nothing is good unless you can look up or turn around in bed—and there he is. Without that, you're not a woman. You're something with a French provincial office or a book full of clippings, but you're not a woman."

Chapter 3

Davis and Merrill became real-life husband and wife immediately after the production completed. Each later admitted they had married their characters. When they divorced ten years later, Davis told Mankiewicz the sequel to the movie didn't work out.

In a twist of fate, Davis' greatest film role was offered to her only after two other actresses became unavailable. Claudette Colbert was the first choice since she resembled a young Ann Baxter. But she had injured her back on the set of **Three Came Home** (1950). Mankiewicz waited for two months, and when location shooting could not be delayed further, Ingrid Bergman was contacted. Bergman, however, was not interested in deserting her husband, Roberto Rossellini, in Italy. Then Davis was approached. She read the script in one setting and accepted the part. Later she told film critic Judith Crist she was the luckiest person on earth.

Perhaps she made her luck. At the time Davis was still seething from her abrupt departure from Warner Brothers. She did not get on with director King Vidor during **Beyond the Forest** (1949) and told Jack Warner to choose between them. To her surprise, Warner sided with Vidor, who viewed Davis as past her prime and an expensive studio commodity. Without a studio and labeled difficult, she put fire into the part of Margo to avenge the critics with stones. Today, it is difficult to imagine Colbert or Bergman lighting the same fires at the theatre. Colbert's forte was sophisticated comedy and poignant drama. Bergman, then 35, was a bit young to worry about encroaching middle age.

All About Eve proved to be a box office and critical delight, earning 14 Academy Award nominations, a record that was tied in 1997 by **Titanic** and again in 2016 with **La La Land**. The awards included best director, picture, screenplay, and supporting actor. Both Davis and Baxter were nominated in the best actress category, effectively canceling each other out since fans of the film voted for one or the other. The winner was Judy Holliday for **Born Yesterday**. Severely disappointed, Davis cried foul in her typical manner. She said she created Margo specifically for the screen while Holliday perfected Billie Dawn on Broadway and then transferred it to film. **All About Eve**

was later musicalized on Broadway as *Applause* with a much-admired performance by Lauren Bacall, another long-term survivor in the Davis mode.

After 1950, once freeing herself from the confines of the movie studio, Davis' movies are more varied. When she appeared in **Whatever Happened to Baby Jane** in 1962, she opened up a new audience of appreciative baby boomers. From then on, despite low-grade stuff like **Burnt Offerings** (1976), fans could still feel her presence.

Fighting breast cancer and impaired by a stroke, one of her last performances was in **Whales of August** (1987). Together with Lillian Gish, Ann Sothern, and Vincent Price, it was a showcase of old fashioned star power. Still strutting her stuff, she made sure we were still thinking about her.

Davis and Ann Baxter would cross paths again late in their careers. Davis was set to appear in the TV series *Hotel*, but bowed out due to health problems. Baxter became her replacement.

The popular Turner Classic Movie Host Ben Mankiewicz is Joseph L's great nephew.

Cast

Bette Davis	*Margo Channing*
Anne Baxter	*Eve Harrington*
George Sanders	*Addison DeWitt*
Celeste Holm	*Karen Richards*
Gary Merrill	*Bill Sampson*
Hugh Marlowe	*Lloyd Richards*
Gregory Ratoff	*Max Fabien*
Barbara Bates	*Phoebe*
Marilyn Monroe	*Claudia Casswell*
Thelma Ritter	*Birdie Coonan*

Production

Joseph L. Mankiewicz	*Director*
Joseph L. Mankiewicz, Mary Orr (story)	*Writers*
Darryl F. Zanuck	*Producer*

Chapter 3

Alfred Newman   *Original Music*
Milton Krasner   *Cinematography*
20th Century Fox   *Production Company*
USA/138 minutes/1950   *Country/Runtime/Year Released*

Chapter 4

A Night to Remember

"I don't think I'll ever feel sure about anything."
—Second Officer Lightoller

In 1912, the British luxury liner *Titanic* struck an iceberg on its maiden voyage and sank, taking 1,500 of the 2,200 passengers down with it. This tragedy holds a morbid fascination for many, due no doubt to the large number of deaths and the fact that many of the doomed travelers were the world's rich and famous. Their violent and senseless departures made the headlines that much more horrific the next day. We naively thought their wealth provided them with some control over their lives. Yet, they, like others on the ship, had a little over two hours to live before death in the freezing waters of the Atlantic.

This fascination also stems from the knowledge that the tragedy could have been prevented. There were a number of variables that preceded the accident. It's best described as an unlucky series of events in sequence that, when added together, equaled disaster. A change in direction, decision, or fate during this pattern of events could have prevented an enormous loss of life and confidence in technology—but more about this later.

Invariably, we as spectators and evaluators find ourselves thinking "what if." What if something else in the sequence had happened. Taking it a step further, we fantasize about what we would have done if we had been aboard the doomed ship. Would we have survived? Away from this fantasy, we all know we cannot turn back time. In **A Night to Remember** (1958), the tragedy unfolds like it did that cold night in April 1912, leaving no room for what ifs.

Based on Walter Lord's 1956 best selling book of the same name, the film is full of real life events and dialogue that is as close to fact as survivors could recount. Lord interviewed over 60 surviving passengers in his research. There are colorful portraits of the passengers, including Molly Brown, the noveau rich gal from Denver who didn't fit into society. Even in her lifeboat, she bucked protocol. When a movie was made of her life, it seemed appropriate to call it **The Unsinkable Molly Brown** (1964).

The *Titanic*'s crew reportedly ignored ice warnings. Instead, they recklessly plowed full speed ahead. The ship was traveling at a high speed since the night was clear and calm. The iceberg they struck had shed its topmost layer of ice, making it harder to see. Frederick Fleet, in the crow's nest, had misplaced his binoculars. As the ship filled with water it split in half. The ship broke into two pieces, separating at the fourth smokestack. When the grave and wreckage were found in 1985, these two pieces were basically intact and separated by a large debris field.

The *Titanic* would have probably suffered less damage if it had hit the iceberg head on. By veering to its side, the ice mountain ruptured a 300-foot long fatal scratch below the waterline. After the disaster, new regulations and standards were instituted for wireless use and the number of lifeboats required for all passengers. Ice patrols were also initiated.

There are other poignant characterizations in this film. The elderly lady who refused a seat in a lifeboat to remain on board with her husband was Mrs. Isador Straus. Her husband owned Macy's, the world's largest department store.

The managing director of the shipbuilding company that built the *Titanic* also was on board. When the chairman of the company couldn't make the voyage for health reasons, Thomas Andrews was unlucky enough to take his place. Then there was millionaire Benjamin Guggenheim, who took off his life vest to put on comfortable evening attire, saying he was going to die like a gentleman.

Crew member stories are memorialized on film. Second Officer Lightoller was the most senior staff member to survive the disaster (by clinging to an overturned lifeboat) and one of the few males to emerge with honor from the tragedy since the lifeboat call was for women and children first. Captain Smith was last seen entering the wireless room, where he told the crew they had done their duty. There were rumors that he committed suicide, but his final minutes are unknown. Poignantly, he had planned to retire after completing this voyage.

The film cuts back and forth between the three class structures on the ship: 1st, 2nd and steerage. A first class ticket cost around $4,000 in 1912, a king's ransom. Only the super rich could afford this fare. They were very easy to spot with their furs, impeccable manners, and speech patterns. Second class passengers included teachers, professionals, and doctors. They were well mannered and orderly but without the airs of the upper class with whom they may have accidentally rubbed elbows. Many of the steerage passengers were coming to the new world to start a new life. With optimism and enthusiasm, they sang, danced, and courted below the decks.

The tempo of the film goes back and forth, between panic and calm. Families are split, men quietly say goodbye to their wives and children, and the band plays a hymn. These moments are interrupted with people trying to rush the lifeboats, distress signals being sent up to no avail, and visuals of a great ship slanting towards the bottom of the ocean. When the ship begins to buckle and shift violently, the contents and remaining passengers plunge into the ocean as if someone is tossing pennies into a fountain. Though inevitable, this is perhaps the most terrifying and sad moment in the film.

This is a British production with a home grown cast. However, some of the film's actors had minor careers in the United States. There is Lawrence Naismith as Captain Smith, Kenneth More as Lightoller, and David McCallum as Jack Phillips. Honor Blackman is also on hand, looking properly dignified, the opposite of the role for which she is most famous: Pussy Galore in **Goldfinger** (1964).

Hollywood has produced at least two major movies on this subject. **Titanic** (1953) starred Barbara Stanwyck and Clifton Webb and was less a documentary than **A Night to Remember**. It offered some soap along with the disaster. Stanwyck and Webb are a fictitious couple in a loveless marriage. Always watchable, Stanwyck's remarkable

Chapter 4

presence dilutes the overall impact of the disaster. Always watchable, those familiar with Stanwyck's long career of playing strong-willed women know she will have a seat in a lifeboat. In contrast, James Cameron's **Titanic** (1997) used a Romeo and Juliet story with mind boggling special effects, making the movie the highest grossing feature film in history. Interestingly, Bernard Fox, who played Frederic Fleet in **A Night to Remember** was also cast in the 1997 **Titanic** as Colonel Archibald Gracie. There is also a German film in circulation entitled **Titanic** (1943). Produced at the height of World War II, the film offers an unflattering review of British culture.

In 1985 and 1986, a Franco-American expedition led by Robert D. Ballard located and photographed the wreckage of the *Titanic*, using high tech sonar and camera equipment. His montage of pictures was published in *National Geographic* and in several books—thus continuing public interest in the most famous disaster of the 20th century. Undoubtedly this paved the way for Cameron's 1997 film, which included footage from these expeditions. The views were haunting and have only heightened the public's fascination with the ship that was supposed to be unsinkable.

One curiosity is why the *Titanic* did not have enough lifeboats on board. At the time, ships were required to carry lifeboats based on the ship's gross tonnage, not the number of people on board. The *Titanic*'s 20 lifeboats were only enough for half of its passengers. Apathy or denial on the part of passengers and crew to the crisis at hand resulted in filling the early boats only half full, before being lowered into the water. Worse, with the exception of one, the half-empty boats made no attempt to rescue dying passengers in the water when the vessel finally submerged.

While White Star Line officials denied any favoritism to the wealthy and privileged passengers, the survivor list is revealing. A disproportionate number of rich were saved, suggesting that the working class was not informed of the consequences they faced if they did not quickly find a lifeboat.

Sadly, a nearby ship, the *California*, did not hear the *Titanic*'s SOS signals. It was within range for a full rescue. The *California*'s Captain,

Stanley Lord, was found negligent after the disaster. His relatives have unsuccessfully tried to clear his name of any wrongdoing. The *Carpathia* was the closest ship to have its "ears on" and it was 58 miles away. It was too late by the time it arrived on the scene.

Today there is a very active international organization, the Titanic Historical Society, which dedicates itself to preserving the memory and history of the Titanic. Members plan a major convention each April (on the day of the disaster) and publish a quarterly journal. Dues for membership are renewed on April 15, the day after the sinking.

The last survivor of the Titanic, Milvina Dean, died May 31, 2009 at 97. She was the youngest survivor of the disaster, barely two months old when her mother carried her and her brother Bertram to lifeboat number 10. Her father stayed on board the ship and did not survive.

For many years, Dean was a positive and enthusiastic guest at the annual Titanic Historical Society Meetings. In late 2008, when it was announced that Ms. Dean was confined to a nursing home and her Titanic mementos were to be auctioned off to pay for her medical care, there was an outpouring of affection from all over the world to ensure that her expenses would be covered and she would be able to keep her personal items.

Cast

Kenneth More	*Second Officer Charles Herbert Lightoller*
Ronald Allen	*Mr. Clarke*
Robert Ayres	*Major Arthur Peuchen*
Honor Blackman	*Mrs. Liz Lucas*
Anthony Bushell	*Captain Arthur Rostron (Carpathia)*
John Cairney	*Mr. Murphy*
Jill Dixon	*Mrs. Clarke*
Jane Downs	*Mrs. Sylvia Lightoller*
James Dyrenforth	*Colonel Archibald Gracie*
Michael Goodliffe	*Thomas Andrews*
Kenneth Griffith	*Wireless Operator John "Jack" Phillips*
David McCallum	*Assistant Wireless Operator Harold Bride*

Chapter 4

Laurence Naismith	*Captain Edward John Smith*
Bernard Fox	*Frederick Fleet*

Production

Roy Baker	*Director*
Walter Lord (book), Eric Ambler (screenplay)	*Writers*
William MacQuitty, Earl St. John	*Producer*
Geoffrey Unsworth	*Cinematography*
William Alwyn	*Original Music*
Yvonne Caffin	*Costumes*
Rank Film Organisation	*Production Company*
United Kingdom/123*/1958	*Country/Runtime/Year Released*

The actual sinking of the Titanic took place in approximately 160 minutes.

Chapter 5
A Shock to the System

"I forgive you for failing."

—Leslie Marshall

Whenever the number of employees at the workplace is more than one, politics exist. Anyone who has worked in a situation where politics are rampant or out of control, and where work style is more important than the amount and quality of work produced, will enjoy **A Shock to the System** (1990).

Who hasn't had at least one bad experience with a supervisor who exploits the staff or stockholders? Many people count themselves lucky to have had only several of these experiences in a lifetime of work. When an outfit goes bankrupt because of gross mismanagement, those accountable are usually described in the headlines as arrogant, critical and without the necessary skills to do the job.

A Shock to the System is a delicious black comedy, putting into practice what those on the frontlines often dream of doing to terrible bosses who drive down profits and office morale. It is a fitting tribute to the office soldiers who have fought and been fired somewhere along the battle lines in the corporate game. This becomes a perfect fantasy for Walter Mitty types everywhere who stand in the dark shadows of something powerful and evil.

On a smaller scale, the movie makes jabs at corporate greed. Minor conversations during the work hours reveal ill-advised decisions that affect thousands of employees. The movie's release date was properly timed. The nation was reeling from an economic downturn and the unemployed could use a few laughs.

Michael Caine stars as an assistant marketing chief in a Madison Avenue advertising agency. He has been loyal to the system for the best years of his life. Now in late middle-age and in line for the

Chapter 5   39

coveted role of marketing director, his promotion appears to be in the bag. Both the office staff and his wife (Swoosie Kurtz) expect him to receive this crowning achievement, a reward for his good service. His wife even spends his raise before it is announced, explaining "you always get what you want." But when he fails to win the position, losing it to someone younger and inferior, he takes matters into his own hands. Perhaps going off his rocker a bit, he dabbles in murder.

Essentially he is the shock to the system, the learned social rules that everyone plays to either retain their position or to get ahead at the work place. The system supports hard work. But it also supports bonding with the powerbrokers and knowing who your enemies are. Caine decides to play this game his way, without a conscience, because the system has failed him. As he explains, he's forced to change his technique because "the magic was draining out of him every day."

By outright appearance, Caine appears successful. He owns a splendid home in Connecticut. Though childless, he is married to a wife who is always arranging a dinner party or social gathering. Yet, there is also a slight maverick side to him. Perhaps it is the cowboy he longed to be. Notice that he drives a Jeep Wagoneer with wood grained panels. He has also worked his way up the hard way. He mentions to a friend that his father was a bus driver. In real life, Caine's father was in this same line of work.

Beneath this successful exterior, something is missing and wrong in his unhappy life. His wife doesn't appreciate him. She spends, spends, and spends. When he tells her the bad news about not getting the promotion, she tells him that she forgives him for failing. Sadly he has no support at home when an incompetent supervisor he's propped up for years betrays him. He also feels the pinch of advancing age. His new boss is much younger, representing change, a new order, a new drain on the power base Mr. Caine has so carefully groomed through his years of loyal service. This antagonist and new supervisor is "Big Bad Bobbie" (Peter Riegert). Caine views his enemy as an arrogant social climber, full of savvy, including smooth plans to impress those on the highest floors. Caine cynically speaks of Bob's nobility: "Hail to the conquering hero," he says. When "Sir Robert" initiates changes that adversely affect Caine's standing, he increases the title to Emperor Bob.

Attempting to take care of the situation, he becomes fixated on magic. He refers to his shrew wife as a witch whose spell must be broken. He chants magical phrases and refers to himself as a sorcerer. "Every sorcerer needs an apprentice," so he manipulates an office worker (Elizabeth McGovern) into his diabolical plans. The first victim is his unaffectionate wife. His line "what a shock" when he finds out she has been electrocuted, is a real hoot. When he discovers how easy murder can be at home, he decides to hone his newfound craft at the office. Thus, he becomes the opposite of a monster boss. He is now the toxic employee. Caine's performance as someone who moves gracefully toward crime is also manipulative. Though poisonous, we sympathize and ghoulishly urge him on. We dislike the other distracting characters, too, and hope he is successful in rubbing them out. Our support of his crimes gives credit to the movie's fun and wild sense of darkness. This time our lack of remorse is excused. It is all a fun fantasy.

Performances in small roles are rewarding. Swoosie Kurtz is the annoying wife. Her self-centered world this week is fitness. Next week it will probably be crafts. More disturbing is the way she manages their income. Carelessly borrowing funds from their money market account, she has no idea the high penalty she will pay at the hands of her husband.

Ingenue Elizabeth McGovern (**Ordinary People**, 1980; **Ragtime**, 1981) reflects proper innocence as one of the girls in the office and the love interest of Caine. Green as celery, she does not fully understand the rules of the game.

Caine, then 57, continued this period of intense activity in his cinematic career. A leading international star since the 60s, he filmed nonstop, often making two or three films per year during this phase in his career. **A Shock to the System** remains one of the lesser-known bright stars in this constellation. After accepting a 1999 supporting actor academy award, his first, for his work in **The Cider House Rules**, he told the audience he is a survivor. Indeed he is.

Chapter 5

Cast

Michael Caine	*Graham Marshall*
Elizabeth McGovern	*Stella Anderson*
Peter Riegert	*Robert Benham*
Swoosie Kurtz	*Leslie Marshall*
Will Patton	*Lieutenant Laker*
Jenny Wright	*Melanie O'Conner*
John McMartin	*George Brewster*
Barbara Baxley	*Lillian*

Production

Jan Egleson	*Director*
Simon Brett (novel), Andrew Klavan, Alice Arlen, Patrick McCormick	*Writers*
Leslie Morgan	*Producer*
Gary Chang	*Original Music*
Paul Goldsmith	*Cinematography*
Brigand Films	*Production Company*
USA/91/1990	*Country/Runtime/Year Released*

Chapter 6

Attack of the 50 Foot Woman

"Harry, I saw a satellite tonight!"

—Nancy Fowler Archer

Perfectly awful movies often become hysterical (and watchable) when they age, especially those that were created with the best intentions. One wonders what the story is behind some of cinema's most dreadful films. Some directors and writers create these camp classics because they are hopelessly out of sync with the public's taste and intelligence. In other instances, it may be a question of money. They may be struggling with funding and not have the ability to creatively cut corners without hampering the style of the film. Thanks to Tim Burton's film **Ed Wood** (1994), one can now imagine the inspiration schlock director Edward D. Wood Jr. must have had to create **Glen or Glenda** (1953) or his infamous **Plan 9 From Outer Space** in 1959. However, in direct contrast to Wood, Roger Corman turned out a number of excellent movies on a tight budget—and so did the folks at American International Pictures (AIP).

It's not always the low budget or weak script that causes the filmmaker's stress. For example, did the car dealer supplying the convertible bargain for a role for his woman? Did the gangsters putting up the capital pull out during production when they realized they could make more money on gambling or beef? There may also be creative differences among cast and crew, prompting sabotage. The producer may also have gambled on the ability of the director, cast and crew. Or there may be just enough film available for one take—if even that.

Any of these reasons could be the excuse for the quirky sci-fi classic **Attack of the 50 Foot Woman** (1958). Compared to the normal standards and practices of the day, artistic merit is lower than zero for what turns out to be a science fiction soap opera. But current audience

Chapter 6

members can use this to their advantage because it opens the door to a broad comedy of errors. With little effort, audiences who find the right pulse of this film can have a good time. It may help to supplement your popcorn with a high-octane beverage to safely view the hysterics. When something does appears ridiculous and you detect sarcasm from within, just remember this is what happens when a man from outer space causes an angry rich woman to grow to 50 feet.

The movie opens with a serious news flash. As if it is Christmas Eve, a smirking television journalist says a satellite has been spotted racing towards the California desert. Since a satellite is a man-made device, the correct term to use should have been unidentified flying object (UFO). Meteor would have also been acceptable.

Next is a cut to the Mojave Desert where an excessively large car with huge fins and lots of chrome speeds along Route 66, throwing up dust as it makes it way. Suddenly there is a flash in the sky. The large car brakes into a skid to avoid a huge white sphere in the road. The woman driver, now hysterical, stops just short of the object. Screaming and moaning, she tries to restart her Chrysler Imperial convertible. There's a weird high-pitched noise and something off camera starts to approach her. Getting out of the car, she reveals a healthy bosom, home to a very large diamond necklace. There are more screams from this terrified woman. She clutches her chest, as if to protect her jeweled assets. Then a large rubbery hand with hair splotches reaches towards the diamonds. Regaining some sense of survival instinct, our lady friend then turns sharply on her high heels and runs several miles through the scorching desert, back to the safety of the town. Out of breath and haggard, she tells her incredible story to the sheriff. "I almost hit it with my car," she screams. The sheriff is smart though, and humors her. She is Mrs. Archer, a woman worth $50 million dollars who pays most of the taxes in this sleepy desert community.

As the fun story develops, we find that Mrs. Archer has a history of mental and drinking problems. She also picks the wrong men. Her husband, known in the gossip columns as Handsome Harry, is having an affair with Honey, the town temptress. Harry and Honey quickly realize that Mrs. Archer's desert experience is an opportunity to move her out of the picture, take her money, stay and romp in bed all day and not have to work for a living.

But all is not well. Mrs. Archer apparently was touched in some way by the man in the satellite and grows to be 50 feet tall. That levels the playing field, somewhat, between her and Harry. While the dialogue is corny, the cast and crew may have been in on the joke. For example, when the police car driven by a bespectacled deputy nearly hits the sheriff, they make out like Andy Taylor and Barney Fife, all to good comedic effect.

The voluptuous lady who increases in proportions is Allison Hayes. She starred in a number of poverty row films, including such non-classics as **The Steel Jungle** (1956), **The Unearthly** (1957), **Zombies of Mora Tau** (1957), and **Wolf Dog** (1958). Unlike **The Attack of the 50 Foot Woman**, they have not been heard of since. The distinction, of course, is that B movie lovers continue to seek out this masterpiece. Miss Hayes, like a lot of women in movies who are used for decoration, entered the profession through a beauty contest as Washington, D.C.'s entry into the 1949 Miss America pageant. By the early 50s she was on her way to Hollywood where she was groomed by Universal Studios to star in grade B fare. In later years, her acting improved and she worked regularly on daytime soaps. She died relatively young at 47 of a blood disorder in 1977.

Yvette Vickers, the actress hired to play Honey, the dime-store blonde, occasionally turned up in bit roles during this period. Her beauty is very much in evidence. In fact, she was a *Playboy* magazine centerfold shortly after this film tried to find an audience—Miss July, 1959. She made appearances at film gatherings fielding questions from receptive and adoring fans who admired her performance and this movie. The DVD release includes her on the audio commentary. Vickers died in 2010 under macabre surroundings. Withdrawn and alone in her Benedict Canyon home, her mummified body was found by a worried neighbor. Apparently Vickers had been dead for months before this gruesome discovery. An autopsy ruled her cause of death was due to heart failure.

Chapter 6

The fellow charged with playing sleazy Handsome Harry is William Hudson. Like Ms. Vickers, his body of work lacked distinction. This was one of his rare starring roles. He worked fairly steadily in movies and television in the 50s and 60s—typically down in the cast list and in uniform. He also died relatively young, at 49 in 1974.

The unintentional comedy gets a boost from the movie's brisk pace. There is a string of ludicrous situations featured in rapid succession. At one point, our illicit couple is dressed in tacky 50s garb, with guns and ammunition, and drive around in the desert looking for the satellite in their convertible with the top down. The local news media continues to spread vicious rumors, and there is a craggy face butler named Jess who only takes orders from Mrs. Archer.

The conversations are sprinkled with tawdry remarks, increasing the wit quotient considerably. When Mrs. Archer accuses her husband of philandering, he says "For heaven's sake, Nancy, why I hardly nodded to the girl." When the sheriff sees a giant footprint in the desert, he says it obviously "wasn't made by a Japanese gardener." When the two doctors confer over the title character's condition, one with a thick European accent says "we'll find our answer when we operate."

One of the best tidbits comes from the mouth of Honey. In plotting Mrs. Archer's demise, she advises Harry to "just hide out and let her blowup like a balloon." After Mrs. Archer does just that, her nervous physicians order chains, meat hooks, 40 gallons of plasma, and an elephant syringe to keep her sedated. When she wakes up and realizes her condition, she starts screaming and practically pierces everyone's eardrums.

Director Nathan Hertz usually lists Nathan Juran as his credit signature. Perhaps he thought he had a bomb on his hands with this film and decided to hide. A graduate of MIT, he was an architect before making it as an art director in Hollywood. His accomplishments in this field include winning an Academy Award for art direction in **How Green Was My Valley** (1941). Another excellent example of his work is **The Razor's Edge** in 1946.

In the 50s, Juran turned to directing. **The Seventh Voyage of Sinbad** (1958) has special effects by Ray Harryhausen, a score by

Bernard Herrmann and fine production values. One can only wonder why, in contrast, **Attack of the 50 Foot Woman**, released in the same year, offers such crude special effects.

A made-for-cable remake of this film surfaced in 1993, starring statuesque Darryl Hannah in the title role. It approached the subject tongue and cheek, even using footage from the original in a drive-in movie scene. The movie's slant was changed, though, with Hannah becoming more of a feminist than a victim. The original version remains the one with the high fun quotient.

Cast

Allison Hayes	*Nancy Fowler Archer*
William Hudson	*Harry Archer*
Yvette Vickers	*Honey Parker*
Roy Gordon	*Dr. Cushing*
George Douglas	*Sheriff Dubbitt*
Ken Terrell	*Jess Stout*
Otto Waldis	*Dr. Von Loeb*
Eileen Stevens	*Nurse*
Michael Ross	*Tony & Space Giant*
Frank Chase	*Charlie*

Production

Nathan Juran	*Director*
Mark Hanna	*Writer*
Jacques R. Marquette, Bernard Woolner	*Producers*
Ronald Stein	*Original Music*
Jacques R. Marquette	*Cinematography*
Allied Artists Picture Corporation/Woolner	*Production Company*
USA/66 minutes/1958	*Country/Runtime/Year Released*

Chapter 6

Chapter 7

The Bad Seed

"She knows what she wants and asks for it."
—Monica Breedlove

Very few Broadway productions survive intact when transplanted to the big screen. The cast, script, and other logistics that play so well on stage usually receive a major transformation by the time the film crew arrives. In less than a minute, you can count on one hand the number of Broadway productions that retain the original leads. It's a pity since they hone their craft to perfection in front of a live audience.

There are many reasons for this switch in personnel and it is not a question of having ability or talent. For example, Bette Davis played Maxine in **The Night of the Iguana** (1964) on Broadway, but Ava Gardner won the movie role because director John Huston loathed Davis and loved Gardner.

It can also be a question of box-office pull. When it was announced that **My Fair Lady** (1964) was to be filmed, everyone in the industry presumed Julie Andrews and Rex Harrison would repeat their Broadway triumph. But that wasn't to be: Audrey Hepburn was paired with Rex Harrison, since producers believed that an established box-office gun was necessary to coax people to the movie theatres. Andrews was untried in that area, though she proved her worth shortly thereafter with **Mary Poppins** (1964).

One of the more fortunate transformations to the screen is **The Bad Seed** (1956). Based on Maxwell Anderson's play, the original cast members arrived in Hollywood without much fuss, except that Joan Crawford was offered but declined to play the mother role in the film. Based on what we learned later about Ms. Crawford's mothering skills, it could have been poetic justice. Despite considering Crawford, producer-director Mervyn LeRoy apparently did not question the bankability of the complete package. He correctly theorized that expert performances were needed to carry off this unusual examination of a demon child. If a big name had been hired for the movie, attention would have been drawn to that person's star personality and spoil the ensemble effect. Thus, lucky Nancy Kelly was hired to repeat her Tony award winning performance. It was her first Hollywood film in a decade.

The movie's subject was quite chilling in its day. Even now it packs a big wallop. The story centers on what first appears to be a sweet little girl, played to perfection by young actress Patty McCormack. She is a bright-eyed, cherubic 10-year-old with pigtails and frills on her nicely pressed dress. She roller skates and plays out in the yard with her tea set like any other child who is full of innocence and life. But as the story unravels, we suspect that she may be responsible for the deaths of several people.

McCormack is a very effective psychopath. You could easily imagine her growing up to be something like the Kathy Bates' character in **Misery** (1990). As with Ms. Bates' Oscar-winning performance, we only see subtle hints of evil behind a mask of normal behaviors expected from a child. Furthermore, everything is further disguised in a pretty package of middle- class surroundings. McCormack's mother (Nancy Kelly) and father (William Hopper) are attractive, educated, and gainfully employed. They live in an apartment complex surrounded by a white picket fence. It all plays like an unremarkable town in the Midwest. In contrast to this normalcy, there is the creepy handyman, Henry Jones. He's the kind of guy caregivers warn children to avoid. He appears grubby, illiterate, and talks dirty under his breath. Appearances are deceiving, though. He is on to the child's game long before anyone else—and suffers greatly for it.

The landlord neighbor, Evelyn Varden, is loud, bossy, and doting. She dabbles in amateur psychology and her knowledge in this field makes her more harmful than good.

Eileen Heckart is excellent in her two scenes as the grieving mother of a drowned boy. Her sadness and loss are uncomfortably real.

Nancy Kelly deserves strong praise for her performance. She at first realizes there is an immature quality in her only child. She becomes

Chapter 7

increasingly vigilant and gathers proof of her other violent acts, leading to the eventual confrontation. Kelly captures the complexity and strength of motherly love as she agonizes over the right thing to do.

The movie ends with an unusual send-off. Retaining its theatrical origins, the smiling cast comes out for a curtain call—implying that all is well. This epilogue is usually cut off on TV showings but is intact on the video version. However, it does not soften the aftertaste. The movie is as chilling and shocking as any Hollywood excursion into the life of a murderer.

Kelly, Heckert, and McCormack received Academy Award nominations for their performances.

Kelly was born in 1921 and started out as a child star in silent movies. She eventually graduated to ingénue roles in the late 30s. Her roles were not worthy of her talent, and in 1946, she quit Hollywood to pursue a career on Broadway. In 1956, she returned for this role, a one-shot comeback. Apart from small roles in two made-for-television films in the 70s, she did not work again in Hollywood.

McCormack continued to work in movies following **The Bad Seed**. She played troubled teens in the 60s, mainly in second-rate films, with titles like **The Miniskirt Mob** (1968). Like many child stars that cease to be overly cute in adulthood, her career dried up after adolescence. Heckert went on to appear in many movies in supporting roles, often stealing the notices from the more illustrious stars who had proper lighting and makeup. She eventually won an Academy Award as best supporting actress for her performance in **Butterflies are Free** (1972). She was actually drawing on unemployment insurance when she accepted the award. Her situation once again emphasized that it isn't always a question of talent or ability to find steady, gainful employment in Hollywood.

Hopper is the son of influential gossip columnist Hedda Hopper. He later became well known on TV as *Perry Mason*'s friend, private investigator Paul Drake.

Henry Jones, a familiar face to comic and sinister roles on TV and the big screen, proved his metal in this performance, but it is one of his many, many memorable outings.

Watch closely at the beginning of the movie. You'll see a young Kathy Garver (later to become older sister Cissy on TV's *Family Affair*), and Shelley Fabares. They play two of Rhoda's classmates at the school picnic.

The Bad Seed was remade in 1985 with Blair Brown, David Carradine, and Carrie Wells (as the child). The 80s version remains more interesting than bone chilling and lacks the strong audience manipulation found in the original.

Cast

Nancy Kelly	*Christine Penmark*
Patricia McCormack	*Rhoda Penmark*
Henry Jones	*LeRoy Jessup*
Eileen Heckert	*Hortense Daigle*
Evelyn Varden	*Monica Breedlove*
William Hopper	*Colonel Kenneth Penmark*
Paul Fix	*Richard Bravo*
Jesse White	*Emory Wages*
Gage Clarke	*Reginald "Reggie" Tasker*
Joan Croydon	*Claudia Fern*
Frank Cady	*Henry Daigle*
Kathy Garver	*Rhoda's schoolmate*
Shelley Fabares	*Rhoda's schoolmate*

Production

Mervyn LeRoy	*Director*
Maxwell Anderson (play), William March (novel), John Lee Mahin (screenplay)	*Writers*
Mervyn LeRoy	*Producer*
Harold Rosson	*Cinematographer*
Alex North	*Original Music*
Warner Brothers	*Production Company*
Moss Mabry	*Costumes*
USA/129/1956	*Country/Runtime/Year Released*

Chapter 7

Chapter 8
The Bank Dick

"We're making motion picture history here."
—*Egbert Sousè*

To a small and discerning group of film buffs, W.C. Fields is a comic genius. Certainly he was one of the funniest men of his generation to be in the movies. Like all great stars from the golden age of Hollywood, there was a unique and strong personality at work. With that inimitable voice that sounded like a cross between a foghorn and a Las Vegas huckster, it didn't take him long to have the audience completely satisfied and under his influence. What one remembers most are his casual observations on the state of things. He was constantly evaluating and supremely negative. His glass, from his view, was always half empty.

Fields was delightfully eccentric with several distinctions other film personalities try to hide or avoid. Apart from not liking children and animals, he's boastful, cranky, dishonest *and* very dependent on alcohol. In fact, there's a routine that has his character drink water accidentally and the incident is treated with the same alarm as taking poison. Despite the warning flags, we're inclined to usually overlook these flaws. His character does exude tremendous warmth. If he does overindulge with spirits, it's usually in response to an insane situation.

The film roles he essayed included a carnival barker, the President of a small country, a lazy sheriff and an ordinary office worker. There are instances when he didn't have a job or had just been fired for good reason. Despite his vocation or status in the community, he never seemed to be in control of the situation. The responsibilities, obstacles and competition he faced sometimes got the best of him. Automobiles, furniture, clothing, even pool cues gave him a hard time.

There were dreams of wealth and that made him gullible to a con. He was easy prey for phony stock, orange groves in the desert and other dangling carrots that offered the promise of an easy life for his family.

Fields grew funnier as he aged. This was probably due to his increased drinking, which heightened his eccentricities and lowered his inhibitions. It's remarkable that he was at the zenith of his comic powers when his health was at its worst.

Campus and art theatres began to regularly screen his films in the 60s and established him as a cult figure. Today, his routines have stood the test of time. Perhaps his cynicism is very much in touch with today's world. His genius was in knowing the core of our interests and what makes us smile.

The films he wrote appear to be semi-autobiographical. It's widely known that his early years were very difficult. Developing a sense of humor was probably a survival tactic he was forced to take on early in life. It may also explain why he was comfortable playing the underdog, one with more enemies than friends. However, there is usually at least one person in his circle who believes in him, making the final reel more palatable. Generally, a levelheaded daughter would provide support and encouragement. In the end he would emerge as a hero in an unfair world.

His next-to-last feature, **The Bank Dick** (1940), was a prime example of his genius. Early on in the film, there is a neat little family breakfast scene. He hasn't arrived from downstairs so we have an opportunity to hear what his family really thinks of him. It's rather frightening. After he does appear, the interactions are, to put it mildly, rather extreme. There is the flaky wife, a hawk-eyed mother-in-law and an older daughter offering unique perspectives on the family unit. In one grand moment, Fields is ready to heave a large cement pot toward his youngest daughter after she beans him on the head with a sharp object.

His day fatefully begins when, heading for the local bar, Fields unknowingly walks into the middle of a bank robbery. When the thief is caught, the townspeople mistakenly give Fields credit for foiling the gunman. Still in a drunken stupor, he seizes the opportunity and milks it for the reward. The bank complies by hiring him as a security guard or "bank dick."

The newly acquired job is rife with laughter. After accepting the position, he soon finds out that he isn't getting a salary. He has fallen behind in his mortgage payments, which he owes to the bank, so he essentially works for nothing. He also fails to muster any authority, taking a barrage of insults from customers. One lady asks her small son if he'd like to have a bag a nickels the size of that man's nose.

Outside of work, there is a minor collision with a car. Pointing to a piece of chrome trim on the vehicle that just goosed him, he says that putting funny looking things on motorcars is what kills people. His observation is prophetic and a good example of his vision. It's now a federal safety violation to place or design sharp objects on cars.

Fields sprinkles his films with subtle humor that wouldn't pass the censors if they were fully aware of the implications. For example, the film's title and the name of the local bar mask male and female genitalia. There are other less obvious teases. When a brick lands on his head, he exclaims "Godfrey Daniels." This is his invented slang for mad dog spelled backwards. Listen carefully to Fields' when he offers an evaluation of his daughter's fiancé, flabby Grady Sutton. Fields says the man sounds like a bubble in a bathtub—or flatulence.

His films also reveal his prejudices. There was a strong personal dislike for doctors. In declining health, Fields' scoffed at their advice to give up drinking. He gets revenge in this film. The physician, in a minute role, is seen as greedy and cold. His establishing scene has him examining an emaciated man; telling him that he better stop eating health food!

Movie directors were also on the Fields' hit list. In this film, his bragging places him in the director's chair when a movie is being filmed on location in the small town of Lompac. His ideas seem witless to the cast and crew, but Fields, as always, has the last laugh.

Director Charles Cline was one of the few men in the industry who could handle Fields' behavior on the set. Apparently he had to let Fields direct himself, as he did when they worked together in earlier films. Production could be tedious since Fields excessive drinking could hamper the marginally financed productions. Still, they always returned a modest profit and excellent reviews. However, studios were cautious offering him a lengthy production: the features he carried generally have very short running times.

Fields wrote the screenplay for **The Bank Dick** under the pseudonym Mahatma Kane Jeeves, an old vaudeville term meaning "My hat, my cane, Jeeves." Another name he sometimes used was Otis Criblecoblis. Usually he submitted a script proposal to studio heads in a very unorthodox way, like the back of an envelope. Visually it was unintelligible, but Fields was paid a salary for the sketchy idea much to the annoyance of polished studio writers. The fact is Fields knew exactly what he was going to do on camera, but could not or would not communicate it on paper.

The chase segment and finale are memorable. He plays driver/hostage to Filthy McNasty, the escaping bank robber. His calm observations during the journey are very funny.

The supporting cast is first rate. Una Merkel plays the older daughter and her opening speech on starving herself to death is a hoot. Franklin Pangborn offers further comic relief as the stuffy bank examiner. Three Stooges fans can spot Shemp Howard as Joe the bartender.

There were numerous classics before **The Bank Dick** that offer variations of his comic genius. His vaudeville roots of juggling and showmanship are evident in all of them. **It's a Gift** (1934) put him at war with a nagging wife and embracing another get rich scheme. **Man on a Flying Trapeze** (1935) was worth the price of admission to see him receive four tickets in a row from a traffic cop. He was one of the many stars in the episodic **If I had a Million** (1932). In this movie, he was beautifully partnered with Alison Skipworth. Together, they dueled road hogs, another of his pet peeves.

He did have a serious role, once, in **David Copperfield** (1935), as Micawber. His performance suggested that his dramatic range had not been fully exploited. There was also a memorable teaming with Mae West in **My Little Chickadee** in 1940. West shrewdly insisted on a no drinking clause in their contract to prevent production delays.

Chapter 8

His name was mentioned when MGM was casting the wizard in **The Wizard of Oz** (1939), but everyone knows the role went to Frank Morgan. Fields' last feature in a starring role was **Never Give a Sucker an Even Break** in 1941, directly after **The Bank Dick**. In this outing, he played himself trying unsuccessfully to sell a screenplay. The situation may not have been too far from the truth. He made appearances in several films after that, but only in isolated segments since his health was not up to carrying an entire movie. He died of cirrhosis of the liver on Christmas Day in 1946, a holiday he did not care for. He was one month shy of being 67 years old.

Carlotti Monti published an interesting perspective on Fields in 1972. Monti was Fields' mistress for the last 13 years of his life and can be seen in bit parts in several of his movies. Thus, **W.C. Fields and Me** was adapted to the screen in 1976 with Rod Steiger and Valerie Perrine taking on the roles of Fields and Monti.

Cast

W.C. Fields	*Egbert Sousè*
Cora Witherspoon	*Agatha Sousè*
Una Merkel	*Myrtle Sousè*
Evelyn Del Rio	*Elsie Mae Adele Brunch Sousè*
Jessie Ralph	*Mrs. Hermisillo Brunch*
Franklin Pangborn	*J. Pinkerton Snoopington*
Shemp Howard	*Joe Guelpe*
Dick Purcell	*Mackley Q. Greene*
Grady Sutton	*Og Oggilby*
Russell Hicks	*J. Frothingham Waterbury*
Pierre Watkin	*Mr. Skinner*
Al Hill	*Filthy McNasty*

Production

Edward F. Cline	*Director*
W.C. Fields, Richard Carroll	*Writers*
Jack J. Gross	*Producer*
Milton R. Krasner	*Cinematographer*

Charles Previn	*Original Music*
Universal	*Production Company*
Vera West	*Costumes*
USA/74/1940	*Country/Runtime/Year Released*

Chapter 8

Chapter 9

Beach Blanket Bingo

"Why me? Why me all the time?"

—Eric Von Zipper

Beach Blanket Bingo (1965), like other movies from its era that featured young people frolicking near the ocean and singing about love, was targeted to a specific audience. They were not designed to elicit favorable reviews or win an award for superior writing. They were designed to make money. Like teenagers, these films had to have a sense of rebellion about them. If you were in puberty, it was cool to go with your buddies to see them. It was even cooler that your parents didn't like or approve of them.

The mature audience had reason to pick other movies. The plot is as thin as its budget. The characters have no source of income and responsibilities. They hang out on million-dollar beach property without parental supervision. Usually there's an innocent tangle with the neighborhood toughs or the police, but no one really gets hurt. On the other hand, parents could be grateful that these kids spend most of their time flirting and surfing in the Southern California sunshine, never thinking about racial strife, Vietnam, or other social concerns in the mid-60s. That was to come a few years later.

The six beach movies produced by American International Pictures remain of interest to hardcore baby boomers and diehard fans of this genre. To the rest of the population, they are pleasant time fillers of a time gone by, before the seed of cynicism arrived and brought realism to the youth oriented film.

You must turn back your clock to this special illusion of innocence. The sands are full of beautiful young people with cropped hair and bright teeth. They are just beginning to experience adulthood and all the responsibilities it brings. Unlike today's teen pictures, they are not flaunting or testing out their equipment (at least not on the screen). They have normal teenage insecurities, but are filled with a sense of excitement, awe, and adventure. They remind us to not take life so seriously; to stop worrying about leaky plumbing, if the grass needs fertilizer, or whether your boss liked you on Tuesday.

The movies, of course, are not realistic interpretations of teenagers, then or now. It didn't matter. All of the beach movies were extremely popular at the time and made millions for the producers, who were savvy enough to see an opportunity and cash in. The AIP produced beach films were probably influenced by the box office might of **Where the Boys Are** (1960), a good movie about college guys and gals in Fort Lauderdale during spring break. Unlike this story, the beach series lacks serious pretensions. Welcome to their adventure. They are simply a bunch of young people dancing on the beach having a good time, thinking about sex, and little else.

Perhaps the peak of the series came with **Beach Blanket Bingo** in 1965. The producers spent more money than usual (well, not much more) and the finished product has a gloss the others failed to muster. This time our couple is involved in skydiving, a kidnapping, and some jealous suitors (Deborah Walley and John Ashley, who later were married in real life). A subplot involved series regular Bonehead (Jody McCrea) falling in love with a mermaid named Lorelei.

Don Rickles returned as Big Drop, a skydiving operator. He brought an extra panache to the proceedings with his now famous insult routine. At one point he tells Frankie that he can't sing and he's getting too old for this sort of thing. Rickles was half-right. Avalon was 30, but he could sing a pleasing tune, given good material and an arrangement. The other songs, by a band called *The Hondells*, are corny and contrast widely with today's more provocative teenage music.

Annette Funicello, once a Disney Mouseketeer, sticks to a one-piece swimsuit, perhaps in reverence to Uncle Walt, not that it detracts from her healthy upper body. She later said she had to have Walt Disney's permission to do these pictures.

Traditional to the series, Avalon and Funicello have a break-up somewhere during the course of action. This battle of the teenage sexes does not last too long. He eventually learns Annette's okay, even if she does assert her rights as a woman. Annette learns by the last reel that Frankie really does love her, despite his macho calf routines and the fact that she refuses to have sex with him until they're married.

Paul Lynde is very funny as Bullets, Linda Evans' cynical press agent. Evans, who would probably like to forget she was in this film, is pop star Sugar Kane. She's on the beach to promote her new album *Come Fall With Me*. (She's a skydiver, no less, no more). The original choice for the role was Nancy Sinatra since her dad's hit *Come Fly With Me* was high on the charts. However, she bowed out after Frank Sinatra, Jr. was kidnapped and father put a serious protection net around his offspring.

Harvey Lembeck plays roughhouse wannabe Eric von Zipper, leader of the Rat Pack. His biker character, as he thoughtfully explains, is a takeoff on Marlon Brando's interpretation in **The Wild Ones** (1954). His lovely cohorts in the mayhem are named Puss and Boots. He is about as frightening as a toddler going door to door for treats on Halloween.

Soap opera addicts can also spot a young Michael Nader as one of Frankie's buddies. He has a few lines, but no billing. It would be several years before he wooed the females with his work on daytime and nighttime soaps. In fact, he would be reunited with Evans on TV's *Dynasty* in the early 80s. When he reminded her they had worked together years before, the response she provided wasn't going to elicit further comments on the subject.

The beach series formula seldom varied, beginning with **Beach Party** (1963). This first in the series has anthropologist Robert Cummings studying the behavior of teenagers, hoping to discover what ails them. He picks Frankie and Annette, basic all-Americans, for his control group. What he finds out doesn't shock him.

The success of this film prompted a sequel, **Muscle Beach Party** (1964), which dropped anybody over 30 from star billing. The top slots now belonged to Frankie and Annette. In this outing, Frankie and company are bullied by Don Rickles and his stable of weightlifters, a curious phenomenon on California beaches at the time. Again the box office was strong, so **Bikini Beach** (1965) was produced as the next in the series. In this one, Avalon played dual roles, at one point our favorite teen crooner and at another point, a British pop star cleverly named the Potato Bug. The pun was directly aimed at the four young men from Liverpool who at the time were setting the charts on fire (and putting out to pasture crooners like Avalon, Bobby Darin, and Fabian).

The follow-up to **Beach Blanket Bingo** was **How to Stuff a Wild Bikini** (1965), but Avalon was inconceivably relegated to a cameo. The new leading man was Dwayne Hickman, fresh from his canceled television show. The return on investment was only a trickle, so the series producers moved from the sand to the south. In **Fireball 500** (1966) they traded beach balls for stock car racing and moonshine and added then teen heart throb Fabian, but this did little to keep interest from waning for this series. The times were changing and the surfer dude was going out. The new hero was the antihero. He had long hair, didn't conform to established rules of social conduct, and probably smoked pot in a beat up VW bus. Mike Nichols' **The Graduate** (1967) added a new dimension to the new "youth" film. And the girls—well, they were burning their bras and thinking about professional careers outside the ranch house in the suburbs.

There was a semi-private reunion of sorts for all of the players in this series in 1985, and it's well documented in the book *The Beach Party Phenomenon* by Stephen J. McParland. It's a must read for fans who admire this film genre.

In 1987 Frankie and Annette returned in **Back to the Beach**. Now middle-aged and married (to each other), they focused on the problems of being parents to teenagers. It was payback time, so to speak. Cashing in on the nostalgia craze, the movie tried hard to capture the original flair of the series (Connie Stevens and stars from classic television programs from the 1960s were brought in for some fun). The movie does have its moments. Lovely Annette still looked pretty good in her suit.

Following **Back to the Beach**, Frankie and Annette continued to work on projects related to their past glory. Avalon toured with Fabian and Bobby Rydel as a trio and with Funicello for some concert

Chapter 9

dates in the 90s. Sadly, Funicello revealed in 1992 that she had been battling multiple sclerosis for quite some time, and began to severely limit her personal appearances. She died of complications from the disease in 2013 at the age of 70.

Cast

Frankie Avalon	*Frankie*
Annette Funicello	*Dee Dee*
Deborah Walley	*Bonnie Graham*
Harvey Lembeck	*Eric Von Zipper*
John Ashley	*Steve Gordon*
Jody McCrea	*Bonehead*
Donna Loren	*Donna*
Marta Kristen	*Lorelei*
Linda Evans	*Sugar Kane*
Timothy Carey	*South Dakota Slim*
Don Rickles	*Big Drop*
Paul Lynde	*Bullets*
Donna Michelle	*Animal*
Michael Nader	*Butch*
Patti Chandler	*Patti*
Buster Keaton	*Buster Keaton*
Earl Wilson	*Earl Wilson*
Bobbi Shaw	*Bobbi*

Production

William Asher	*Director*
William Asher, Leo Townsend	*Writers*
Samuel Z. Arkoff, James H. Nicholson, Anthony Carras	*Producers*
Les Baxter, Roger Christian, Jerry Styner, Gary Usher	*Original Music*
Floyd Crosby	*Cinematography*
AIP	*Production Company*
USA/98 minutes/1964	*Country/Runtime/Year Released*

Chapter 10

Beat the Devil

*"They're desperate characters—
not one looked at my legs."*

—*Gwendolen Chelm*

Humphrey Bogart remains one of the most popular male personalities created during the golden age of movies. In fact, his popularity reached dizzying heights long after his premature death in 1957, thanks to television, college campus replays and art house revivals of his movies, and an affectionate valentine from Woody Allen.

Bogart's career is made of solid gold. His body of work contains more than his share of good films. In fact, a large number of his movies consistently rank among the top films of all time. To have the success he achieved, he must have been as resilient as the characters he played. When he arrived in Hollywood, there was a sea of handsome actors vying for the top spots. He wasn't handsome, suave, or dashing in the traditional sense. Thus, it took awhile for him to be fully established as a leading man, to be the tough cynical loner able to survive in a difficult world. When he found his film niche and had the power to pick and choose his roles to hone this image, audiences flocked to see their hero. Unlike some other cult figures in the film world, the relationship Bogart had with his fans was very healthy. Men wanted to be like him, and women wanted to be with him.

In his early films, Bogart was often cast as a gangster or someone from the underbelly of society. Later, when he became a man of integrity, he embraced solitary professions like private eye or adventurer. When he switched to being a good guy, he still carried the baggage of the earlier career, nosebleeds and all. His scars wouldn't allow him to get close to anyone. Thus, he was very careful with whom he chose to drink and sleep with. It's also remarkable that the characters in his films are frequently older beyond their real years. They have learned from their mistakes.

Subsidiary characters in his gallery of work are filled with manipulative females, sly or arrogant members of the underworld, and gangsters like ones he once played. The results are always unpleasant for them. He sees through the veneer, despite the size of their bank account, the quality of the clothes they wear, or the excuses they give for their behavior. He is wise enough to walk away from a problem, but if pushed, he uses his brains to deflate the intellectual snob or his fists to end that difference of opinion. Or both.

He moves from tough to sensitive with ease. Women find his charm and power irresistible. In his interactions with females, he always does the choosing. He's always in charge and never allows his feelings for them to get in the way of justice. Men loved this aspect of his personality—the ability to control one's emotions.

This image, lovingly worshiped by fans both young and old, was established or consolidated in three films: **The Maltese Falcon** (1941), The **Treasure of the Sierra Madre** (1948) and The **African Queen** (1951). His good friend, Director John Huston, directed all three of these classics. He was also fortunate that his rival, George Raft rejected many of the scripts he received, including those for **The Maltese Falcon**, **Casablanca** (1942) and **High Sierra** (1941).

While he appeals to both sexes, males are more likely to be part of his core fan mix. He acts out male fantasies. He's the guy that does not play by the rules. Women are used primarily for sex and it takes a long time for him to warm up to a dame. He is a true existential hero, one that is opposed to any type of authority. He doesn't say he's sorry—unless he really means it. The core of his character is not unlike the personality Clint Eastwood adopted for **Dirty Harry** (1971).

It's uncertain how Bogart injured his lips. The studio publicists said it was from a World War I injury, but other reports said it was from a childhood accident. Whatever the cause, his vocal defect and drooping mouth could have been the kiss of death to some actors. For him it was turned into an asset and became a distinguishing trademark. Early in his career he used his appearance to menace society. Later, it made him appear weary of the world.

His first impact was in **The Petrified Forest** (1936), when his gang terrorized Bette Davis and other innocents at a roadside diner. When he developed into the good guy, you knew he'd never be completely on your side. It is his nature to not trust anyone.

In the early 50s, when the Bogart image was permanent, almost legendary, and very popular, the star tackled a series of creative projects to flex his acting might. **The African Queen** was like his other antiheroes, but teamed with fiery Katharine Hepburn brought fireworks and a Best Actor Oscar.

While other directors enhanced his appeal, Huston completed Bogart's transformation from featured villain to tough hero, thus widening his audience appeal immeasurably. With this success, Bogart and Huston collaborated for a fourth and final time with **Beat the Devil**. Based on a novel by James Helvick, it was originally intended as a follow-up to his earlier espionage tales. But the story didn't gel. After reading the first draft, Bogart reportedly said "it stinks."

Rather than drop the project entirely, Huston hired novelist Truman Capote(!) to jazz things up. The salvage idea was to satirize Bogart's and Huston's previous work and send-up the Bogart image. Their investment was high (Bogart owned the rights to the story and was one of the producers), so they went ahead with it, despite reservations. Bogart thought the end results were a mess. Most critics agreed and the audiences stayed away.

After his death from cancer in 1957, a growing legion of Bogart fans began to see **Beat the Devil** as a witty, clever spoof, worthy of their hero. They could also see it as a bold move. Creating a caricature of your image in an entire film was something new in 1953. At the time it was a footnote in his long career. Today, time has served it well. It helps put his career in perspective. The elements of the classic Bogart movie are all there and intact. There is a generous assortment of shady characters with different nationalities. Most prominent are Robert Morley and Peter Lorre, past alumni from other Huston-Bogart movies.

Chapter 10

The females are also very interesting. For decoration there is Gina Lollobrigida. In a bit of inspired casting, Jennifer Jones is a flaky woman with a penchant for making up stories when the conversation becomes routine. This motley crew assembled in Italy to make their sordid plans to control the uranium market in a backward Central-African country. With the atomic age in full blast, this mineral was the stuff bad guy dreams are made of.

The plan, however, is wrought with disasters. First, a leisurely business lunch meeting turns into an embarrassing freak accident when their antique limousine goes over a cliff. Later, the dilapidated ship they board to Africa stalls and eventually sinks. Struggling toward shore, they are confronted with hostile natives.

Sex is also on everyone's mind, in the subtext. There are hints of wife swapping. Bogie is married to luscious Lollo, but Jones is also in the game.

Unlike the characters he is spoofing, Bogart appears to be something of a dilettante in this role. He dabbles in things, not showing real substance. He buys a seasonal restaurant only because he likes the food. He loses it to the bank, but still gets to eat there all year long. This is what's important to him.

Though his behavior is strange, he is not without his smarts. He's involved with a group of associates, being very careful to not call them friends. On their journey to Africa, all are suspicious of each other's motives and are pretty frank about it. One of Bogart's best lines from the adventure is "I must have a lot of money, otherwise I become dull and listless."

Jones is surprisingly the funniest performer of the bunch. She is married to a fellow who fancies himself an English squire. Their chess match is perhaps a summary of their relationship and reveals his lack of blue blood. She admits to being a witch. Her art is throwing red herrings to mess up everyone's plans. When Morley suspects a swindle, he asks her what her real game is. Without flinching, she responds with "sin." When Morley's triple chin drops in astonishment, she asks him "isn't that what we're most concerned with? Sin?" This sounds like Truman Capote having a very good time. As in other

Bogart films, she is the central female character that drills holes in the established rules.

Morley is cast as "Fat Guy," a direct spoof of Sidney Greenstreet's fat man in search of a rare bird. His conversation with the African leader is a highlight. Hiding their real intentions, he says he's there to sell sewing machines and vacuum cleaners—hut to hut.

Bogart makes friends with the African Leader and turns their release negotiations to his advantage. The leader idolizes actress Rita Hayworth and has a shrine to her in his bungalow. Bogart promises an introduction to the actress (although the two never made a movie together). The scriptwriter may be referencing Hayworth's then current exotic husband, Aly Khan.

After **Beat the Devil**, Bogart was powerful enough to expand his acting range, though still within his acceptable image. He was the psychotic Captain Queeg in **The Caine Mutiny** (1954), courted Audrey Hepburn in **Sabrina** (1954), and made Ava Gardner a star when she was **The Barefoot Contessa** (1954). But his fans adore the character he spoofed in this movie. Aside from Huston's work, the image was perfected in Howard Hawks' **To Have and Have Not** (1944) and **The Big Sleep** (1946) with wife Lauren Bacall. There is also fond affection for the wartime love story, **Casablanca** (1942).

The late 60s brought a renewed popularity for Bogart. Riding the crest of this wave was Woody Allen's **Play it Again, Sam** (1972). An actor played Bogart's ghost and the character provided nerdy Allen with much needed advice on love, and other survival skills.

Jennifer Jones was married to **Gone with the Wind** (1939) producer David O. Selznik. She won the Best Actress Oscar for their first movie together, **The Song of Bernadette** (1943). Her career is interesting, but he could have managed it better. Through the 50s she had plum parts in many of his highest quality productions but she virtually retired from the screen after his death in 1965. Her last film was a good one, **The Towering Inferno** (1974). She had hoped to film **Terms of Endearment** (1983) but when it became clear that no one would make it with her (she was too mature for the role), she turned the rights over to James Brooks and it became an Oscar winning vehicle for Shirley MacLaine.

Chapter 10

Robert Morley enlivened many Hollywood and international productions in supporting roles for over 50 years. A catchphrase in Hollywood noted his professionalism. When a movie was bad, industry insiders were heard to say "even Robert Morley could not have saved it." The thought has merit. Morley had a way with a line and could extract wit from the most banal script. His aristocratic English humor, with a dose of haughtiness, is very much in evidence in this movie.

Gina Lollobrigida, known as La Lollo in her Italian homeland, became the first European sex star to make it big in Hollywood. It almost didn't happen. She was tied to a contract under Howard Hughes, preventing her from filming in Hollywood for years. However, the contract didn't carry weight outside the United States. Since this is a British production filmed in Italy, it is one of her first English speaking roles. Later in the decade, once free from Hughes, she enlivened many Hollywood productions with her earthy brand of Italian temper and sensational figure. She retired from the screen in the mid-70s to become a photojournalist, scoring a major scoop with an interview with Fidel Castro. She still looked marvelous when she was invited back to Hollywood in the 80s for some guest shots on TV. In 2015, she appeared at the TCM Film Festival and shared Hollywood anecdotes with an attentive audience. She said David Selznick asked her to withdraw from the picture because her beauty would overshadow his wife Jones. She told Selznick that she had signed a contract and had no intention of backing out of her commitment.

Peter Lorre's first role was the child murderer in Fritz Lang's **M** (1931). Its international success typecast him as something sinister for the next 35 years, including one of the dubious characters in **The Maltese Falcon**. Along with Sidney Greenstreet, Lorre was a top villain at Warner Brothers in the 40s. He had been off the screen a few years when Huston and Bogart persuaded his return to **Beat the Devil**. After re-emerging, he worked steadily in small roles until his death.

Cast

Humphrey Bogart	*Billy Dannreuther*
Jennifer Jones	*Gwendolen Chelm*
Gina Lollobrigida	*Maria Dannreuther*
Robert Morley	*Peterson*
Peter Lorre	*O'Hara*
Edward Underdown	*Harry Chelm*
Ivor Barnard	*Major Ross*
Marco Tulli	*Ravello*
Bernard Lee	*C.I.D. Inspector*

Production

John Huston	*Director*
James Helvick (novel), Truman Capote,	*Writers*
John Huston, Anthony Veiller, Peter Viertel	
Jack Clayton, John Huston, Humphrey Bogart,	*Producers*
Angelo Rizzoli, John Woolf	
Oswald Morris	*Cinematographer*
Franco Mannino	*Original Music*
Rizzoli-Haggiag/Romulus Films Ltd/Santana	*Production Company*
United Kingdom/100/1953	*Country/Runtime/Year Released*

Chapter 11

The Big Heat

"We're sisters under the mink."

—Debby Marsh

A basic plot element of a movie is to have a good force pitted against a bad force. Their collision, friction, and difference of opinion keep our attention. This premise is especially prevalent in movies concerning the underworld. In the golden years, Hollywood typically presented the police as noble and upstanding citizens, sworn to uphold the law despite any stress placed on them. These uniformed citizens may be detached from their work and may not even like what they're doing, but there is an honor and respectability to their profession because they guard our safety. Many of us sitting comfortably in a movie theatre have little contact with the seamy side of life or with the police (and it's usually when we receive a traffic violation). Thus, we may harbor the illusion that members of our law enforcement agencies are sincere, thoughtful, above board, extremely competent and can always be counted on to look after our best interests.

On the other side of the fence, the bad guys and gals are pretty scary. They exploit, assault, harass, rob, or intimidate anyone who blocks their cruel path to wealth and power. There are no rules to their behavior. They have a bag full of dirty tricks just waiting to be used on the unsuspecting. When these individuals are carted off to jail or the morgue in the end, it is both justifiable and a relief. We feel safer that they will no longer be a problem to society.

There are always distinct lines of behavior to these opposing parties. However, Fritz Lang's **The Big Heat** is a variation of this idea, but with more grit and dimension than most film noirs can muster. The leading man/hero, Glenn Ford, is the "good" detective. He is a family man, the model citizen. He pays taxes, has a mortgage, and drives a Ford. Then he snaps.

The story is relatively simple. Ford suspects the mob has infiltrated the police department. He makes a lot of noise and accuses his supervisors of sandbagging. He eventually pushes too hard in his investigation and his wife becomes a victim in a retaliatory measure meant for him. This destroys the only warm and safe place he knows—his home. Bitter, angry, and driven, he seeks revenge by thinking and acting like a criminal. He turns the screws on the mob and does not let up.

Crime fighting becomes a personal crusade to him. He becomes almost suicidal and doesn't seem to care if he returns home after calling it a day. This increases his ability to take risks and evens the playing field. Suddenly he doesn't blink when fighting the mob. By removing boundaries of good conduct, he freely uses his fists, tools of the gangster trade, and other crude forms of manipulation on the criminals. He hits below the belt. It's as if he's saying, "an eye for and eye." When he uses his poison, the lines between good and bad become blurred. It becomes difficult to distinguish who is morally right. Lang suggests that good must become bad to rid the world of all that is evil. And that causes us to ask ourselves how far over the line the righteous can go to stop corruption before they become part of the problem. That is the most intriguing nature of **The Big Heat.**

This is but one film in Fritz Lang's catalog of corruption and cynicism. He frequently explores the seamy side of life. **M** (1931), his personal favorite, creates an atmosphere of terror in a city besieged by a child murderer. **Fury** (1936) is about lynch mobs and **The Woman in the Window** (1944) details a story of lust and murder.

Like these films, **The Big Heat** is a superbly crafted movie. Lang shoots most of the scenes at night with stark lighting. He uses soft tones of gray inside Ford's house to suggest warmth. Otherwise the lighting contrasts create jarring images. For example, when Ford visits the mob-financed mansion, calls on the policeman's widow, or goes to the cocktail lounge populated by the underworld, it is well

Chapter 11

lighted and white. But in this case, white is not pure. The fixtures, lack of shading, and straight lines signal opposition and conflict. This use of shading reveals the tension between good and bad. He takes image of good and bad—black, white, night, day—and mixes them up, all to great effect.

Lee Marvin is the key player in the collision. He is your basic psychopath and gets his kicks from physically hurting women. He throws a pot of hot coffee into Gloria Grahame's face when she tries to split—a scene that still shocks us today—and he stubs out a cigarette on Carolyn Jones' hand when she doesn't roll the dice to his satisfaction.

Pitting Ford against Marvin creates tremendous friction, which becomes the source of **The Big Heat**. Grahame puts herself in the middle of these opposing forces, a hell spot if ever there was one. As a gray area in the film, she is willing to make the ultimate sacrifice for the man she loves. Her experience also implies that once you start down a particular path of destruction, it's difficult to change direction, no matter how good your intentions are.

As Ford pushes the rulebook aside, he pits the criminals against each other with greater frequency. He threatens them in public places, telling Marvin "why don't you get out of here while you can still walk." He threatens to expose people hiding behind a mask of respectability. He tangles innocently with B-girls—the ladies that hang out at the bar—and know the score.

The prime B-girl is Gloria Grahame. She is attracted to power, clothes, travel and expensive entertainment. Like others of her same breed, she gets biffed around every once in a while, but she knows it is part of the deal. She comes across as hard, but not without compassion. This ounce of pride contributes to her downfall. Grahame is quite excellent here. Her sensuality is open and exciting, especially when she follows Ford to his hotel room and draws down the covers on the bed.

Ford's obsession for revenge unleashes his terror on Marvin and anyone else that stands in his way. The establishment tries to restrain him, so he resigns from the force. They ask for his gun, but he refuses. He calls them chicken-hearted and storms out.

The mob is especially worried about this turn of events. They are used to having the boys in blue take bribes and respect the rules. In an attempt to shock some sense into Ford, Grahame questions his objective with the telling remark "there isn't much difference between you and Vince Stone."

Ford's easygoing acting persona is perfect for this type of complex character. He typically played the fresh egg, always intelligent, slow to rile up. He first scored with Rita Hayworth when she was **Gilda** (1946). His work peaked in the 50s in dramas like **The Blackboard Jungle** (1955); in comedies like **The Teahouse of the August Moon** (1956); and in westerns like **The Sheepman** (1958). His 60s work is solid but his acting style of relaxed niceness had run its course. It is something of value to have, and was put to good use as the adopted dad to **Superman** (1978).

Grahame remains one of the screen's best ladies of easy virtue. Her appeal was strong enough to move out of bit parts (she's the blonde who flirts with Jimmy Stewart in 1947's **It's a Wonderful Life**) to a co-starring role with Humphrey Bogart in Nicholas Ray's **In a Lonely Place** (1950). She was married to Director Ray at the time, and the teaming with Bogart pushed her up the ladder a notch or two. She won the Best Supporting Actress Oscar for being bad in **The Bad and the Beautiful** (1952) and played Ado Annie in the screen adaptation of **Oklahoma!** (1955) as the girl who can't say no. Another variation of her film persona can best be seen in **Sudden Fear** (1954), when she and Jack Palance plotted unsuccessfully against Joan Crawford.

Grahame eventually divorced Ray and married his son—her step-son—and stayed away from film to raise her family. She returned in the 70s for character parts. One of her last roles was in a good film, **Melvin and Howard** (1980).

It would be ten years before Lee Marvin would graduate to stardom. After playing Liberty Valance in **The Man Who Shot Liberty Valance** (1962), he cleaned up his act. After all, major stars have to

Chapter 11

be respectable members of society. Once he became one of the good guys, audiences lost one of the best of the screen villains.

Fritz Lang followed up this movie with **Human Desire** (1954), reuniting Ford and Grahame. Again, it detailed Lang's interest in violence and social themes. His familiar style and craftsmanship were there, as always, but it doesn't pack the heat of this film.

Cast

Glenn Ford	*Dave Bannion*
Gloria Grahame	*Debby Marsh*
Jocelyn Brando	*Katie Bannion*
Alexander Scourby	*Mike Lagana*
Lee Marvin	*Vince Stone*
Jeanette Nolan	*Bertha Duncan*
Peter Whitney	*Tierney*
Carolyn Jones	*Doris*

Production

Fritz Lang	*Director*
William P. McGivern (story), Sydney Boehm	*Writers*
Robert Arthur	*Producer*
Charles Lang	*Cinematographer*
Henry Vars	*Original Music*
Jean Louis (gowns)	*Costumes*
Columbia Pictures	*Production Company*
USA/89/1953	*Country/Runtime/Year Released*

Chapter 12

The Blues Brothers

"We're on a mission from God!"

—*Elwood Blues*

When NBC's *Saturday Night Live* burst onto the TV scene in 1975, it was funny, fresh, and innovative. It was a showcase for a group of young comics, a bridge between old hats like Jack Benny and Bob Hope who had honed their craft on vaudeville, and middle-agers like Alan King and Carl Reiner who did their work on television and in Las Vegas. The original cast members in the SNL ensemble included Dan Ackroyd, John Belushi, Chevy Chase, Jane Curtin, Gilda Radner, and Garrett Morris. Bill Murray joined the cast in 1977.

After a couple of seasons most of these performers left to pursue their careers. Inevitably, they made a pitch for stardom on the big screen.

The first to leave the fold was Chevy Chase. He did well in movies initially, but a string of very weak comedies in the 90s dampened his hopes of a long-term career in film. Bill Murray found a niche in character roles. Gilda Radner lost a courageous and public fight with cancer at 42, never realizing her full potential in movies. Jane Curtin found herself in a successful TV series, *Kate and Allie*, one of the better sitcoms in its day that enjoyed a long run.

Of all of the original cast members, Dan Ackroyd and John Belushi were probably the most successful big-screen hitters. Ironically their overwhelming popularity in movie theatres was based on a pair of characters they created for the TV program.

Their creation was a pair of siblings who sang rhythm and blues punctuated by rock and roll. They called themselves **The Blues Brothers**. They wore dark suits and hats, white socks, sunglasses (indoors and outdoors), and performed acrobatic dances on stage. The two actors said in interviews that their inspiration was blues legend Sam Cook. If so, they were modeling themselves after one of the best. Even if their gig was just okay musically, they opened up a floodgate of enthusiasm for something with rhythm. This was especially apparent in 1980 when the repetitive sounds of disco were on the wane and new wave wasn't yet strong enough to take the country by storm. **The Blues Brothers** sound was what young people needed to grab onto at the time, making this the perfect summer movie of 1980.

Always affable with just the right amount of farce, **The Blues Brothers** never takes itself seriously. It has an updated, very modern charm about it. And as a musical, it stands on its own creativity. In contrast, 1978's **Grease** satirized the style of the 50s by poking fun at an era of milkshakes and Sandra Dee, often in a condescending manner.

The movie duo is the brainchild of Dan Ackroyd. With director John Landis, they fashioned a simple screenplay into a fun, large-budget film. The premise is an update of the old Judy Garland/ Mickey Rooney films in which the gang puts on a show to raise money for themselves. Set in 1980, though, this film has slapstick violence and rough language, much to the delight of young people.

The Blues Brothers wanted you to believe they learned their craft from performing and sweating in small smoke-filled bars near Maxwell Street. In the movie, their history is vague but we do know they're a deadpan act from Chicago. There is Elwood Jake (John Belushi) with his name tattooed on his fingers to prove it. He is pudgy but still manages some nifty acrobatics, courtesy of a more lithe stand-in. Warming up to a song, he twirls a watch on a chain. He is slightly more obnoxious than his taller brother, Dan Ackroyd, who goes by the name of Jake.

As the story unfolds, we learn Jake and Elwood grew up in a city orphanage run by a strict nun they nicknamed Penguin (gloriously realized by Kathleen Freeman). Their father figure was itinerant handyman Curtis (Cab Calloway), who also is an excellent blues man. There is a problem, though. The Chicago Tax Authority has revalued the orphanage property and the Penguin owes $5,000 in taxes. If the nun doesn't pay, the orphanage will fold and all the hapless children that live there will be thrown into the cold street. Earning the $5,000 to save the orphanage becomes the noble reason the Blues Brothers create a living nightmare for Chicago's finest.

The brothers receive a message from God in the person of James Brown, telling them to regroup their band. As they try to organize a reunion of band mates, funny things keep happening to the duo. There is a mysterious girl (Carrie Fisher) who keeps trying to assassinate them. They become involved in a grudge match with some Chicago Nazis (led by Henry Gibson) and try out their stuff at a hardcore country and western bar. Most prominent are their frequent run-ins with authority, usually involving some driving infraction.

The film's highlights belong to the music, which gives viewers a perfect opportunity to see and hear professional singers strut their stuff in cameos. Aretha Franklin's reprises her *Respect* number in a greasy spoon diner. She's in top form, traveling around each note like it's a cuddly baby. Unlike the elaborate costumes she wears in concert, she sports a foodstained apron and fuzzy pink bedroom slippers. It's a great comedy number and her last line is a riot.

Ray Charles gives a performance that contains the usual boundless energy his fans are accustomed to. There is a too brief sequence of *Boom Boom* with Johnny Lee Hooker, plus James Brown in a singing and dancing call to the lord. Gleefully, another old timer, Cab Calloway, puts on permanent record his audience participating number *Minnie the Moocher*. This is the same guy who sang *Reefer Madness* in 1933's **International House**.

Chicago is a wonderful backdrop for the film. You can almost smell the hot dogs and pizza in the streets. There are frequent jokes (and landmarks) concerning the city's long running mayor, the late Richard J. Daley. The Daley machine was a familiar catchphrase to Chicagoans. It began in 1955 and ended when the powerful figure died peacefully at work in 1976 while sitting at his desk. A few years later, when **Blues Brothers** was being filmed, Jane Byrne held the reins to one of the most interesting cities in the world. She apparently got into the blues festivities during filming, and the national media

Chapter 12

published a photograph of her decked out in a black blues outfit complete with sunglasses and fedora. Embarrassed and crying foul, she claimed the photo of her with Belushi and Ackroyd was private and not for public consumption. Some heads from her office did sing the blues when the pictures escaped their scrutiny. Later, the dark suits and sunglasses worn by the boys sold at auction for $12,000.

Director John Landis reportedly crashed over fifty 1974 Dodge four door sedans for the film's series of stunts. There are also several spectacular chases featuring a good deal of ribbing about Chicago's Wacker Drive and the structural girders of the Chicago Loop.

Unfortunately, **The Blues Brothers** was a career high for the Belushi and Ackroyd team. They reunited in the terribly unfunny **Neighbors** in 1982. Belushi died of a drug overdose shortly before its release. He was only 33. A subsequent investigation, book, and movie filled in the details of his tragically short life.

Belushi's death left Ackroyd with a number of unfinished projects. **Spies Like Us** (1985) was to have reunited the pair with Landis. Instead, fellow SNL alum Chevy Chase took the role and the film was very popular. Ackroyd has gone on to solid straight performances in major films like **Driving Miss Daisy** (1989), **Chaplin** (1993), and **Pearl Harbor** (2001).

However, Ackroyd mistakenly tried to produce a **Blues Brothers** sequel twenty years after this classic. With Director Landis and actor John Goodman, **Blues Brothers 2000** reunited many of the original cast members but the finished product was not as inspiring as its predecessor.

Cast

John Belushi	*"Joliet" Jake Blues*
Dan Aykroyd	*Elwood Blues*
James Brown	*Reverend Cleophus James*
Cab Calloway	*Curtis*
Ray Charles	*Ray*
Aretha Franklin	*Mrs. Murphy*
Steve Cropper	*Steve "The Colonel" Cropper*

Donald Dunn	*Donald "Duck" Dunn*
Murphy Dunne	*Murphy "Murph" Dunne*
Willie Hall	*Willie "Too Big" Hall*
Tom Malone	*Tom "Bones" Malone*
Lou Marini	*"Blue Lou" Marini*
Matt Murphy	*Matt "Guitar" Murphy*
Alan Rubin	*Alan "Mr. Fabulous" Rubin*
Carrie Fisher	*Mystery Woman*
Henry Gibson	*Head Nazi*
John Candy	*Burton Mercer*
Kathleen Freeman	*Sister Mary Stigmata (a.k.a. The Penguin)*
Steve Lawrence	*Maury Slime*
Twiggy Lawson	*Chic Lady*
Frank Oz	*Corrections Officer*
Charles Napier	*Tucker McElroy*
Chaka Khan	*Choir Soloist*
Steven Bishop	*Charming Trooper*
John Landis	*Trooper La Fong*
Paul Reubens	*Waiter*
Steven Spielberg	*Cook County Assessor's Office Clerk*
John Lee Hooker	*Street Slim*

Production

John Landis	*Director*
Dan Ackroyd, John Landis	*Writers*
Bernie Brillstein, George Folsey Jr., David Sosna, Robert K. Weiss	*Producers*
Stephen M. Katz	*Cinematographer*
Elmer Bernstein	*Original Music*
Deborah Nadoolman	*Costumes*
Universal Pictures	*Production Company*
USA/133/1980	*Country/Runtime/Year Released*

Chapter 12

Chapter 13

Bob & Carol & Ted & Alice

*"First, we'll have an orgy. Then
we'll go see Tony Bennett."*

—*Ted Henderson*

Bob & Carol & Ted & Alice was one of the breakthrough sex
comedies of the 60s, at least for those put out by major Hollywood
studios. Just a few years before, Doris Day was doing her best to titillate audiences by discussing her lack of bedroom experience. The
big screen turned daring and sexy as the decade came to close. The
phrase turning on and tuning out became familiar, as well as something called free love. The feminist movement also pushed things
up a notch a bit. Suddenly, women wanted their share of foreplay.
Hollywood took notice that the buying public was actively seeking
mature, adult themes. While the big and established stars were not
willing to roll around in bed, plenty of star-hopefuls were willing to
showcase their physical gifts. However, a number of actors, including
established performers were willing to talk about sex in great detail
without blushing. By the 70s, our sensitivity to sex on the big screen
had diminished. What was once left to the imagination was now in
full view.

Bob & Carol & Ted & Alice is a month in the sex lives of two
Californian couples. The hip couple is Bob (Robert Culp) and his
beautiful wife Carol (Natalie Wood). He is a film producer and she is a
typical film producer's housewife. The film opens with Bob and Carol
attending an educational workshop. It is one of those self-exploratory
classes conducted by a self-ordained guru, a man whose advice is
probably more superficial than they realize. Their interpretation from
this heady experience: They now have permission to seek out their

80   Chapter 13

darkest desires. Not wasting time to put them in practice, they develop a whole new set of values and mores, heartily sprinkled with the proper language of the day, including words like hip, cop-out, head trip, cool, and groovy.

Greg Mullavey (later the husband to Mary Hartman on TV's *Mary Hartman, Mary Hartman*) plays the leader who unleashes their power, so to speak. Interestingly enough, many of the conflicts that come out in this free-for-all are the topics we now hear on programs from Oprah Winfrey to Phil Donahue. People speak of promiscuity, demanding better sex, unfulfilling sex, and not being able to have sex. Mullavey's rule of thumb is "don't talk how you think, tell them how you feel. Deal with your feelings, give more of yourself." He also instructs them on a form of primal therapy, 1969 style, where participants actively beat pillows and scream.

Since this intense workout changes Bob and Carol's perceptions of their universe, they boldly push their nonsense onto a waiter at an expensive restaurant. It's a very funny scene, unless you are the waiter. More seriously, though, Bob and Carol decide to explore alternative relationships within their newly found karma. Bob has an affair and confesses the sordid drama to Carol. She grins and says okay, that was nice. Then she sleeps with a tennis pro hunk. Bob, afraid of being a hypocrite, offers a cocktail with the bewildered man to prove that he plays on the same playing field with his wife. It really bothers Bob when the man asks for the expensive liquor.

The fireworks begin to fly when they increasingly push their views on the more uptight Ted and Alice. They are their closest friends, but have a more conservative set of values. Bob and Carol drive a Jaguar and live in a contemporary southern California ranch. They wear medallions and the latest fashions in polyester. In contrast, Ted (Elliott Gould) and Alice (Dyan Cannon) drive a Cadillac, a symbol of American prosperity and conservatism. They are strictly button-down types and live in early-American Ethan Allan splendor. Ted is the first to cave in to the new sport. Too bad for him that he tells Alice of his affair at the most inopportune time. Meanwhile she has some seriously funny sessions with her analyst.

Chapter 13

The ads for this film openly flaunted the wife-swapping theme. Will they really do it? The four do have a serious get together before a Tony Bennett show in Las Vegas. But the ending is very open-ended. It is up to the audience to decide if they go all the way.

Wood is the perfect Carol. Though very popular with audiences, many critics found her acting limited and one-dimensional. However, she is quite competent in this role. She was one performer who had more style than substance. In fact, Wood knew she was no heavyweight in the drama department and had a sense of humor about it. When *Harvard Lampoon* voted her the worst actress of the year, she went to the ceremony and accepted the award. After her death in 1981 in a drowning accident, her sister Lana wrote a candid and loving book, *Natalie—a Memoir by Her Sister*. Lana Wood said her older sister was nervous during the filming and concerned over her faltering career. Distributors had labeled her box-office poison after a series of expensive failures. Believing her cleancut image was a liability, she was also afraid that newcomer Dyan Cannon would draw attention away from her. In an industry that is heavily dependent on beauty, one might be able to justify her insecurities. However, in retrospect, Ms. Wood didn't have anything to worry about. She's wonderful and sexy, like a light bulb that refuses to dim. In fact, this film was a worldwide hit, one of the most successful of her career. Wisely, she accepted a percentage of the profits and reaped a bonanza.

As if resting on her laurels (and to spend time with her children), she stayed away from the screen, only to return in the late 70s in several forgettable roles. Her last film **Brainstorm** (1983) was almost shelved when she died during production. It was a good film. Her role was abbreviated, but she fit into the ensemble cast that included Cliff Robertson, Louise Fletcher and Christopher Walkin. The film was dedicated to her memory. The final credits ended with the message "To Natalie."

Cannon won the coveted role of Alice just as her marriage to Cary Grant was ending. Grant used his connections in the industry to get her the job, thinking it would save their marriage. In reality, it just brought her independence. Her performance was good enough to resurrect a dormant career. She was justifiably rewarded with an academy award nomination for best supporting actress (as was Gould for supporting actor, and Mazursky and Tucker for their original screenplay). Popularized by this performance, she became a very busy leading lady during the 70s, playing cheerful, lusty, and somewhat flaky broads. She gave that image a middle-aged slant when she played a reoccurring role on TV's *Ally McBeal* as Judge Whipper.

Gould was married to Barbara Streisand, and while in the shadow of her success, he was known as Mr. Barbara Streisand. That changed when he scored big in his next film **M*A*S*H** (1970). Culp, more of a TV star than film personality, has seen most of his work on the small screen.

This hit movie inspired a television series of the same name, though none of the movie cast participated. Since that medium was not as free to explore the mores of society, it played flat and was cancelled after a brief run.

The appropriately titled song *What the World Needs Now is Love* was composed by Burt Bacharach and Hal David, and with vocals by Jackie DeShannon.

Cast

Natalie Wood	*Carol Sanders*
Robert Culp	*Bob Sanders*
Elliott Gould	*Ted Henderson*
Dyan Cannon	*Alice Henderson*
Horst Ebersberg	*Horst*
Lee Bergere	*Emilio*
Donald F. Muhich	*Psychiatrist*
Noble Lee Holderread, Jr.	*Sean*
K.T. Stevens	*Phyllis*
Celeste Yarnall	*Susan*
Greg Mullavy	*Group Leader*

Production

Paul Mazursky	*Director*
Paul Mazursky, Larry Tucker	*Writers*

Chapter 13

Larry Tucker	*Producer*
Charles Lang	*Cinematographer*
Quincy Jones, Burt Bacharach	*Original Music*
Moss Mabry	*Costumes*
Columbia Pictures	*Production Company*
USA/104/1969	*Country/Runtime/Year Released*

Chapter 14

Bye Bye Birdie

"The next time I have a daughter, I hope it's a boy."
—Harry McAfee

Elvis Presley's tremendous influence on American pop music and culture in the 50s and his enduring legacy following his death at 42 in 1977 speak well for him as an artist and as a pioneer in the field of entertainment. He was one of the true greats. Elvis didn't just sing to audiences, he mesmerized them.

When Elvis first appeared to the entire nation (in the mid50s), he made every other male performer in his peer group look as though they were standing still. An historic appearance on *The Ed Sullivan Show*, the most popular variety program on Sunday night, confirmed his forward motion. His guest shot for Mr. Sullivan became legendary because word got out that swivel hips could only be filmed from the waist up, so as to not morally offend anyone. By cleverly announcing this filming policy to the public, Elvis called even more attention to his physical presence, which could only be imagined. Millions of viewers tuned in to experience on camera what they could of this man called Elvis.

When Elvis had a dozen or more hit records and his popularity was assured for the long run, he branched out into movies. His early films did well and are much appreciated by his fans, if not critics. Then Uncle Sam called. Unable to get an exemption from the Army, Elvis put his career on hold and became an enlisted man, one who was honored to serve his country.

Industry insiders and other people envious of his appeal unwisely predicted that Elvis would be forgotten after he completed his two-year stint (he was stationed in Germany like other American soldiers of this period). Returning to the civilian fold in 1960 with a series of hit movies and records, his popularity soared. He was really in a class by himself. His fans were loyal and remain so beyond anyone's imagination. When they got married, had children and stopped going to his movies, Elvis turned them on to his TV specials and live concerts. Before he had become too much of a caricature of his former glory, he passed on, joining the likes of Marilyn Monroe and James Dean, two other mythical figures from the 50s who died before their time.

Elvis was more than records and movies. He was a cultural icon with a strong sense of style. That made him ripe for impersonators and parody. The first popular send-up of the legend was **Bye Bye Birdie** (1962). This film was based on a hit Broadway musical about a pop singer named Conrad Birdie who is drafted into the army at the height of his appeal.

Early on in the movie, a newscaster explains the Birdie phenomenon in a series of still photos. It reprises many Elvis Presley trademarks including the full body suit, greased back black hair, half-sneer, and long sideburns. This deal also has shades of Frank Sinatra, one of the originators of mass female swooning. It was later revealed that girls attending Sinatra's early concert appearances were hired to scream during his performance.

Like Elvis, Conrad Birdie (Jesse Pearson) is a popular singer with the ladies. He swivels and shakes and causes herds of girls to swoon with delight—and that's before he starts singing. And like Elvis, Birdie has just been drafted into service. Struggling songwriters Dick Van Dyke and Janet Leigh devise a publicity gimmick to guarantee another hit song for Birdie before he goes off to the Army. The idea is for him to sing a song entitled *One Last Kiss* on *The Ed Sullivan Show*. Then, under great fanfare, and in front of millions of viewers, Conrad will ceremoniously kiss one of his most ardent fans, an innocent 15-year-old girl. This pure girl, plucked from middle America in a random drawing, turns out to be attractive Ann-Margret.

This media campaign does have complications, though. The first is Ann-Margret, who has suddenly bloomed and seems to turn on Conrad. She has a protective dad, Paul Lynde, who has good reason to be afraid that his daughter will be sullied. Dick Van Dyke has a parent problem also, of another type. His domineering mother, Maureen Stapleton, wants to keep Van Dyke from marrying Leigh. And Ann-Margret's beau, young Bobby Rydell, does not want a strange pop star kissing his girl in front of millions.

Surviving songs from the original Broadway play are shortened a bit, but still retain their snap. They capture the spirit of small towns, romance, and the pursuit of fame. *The Telephone Hour* has the teen girls tying up the town's phone lines to exchange gossip. Birdie's introductory song to Sweet Apple, Ohio, *Honestly Sincere* causes mass swooning and fainting. And if you are curious about where those bright yellow smiley faces originated, then *Put on a Happy Face* is the thing for you. Other fun stuff includes addressing unruly children with *What's the Matter with Kids Today*. The tribute to Mr. Sullivan is for real. The program was on the air each Sunday from 1948 to 1971 and an appearance on *The Ed Sullivan Show* signaled that you were on your way to the big time.

The standout number in the movie is the swinging *I've Got a Lot of Living to Do* by Ann-Margret, Rydell, and Pearson. It's about the signals that pass between young men and women: the three of them make the idea of hanging out at the malt shop look very appealing indeed.

The opening and closing credits offers Ann-Margret the opportunity to sing the title track and look sexy. The producers added this scene after principal filming was complete. It was a marketing rather than creative decision. Apparently, the money people thought she had more box office pull than Van Dyke and Leigh. The movie did brisk business but it's unclear whether she had anything to do with it. It turned out to be her last ingénue role (she was 22) before taking on more mature characters. In this movie she is wholesome and sweet. However, her fans say the sizzle she puts in the title track makes her the female equivalent to Elvis.

Showcasing Ann-Margret at the expense of Van Dyke and Lynde caused some ill feelings behind the scenes. Van Dyke and Lynde were reprising their roles from the Broadway hit, and they both said they didn't care for the screen adaptation. Van Dyke told his colleagues to

Chapter 14   87

not go see the movie if they were friends of his. Despite the limitations imposed on them, they do shine in their roles. Lynde's caustic delivery is in fine form when he cynically asks his wife what they did to deserve such a daughter. She replies "we got married."

Dick Gautier played the part of Conrad Birdie on Broadway. Under Pearson's interpretation, there is little character development beyond obnoxious behavior. He also has a slight paunch—something that would later plague Elvis.

Leigh replaced Chita Rivera for the film version and the number *Spanish Rose* suffers from this switch in casting. The bigoted aspects of the play are erased with this change in nationalities. Stapleton's incongruous putdowns to Leigh are on age and appearance (in real life, Leigh is several years younger than Van Dyke). On Broadway, Mama's anger was prejudice toward her Spanish origins. While Leigh is a competent leading lady, she needs more than a black wig to convince us she is a Spanish senorita. Leigh is also known more as an actress than a dancer. Though she proves herself to be a capable performer, the Shriner dance would have been quite different with athletic Rivera.

Bobby Rydell, a 1963 teen idol, is fine as a love interest for Ann-Margret. He reveals a pleasant singing voice. Interesting enough, the Rydell High School from **Grease** (1978) was named in his honor.

Director George Sidney was an old hand at screen musicals. An alumni of Metro-Goldwyn-Mayer, he directed a good portion of that studio's staple product, including **Anchors Aweigh** (1945), **Annie Get Your Gun** (1950) and the classic **Showboat** (1950). His next project was one of the King's most popular movies: **Viva Las Vegas** (1964). Hired as Elvis' love interest was none other than Ann-Margret. Apparently they fell in love off-screen too. He reportedly sent her flowers each time she opened in Las Vegas until his death.

Ann-Margret's honeymoon period with the critics and fans ended with **Bye Bye Birdie**. In the next decade, critics sniped at her movie performances, yet she revealed herself to be a plucky performer in Vegas and in spectacular TV specials. Her work in **Carnal Knowledge** (1971) as a ripe lady wanting desperately to get married, finally turned the tide to her favor. A follow-up opportunity in **Tommy** (1975) proved she was as strong and capable as anyone else of her generation. That potential was much in evidence when she was cast as Blanche Dubois in the TV version of *A Streetcar Named Desire* (1984).

Fans of **Grease**, the top grossing musical of all time and a parody of the 50s, will enjoy **Bye Bye Birdie**. There are similarities. Both use the same cars, home furnishings, and punch lines. However, there is a difference. **Bye Bye Birdie** takes itself seriously and is the real thing. **Grease**, on the other hand, makes jokes at the 50s culture and morality to enhance its appeal.

Bye Bye Birdie was remade in 1995 for television, and the effort won several Emmys. However, like **Grease**, its charm was in the spoof of the 50s and early 60s culture. But the 1963 original is where their ideas and excitement were created.

Cast

Janet Leigh	*Rosie DeLeon*
Dick Van Dyke	*Albert Peterson*
Ann-Margret	*Kim McAfee*
Maureen Stapleton	*Mama Peterson*
Paul Lynde	*Harry McAfee*
Bobby Rydell	*Hugo Peabody*
Jesse Pearson	*Conrad Birdie*
Ed Sullivan	*Himself*
Mary LaRoche	*Mrs. McAfee*
Frank Albertson	*Mayor*

Production

George Sidney	*Director*
Michael Stewart (play), Irving Brecher	*Writers*
Fred Kohlmar	*Producer*
Joseph Biroc	*Cinematographer*
Charles Strouse, Lee Adams (lyrics)	*Original Music*
Gower Champion	*Choreography*
Columbia Pictures/Kohmar-Sidney Productions	*Production Company*
USA/112/1963	*Country/Runtime/Year Released*

Chapter 14

Chapter 15

Charade

"I'm beginning to think women make the best spies."
—Regina Lambert

With the overwhelming artistic and commercial success of Alfred Hitchcock in the suspense genre during the 50s and 60s, it is no surprise that other directors attempted to imitate his stylish thrillers. Besides flattering Mr. Hitchcock, moviegoers craved Hitchcock's lethal doses of sex, dark humor, and murder. Unfortunately, many of the imitations were weak and relied on a rehash of his most famous sequences. These lesser directors simply raided his garbage cans. However, several efforts stand on their own two legs without fear of comparison. Stanley Donen's **Charade** is one such contender. On its own merit, the film offers a good story, a subtle mix of sex and humor, and of course, murder. In fact, there are several murders to keep everyone guessing and on their toes.

To be perfectly fair, one has to admit this movie flourishes in a genre created and cultivated by Hitchcock. With that caveat cast aside and ignoring Hitchcock's influence, **Charade** comes within throwing distance of the master of suspense at his peak.

This film has all the trappings of a good Hitchcock film. It offers fine performances from elegantly chic Audrey Hepburn and suave Cary Grant. Along with this star power, supporting roles feature a trio of soon-to-be stars: Walter Matthau, James Coburn, and George Kennedy. Other components of a Hitchcock production include famous locations. In this case, we get a beautiful sightseeing tour of Paris to view the Seine River, Notre Dame, the Colonnade, and the French Alps. The lively dialogue combines passing bits from bystanders in minute roles, another favorite Hitchcock trick. The music is by Henry Mancini, and, while he doesn't try to emulate Bernard Herrmann, the mood and tempo of the soundtrack add much to create full-bodied suspense. There is also plenty of sexual fencing between the stars, though not as dark and subtle as Hitchcock would have it. Grant doesn't have mother fixation problems (like he did in **North By Northwest**) and dear Audrey is not frigid (like Tippi Hedren in **Marnie**).

Charade begins with a murder—Hepburn's husband—when he is thrown off a train. We learn that he was somehow mixed up in a quarter of a million-dollar robbery of World War II gold. His former war buddies (Kennedy, Coburn, and Ned Glass) all want their share. Grant and Matthau have their interests in the money, too, so everybody is a suspect. **Charade** is, indeed, the appropriate title to this concoction since the characters keep changing their identity to protect their secrets. The audience keeps guessing until the very pleasant surprise ending.

Coburn is the lanky Texan, full of southern charm and embellishment. Kennedy is the steel-clawed tough who probably later inspired a James Bond villain. Ned Glass looks like a friendly bank examiner with a touch of weasel. (Mr. Glass had, in fact, a small role in Hitchcock's **North By Northwest**, as the ticket man who alerts the police to Grant's whereabouts). However, Matthau comes off best and his comic timing is perfect in support of Hepburn's doe-eyed innocence.

It is her innocence that propels the story. The opening scene in which Grant comes on to Hepburn sets the tone and mood for the picture. She tells him that she can't have any more friends until someone dies. When he starts to walk off, she calls him a quitter. Despite this rather racy pick-up line, she still is vulnerable. Apparently she has grabbed every hook, line, and sinker thrown at her. She married someone with four identities and never did know what he did for a living, how much he made, or who any of his friends were. She finally says in exasperation "I don't know who anybody is."

Hepburn speaks of honesty throughout the movie. This guileless nature she brings to the role makes her very attractive to the audience and to her male costars. When she wonders out loud why people lie, her Girl Scout personality is at its most appealing.

In a Hitchcock movie, the real story is in the relationships. In

Chapter 15

Psycho (1960), it was a story of a son and his mother—not stolen money. In **North by Northwest** (1959), it was an innocent man drawn into an affair with a double agent, not a story about international intrigue. **Charade** follows this course. The real story is the relationship between Hepburn and Grant and how they are drawn together despite the charade they are involved in. If you overlook this pleasant journey and focus on solving the murder, you will miss most of the fun.

Casting 59-year-old Grant to 35-year-old Hepburn poses no problem for fans of the two stars, though Grant initially seemed to have problems with the age difference. Before signing for the role, Grant insisted that no love and kissing scenes take place, for fear of being laughed at. He also wanted it clear that it was his character who was being pursued by a younger woman, not the other way around. At his insistence, jokes about his late middle-age were included so the audience could savor the idea, instead of being forced to believe that the May/December romance was automatic. Accompanying Hepburn to her flat, he says "I can be arrested for transporting a minor above the first floor."

Hepburn receives her share of scrutiny too. There are frequent thin jokes, with Grant telling her, "it's infuriating that your happiness doesn't turn to fat." In a sea of curvaceous actresses, Hepburn's reed-thin figure is a standout from her peers.

Hepburn was actually set to star in a Hitchcock production in the early 60s—between **Psycho** (1960) and **The Birds** (1963). She was a logical choice for his type of heroine. She had the style, class, and grace of his typical leading lady. But the director, who apparently had a penchant for the perverse, altered the script at the last minute, throwing Hepburn into a degrading rape scene. She balked and the production never got off the ground. It was Hitchcock's loss and Donen's gain.

Givenchy was Ms. Hepburn's chosen costume designer. She requested his services whenever she made a film and, per her contract, she kept all of the designs once the picture wrapped. Not only did she have looks and style, apparently she had brains too.

Unlike many of her peers, Hepburn's career went upward from the start. It began with an Academy Award for her first American movie, **Roman Holiday** (1953). After that she seldom missed a beat, receiving a total of five Oscar nominations, including best performances for **Sabrina** (1954), **The Nun's Story** (1959), **Breakfast at Tiffany's** (1961) and **Wait Until Dark** (1967).

Nearing 40, she retired from the industry in 1968 to raise her two sons at a Swiss villa. She was almost coaxed out of retirement with **40 Karats** in 1972 (Liv Ullman took the role). She finally agreed to star with Sean Connery in **Robin and Marian** in 1976, in which hero and heroine were middle-aged and still hanging out in Sherwood Forest. It was a welcome return to the fold. However, appearances after that were sporadic and not worthy of her abilities. She was also increasingly devoting her time to charitable causes. In 1988 she was appointed Special Ambassador for UNICEF, bringing hope to starving children all over the world. When she died of cancer in 1993, the world lost one its most beloved stars.

Grant retired from acting in 1966, finishing a lengthy career of extraordinarily good movies. Many are now regarded as classics, including the three he did with Hitchcock—**North By Northwest** (1959), **Notorious** (1946), and **To Catch a Thief** (1955). In interviews he admitted that his range was narrow and that he was lucky with his material. His fans might disagree with this harsh assessment. He remained a popular Hollywood dignitary in the eyes of the public until he died in 1986 at age 82.

Tall and thin James Coburn moved from supporting player to leading man in a few years after this film. His career as a box-office movie star would peak in the late 60s with films like **In Like Flint** (1966) and **The President's Analyst** (1967). After that, he became a working actor frequently saddled with routine parts. The late part of his career received a boost when he played with relish Nick Nolte's angry father in **Affliction** (1997). It must have been particularly rewarding for him to win the Best Supporting Actor Oscar.

George Kennedy won the Best Supporting Actor Oscar for his part as Paul Newman's prisoner pal in **Cool Hand Luke** (1967). He continued to work regularly in meaty supporting roles, often stealing scenes from the more illustrious star.

Chapter 15

Stanley Donen was responsible for many of Metro-Goldwyn-Mayer's classic musicals. Along with Gene Kelly (Donen started out as a hoofer), they created three of the best screen musicals ever made: **On the Town** (1949), **It's Always Fair Weather** (1955), and **Singin' in the Rain** (1952). On his own he directed one of the last musicals written specifically for the screen: **Seven Brides for Seven Brothers** (1954), as well as **Funny Face** (1957), which starred Audrey Hepburn. At Warner Brothers, he directed **The Pajama Game** (1957) and **Damn Yankees** (1958), more highs in the musical genre. When musicals went out of fashion, he turned to sophisticated comedy and **Charade**, with much success.

The remake of **Charade** entitled **The Truth About Charlie** appeared in 2002. Singer and model-turned-actor Mark Walhberg courageously took on the Cary Grant role and the film passed unnoticed.

Cast

Cary Grant	*Peter Joshua/Alexander Dyle/*
	Adam Canfield, Brian Cruikshank
Audrey Hepburn	*Regina "Reggie" Lampert*
Walter Matthau	*Hamilton Bartholmew/Caron Dyle*
James Coburn	*Tex Panthollow*
George Kennedy	*Herman Scobie*
Dominique Minot	*Sylvie Gaudel*
Ned Glass	*Leopold W. Gideon*
Jacques Marin	*Inspector Edouard Grandpierre*
Paul Bonifas	*Mr. Felix, Stamp Dealer*

Production

Stanley Donen	*Director*
Peter Stone, Marc Behm	*Writers*
Stanley Donen, James H. Ware	*Producers*
Charles Lang	*Cinematographer*
Henry Mancini	*Original Music*
Universal International Pictures	*Production Company*
Hubert de Givenchy	*Costumes*
USA/113 minutes/1963	*Country/Runtime/Year Released*

Chapter 16
Cool Hand Luke

"What we've got here is failure to communicate."
—Captain

Cool Hand Luke (1967) is one of the best films of the late 60s. It offers a gritty combination of ideas, action and poetry to form a superb movie. The subject—life on a Southern prison road gang—is grim, but the unique script, direction and especially the acting by a first rate cast ensures a terrific film experience. It was very popular then and now. Just about everyone involved in the production benefited career wise. This film consistently makes the cut when someone decides to list the top movies of all time.

The film is unusual in the manner that it maintains our interest. It offers a bit of tension—not nearly as strong as the scene leading up to the shower in **Psycho** (1960), but medium grade. It's there for two hours but we don't get exhausted from it. It's just enough heat to keep us on the edge of our seat.

This tension comes from a number of variables. The characters are placed in a claustrophobic (and humid) setting. Having violated society's rules, their punishment is to have no control over their lives. They need permission to walk, to drink water, to speak. They are forced to sleep in the same room and most of them have severe problems in getting along with others. The resulting group situation creates a pressure cooker atmosphere waiting for something to happen. We anticipate some type of disaster as we head toward an inevitable conclusion.

The setting is the deep South, just after World War II. One character drives this story and his name is Luke. Played by superstar Paul Newman, Luke is gifted with a perfect smile and body. He is also bright, witty and with unlimited charm. These traits provide him

Chapter 16

95

with a lot of power. But a serious character flaw underscores all of his assets. He doesn't conform to the rules of society. He has a serious problem with authority.

The movie spells this out clearly in the opening scene before the credits. The word "violation" covers the entire screen for just a brief second. Then we see a drunken Luke shearing off the tops of parking meters. Very soon we realize that his rebellion isn't directed to any one person, place or thing. He actually can be a nice guy. This is just one contradiction.

There's a particularly telling scene when Luke arrives at the prison and is greeted by the prison warden (whom the guys call Captain), played by Strother Martin. Martin bends his eyebrows ever so slightly when he reads Luke's dossier. We realize the Captain has seen just about everything there is to see. Yet he's surprised at how someone with so much promise has self-destructed.

Martin wonderfully underplays this scene, which actually increases the tension between Luke and authority. A lesser actor would have concentrated on the sadistic side of this character. Martin plays him as a Southern gentleman, with gracious manners and a slow to rile demeanor. When he does hit the ceiling, the Captain utters the most famous and often quoted line: "What we've got here is failure to communicate."

With the delivery of this observation, the Captain is correct. Luke does have a problem with communication. Concerning the parking meter incident, when the police arrive and ask him what he is doing, his answer is barely audible. Other missed signals include the boxing match (he doesn't know when to stop), a visit from his mother (there's an air of resignation on her part), and the card game (his miscommunication works for once as he wins the pot and earns the moniker "Cool Hand Luke").

Luke does understand some forms of communication. He knows that the blonde washing the car is a big tease when all of the other prisoners get overwhelmed. It's also easy for him to manipulate two youngsters into helping him in his escape attempt. It would have been more natural for them to duck and cover when they saw a man walking up the road covered in grime and with shackles on his ankles. But this is no ordinary man. This is Luke.

A fellow prisoner, George Kennedy is especially enamored by Luke. At first he feels that his regal position in the compound is threatened. Later he becomes Luke's protector and confidant—eventually offering explanations for his behavior. Kennedy offers a standout performance among a very strong cast. He won a Best Supporting Actor Oscar for his interpretation of the illiterate Dragline.

It's significant that Luke's name comes from the bible. There are religious symbols carefully placed throughout the movie. After his mother dies, he sings a song (off-key) entitled *Plastic Jesus*. A church and a prayer play a prominent role, but the most subtle image is after he swallows 50 (!) eggs to win a wager. He's sprawled out on a table, nearly nude. He's the image of Christ being crucified on the cross.

Jo Van Fleet is excellent in her five minute role as his dying mother. She was actually only one year older than Newman (he's 42) and she's a credit to her craft that this fact is not obvious. Bette Davis declined this part, saying that she wasn't interested in taking a cameo role and listing her name below the title. It would have been interesting to see her interpretation.

Strother Martin was one of the most recognizable and busy character actors in the 60s and 70s. He started out in Hollywood as a swimming instructor to the stars. He's the diver in the Joan Crawford film **The Damned Don't Cry** (1950). His whiney voice assured him of comedy roles, but he was equally impressive as the villain. He frequently made Westerns, being hired multiple times by Directors John Ford and Sam Peckinpah. He was also a favorite of Newman and they appeared together in **Slap Shot** (1977), **Pocket Money** (1971), **Butch Cassidy and the Sundance Kid** (1969) and **Harper** (1966).

Other cast members were at the beginning of their careers. Wayne Rogers (Gambler) went on to star in TV's *M*A*S*H* and Ralph Waite (Alibi) went on to TV's *The Waltons*.

Lalo Schifrin's musical arrangements brought him an Academy Award nomination. To contrast his range, he was also responsible

Chapter 16

for some classic TV themes around this time: *Mission Impossible* and *Mannix*.

Other Academy Award nominations included Paul Newman for best actor (his fourth nomination) and Donn Pearce and Frank Pierson for the screenplay. The screenplay is based on Pearce's novel. It was inspired from personal experience: The author spent two years time on a prison road gang for safecracking. Despite these multiple nominations, only Kennedy took home the Oscar prize.

Director Stuart Rosenberg was apprenticed in television before advancing to the big screen. His directing style is crisp, efficient and conventional. It works very well with this project.

Rosenberg directed Newman and Joanne Woodward (Mrs. Newman) a few years later for a political film, **WUSA** (1971), but it didn't register with audiences and hasn't been heard of since. This must have been a disappointment for the Newmans. In real life, they are known for their social causes and philanthropy. In the wake of **Cool Hand Luke**, in 1968, they actively campaigned for Democratic Presidential candidate Eugene McCarthy running against Richard Nixon. During the Watergate investigation, leading up to Nixon's resignation from the oval office, it was revealed that Newman was listed 19th on the administration's political enemies list. Perhaps echoing the sentiments of Luke, Newman said the inclusion on this list was his life's proudest achievement.

The beautiful blonde who suggestively washes the car is Joy Harmon. Ms. Harmon's film appearances were memorable and always tailored to display her obvious assets. Assets not obvious in her casting were her business savvy and baking skills. She now owns a very successful wholesale catering business. "Aunt Joy's Cakes" is located in Burbank, California and clients served include the major Hollywood studios.

Cast

Paul Newman	*Luke*
George Kennedy	*Dragline*
J.D. Cannon	*Society Red*

Robert Drivas	*Loudmouth Steve*
Strother Martin	*Captain*
Jo Van Fleet	*Arletta*
Marc Cavell	*Rabbit*
Richard Davalos	*Blind Dick*
Dennis Hopper	*Babalugats*

Production

Stuart Rosenberg	*Director*
Donn Pearce (also novel), Frank Pierson	*Writers*
Gordon Carroll, Carter Dehaven, Jr.	*Producers*
Conrad Hall	*Cinematographer*
Lalo Schifrin	*Original Music*
Warner Brothers, Jalem Productions	*Production Company*
Howard Shoup	*Costumes*
USA/126/1967	*Country/Runtime/Year Released*

Chapter 17
The Court Jester

"The king of jesters, the jesters of kings."
—Hubert Hawkins

He sings, dances, clowns, and courts the leading lady with a dash of flair and charm not at all common in screen comedians. He is Danny Kaye, a rather spirited leading man with a kind face, slight build, and wide range of eccentricities. His distinction among his peers is that he was one of the few comedians of his generation who could play a convincing romantic figure. In the 40s and 50s, Kaye was at the height of his powers. Perhaps the film that best showcases his versatility (and does not age like his other work) is **The Court Jester**.

In this grand outing, his character is asked to act out several complete characterizations and dialects in rapid succession. A superb mimic, he does these intricate scenes with a high degree of skill and energy, which adds much to the fun quotient of this film. The character he plays is a meek and mild subordinate, living during a time when brute strength was viewed as a prime asset to have for survival. He is highly clever but hasn't received all due breaks. To flourish in a system that demands strength, power, and might—things that come from testosterone—he must masquerade as a hero, to be dashing, and cavalier. He is a joy to watch in this film as he plays out these various parts. This is easily the best film in his long and somewhat illustrious career of movies, theatre, concerts, and television.

This movie was produced under his own company and it is a family affair. His wife, Sylvia Fine, provided much of the dialogue, as she did for most of his films. She also receives story credits, and is credited as co-songwriter with Sammy Cahn.

If Kaye was popular in the United States during this time, Great Britain was a bit more enthusiastic to his broad range of gifts. Perhaps it was appropriate that this film take place in medieval England. The story threads itself from a few old standbys. There is a bit of Robin Hood as a group of do-gooders try to usurp power from the king. There is a piece of **The Scarlet Pimperal** (1935), if not in color, then in mistaken identities. And the political and court intrigue reminds one of **Dangerous Liasons** (1988), that the privileged are bored and have nothing to do but guard their power base.

The featured cast is first rate, and they all are given the opportunity to strut their stuff, shine, and be proud that this film is on their resume.

A young Angela Lansbury is particularly effective in a supporting role as the King's recalcitrant and spoiled daughter. Her jabs with her psychic advisor, Mildred Natwick, set up some of the funniest comic sequences on film. As the story goes, Lansbury's in love with the alter ego of Kaye. When he faces certain defeat in a duel, she firmly tells Natwick "if he dies, you die." Natwick's subsequent witchcraft provides the basis for the now classic scene "the pellet of poison is in the vessel with the pestle…or is it in the chalice from the palace…or from the flagon with the dragon." In later years, Kaye said fans would introduce themselves to him by reciting this famous sequence.

Rathbone, one of filmdom's first and most popular Sherlock Holmes, plays the obvious villain. You know he is going to be devious when his name tries to dominate the opening credit sequence. The swashbuckling between Kaye and Rathbone is another finely tuned comic adventure. Kaye's arrogance during this lengthy match makes Rathbone's villain appear quite conventional in a world when most villains display oversized egos. It is also interesting to note that Rathbone was an expert swordsman in real life. Though he is supposed to be inferior to Kaye's machismo, his confidence is apparent in the duel scene, which makes the comedy that much stronger. This power of illusion also exists in Kaye's tights. All that muscle is not real: his thin legs were padded for better definition.

Kaye's leading lady is Glynis Johns, the delicious looking English lady with the sensual voice. Kaye is naturally turned on to Johns, but the film has to heat up before they can get together by the final

Chapter 17

reel. Her role, as his supervisor, is an interesting reversal of gender dominance in a time when women were pretty much told what to do by men.

Most of Kaye's movies have not stood the test of time. **White Christmas** (1954) is a perennial favorite and **Hans Christian Anderson** (1952) was a personal success for him. Yet, after **The Court Jester**, most of his theatrical efforts were tired and unfunny and he turned to a variety TV show in the 60s. His charity work with world children's organizations also increased. One of his last roles, a serious one, was in **Skokie** (1981). He played a concentration camp survivor fighting against a planned Neo-Nazi parade in a Jewish Chicago suburb. It belatedly revealed another facet of his versatility.

Johns went on to make her mark in many productions. The daughter of character actor Mervyn Johns (he was Mr. Cratchit in 1951's **Scrooge**), she had her first role as the hysterical 15-year-old girl in **South Riding** (1938). Although Johns never hit a home run, there were plenty of singles in a long and varied career. She was the intellectual and cultured lady seeking sex in **The Chapman Report** (1962) and Mrs. Banks in **Mary Poppins** (1964). Stephen Sondheim's *Send in the Clowns* was written specifically for her in **A Little Night Music**, her Broadway triumph in the 70s. After a long absence from the screen, she found fruitful work after most of her peers had retired, first in **The Ref** (1994) as the mother-in-law from hell, then in **While You Were Sleeping** (1995) as one of the kind onlookers. She had another fun (and prominent) role as the lame grandmother in **Superstar** (1999).

One of Mildred Natwick's last roles was, coincidentally, **Dangerous Liasions** (1985), as one of the aged members of the privileged set. Perhaps the producers couldn't forget the poison pellet routine in **The Court Jester**.

Cast

Danny Kaye	*Hubert Hawkins*
Glynis Johns	*Maid Jean*
Basil Rathbone	*Sir Ravenhurst*

Angela Lansbury	*Princess Gwendolyn*
Cecil Parker	*King Roderick I*
Mildred Natwick	*Griselda*
Robert Middleton	*Sir Griswold*
Michael Pate	*Sir Locksley*
Herbert Rudley	*Captain of the Guard*
Noel Drayton	*Fergus*
John Carradine	*Giacomo*
Edward Ashley	*Black Fox*
Alan Napier	*Sir Brockhurst*

Production

Melvin Frank, Norman Panama	*Director*
Sylvia Fine (dialogue)	*Writers*
Melvin Frank, Norman Panama	*Producers*
Ray June	*Cinematographer*
Sylvia Fine, Vic Schoen	*Original Music*
Paramount/Dena Enterprises	*Production Company*
Edith Head, Yvonne Wood	*Costumes*
USA/101/1956	*Country/Runtime/Year Released*

Chapter 18

Defending Your Life

"She's going to have a field day with this one."
—Bob Diamond

The idea of reincarnation is believable, compelling, and comfortable to many because it offers the hope of another (and more fulfilling) existence. At one point in time, and this wasn't very long go, the notion of living another life was relegated to the dark parlors of traveling carnivals. Later, the works of Edgar Cayce and researchers popularized it for enthusiastic people receptive to alternative thoughts on death and the afterlife. In some circles today, it is chic dinner conversation alongside white wine and broiled fillets Florentine.

Followers of this ideology are as serious as Christians, Jews, Buddhists, etc. are about their beliefs. Those believing in reincarnation think the life we are experiencing now is just one of many to come. This idea to live again and again, in different times, with different genders, occupations, and ability levels attempts to explain why differences exist in human beings. There is no heaven or hell after death. Instead, life is a growth experience on a continuous path that may seem at times to be like heaven or hell. If one is able to grow spiritually and intellectually, then that person moves to the next step or into the next physical body. It is part of an overall master plan, to grow towards the eternal light. Reaching this light is the goal. Once there, we will find peace, warmth, love, security, hope, happiness and all those other serene things hoped for in our short time on earth.

In **Defending Your Life** (1991), director-writer-star Albert Brooks successfully crystallizes these beliefs into a mainstream movie. His appraisal of the situation after death pokes fun at a subject unfamiliar to most moviegoers. That works to his advantage. Those less familiar with the subject will see another explanation, another story, another philosophy, plus a few surprises along the way. Those who are open-minded have a rare opportunity to view something about a subject rarely spoken of in a direct manner. Even the most skeptical observers, if they can suspend their beliefs, will gain some pleasure in a consistently funny, albeit unusual movie. The movie's overall message is to live without fear. That fear is debilitating. As Torn puts it, "lift the fog and you're in for the ride of your life."

Brooks plays Dan Miller, a name and character as average as average can get. In a brief prologue, we glimpse his lifestyle, which fits exactly in the middle. It doesn't enthrall us, nor does it drive us away. As he approaches middle-age (he is really in the middle of everything), we sense he still hasn't found life's satisfaction. It is his birthday and he is alone at a BMW dealership picking up his new convertible. We suspect he's trying to add some pizzazz to his droll lifestyle and believes an open-topped car will do the trick. It's as if he's pleading with people to "look at me." Thinking that a loud music will draw attention his way, he tries to get high on a Barbara Streisand song. Unfortunately, his musical shortcomings are cut short when, fumbling for CDs that have fallen to the floorboard, he weaves in front of a bus. His resulting death sends him to Judgment City.

We learn that Judgment City is the afterlife. Once there, cheerful Rip Torn greets him. Torn is easily the funniest performer in the film. He explains the situation in concise terms: "You're here to defend your life. This isn't heaven or hell. When born, you have many life-times. After each one, we examine it. We look at it to see if you can move on. We want you to keep going. Keep growing, getting smarter."

Somewhat perplexed, Brooks asks if there is a limit to returns. Torn explains "I've seen people go back 100 times. I've seen them, but I wouldn't want to be around them." Brooks' stay in Judgment City is short—four days in what looks like court. There he views embarrassing pieces of his life on a large screen. Lee Grant, the prosecuting attorney, (AKA Dragon Lady) has a field day reporting on Brooks' past failures, fears, and unproductive life.

In contrast to this is Meryl Streep, a nice woman he can fall in love with (and learn something from). She is also defending her life,

Chapter 18

but without the same level of embarrassment he is experiencing. She's a glowing woman who readily admits that she can make difficult situations work. She was once Prince Valiant (why do people who believe in reincarnation feel they were once someone famous?). In the immortal words of Rip Torn, she seems a natural for going forward.

Brooks the writer cleverly milks Judgment City's culture for every ounce of humor. The television shows include *Face Your Fear*. and there is a Past Lives Pavilion with a special hostess (to reveal her name would spoil the fun) who introduces you to your former lives. There's also a comedy club called "The Bomb Shelter" where a comic sings *That was Life* to the tune of Frank Sinatra's megahit: *That's Life*.

This is also a rather utopian society for the restless. The restaurants are sensational with fast service and one can eat all they want and never gain a pound. Torn suggests taking some food home as well. "They love putting things in bags." Torn, Grant and other residents of Judgment City have a unique quality that sets them apart from visitors. Operating without fear or envy, there's an air of friendliness and camaraderie. Torn and Grant compare their intelligence levels with a dash of good humor. Their dialogue is intense and reeks with intelligence. They're polite, strong, confident, and independent people secure in themselves—apparently something that can happen when you use 50 percent of the brain.

Brooks took special pains to assemble this cast. Apart from Lee, Torn, a nice bit by Buck Henry, and the surprise host mentioned earlier; there is 87-year-old Maxine Elliott Hicks, the elderly lady Brooks encounters on the tram. She was rounding out her career in film; her first film appearance was in a 1914 antique entitled **The Borrowed Finery**!

You typically find Albert Brooks in roles where his position is threatened. He's forced to make a hard decision in life management. When he does make a decision, he worries about it. He questions an unfair system, but has few survival skills to fall back on, outside of walking away from a paycheck. His screen persona resembles early Jack Lemmon. But while Jack is surprised and shocked by the unfairness he is embroiled in, he never loses touch with who he is and what he stands for. Brooks, on the other hand, is neurotic—full of self-doubts but very quick to evaluate those who are at least trying.

One of Brooks' earlier credits was the moderately successful **Lost in America** (1985). Fed up with a dog-eat-dog system, Brooks and his wife drop out to travel cross-country in a trailer home. While it is supposed to be a road to self-discovery, they discover they weren't that bad off before dropping out.

In **Broadcast News** (1987), he is the conscientious newsman uncomfortable in front of cameras, while blond John Hurt, all teeth and rehearsed sincerity, wins rating points with the public and management.

In **Mother** (1996) he went into film therapy again to explore another common malady: mother—son relationships. In this case, mother was Debbie Reynolds. And while it was nice to see her in a good role (Doris Day was the first choice, but said no), the jokes and outcome were pretty flat.

Defending Your Life scored a bull's-eye with the critics, the box office was weak outside the big cities. This was a pity because the message fits universally into many belief systems.

Cast

Albert Brooks	*Daniel Miller*
Meryl Streep	*Julia*
Rip Torn	*Bob Diamond*
Lee Grant	*Lena Foster*
Buck Henry	*Dick Stanley*
Gary Beach	*Car Salesman*
Julie Cobb	*Tram Guide*
Maxine Elliott Hicks	*Elderly Lady on Tram*

Production

Albert Brooks	*Director*
Albert Brooks	*Writer*

Robert Grand, Michael Grillo, Herb Nanas *Producers*
Allen Daviau *Cinematographer*
Michael Gore *Original Music*
Geffen Pictures *Production Company*
USA/112/1992 *Country/Runtime/Year Released*

Chapter 19

Detour

*"It was stupid for me to leave all
that money on a dead man."*

—*Al Roberts*

Detour (1948) was virtually ignored at the time of its release because it lacked technical gloss, big name movie stars, a publicity campaign, and other items usually critical to a movie's success. Today, the vehicle is regarded as one of the most interesting small budget movies ever made. Its reported cost was only $21,000, a fraction of what the major studios invested in comparable offerings during this era. However, from a modern perspective, the money was very well spent, though it probably wasn't apparent at the time to the overstressed accountant. Perhaps these cost constraints prompted creativity. The creative juices are rich and in abundant supply. That this jewel survived and eventually found an audience is food for thought and somewhat of a miracle.

The film moves at a very fast clip and covers a lot of action in a short 65-minutes. The screenplay is compact and precise—with a slight jagged edge feel to it. While you may take away the styles and slang of the day, it's spliced full of unintentionally witty pseudo-intellectualism. That makes it even more palatable in terms of what we accept as good today. Odd films often require a degree of tolerance from the viewer. In other words, you're asked to suspend your beliefs, to temporary alter that frame of reference you walk around with. However, in contrast to a real turkey like Ed Wood's **Plan Nine from Outer Space** (1956), **Detour** reveals some degree of skill involved in the production. It does have shortcomings, but they can be forgiven. Most can be directly related to the miniscule budget. If anything, the poor lighting, rear projection, and the incongruous series of events actually enhance rather than detract from its overall impact. The story is intriguing and a high degree of style simmers throughout this product.

Edgar G. Ulmer directed a large number of obscure films, beginning with silents, on ultra tight budgets. Despite these limitations, the movers and shakers in the French cinema say he was a full-fledged auteur, or his body of work has a clear personal stamp to it. This film's distinction has subsequently made it a very popular item for study and pleasure. As its stature has grown over the years, **Detour** has made back its original investment many times, something that would surprise that overstressed accountant.

The story involves people who are struggling to live in a tough situation. They haven't had many breaks. The central character, played by Tom Neal, is a piano man. Like other musicians who play to empty nightclubs, he doesn't have much going for him. Still at the beginning of his career, the position he holds in life disturbs him. In a business not known for stability, he is trying to hold onto something that will offer him a bit of security. His rugged features and late afternoon beard imply he has been around the club scene for quite some time. He appears weary and approaching burnout. This offers some clue to his decision making process. He isn't thinking clearly.

Like other young men, he fantasizes about women to relieve the tedium. There is one lady in particular that he longs to settle down with, but she just said goodbye. She is on her way to California in an attempt to become a movie star.

Actor Neal frequently narrates portions of the film. We are privy to his thoughts on matters of the heart. He describes this relationship as follows: "I was an ordinary healthy guy. She was an ordinary healthy girl. When you add those two together, you get an ordinary healthy romance. Which is the old story." Sounding experienced, our man goes on to say that "all in all, I was a pretty lucky guy." Neal is at times quite cerebral.

His probing is what keeps the film in motion and interesting. There are instances where he sounds like he should be in front of a classroom, discussing the ramifications of Chaucer or Shakespeare.

He seems to be constantly searching for the truth. Often philosophical about the whole raw mess, his character comes across as multi-dimensional and rather likeable.

As the story progresses, we see his luck change from bad to worse. It is his pursuit of his dream—to line up something for him and his girl out in California—that gets him detoured.

Our guy is really a victim of circumstances. There are some inanimate objects that curse him, including a brick and a phone line, otherwise known as smoking guns. In a bizarre twist of fate, he gets hooked up with an unstable young woman who seems to be slightly clairvoyant. After that, the story becomes very strange, punctuated by a flashback within a flashback scene.

Neal tries to find a system of order in the madness that engulfs his life. After being detoured, he pauses, studies the situation and picks the more unfortunate risk. There is something fatal about his decisions. He explains it with: "but from there something else stepped in and shunted me off to a different destination other than the one I picked for myself." This does not sound like middle America speaking. And it doesn't sound like what you would expect to hear from a lonely piano man in a seedy nightclub.

This intellectual bent he's on doesn't stop. Most tough guys would choose a different metaphor toward someone who gets out of line, but our lead refers to one such jerk as a "piece of cheese."

Neal's co-star is the formidable Ann Savage. She is more than tough. She spits and snarls between coughs that could scare the pants off any man twice her weight. She eats men like Neal everyday for breakfast. Like someone troubled and disturbed, her character is widely inconsistent. The fault isn't in her acting ability, but in a shortage of takes. Whatever her inspiration, her anti-social performance keeps things popping.

Her verbal spars with Neal are special highlights. Because of their mistrust of each other, there's no respect between these two alley cats. To keep things interesting, much dialogue is devoted to some serious sexual fencing. After all, Neal refers to himself as a healthy male. As he narrates, we are privy to his thoughts. Naturally he fantasizes

Chapter 19

about having sex with her, at least for a second or two, but quickly realizes that she would be as "rotten in the morning as the night before." Perhaps the most erotic line between these two losers occurs when they have to share a room for the night. "I'm first in the bathtub," she demands. "I don't know why, but I knew you would be," he responds.

Neal's last line in the movie, where he discusses fate, is worth the entire movie trip. It closes down the picture without much fuss. This unorthodox way of bringing things to a halt quickly with no explanations provides **Detour** an edge over its contemporaries. It wasn't supposed to be this way—the money ran out so they had to stop the production cold turkey. This rather abrupt climax makes the film unique when viewed against its contemporaries. Its lack of a clear resolution lets the viewer imagine what happens next to our hero. Credit scriptwriter Martin Goldsmith for the ending. The movie was based on his 1939 novel.

If the ending is pure low budget truth, the tawdry dramatics are similar to those of writer James M. Cain. His work was popular at the time with **Mildred Pierce** (1945) and **The Postman Always Rings Twice** (1947). But to say more would be unfair. You can't compare these polished classics to a rough diamond like **Detour**.

Believe it or not, the life of actor Tom Neal was more interesting than **Detour**, adding an amazing postscript to this film and confirming that life is more interesting than fiction. He was the son of a banker born with many advantages. In his youth he dabbled in boxing and sports. Cerebral like his character, he earned a law degree from Harvard in 1937. Despite this high level of accomplishment, drama is what really interested him.

He tried Broadway in the 30s, but was cast in three successive failures. Following this he went to Hollywood where he appeared in dozens of run-of-the-mill films throughout the 40s. His career ended in 1951, after he was involved in a notorious love triangle with actor Franchot Tone and actress Barbara Payton. Apparently his jealously over girlfriend Payton erupted into violence, which sent Tone to the hospital. This altercation resulted in bad publicity and effectively ended Neal's career, which was in a slump anyway. He turned to gardening to make a living. This vocation also failed, but the worst was to come.

In 1965, he was convicted of involuntary manslaughter when his third wife was found dead. He said the gun had gone off accidentally during a struggle, but he spent the next six years in jail. Eight months after he was released in 1972, he died of congestive heart failure.

Though not widely released in theatres, Neal's look-alike son, Tom Neal Jr. appeared in a remake of this film in 1992. Also named **Detour**, it followed the original script but added subplots that had been cut out of the original due to lack of funds.

Savage went into television during the 1950s. When parts didn't come her way, she transitioned into secretarial work. In 1979 she became a licensed pilot. There was renewed interest in her work after she started attending film festivals and screenings. She also accepted a small role in a 1986 film **Fire with Fire** because it was nonexploitive. More important, Canadian filmmaker Guy Maddin cast her in **My Winnipeg** (2008) as his tough mom. It required 86 year old Savage to reach back to her "bad girl" days, and she earned raves in an acclaimed film. This introduced her to a new generation of movie fans. She died of a stroke the following year realizing that she had been part of something exciting and not forgotten.

Detour has the honor of being the first poverty row film to be chosen by the Library of Congress for preservation. The position it holds in this catalog of greats is an inspiration to any budding filmmaker with great ideas, determination and a lack of proper funding.

Cast

Tom Neal	*Al Roberts*
Ann Savage	*Vera*
Claudia Drake	*Sue Harvey*
Edmund MacDonald	*Charles Haskell Jr.*
Tim Ryan	*Diner Proprietor*
Esther Howard	*Holly (Diner Waitress)*
Pat Gleason	*Man*
Don Brodie	*Used car salesman*

Chapter 19

| Roger Clark | Cop |
| Harry Strang | California Border Patrolman |

Production

Edgar G. Ulmer	Director
Martin Goldsmith (short story, screenplay)	Writer
Leon Fromkess, Martin Mooney	Producers
Benjamin H. Kline	Cinematographer
Leo Erdody	Original Music
Mona Barry	Costumes
Producers Releasing Corporation	Production Company
USA/67/1945	Country/Runtime/Year Released

Chapter 20

Dinner at Eight

"But everybody's broke, darling."

—*Millicent Jordan*

The years go by, but **Dinner at Eight** still retains much of its charm. This is a remarkable achievement when you realize that the majority of films from this era (1933) are mainly of interest to film historians, oldsters hoping to rekindle memories, and diehard movie buffs whose lifelong goal is to see every film made. **Dinner at Eight** is the exception to all the antiques that entertained the Depression era folks. It maintains your attention despite the wide span of time between then and now. Certainly, the fashions, strength of the dollar, and slang may have changed, but the core of the human condition has not. This film offers a deeper level of understanding of this core—one that is both rotten and sweet. Concurrently, today's audiences may enjoy the breezy antics of a cast strutting their stuff at a time when the film industry was learning to talk, thrill, and enrich audiences.

This is an especially fun outing if you turn back your mental clock and recall what was going on in the world at this time. A few years before **Dinner at Eight** was released, Hollywood was filled with self-ordained aristocracy and gracious living. Silent screen stars portrayed jazz babies, sheiks, vamps, or swashbucklers and brought on a decadence that hadn't raised eyebrows. They sometimes played the parts off screen as well. It was easy to party all night when you didn't have to study dialogue. But after sound arrived, the mood changed for those with thin voices and short memories. Surviving was the real game and the times were especially grim. The buying public would only pay to see people they could identify with. In other words, they had to feel comfortable enough to have them in their home for dinner. The audience also needed to laugh when their world wasn't particularly funny. Many had lost their hard-earned savings in the stock market collapse. Jobs were scarce. Times were tough. Movies reflected this change in national attitude. The most popular stars experienced some degree of suffering during the first reel, but stood tall with courage and convictions. Those that were out of step with the times (such as good timers Clara Bow and Louise Brooks) saw their careers evaporate. Scandals in their personal lives didn't help their cause either. Silent stars that adapted to change, like Joan Crawford with her struggling shop girl routine, thrived.

Dinner at Eight was based on the hit George Kaufman-Edna Ferber play. Top writers Herman Mankiewicz, Frances Marion, and Donald Ogden Stewart fashioned one of the first social comedies, openly dealing with the general depressed state of the country. While there is an attempt at reality, by the final reel, there had to be some offer of promise and hope for the New Deal just around the corner.

Dinner at Eight reflected this new order. By uniting various layers of society at an elegant dinner party, we see old money, new money, lost money, bad money, and no money. The daily lives of these personalities revolve around their bank accounts, their looks, occupations, and whom they know. It is a comedy of appearances. Those that have it, guard it. Those that don't are desperately trying to get it back. Everyone is trying to impress but few are wise enough to pull it off without looking desperate. The impressive cast—all invited to dinner—includes Marie Dressler, brothers John and Lionel Barrymore, Wallace Beery, Jean Harlow, and Billie Burke, all representing a virtual who's who of Hollywood at the time. This multi-star format is one of the best opportunities to view vintage Metro-Goldwyn-Mayer stars in their prime. Until **Grand Hotel** in 1932, only one or two top stars had appeared together in a single picture. The success of **Dinner at Eight** and **Grand Hotel** taught producers that the public wanted lots of stars (in good vehicles).

This genre, along with musicals, was extremely popular in the early 30s. Straight dramas depicting the same social ills were either too depressing or phony. In contrast, a comedy like **Dinner at Eight** approached the audience with wit and style. While the characters are ravaged in some way by the depression, these scrappers offer inspiration to the moviegoer, who is sitting in a dark room in search of hope, encouragement, and better times.

One of Metro-Goldwyn-Mayer's brightest stars, Marie Dressler, is peerless in the film. She's the dowager actress out of husbands, money, and acting roles. While everyone gets a chance to shine, she's the one to watch, not that you are going to take your eyes off her while she is on screen. She's witty, worldly, and rather hip in a time before hip was in. There is very little restraint in her performance. You have a full range of facial expressions and, unlike most actresses who reach a certain age, Dressler is not afraid to mock her years. For example, talking to a woman of her generation, she says "We must have a nice talk about the Civil War." Although she is dressed to the hilt, she cuts through all social pretensions and class. Her remark to Jean Harlow at the end of the movie is justifiably famous.

The rest of the cast is fine, if a bit pale when compared to a steamroller like Dressler. Lionel Barrymore is the honest businessman, fighting health problems and unscrupulous business tactics. He found his film niche in grandfathers, bankers, and favorite uncles. An automotive accident put him in a wheelchair in 1938, but this handicap did not deter his activity. He is best remembered for his mean and wily Mr. Potter in **It's a Wonderful Life** (1947).

Billie Burke is the organizer for **Dinner at Eight**. One of the movie's many priceless moments belongs to her when all of her well-laid plans get screwed up and she spends a minute or two verbalizing her problems. When **Dinner at Eight** was released to art houses some generations later, audiences were known to spontaneously applaud at the end of her emotional tirade. Thanks to its annual return to prime time, she is best known as Glenda, the kindest of all witches, in the **Wizard of Oz** (1939). Audiences wishing to see her dressed in straight clothes will be intrigued by her flighty hostess performance. Once a great beauty, and very popular on stage and in some early silent pictures, she curtailed her activity when she married showman Florenz Ziegfeld. When they lost their fortune in 1929, she returned to movies where her fluttering voice was used to good comic effect.

Chapter 20

Apparently as resilient as Dressler, she wrote in her memoirs "oh that sad and bewildering moment when you are no longer the cherished darling, but must turn the corner and try to be funny."

Wallace Beery and Jean Harlow represent the new game in town. He is the unscrupulous business tycoon and she is young and sexy wife. Their verbal spars (and her slinky clothes) are quite daring, yet surprisingly contemporary. Their characterizations were the inspiration for **Born Yesterday** (1950), also directed by George Cukor.

Wallace Beery was Dressler's costar in **Min and Bill** (1930). They were teamed together in several other efforts around this time and were popular with audiences seeking two familiar mates. Harlow was the original blonde bombshell your great-grandfather dreamed about. Using sex as a blatant come-on, she is one of the first stars to wear gowns to accentuate her body, without the benefit of underclothes. Like Marilyn Monroe, Harlow revealed a special gift for comedy. Her sudden death from uremic poisoning at 25 in 1937 sparked as much public reaction as Monroe's untimely passing in 1962.

Other celebrated guests include a faded matinee idol, John Barrymore. Once known to his fans as the "Great Profile," his looks have gone the same way his popularity did. His performance as a ham actor registered the correct sadness for the movie. Accepting this part took some courage. Few actors would risk tarnishing their careers by taking on a role of an actor who isn't doing so well. While he wasn't down and out at this point in his career, his performance is mighty convincing. Like older brother Lionel and sister Ethel, he was a major theatre star with a celebrated career. In his prime, he portrayed *Hamlet* and other classic roles. Although his talent and name assured him of continual employment, drinking took its toll on his health. An alcoholic since 14, he eventually could not remember lines or read cue cards, and this effectively ended his career. He died broke in 1942 at 60.

Today's audience may find it hard to believe that Dressler, a homely and rather large woman in her twilight years, was one of the most popular stars in 1932. She was a top star at the time mainly because audiences could identify with the old trouper. In fact, she had spent the 1920s practically destitute. Born in 1868, in Ontario, Canada, she was a popular comic star in vaudeville. In 1914, she starred in the first full-length comedy, Mack Sennett's **Tillie's Punctured Romance**, where Charlie Chaplin and Mabel Normand were in the supporting cast. However, when she led a chorus-girl strike (which led to Actor's Equity) in 1917, she found herself out of favor. At her low point she hawked peanuts on Coney Island. She was almost forgotten when a Metro-Goldwyn-Mayer scout happened to see her at a hotel in the late 20s. (She says she was actually on her way to her room to commit suicide when the scout intervened). Working her way up the ladder, she eventually won a straight part in Garbo's **Anna Christie** in 1930 which renewed audience interest. Soon she was in star parts again (and money), eventually winning the Best Actress Oscar for **Min and Bill** in 1930. At the time of her death in 1934, from cancer, she was topping the popularity polls.

Director George Cukor and Producer David O. Selznick produced **Dinner at Eight** and other classic films such as **A Bill of Divorcement** (1932) and **Little Women** (1933). But their friendship came to an abrupt end when Selznick fired Cukor from **Gone With the Wind** (1939) after just ten days of filming. Apparently Clark Gable didn't want to receive direction on his interpretation of Rhett from a person best known for being a woman's director. Cukor, who was gay, survived the setback and had a long and fruitful career. He continued to extract an unusually high number of excellent performances from actresses who were lucky enough to be cast in his productions, as can be seen in **Dinner at Eight**.

Labeling him as a woman's director, however, isn't really an accurate appraisal of Cukor. He was more of an actor's director. A favorite Cukor approach was to maintain the camera on the actor, without cuts, for longer- than-usual periods of time. This allowed both genders to fully connect with their character and the audience. This technique requires acting skill to be successful or the audience will get up and leave the theatre. However, Cukor was confident in material and talent. Both male and female actors were certain to appreciate an opportunity to artistically shine under his masterful direction.

Usually each year The Academy of Motion Picture Arts and

Chapter 20

Sciences presents The Jean Hersholt Humanitarian Award to members of the academy who bring credit to the industry through charitable efforts. For example, Elizabeth Taylor received the award in 1993 on behalf of her work for AIDS. The name behind the award, Jean Hersholt (1886-1956), was an actor in silent films and subsequently became a well-respected supporting player in talkies. He plays the insignificant part of Jo Stengel in this film. Hersholt's most important work was, apparently, off screen. He was a tireless champion for many humanitarian causes, notably the construction of the Motion Picture Country Home and Hospital. The Academy recognized his selfless acts by establishing this award in 1957, shortly after his death.

Shelley Duvall produced a version of **Dinner at Eight** for cable TV in 1989. Lauren Bacall courageously took on the Marie Dressler role. Other cast included Harry Hamlin, Marsha Mason and Charles Durning. This place setting was not a distinct improvement on the original.

Cast

Marie Dressler	*Carlotta Vance*
John Barrymore	*Larry Renault*
Wallace Beery	*Dan Packard*
Jean Harlow	*Kitty Packard*
Lionel Barrymore	*Oliver Jordan*
Lee Tracy	*Max Kane*
Edmund Lowe	*Dr. Wayne Talbot*
Billie Burke	*Millicent Jordan*
Madge Evans	*Paula Jordan*
Jean Hersholt	*Jo Stengel*
Karen Morley	*Mrs. Talbot*
Louise Closser Hale	*Hattie Loomis*
Phillip Holmes	*Ernest DeGraff*
May Robson	*Mrs. Wendel*
Grant Mitchell	*Ed Loomis*
Phoebe Foster	*Miss Alden*
Elizabeth Patterson	*Miss Copeland*

Production

George Cukor	*Director*
Edna Ferber (play), George S. Kaufman (play), Herman J. Mankiewicz, Frances Marion, Donald Ogden Steward (additional dialogue)	*Writers*
David O. Selznick	*Producer*
William H. Daniels	*Cinematographer*
William Axt	*Original Music*
Mona Barry	*Costumes*
Metro-Goldwyn-Mayer	*Production Company*
USA/113 minutes/1933	*Country/Runtime/Year Released*

Chapter 21

Dirty Harry

"Well, I'm all broken up about that man's rights."
—Harry Callahan

In the late 60s, John Wayne turned down the offer to play a maverick detective working the beat in San Francisco. Frank Sinatra was also asked but he had decided to retire (briefly). Paul Newman is also said to have vetoed this role. Thus, a fourth choice, Clint Eastwood, became Detective Harry Callahan, also known as **Dirty Harry**.

Since the movie became very, very popular, especially among young males, all three of these powerful stars probably had regrets. Its immense popularity spurned four sequels, as well as catch phrases that have become a solid part of American culture. The success of the Dirty Harry series placed Eastwood in the superstar category, where he continues today. In a career that will go on as long as he wants it, he can pick his own roles and pull his own shots. This rare status has also allowed him to branch out to directing, and to win the Best Directing Oscar for **The Unforgiven** in 1992.

Dirty Harry's intrigue and interest are the results of the tight direction by Don Siegel. Siegel was the first to establish the Eastwood screen persona, if you don't count his Italian Westerns, beginning with **Coogan's Bluff** in 1968. This time around, Siegel creates a San Francisco under siege. His clever evening shots of the Frisco skyline and neon artwork evoke the correct mood of the waning days of the psychedelic period. Eastwood, just on the other side of 40, has the experience and authority we have come to expect and admire in his characterizations. He only speaks when it's necessary. He despises regulations that prevent him from doing his job. This directness, sometimes confused with common sense, is what his supervisor lacks. Eastwood frequently and hilariously bucks authority, something that many male breadwinners would like to do. Rebellion forms the core of his appeal and is why males flock to his movies in droves. He lives out their fantasy. He is what every working stiff with job stress and a mortgage would like to be: independent with his own set of rules. Of course, this doesn't work in the real world. He would have been booted from the force the first time he ignored authority, policy and procedure.

Eastwood's appeal isn't limited only to males. Females see his soft, gentle side. He has very good manners and is very careful in his choice of friends. Once close to someone, he is very loyal. He has an old fashioned morality about him, and is a gentleman at heart. These qualities, plus rock hard confidence, is a great turn-on for the opposite sex.

The story line in **Dirty Harry** is loosely based on one of this country's first notorious serial killers. In the late 60s, a maniac who called himself the Zodiac Killer terrorized Los Angeles. In cryptic statements to authorities, the Zodiac Killer explained his dementia and described several of his grisly acts. Apparently his half-dozen victims were picked at random. His most horrifying message revealed his desire to follow a school bus and "pop off the kiddies as they bounded out." Panic-stricken parents started driving their children to school and yellow buses were escorted along their routes by patrol cars. Unlike this film's demented antagonist, the Zodiac Killer was never caught, but disappeared suddenly. Criminal experts theorize he eventually committed suicide—they hope. The Zodiac's actual cryptic handwriting was used in this film during the opening credits. When it came time to present the **Zodiac** (2007) on the big screen, a film poster of **Dirty Harry** can be seen in the film's montage.

Dirty Harry's nemesis calls himself Scorpio, another borrowed astrological sign. He picks people at random and shoots them with a high powered rifle. Unlike most serial or spree killings, he tries to extort money from the City of San Francisco. Harry is summoned because of his track record of bringing them in when nobody else can. He's the clean-up man and that is how he earned his nickname. He gets recruited for every dirty job that comes along.

Chapter 21

This film provides Eastwood with one of his best catchphrases. It has become folklore, a celebrated Hollywood anecdote. The movie opens with Harry preventing a bank robbery. Apprehending one of the suspects, who is reaching for a gun, Harry says "Uh uh, I know what you're thinking. Did he fire six shots or only five? Well to tell you the truth in all of this excitement I kinda lost track myself. But being this is a .44 Mangum, the most powerful handgun in the world, and would blow your head clean off, you got to answer yourself one question: Do I feel lucky? Well, do ya punk?"

Harry Guardino does a nice turn as Harry's frazzled supervisor. John Vernon is effective as the Major, as is Reni Santoni as Harry's partner. Andy Robinson is chilling as Scorpio, though he was not the producer's first choice. Audie Murphy, the war hero turned actor, was approached first. Unfortunately he was killed when his private plane went down in the Appalachian Mountains in 1968. Robinson said he received death threats after **Dirty Harry** and found other jobs scarce because of the resulting typecasting.

Sequels that followed the success of this formula were popular. If they seemed opportunistic, they provided another glimpse of this very complicated person, Dirty Harry. In **Magnum Force** (1973) Harry took on police corruption. **The Enforcer** (1976) gave him a female partner and audiences lapped up his version of a sensitive male. **Sudden Impact** (1983) was about a victim taking the law into her own hands, a topic to which Harry could relate all too well. **The Dead Pool** (1988) found our man in a full-blown relationship, perhaps with someone to care for him in his old age.

You could also say that Eastwood's role in 1993's **In the Line of Fire** was a reworking of **Dirty Harry**. Now middle-aged, his character has worked for the Secret Service (unsuccessfully) guarding President Kennedy. This time his supervisors are arrogant AND younger. But he continues to prove that this old dog still has a few tricks up his sleeve. It turned out to be one of the best movies of that summer.

In 2004, Eastwood directed and starred in **Million Dollar Baby**. The film won academy awards for best picture, directing, actress (Hilary Swank) and supporting actor (Morgan Freeman). The subject was female boxing and he was Frankie Dunn, an aging trainer to a determined young woman. Eastwood's character faced a heartbreaking decision at the end of the movie. One could imagine that Harry Callahan would approve of Frankie Dunn's final action.

The most recent development in the franchise is an interactive video game entitled **Dirty Harry.** Clint Eastwood lends his voice and likeness to the product that entertains and introduces Harry to a younger group of fans.

Cast

Clint Eastwood	*Harry*
Harry Guardino	*Bressler*
Reni Santoni	*Chico*
John Vernon	*The Mayor*
Andrew Robinson	*Killer*
John Larch	*Chief*
John Mitchum	*Di Giorgio*
Mae Mercer	*Mrs. Russell*
Lyn Edgington	*Norma*
Ruth Kobart	*Bus Driver*

Production

Don Siegel	*Director*
Harry Julian Fink, Rita Fink, Dean Riesner,	*Writers*
John Milius, Donald Ogden Steward	
(additional dialogue)	
Robert Daley, Carl Pingitore, Don Siegel	*Producers*
Bruce Surtees	*Cinematographer*
Lalo Schifrin	*Original Music*
Warner Brothers/Malpaso	*Production Company*
USA/102/1971	*Country/Runtime/Year Released*

Chapter 22

Dr. Strangelove:
Or How I Learned to Stop Worrying and Love the Bomb

"You can't fight in here, this is the war room!"
— *President Merkin Muffley*

There's a wonderful moment of dialogue in **Dr. Strangelove: Or How I Learned to Stop Worrying and Love the Bomb** between the President of the United States and the Premier of Russia. The date is 1963 and international relations between these two superpowers are fragile and overstressed. The country has had Francis Gary Powers, the Bay of Pigs, and the Cuban Missile Crisis, and other events fueling the cold war. The rather intimate and informal phone conversation between these two world leaders takes place because a military accident has occurred. Our President is forced to tell the Premier that a group of B-52s is heading to Russia and planning to drop nuclear warheads. "It's a big mistake," he explains rather tactfully. "One of our commanding officers... well...he went a little funny in the head." The subject is dark, disturbing, and incomprehensible, and that makes this scene one of the funniest ever made on film. It raises black comedy to heights previously unseen and should be required viewing for anti-nuclear activists, world leaders, and anyone who wants to make a message film. It is a rather delicious moment in what has become the most powerful film ever made on world destruction.

Compare **Dr. Strangelove** to Russian roulette. It details–in short trigger pulls—the events leading up to a nuclear confrontation. The main characters have symbolic names like J.D. Ripper, Bat Guano (guano is another term for feces), Major King Kong, and Premier Kissoff. Underlying all of this funny business is a topic that is usually

126   *Chapter 22*

taken very seriously. Each scene becomes yet another tragic confrontation between two opposing forces. These series of confrontations snowball into a world crisis, eventually ending of the world as we know it. This is pretty heady stuff, then and now. Stanley Kubrick shows us how we do not peacefully co-exist and how our society has the potential to self-destruct. We all want to believe that someone in charge will be able to stop the insanity, but it doesn't happen. Thus, that bubble we live in is illusion and that makes us feel very vulnerable. We are never safe in Kubrick's world.

The insanity starts when a high level U.S. base commander blames his impotence on the communists. He mumbles something about the Russians zapping his "precious bodily fluids" and then orders his pilots to bomb Russia with nuclear warheads. This starts a whole series of arguments from within his base, proceeding all the way to the Pentagon. One of the principal players in this game of distrust is General Buck Turgidson, who briefs the President on the situation. Played brilliantly by George C. Scott, he's the typical macho solider, all gung ho and excited to launch to a full-scale attack. He believes we should finish the job that the crazy commander started since the Russians are going to counterattack. By doing that, he theorizes that we save ourselves and wipe out the communists at the same time. Turgidson's dialogue with the President is just another peak in the fun in this nearly perfect black comedy.

There are many other tidbits that make this experience pleasurable. They are often items that require multiple viewing to catch. For example, when the Commanding Officer's base is attacked, hovering above all of the mortar smoke and gunfire is a billboard proudly claiming, "Peace is our Profession." And when a British Officer tries to call the President on a pay phone to give him a crucial piece of information that could save the world, he lacks the capitalist cash to do so. When he orders a soldier to shoot a vending machine for its change, the soldier says "you're going to have to answer to the Coca-Cola Company if you don't reach the President." In contrast to the world situation, the principal players in the political nightmare still find plenty of time for sex. It metaphorically rises during the credits when two airplanes are scene mating in the sky. Then it goes down

Chapter 22   *127*

to ground level where Buck Turgidson's girlfriend seems privy to an awful lot of national secrets. Apparently, Buck's quite a womanizer. Later, when making plans for a fall-out shelter, he insists on having a strong ratio of beautiful women for each man. There are other parallels to sex, or lack of it. If Viagra had been around, perhaps Jack D. Ripper might not have gone bananas.

Something called "The Doomsday Machine" adds a concluding epitaph to the film. This plan has a simple premise and goes like this: if any bomb is dropped, it will trigger a series of bombs, resulting in the total destruction of the earth. Of course, the whole point is lost if you keep it a secret, which is what the Russians have done most brilliantly. The character of Dr. Strangelove is probably based on Dr. Wernher von Braun, the German rocket scientist recruited by the United States after he worked for the Nazis. His big and telling scene is at the end of the film. He begins his presentation by accidentally calling the President "Der Fuhrer" when his actual name is Merkin Muffley—another word for fake pubic hair. Dr. Strangelove then spews out some master race philosophy, but is sidetracked by a number of physical ailments that permit some amusing self-inflicted pain. It is Peter Sellers at his most hysterical. From the looks of it, it must have been a laugh riot on the set during filming. If you watch actor Peter Bull, you can see him break concentration and laugh when Dr. Strangelove starts doing his uncontrollable arm bit.

Director Stanley Kubrick originally intended to have Sellers play several other key roles. As good as he is at playing Strangelove, the President, and Mandrake, the film would have suffered from too much of a good thing. Sterling Hayden, George C. Scott, and Slim Pickens filled out these other roles quite colorfully and add much enjoyment to the film. Casting Hayden was an interesting choice. Though he is cast as a hardcore American in the movie, his personal life was a different matter. During Hollywood's red scare in the early 50s, he testified to the House Un-American Activities Committee and regrettably confessed membership in the communist party. Since his information was forthright, he protected his career. However, apparently doing this took a toll on his friendships—and self-worth.

George C. Scott said he had a blast playing Buck. He was nominated for Best Supporting Actor but did not win. At that time, he made it clear that, if selected, he would refuse an award that he could not respect. Several years later, he was given another chance to turn down the award when he was nominated as Best Actor for **Patton** (1970). Instead of removing his name from consideration before the awards, he simply didn't show up. His award remains unclaimed in the Academy's vaults.

Slim Pickens was a former rodeo star before settling in Hollywood. He made good use of these skills, riding the ultimate bucking bronco. Kubrick asked Pickens to play his role with the utmost seriousness. This manipulation from the director resulted in a very funny performance.

Composer Laurie Johnson's music adds much to the film's humor. His mixture of complicated and repeating chords produces the proper sound needed for black comedy. London born Johnson is best remembered for his catchy theme from TV's *The Avengers*.

The final song, vocalized by Vera Lynn, *We'll Meet Again* is strangely ironic. The song was popular during World War II since it offered some degree of hope and optimism for the soldiers to return home safely after combat. Kubrick originally planned to end the film with a pie fight. This slapstick scene was filmed but not included in the final version. However, the large table of food in preparation for the scene in the War Room remains in view. It has been reported that Kubrick originally planned Dr. Strangelove as a straight, serious film. But during pre-production, (he scripted it with Terry Southern and Peter George, basing it on George's serious book *Red Alert*), he said he couldn't find the right tone. It is quite possible he wanted to contrast this project with another film in production during this same time, Sidney Lumet's **Fail-Safe** (1964), a more sobering effort on the same subject. **Fail-Safe** starred Henry Fonda as the President, the man who had to make difficult and personal choices. This film is also worth watching to see a different perspective on the subject. In 2000, CBS revived live drama by showcasing this story with big gun actors (George Clooney, Richard Dreyfuss, Harvey Keitel, etc.).

Chapter 22

Also of interest to film buffs is that "men in black" visited Kubrick to ask how he was able to detail the cockpit of a B-52 so accurately. He told these curious government workers that he saw the controls pictured in a magazine advertisement.

Today, **Dr. Strangelove** is a popular fixture on campus and in art theatres, continuously receiving applause from a legion of new admirers as the years go by. While it is frequently studied in film classes, Kubrick has said he didn't conceive of the film as fully as it has often been interpreted. Still, the film is more pertinent now than when it was originally released. The issues are the same; only the players have changed. Today, Jack D. Ripper can be a terrorist or a maverick leader of a third world country. Just thinking about the possibilities can create a bit of anxiety for all of us.

Cast

Peter Sellers	*Group Captain Lionel Mandrake,*
	President Merkin Muffley, Dr. Strangelove
George C. Scott	*General "Buck" Turgidson*
Sterling Hayden	*Brigadier General Jack D. Ripper*
Keenan Wynn	*Colonel "Bat" Guano*
Slim Pickens	*Major T.J. "King" Kong*
Peter Bull	*Russian Ambassador Alexi de Sadesky*
James Earl Jones	*Lothar Zogg*
Tracy Reed	*Miss Scott*

Production

Stanley Kubrick	*Director*
Peter George (from novel), Stanley Kubrick,	*Writers*
Terry Southern, and Peter George	
Stanley Kubrick, Victor Lyndon, Leon Minoff	*Producers*
Gilbert Taylor	*Cinematographer*
Laurie Johnson	*Original Music*
Hawk Films	*Production Company*
Wally Veevers	*Special Effects*
USA/93/1964	*Country/Runtime/Year Released*

Chapter 23

$ (Dollars)

"Stick with it, Joe!"

—Bank Employee

When Goldie Hawn's character, a fun-loving hooker, finally puts her hands on the $1.5 million she and friend Warren Beatty steal from a trio of crooks, it turns into an intimate affair. Never dreaming of having so much money, she dramatically breathes deep, rolls her big blue eyes, and seductively sighs. She asks immediately, perhaps in place of a cigarette, "do you think there's any connection between crime and sex?" For director Richard Brooks, the answer is yes. And it's just one of the fetching moments in $ (1971), a caper film that boasts colorful characters, an unusually long chase, and a surprise twist at the end. And yes, money and sex are used alternatively in this film: both are viewed as the way to pleasure and happiness.

$ (or **Dollars**) stars Warren Beatty as a regular guy named Joe, an American living and working in Germany. His job is to monitor the security system at a Hamburg bank. He's affable, charming, and just as precise and exact as any German. A top priority of his work is to protect a vault of safe deposit boxes and a priceless gold bar prominently displayed in the lobby of the bank.

As the movie develops, we learn Beatty is mastermind to an almost perfect heist. The word "almost" is key since there are plenty of roadblocks to keep suspense high. His friend Goldie uses her skills and charms to uncover information enabling him to raid three safe deposit boxes that belong to criminals, all of whom operate in notoriously profitable circles. His theory: "they can't call the police and report the crime." Robert Webber is the first safe deposit box owner. A buttoned-down Las Vegas lawyer with mob connections, his large cache is from gambling and unreported income. When he finds his money gone, his remark is what you would expect from a narcissistic criminal: "Jesus, when you can't trust a bank."

Scott Brady is the second. A temperamental American Sergeant running a black market operation under military guise, he rips off Uncle Sam and patriotically explains America's success: "We got three things: God, guts, and get-up and-go."

The third crook to own a safe deposit box under Beatty's watchful eye is a burned-out drug racketeer (Arthur Brauss). With his Aryan appearance, he turns out to be the most clever of the three—and the most frightening. He is our tour guide for Hamburg's red light district. Through his eyes, we see the seedy strip joint where drug deals are made and nude women dance in front of a large American dollar bill. Perhaps Hamburg was the logical choice for the misdeeds. It is a major industrial seaport for Germany and a perfect lane for drugs, smuggling, and other illicit stuff.

Gert Frobe is the Bank President. You may remember him as James Bond's arch villain in the thriller **Goldfinger** (1964). This time around he is jolly and harmless around gold and not at all like the villain who tried to hog the world's entire supply of this precious metal.

Director Richard Brooks wrote the original screenplay for $. This was a departure from his norm since he usually adapts his screenplays from novels (**Elmer Gantry** (1960) and **Looking for Mr. Goodbar** (1977) or from plays (Tennessee Williams' **Cat on a Hot Tin Roof** (1958) and **Sweet Bird of Youth** (1962).

Brooks' screenplay for $ puts sex and crime on the same dollar bill. The illicit nature of Hawn's activities is obvious. Prostitution is a sex crime; you have to pay for it to get it. Many of her tricks resort to sexual games for gratification, and the trio of crooks are drawn into the heist because they wander into Hawn's sexual web. She passes their account balances and deposit box keys to Beatty.

Brooks has remarkable skill at suspense and action, as evidenced in **The Blackboard Jungle** (1955) and **The Professionals** (1966). This keen ability surfaces in the last 25 minutes of $ in a grueling chase scene. There are cars, trains, cold weather, and a unique duel on a Scandinavian frozen lake. The action is taut against the grimy backdrop of a Hamburg winter. The Bavarian views are not picturesque and their bleakness sets the serious tone for this deadly game.

Beatty is good as usual in a role that demands him to be charming and articulate. In a career that began based on good looks and style, he evolved to one of the most enduring leading men. From the beginning he was very much in charge of his career. Often producing (**Bonnie and Clyde**, 1967) or directing his work, there have been few misses in a career of profitable films. He was reunited with Hawn in **Shampoo** (1975) and in **Town & Country** (2001). In 1991, at 54, to the surprise of all, he celebrated fatherhood and marriage, in that order. After dating some of the screen's most beautiful women for years, he settled down with Annette Bening, who co-starred with him in one of 1991's best films, **Bugsy.**

Hawn uses her *Laugh-in* personality to her advantage in a fairly unglamorous role. She pleases moviegoers, but infuriates feminists. Still developing her film persona, she's childlike, affectionately dizzy, and full of self-doubt. Yet, there are hints of steel underneath that frailty. When her unique logic is questioned, she says "I may be ignorant, but I'm not stupid." Today, Hawn is one of the most respected women in Hollywood, pleasing moviegoers with performances full of charm. She survived the 70s, a time when there were few good roles for women. She admitted in a 1985 *Playboy* interview that her least favorite role was the part conceived for her in **$**. Now, both in her career and life, she is seen as a good role model for women in film.

In 1980, she became executive producer of **Private Benjamin** and began a series of mature, interesting women (**Swing Swift**, 1984; **Overboard**, 1987). When the buying public started to avoid her films, she turned to Disney's Touchstone Division to revive her career. Her first film was a neat thriller—**Deceived**—in 1992. Her most recent hit was **The First Wives Club** (1996). Her look alike daughter actress Kate Hudson inherited a good deal of her good looks and charm from mom and effectively carved out a film career of her own.

By 2002, it was thought that Hawn and Beatty had permanently retired from film. However, both returned to the big screen in separate, unremarkable roles after a 15 year absence: Hawn appeared in

Chapter 23

Snatched (2017) and Beatty played Howard Hughes in **Rules Don't Apply** (2017).

Little Richard sings the title tune in $ with his usual frenetic energy. The soulful instrumentals are by Quincy Jones.

Cast

Warren Beatty	*Joe Collins*
Goldie Hawn	*Dawn Divine*
Gert Fröbe	*Mr. Kessel*
Robert Webber	*Attorney*
Scott Brady	*Sarge*
Arthur Brauss	*Candy Man*
Robert Stiles	*Major*
Wolfgang Kieling	*Granich*

Production

Richard Brooks	*Director*
Richard Brooks	*Writer*
M.J. Frankovich	*Producer*
Petrus R. Schlömp	*Cinematographer*
Quincy Jones	*Original Music*
USA/121/1971	*Country/Runtime/Year Released*

Chapter 24

Eating Raoul

"He was a man. Now he's just a bag of garbage."
—Mary Bland

A Paul Bartel production offers a new twist to the strange, bizarre, or offbeat. His films offer unique qualities on the other side of off beat. They tease, are slightly smutty, and frequently amusing. Not surprisingly, his work is not for mass consumption, but personally tailored to his loyal following of admirers. Unfortunately, he seemed to be most creative when working under the constraints of a low budget. His first work was a short called **Secret Cinema** (1969). It was an odd variation of something Alfred Hitchcock would have done on his TV show if the censors had allowed it. It did have merit, though, and paved the way for feature length films. **Death Race 2000** (1975) was his first film that made an impact. But the medium budgeted **Scenes from the Class Struggle in Beverly Hills** (1989) set him back a bit, despite the expensive locale. It just wasn't very funny. However, between this seesaw is **Eating Raoul**, one of the funniest films of 1982. Apparently Bartel worked on this film for quite some time, as funding permitted. Thus, it has his personal stamp as producer, director, writer, and co-star. From the title to the closing credits, his soufflé is a very neat satire on sex and food and how they go hand in hand (or in this case, hand-to-mouth).

The opening scenes offer a straightforward narration by Mr. Bartel. He asks the audience to hear Paul and Mary Bland's story. He says in a deadpan: "it is not a pretty one, but it needs to be told."

The Blands are a pair of puritans living in dirty old Hollywood. They're hopelessly out of sync with today's hip-hop crowd. They seem to represent the Eisenhower era as it was supposed to be. Their apartment is furnished with stylish furniture from the 50s. They wear matching

Chapter 24   135

pajamas (both top and bottoms) and sleep in twin beds. Their blandness is punctuated by their compatibility. After having a terrible day, they rush home and say in complete unison: "we're so lucky we found each other." This couple finds their current economic situation frustrating. Each time they try to improve their lives, something out of the ordinary blocks their goal. Their weirdness makes them easy targets. At work or play they seem to have "I'm a victim" painted on their foreheads, thus bringing out the worst in bullies, crooks and sexual predators. They also have a sense of entitlement. They believe they deserve to succeed even if their plans for the future are unexciting to loan officers, people in touch with reality or who have the vision to make things happen. They hope to open up a restaurant with a fancy kitchen out in the country and call it—what else—"The Country Kitchen." When they are in danger of losing this dream and everything else they've devoted their colorless lives to, they search for a solution.

When the Blands accidentally kill a swinger (who was hitting on Mary), an idea surfaces—one that's as easy as a piece of cake. They decide to lure rich swingers to their apartment under the promise of a good time. When the swingers get there, instead of pleasure, they get murdered. It seems entirely appropriate for Paul to use a frying pan for this dirty deed. He says without wincing: "these swinger types always seem to have a lot of money" and "this city is full of rich perverts." Thus begins their recipe for a very lucrative business arrangement.

Despite the subject of murder, the film is very appealing. It offers the right tone for this type of exercise in black comedy. It doesn't take itself seriously and it carefully avoids the legal and moral implications. Its matter- of-factness adds to the humor. Mary tosses off murder with the same level of concern associated with burning the morning bacon. Further proof that she's a bit wacky are her thoughts on the matter: "Nobody will miss these types of people anyway."

That is, until Raoul arrives in their lives. A self-described, hot-blooded Mexican-American opportunist, he swoons over Mary like the other sexually charged males in the movie. This is because Mary dresses rather provocatively and is a big turn-on. Unlike the others, however, he succeeds in seducing her. First he slips her a mind-altering drug, then carefully places money on her nude body. Poor sexless Paul has to win her back, and the outcome is pretty spicy.

Bartel moves the film along at a quick pace, supplying lots of opportunities to mix food, murder and sex. They are more surprising than shocking, and most of the action is left to your imagination. For example, think about the possibilities between a midget and a Great Dane. One especially funny scene occurs in a sex shop in which greenhorn Paul gets a lesson in sex enhancers.

Some of the players in the sex games are very recognizable, including Ed Begley, Jr., whose character has a passion for groovy hippie chicks. Buck Henry does an interesting turn as a lecherous banker. Another familiar face to diehard movie buffs is Edie McClure, who plays the swinger in fur. The mentor to the Blands is a nice lady who calls herself Doris the Dominatrix. Brandishing a whip and snarl, the actress who accepted this role, Susan Saiger, truly deserves an honorable mention.

The director and his two co-stars, Mary Woronov and Robert Beltran, were reunited in **Scenes from the Class Struggle in Beverly Hills** (1989). Despite this and other opportunities up to his death in 2000, none of Bartel's subsequent work put a dent into mainstream Hollywood. However, his special place in the Hollywood hierarchy of "different" is secure through **Eating Raoul**.

Cast

Mary Woronov	*Mary Bland*
Paul Bartel	*Paul Bland*
Robert Beltran	*Raoul*
Susan Saiger	*Doris the Dominatrix*
Lynn Hobart	*Lady Customer*
Richard Paul	*Store Owner*
Mark Woods	*Hold-up Man*
Buck Henry	*Mr. Leech*
Ed Begley, Jr.	*Hippie*
Billy Curtis	*Little Person*

Chapter 24

Production

Paul Bartel	*Director*
Paul Bartel, Richard Blackburn	*Writers*
Anne Kimmel, Richard Blackburn	*Producers*
Gary Thieltges	*Cinematographer*
Arlon Ober	*Original Music*
Bartel/Films Incorporated/Quartet	*Production Company*
Katherine Dover	*Costumes*
USA/90/1982	*Country/Runtime/Year Released*

Chapter 25

Enter the Dragon

*"Never take your eyes off your opponent,
even when you bow."*

—Lee

Despite **Enter the Dragon**'s technical limitations in dubbing, acting, direction, and other various items that can put a gloss on the
finished product, it still emerges as a must-see film for devotees of
action-adventure movies—especially for those with an interest in
martial arts. More importantly, the film is a showcase for its engaging
star-hero, Bruce Lee, an actor who died before his time.

It has been generations since Lee's surprising and unfortunate
death. In the time that has lapsed, Lee has emerged as something
larger than life. To some extent, he belongs in that macabre galaxy of
lost stars that includes James Dean, Marilyn Monroe, Health Ledger
and John Belushi. Certainly he could perch comfortably on the mantle that displays the handful of ill-fated actors who died just as they
were hitting their stride or prime. Like other performers in this category, who set the world on fire and then abruptly leave it, Lee did at
least one thing extremely well. For example, Dean represented angry
youth. Monroe titillated audiences with her obvious sex in the puri-
tanical 50s. Perhaps Belushi was one of the funniest performers of his
generation. Most would agree that Lee was as close to perfection in
martial arts as anyone who had ever been on the screen. He was and
is the standard by which all are measured. His status remains almost
mythical, and continues to be supported by a small, devoted group
of martial arts fans happy to worship his achievements. He still has
active fan clubs around the world. **Enter the Dragon**'s plot is much
in the same vein as other garden-variety gangster yarns. He's hired

to infiltrate a white slavery ring and opium den. His mission is also personal—the bad guys involved are responsible for his sister's death.

While the fight scenes are incredible to watch, there is also a great deal of interest in watching the star use his powers wisely. The philosophy he included in the film was thoughtful and positive for his young fans. Though his character can literally dust off anything that moves, he avoids confrontations at all costs. A snake does his dirty work in one creative instance. While the reptile clears the room of the bad guys, Lee puts his chin in his hand as if to say this is sooo boring. In another place, a bully finds himself outfoxed and out to sea after tangling with Lee. It is also obvious that Lee is not a supporter of the National Rifle Association, saying "any bloody fool can pull a trigger."

At his best, he is an effective role model for young people. He instructs a young boy "to feel rather than to think." He goes on to say that the mind is the center of your power and not the strength or youth of your body. He also stresses family values and loyalty at all costs (way before presidential elections brought it into vogue). He says that family is the most important thing we have and we must do everything we can to protect and nourish it. With only this to his credit, Lee comes off as a pretty nice guy. Like James Dean, Lee's stardom was just beginning to happen when he died unexpectedly, right when the masses were noticing and complimenting his style and charisma. A good film was already playing to appreciative audiences and another film was in the works. Then poof—he was gone. Perhaps because he was so physically fit and appeared indestructible in his films, his passing was that much more of a shock to his fans. Whether he could have sustained a long career in films will never be known. From what can be viewed in his abbreviated career, it looked as though his charm could keep everybody on the edge of the seat for hours at a time. Though only 5'2", he was physically gifted and a superb athlete. So much so, that on film you question whether the playing time is being speeded up. He is that quick with a chop, spin, or kick. But if you study other non-stationary objects around Lee that are in the same visual range, amazingly enough, you're actually viewing Lee without the usual Hollywood illusion.

His connection to Hollywood was through these lightning-quick skills and techniques. A number of Hollywood stars and celebrities enrolled in his school of jeet kune do. The A-list included Steve McQueen, James Coburn, and Kareem Abdul Jabber. Lee taught his own brand of martial arts, one that he had developed himself. Camp followers all agree that his moves were more fluid and smooth than the other fighting styles. Even his cries were original and distinct. With movie stars in his gradebook, it was only natural for him to find himself in Hollywood.

At first, Lee faced the problem of typecasting. Because he was Asian, he was relegated to roles that were sexless and of servitude. He was required to speak in monosyllables, offer no emotion, and appear tough. He had little to do except destroy an opponent or break up the room as he did in **Marlowe** (1969), or play a third banana to the hero as he did in TV's The *Green Hornet*. When he failed to land the main role in the *Kung Fu* series (it went to American actor David Carradine) he cried foul. At that time, the producers believed viewers wouldn't support an oriental in an hour-long program. Although Lee was born in San Francisco, his parents were from Hong Kong. So Mr. Lee packed up his nunchaks and went to his parent's land where he was welcome. There he signed a two-picture deal. These films, **The Big Boss** (1971) and **Fists of Fury** (1972) showcased him as an action hero. He was good in them, and they became international hits. This was the box office clout he needed, so he asked for and received the job of directing **The Way of the Dragon** in 1973. This was an even bigger hit than the previous two films, Hollywood took notice and made an offer. Coincidentally, President Nixon took his famous trip to China around this time, which made the Orient that more accessible and interesting. Thus, Lee was a pioneer in opening doors in mainstream Hollywood for other artists from the Orient.

The Hollywood offer was for **Enter the Dragon**. It boasted a modest budget and American co-star John Saxon, who, incidentally, has a black belt in karate. Lee negotiated creative control and choreographed the action. The fight scenes, like a good dance with poor music, are what the film is best remembered and most famous for.

Chapter 25

In July, 1973, several weeks before **Enter the Dragon** premiered in U.S. movie theaters, Lee died suddenly at 32, apparently from a burst blood vessel in his brain. **Game of Death,** the feature he was working on when he collapsed, was eventually released in 1978, using a double. After his death, Lee was the subject of intense media attention. Unfortunately many inferior martial arts films flooded the cinema around this time, starring some dreadful Bruce Lee copycats. There was even a parody, an item called **They Call Me Bruce?** (1982) in which comic actor Johnny Yune says people mistake him for Bruce Lee. Amazingly, it was successful enough for a sequel, **They Still Call Me Bruce** in 1987, proving that Mr. Lee's tailcoats were very strong.

The phenomenon Lee brought to the mainstream continues today in some form or another. For example, **The Karate Kid** (1984) films incorporated Eastern philosophy and are very popular. Most action films after 1975 include some type of martial arts—along with a philosophy about fighting. A sad postscript to the Lee legacy occurred when his son, Brandon Lee, died on the set of **The Crow** in 1993, when a stunt gun misfired. The media tried to draw mysterious comparisons but no foul play was every confirmed in the death of the father or the son. **The Crow** was released posthumously. For the second time, audiences were sadly greeted with the end of what may have been a very promising career.

A 25th anniversary version of **Enter the Dragon** in 1998 restored some footage that was deemed too violent when first released. Audiences once again had an opportunity to hold their breath to some mind-boggling action scenes.

Cast

Bruce Lee	*Lee*
John Saxon	*Roper*
Jim Kelly	*Williams*
Ahna Capri	*Tania*
Kien Shih	*Han*
Robert Wall	*Oharra*
Angela Mao	*Su Lin*

Betty Chung	*Mei Ling*
Geoffrey Weeks	*Braithwaite*
Peter Archer	*Parsons*

Production

Robert Clouse	*Director*
Michael Allin	*Writer*
Raymond Chow, Paul Heller, Bruce Lee,	*Producers*
Leonard Ho, Andre E. Morgan, Fred Weintraub	
Gilbert Hubbs	*Cinematographer*
Bruce Lee	*Fighting Sequences*
Arlon Ober	*Original Music*
Louis Sheng	*Costumes*
Warner Brothers	*Production Company*
Hong Kong-USA/110/1973	*Country/Runtime/Year Released*

Chapter 26

Emperor of the North

"Sounds like a ghost story to me."
—"A" Number One

Visualize two trains speeding toward each other on the same track. They are aware of each other, and that a horrific collision is inevitable. There are opportunities to stop, yield, switch tracks, or reverse direction, but they choose to remain on course toward the target.

Metaphorically speaking, this dance of destruction is what **Emperor of the North** holds for the viewer. It offers two inflexible characters with different opinions, riding the rails during The Great Depression. Heading for an eventual showdown, they do everything within their power to protect their honor or turf, to the point of no return.

What a ride this is, made even more enjoyable because the two formidable opponents of might in this exercise pit Hollywood's most notorious screen heavies against each other—Lee Marvin and Ernest Borgnine.

This wasn't the first film in which they appeared together. Early on in their careers, Borgnine and Marvin were usually cast as one of the thugs in support of a gang leader. When things got tough, they usually went down swinging, allowing the hero to face off with the true villain. In **Bad Day at Black Rock** (1955), both terrorized Spencer Tracy with unpleasant results. They also tangled unsuccessfully with Victor Mature in **Violent Saturday** (1955). Together or individually, Marvin and Borgnine consistently offered characterizations so good that it would only be a matter of time until they moved to the sunny side of the street. When this happened and they became honorable, you didn't forget where they originally came from. That toughness, that dirt that remained behind their ears is what keeps our interest in this story.

Rather surprisingly, in an industry that promotes youth and beauty, both actors moved into leading roles in their middle years. Borgnine's breakthrough role occurred when he played **Marty** (1955), the ugly butcher looking for love. In the end, he wins the girl and the Academy Award for Best Actor. One of Marvin's last bad guy roles was Liberty in **The Man Who Shot Liberty Valance** (1962). It seemed fitting that the man who shot him (and survived the ordeal) would become a hero.

The Dirty Dozen (1967) was a big commercial success for both of them, under the direction of Robert Aldrich. As coaches to a group of misfits, both were respectable men in uniform fighting for the allied cause. They had an important mission to complete, but could only use people opposed to authority, as they once were, to complete a crucial exercise in patience. It was one of the year's most popular films. Director Robert Aldrich and stars Marvin and Borgnine were reunited in **Emperor of the North**.

Like **The Dirty Dozen**, **Emperor of the North** offers a good serving of violence, but at least there's a point to it all to keep our interest. It goes beyond pitting good against evil—and having good win for goodness sake. Both opposing forces reveal their flaws, thus defying stereotypes. Marvin plays "A" Number One. He calls himself number one because he's lost everything—family, security, self-respect—in the depression. Like many men down on their luck, he's forced to move around on the rails and scratch at anything just to survive.

Borgnine, on the other hand, is the one with the job, the one who can take a bath each day. He wears pressed clothes and pays taxes. His obsession, though, as trainmaster, is to not allow hobos on his rail. His compulsive nature includes murder to prove his point. His clear advantage is that he appears to be the respectable member of the community. The poor souls he attacks and throws off his train (usually to their death) are nameless, forgotten folks, lost in the economic downslide. Nobody seems to care about them until Marvin gets wind of this practice.

The conflict starts rather simple with a few verbal jabs, but grows increasingly complex. Both men are very determined and have a deep bag of survival tricks. They are experienced in fights and good at what they do. That is what makes this film worth the ride. The details are thoughtful and make for some very good tension and excitement. For example, there is one scene involving dangling chains to discourage men from hiding underneath the cars. You can almost feel the pain when the forged steel comes in contact with flesh and bone.

Pay close attention to the sound effects of moving metal parts, steam, and other objects related to old trains. Their use heightens the suspense and tension, which never lets up once the movie starts.

There are many fine moments in this film, including some interesting communication. When one particularly tense moment occurs because both men will not yield and it places the entire train in jeopardy, Borgnine questions Marvin's motivation. Marvin's response: "It sounds like a ghost story to me." The highlight comes at the end with a physical and brutal showdown between these two. At times they laugh and smile. This reveals yet another relationship: both appear to enjoy giving and receiving pain. Another layer of complexity comes from youthful upstart Keith Carradine. As a young man with less experience in matters of rail travel, Marvin takes him under his wing. Their relationship fills in some of the blanks about Marvin, the aging father figure who realizes he can't remain number one forever. This friendship, though fleeting is important to Marvin's character development. It shows that he has the ability to care about another human being, thus achieving great audience sympathy. The all-male cast has many familiar faces in small roles. Several standouts include film noir actor Elisha Cook Jr., Simon Oakland, and Vic Tayback, (just before he went on to do TV's *Alice*).

The general theme director Aldrich weaves into his movies is to have two headstrong people square off against each other to force a resolution to the conflict. That resolution may not be satisfying to all. You leave the cinema understanding that the struggle will continue. Clearly this is the case here, as it was in **The Big Knife** (1955) when actor Jack Palance collided with studio chief Rod Steiger. **The Dirty Dozen** offered conflict within a team. Another example occurred in **Whatever Happened to Baby Jane** (1962) when two sisters feuded over childhood jealousy and lost opportunities. **The Longest Yard** (1974), in which prisoner Burt Reynolds goes against Warden Eddie Albert, supports the theme of conflict and self-sacrifice. Perhaps more cerebral than other Aldrich work, **Emperor of the North** remains a joy to watch because it works on several layers of intrigue and offers two great actors at the height of their powers.

Cast

Lee Marvin	*"A" Number One*
Ernest Borgnine	*Shack*
Keith Carradine	*Cigaret*
Charles Tyner	*Cracker*
Malcom Atterbury	*Hogger*
Simon Oakland	*Policeman*
Harry Caesar	*Coaly*
Hal Baylor	*Helper*
Matt Clark	*Yardlet*
Elisha Cook, Jr.	*Gray Cat*
Joe Di Reda	*Dinger*
Liam Dunn	*Smile*
Vic Tayback	*Yardman*

Production

Robert Aldrich	*Director*
Christopher Knopf	*Writer*
Stanley Hough, Kenneth Hyman	*Producers*
Frank De Vol	*Original Music*
Joseph F. Biroc	*Cinematography*
Eli Wynigear	*Costumes*
20th Century Fox/Inter-Hemisphere	*Production Company*
USA/118 minutes/1973	*Country/Runtime/Year Released*

Chapter 26

Chapter 27

Female on the Beach

"A woman's no good to a man unless she's a little afraid of him."

—Drummond Hall

One didn't tangle with Joan Crawford in the movies. The characters that attempted to block her personal action plan usually left the scene with their tails tucked between their legs. Even those who tried to make love to her would quickly learn that it was easier to swim with a barracuda. Apparently, this image mirrored life as well. Miss Crawford was as tough off screen as on, and when she died in 1977, *Newsweek's* profile of her departure was titled *Iron Woman*. It was a fitting tribute to her strength, which was required if one considers the length of her career measured against her ability as an actress.

Not surprisingly, it has been widely reported that Crawford had an endless supply of determination. That instinct, which made her so endearing to her legions of fans, is featured in every Crawford performance. Her career began in silent movies. In the 20s, when flappers were the rage, she was the best of them, dancing on tables as she progresses from rags to riches. Most of her 30s roles are the same, with only the clothing, leading men, and furnishings changed. After she had firmly established herself with her audience, she fought for meaty roles but had to contend with Norma Shearer leftovers due to the order of the food chain at Metro-Goldwyn- Mayer. Toward the end of that decade, feeling a draft in her career, she latched onto the working shrew role in **The Women** in 1939. It cemented her screen personality as a tough, resilient female from lower class origins seeking to better herself socially and economically. It is also significant that she would willingly sacrifice her self-respect to gain power.

This was the image she nurtured for the rest of her career. The formula seldom varied. She was very lucky with it and appeared in a number of entertaining movies. She mopped the floor with an ungrateful daughter and won an Academy Award for best actress in **Mildred Pierce** (1945), tangled with a corrupt politician in **Flamingo Road** (1949), found security with gangsters in **The Damned Don't Cry** (1950), and played mind games with a philandering husband in **Sudden Fear** (1952). In all of these circumstances, she was able to use her looks, charm, and intelligence to turn the tables against people who tried to take something unfairly from her. Crawford was not a great beauty or an actress with a wide range of emotions. But audiences liked what she could do in these limited circumstances. Most of her fans were females. Their loyalty through the years kept her name above the title long after most of her peers had retired or could not find suitable roles.

When Crawford reached late middle age, she had difficulty finding a suitable leading man of her stature. Few established stars were willing to handle her mercurial personality. They had to be up and coming, and usually they were much younger. An older woman being wooed by a younger man created special problems in the provincial 50s, but she had a bigger problem than age. The mannerisms she had cultivated so gingerly had reached the point of caricature. Determined to keep her name in the public, she cleverly exploited this increasingly narrow range. Perhaps she was at the height of caricature as the **Female on the Beach**, released in 1955. It is the definitive study of Crawford's independent yet vulnerable woman.

Since Crawford was dating Universal's chairman at the time, **Female on the Beach** was one of the studio's slightly more ambitious projects for 1955. This connection ensured that the star got pretty much what she wanted. Jeff Chandler, primarily a rugged actor in action movies and under contract at the studio at the time, was assigned to co-star. In the film, Crawford is packaged as a gambler's widow who goes to her beachfront home for some much needed rest and relaxation. Instead of rest, the local beach gigolo, Jeff Chandler, amorously pursues her. When Chandler shows an increasingly sexual

Chapter 27

interest in her, sparks begin to fly because she thinks he only wants her for her money and not for love. Fans will savor the trashy dialogue by Robert Hill and Richard Allen Simmons. There is a rich variety of insults for her to heave on Chandler and other unfortunate people who get on her nerves.

Chandler is the perfect Crawford nemesis. Not only is he younger (and can probably seduce most any girl he wants), he turns out to be very needy with scars brought on by an abusive childhood. Crawford's mother instinct kicks in and he is, to coin no better phrase, "In like Flynn." Crawford is experienced and very wealthy, but afraid of commitment. However, coupled with her loneliness, a surprising ability to nurture overrides this tough exterior.

The tennis match, or insult volley, is the best part of the fun. When she finds him nosing around in her kitchen in the morning, she says "I have a long list of dislikes. It's getting longer." Later when she turns frigid to his come on, she explains her lack of interest with "you're about as friendly as a suction pump." And after their first quarrel, she paints him a sharp visual with "I wouldn't have you if you were hung with diamonds upside down."

In fact, nobody remains unscathed by the sharp tongue of the Crawford bitch. When the relationship with Chandler does sets sail, Crawford tells a competitor (Jan Sterling) "so this is where the loser tells the winner she's making a terrible mistake. On the way out, think of something original, will you?" And when two uninvited guests get wind of her animosity toward them (Cecil Kellaway and Natalie Schafer), they demand clarification. Thus, she makes it very clear that they should leave "preferably to another continent."

Naturally, the movie is a showcase for all of the famous Crawford trademarks. She slaps her lover and throws a drink in his face. Her shoulders are wall-to-wall and her eyebrows resemble two furry worms. She balances a constantly lit cigarette between long nails, inhaling with the force of a wind tunnel. And those heels—they form the base to a pair of terrific looking legs that command our interest and attention. In real life, Crawford was obsessed with her body and constantly worked out. And it shows. She's in great shape for a lady of 51 and this was all before Jane Fonda's aerobic workout tapes. Her famous figure proudly displays various swimsuits and cocktail dresses. She probably thought this exhibition was a gift for her fans. They would need to know what was proper to wear at the beach or to a party.

Sex, of course, is the key element to the proceedings. But it isn't normal sex in the way two healthy people relate to one another in an intimate way. Crawford and Chandler have some sexual hang-ups. Chandler's been scarred by his mother, who attacked him with a fishhook (and then committed suicide). He tells Crawford that women are not soft or gentle. And it is implied that after he has sex with a woman, he becomes very cold and distant. Former conquest Jan Sterling even accuses him of hating women. Crawford also has a dubious past. She is a former fan dancer. Somewhere along the line she married a wealthy older man, but the marriage was loveless. Pretending to enjoy widowhood, she frequently barks to anyone who shows interest in her that she would like to be alone. She eventually defrosts to Chandler, but not before several tantrums.

Most of the dialogue relates to some sort of sexual dance. She tells Chandler "I was on an island once. They all look alike—round." The passion turns hot when she finally steps aboard his boat for the first time. Wearing black and looking at him, she says "it's smaller than I thought." But he counters with "it sleeps two." After generating some passion in the cabin, she tells him "don't move your boat." One has three guesses to determine what part of the male anatomy they are referencing. Silver haired, muscular, and standing 6'5", Jeff Chandler would be easy to spot on a crowded street. He was also quite hirsute. Studio executives made him shave his chest for this role. As the male on the beach, at least he had a valid reason to show off his torso. During the 50s Chandler was a popular rugged action and western hero, with occasional forays into soap opera. He also dated swimming star Esther Williams. She revealed in her 1999 book, *The Million Dollar Mermaid: An Autobiography,* that Chandler was a cross-dresser. She terminated their relationship after seeing him dolled up in chiffons and heels.

Chapter 27

In 1962, Chandler unexpectedly developed blood poisoning after having spinal surgery, and was dead at 45.

The muscular lad that takes Chandler's throne at the end of the film, adopted by Osbert and Queenie, is Ed Fury. Mr. Fury would also be easy to spot on the street or beach. He appeared frequently in muscle and fitness magazines in the 50s. He later packed his thong and went to Italy to star in minor league sword and sandal epics.

Another Crawford vehicle released the same year was **Queen Bee**. In this variation of her determined woman doing battle, she spent all her time manipulating the lives of a large dysfunctional family. It was fun to watch her duke it out in a hysterically grim setting. When she was killed at the end, it was a relief to know she wouldn't be able to torture anybody else. Also, during this time in her life, Crawford accepted a different role: corporate executive. A third marriage to Pepsi-Cola Chairman Alfred N. Steele was probably her happiest. Together they traveled around the world to promote this soft drink. When Steele unexpectedly died of a heart attack in 1959, she continued her successful role in public relations for the firm. In fact, films after 1963 usually sprouted a bottle of familiar soda pop on camera near the star.

After a longish absence, she returned to movies in the inspired **Whatever Happened to Baby Jane** (1962). It was a black comedy about feuding sisters who had once worked in Hollywood. One happens to be going insane, leaving the other—an invalid—helpless. Bette Davis was co-star and got all the juicy lines, but Crawford nicely underplayed her role and her diehard fans believe it is her best performance. Certainly it is one of her least mannered and controlled. In 2017, HBO aired a fascinating eight part series entitled *Feud*, a behind the scenes analysis of the Crawford-Davis goings on during the making of **Baby Jane**.

After the rather surprising success of **Baby Jane**, she kept working, but the roles became very embarrassing, especially her last, **Trog**, in 1970. In this grade Z effort she was an anthropologist playing mentor to the missing link. One would hope that keeping a straight face in her first and last science fiction movie deserved some type of award. She later admitted in interviews that all of the films after **Baby Jane** were done for money or to just keep working and that she was ashamed of them.

After Crawford died in 1977, her adopted daughter Christina wrote a tell-all book. It detailed Crawford's abusive and cruel behavior—something Hollywood insiders had known for quite some time but were afraid to talk about openly. The book became a national bestseller and was later crafted into the bio-movie **Mommie Dearest** in 1981 with Faye Dunaway in the title role, an actress that Crawford greatly admired. The book and subsequent film did nothing for Crawford's image.

After her death, a soft core porn film surfaced, purportedly starring Crawford. Allegedly, Metro-Goldwyn-Mayer spent lots of money trying to buy the copies to protect their precious commodity. However, nude stills of Crawford have been documented and published. It was only fitting that this kind of production is where she started. She truly was determined to become a star and was prepared to do anything to reach that goal.

Cast

Joan Crawford	*Lynn Markham*
Jeff Chandler	*Drummond Hall*
Jan Sterling	*Amy Rawlinson*
Cecil Kellaway	*Osbert Sorenson*
Judith Evelyn	*Eloise Crandall*
Charles Drake	*Lieutenant Galley*
Natalie Schafer	*Queenie Sorenson*
Stuart Randall	*Frankovitch*
Marjorie Bennett	*Mrs. Murchison*
Ed Fury	*Roddy*

Production

Joseph Pevney	*Director*
Robert Hill (play), Richard Alan Simmons	*Writers*
Albert Zugsmith	*Producer*

Chapter 27

Charles Lang	*Cinematographer*
Heinz Roemheld, Herman Stein	*Original Music*
Sheila O'Brien	*Costumes*
Universal International Pictures	*Production Company*
USA/97/1955	*Country/Runtime/Year Released*

Chapter 28
The Front

"So who can you sue?"

—*Howard Prince*

It was not one of Hollywood's prouder moments when the House Un-American Activities Committee began their bold search for communist infiltration in Hollywood. Their investigation is probably one of the film industry's most regrettable embarrassments in terms of ruined careers and unfulfilled ambitions. The results of their probe stifled talent and brought fear, persecution, and deceit to an industry already not known for its security. At its most extreme, some of the performers struck by vicious rumors couldn't find work, became despondent, and in rare instances, committed suicide. Today, over half a century later, thanks to some documentary filmmakers, there appears to be an outreach of sympathy for the artists and their families who were blacklisted by the industry because they were thought to have some affiliation to communism.

The beginnings of the red scare probably surfaced during the Great Depression when unemployment was high, wages were low, and labor unions were being formed to provide individual workers with some security and a voice. Following World War II, the mortar was set when the Soviet Union rejected the Marshall Plan and initiated its very own campaign to rebuild war torn Europe. This situation intensified when a small group of individuals within the Hollywood community became convinced that a secret organization of evil communists were plotting to sabotage the American way of life. The most feared method of contaminating the minds of the American public was thought to be through movie houses exhibiting films that contained political messages designed to corrupt American values.

This red scare reached hysterical proportions when the House

Committee on Un-American Activities indicted ten powerful men affiliated with Hollywood. These ten individuals refused to confirm or deny their involvement in the communist party on the grounds that what they did in their spare time was private. The committee disagreed and all were cited for contempt of Congress. They were fined and ordered to serve jail time. Unfortunately, Citizen Hollywood took their silence as pleas of guilt. A blacklist began circulating around to prevent them (and anyone else with the same credentials) from finding employment. That being the case, one of the unfortunates, Edward Dmytryk, broke rank from "The Hollywood Ten," admitted his error in judgment and named other actors and artists with ties to the communist party. The witch-hunt was on, and, unfortunately, it brought down many of Hollywood's most creative forces.

Since the industry does have the ability to inform or influence culture, trends, and mores, there was paranoia. When push came to shove, the players within the Hollywood circle played the game they knew best: self-preservation. That meant indicting friends in the hopes of having the committee look the other way.

One of the best perspectives of the blacklist terror is in Martin Ritt's **The Front** (1976). As entertainment, it makes no attempt to evaluate whether the artists were guilty of anything. It does detail the intrusion into their lives and the resulting chaos. As one can discover, many of the entertainers who were blacklisted were singularly unlucky.

The film's opening sequence begins with the playful song *Young at Heart*. We see and feel the innocent 50s in newsreel footage. It begins with the Eisenhower years, with optimism and hope. Then the montage progresses to the more garish moments of that time, which pitted the celebrity against the politician. Through this introduction, the filmmakers suggest the hypocrisy, anger by those unfortunate souls caught in the madness. The star of the movie, Woody Allen, takes a role not written or directed by Woody Allen. It's refreshing to see him do a variation of this New Yorker character. His current base of fans won't be disappointed since he doesn't veer too far from the eccentricities and neuroses he's nurtured for years with this persona.

During the course of the film, co-star Michael Murphy called his character a schnook. However, a more accurate description would be a pesky insect that ventures too close to the spider's web. The only defense he can muster is to squirm.

Allen plays a front to blacklisted writers. In other words, he puts his name on their work since no one will hire their talent. A failure at many things, he suddenly becomes a successful writer in the eyes of the producers and viewers. His newfound status does create stress. Quick rewrites are out of the question, and there is a funny scene where he scolds his writers for work that is below the standard that he has been accustomed to fronting. His occupation also places him with people that he wouldn't ordinarily come in contact with. He becomes a kid in a candy store and even falls in love with a nice girl. But the job of fronting, as we are allowed to discover, has risks and rewards. His particular innocence brings the real terror down to a level that we can all understand. The relationship between spider and the stricken insect provide the movie with both bite and sentiment.

The practice of fronting work was based on real events. As proof, the industry was embarrassed to learn after the fact that two academy award winning screenplays—one for **Roman Holiday** (1953) by "Ian McLellan Hunter" and for **The Brave One** (1955) by "Robert Rich"— were actually written by blacklisted writer Dalton Trumbo.

Allen's box office might probably brought financing to this project, because many of the other talents involved had major setbacks to their careers. What's unique is that the film's producers hired a number of performers who suffered setbacks due to blacklisting. It's as if these performers have risen from the ashes to bring fire to this project. The standout performance in this group is Zero Mostel. He must have been grateful to present some of the living terror he experienced firsthand. Other survivors from this period include Herschel Bernardi, Joshua Shelley, Lloyd Gough, Walter Bernstein, and especially director Martin Ritt. Ritt was active in early television productions but his promising career suddenly stopped dead in 1951 when it became known that he had been a member of the communist party. He turned to coaching at the Actor's Studio before finally landing a

Chapter 28

job in 1957 to direct **The Edge of the City**. His entire body of work, including **Hud** (1963) and **Norma Rae** (1979) involve strong social themes. It must have been particularly reassuring for him to direct a film that is deeply moving and personal.

Also of significance is the Julie Garfield appearance. She is the daughter of actor John Garfield and appears in the small role of Margo. Her father co-founded the Hollywood Canteen with Bette Davis and starred in **The Postman Always Rings Twice** (1946) and **Body and Soul** (1947). Known for left-wing sympathies, elder Garfield was called to testify before the House Un-American Activities Committee. Though no evidence of communist affiliation was found, his career went into a sharp decline. His death at 39 of a heart attack in 1952 may have been exacerbated by the situation.

One of Garfield's last films, **Force of Evil** (1948) was supposedly a political metaphor for the terror that was creeping into Hollywood at the time. Its director, Abraham Polonsky, was a good friend to Garfield and found himself on the blacklist shortly after the film was released. He didn't direct another film until 1969's **Tell them Willie Boy is Here**. In retrospect, maybe it did matter at the time if communists were involved in Hollywood products. That is, if they were actually communists with evil intentions. But many of those involved, and it didn't matter which side they were on, were ignorant of what communism actually meant. Lenin's ideals were not the same as Stalin's, yet both were communists. The resulting blows to the many careers and livelihoods would be inexcusable today—perhaps. If you have an opinion on a subject, you are supposedly protected under the constitution since voicing one's opinions without fear of retribution and coming to some agreement is how problems are solved. However, Jane Fonda's anti-war standing created much grief for her—though the problems associated with her extreme outspokenness were more personal than professional.

Interestingly, actor Robert Vaughn earned a Ph.D. in Political Science with his analysis of the events that took place during the blacklist. His book *Only Victims: a Study of Show Business Blacklisting* offers anyone interested in this topic a perceptive outline. Vaughn contacted many of the actual victims for this thesis, and it was published in 1972.

Cast

Woody Allen	*Howard Prince*
Zero Mostel	*Hecky Brown*
Herschel Bernardi	*Phil Sussman*
Michael Murphy	*Alfred Miller*
Andrea Marcovicci	*Florence Barrett*
Remak Ramsay	*Hennessey*
Marvin Lichterman	*Myer Prince*
Lloyd Gough	*Delaney*
David Margulies	*Phelps*
Joshua Shelley	*Sam*
Charles Kimbrough	*Committee Counselor*
Norman Rose	*Howard's Attorney*
Josef Sommer	*Committee Chairman*
Danny Aiello	*Danny LaGuttuta*
Julie Garfield	*Margo*

Production

Martin Ritt	*Director*
Walter Bernstein	*Writers*
Robert Greenhut, Charles H. Joffee,	*Producers*
Martin Ritt, Jack Rollins	
Michael Chapman	*Cinematographer*
Dave Grusin	*Original Music*
Sheila O'Brien	*Costumes*
Columbia Pictures/Rollins-Joffe Productions	*Production Company*
USA/94/1976	*Country/Runtime/Year Released*

Chapter 28

Chapter 29

The Graduate

"I'll see you later, Mrs. Robinson."
—Benjamin Braddock

There are movies before and after **The Graduate**. They are as different as apple and oranges, or in cinematic terms as different as Greta
Garbo and Marilyn Monroe. **The Graduate** reached a new plateau
for the art form called movies, especially for those originating in the
United States. Like three other films that came about in this era of
movie making—**Bonnie and Clyde** (1967), **The Wild Bunch** (1969),
and **The Godfather** (1972)—it was and is a landmark film for all of
the senses. However, its distinction from some of the most critically
acclaimed movies from this era is that it is a comedy. It is very, very,
funny, then and now. Not surprisingly, nearly everyone associated
with this movie secured a long-term future in film. To begin, it made
a movie star out of a young, unknown actor, Dustin Hoffman. He is
still as busy as ever turning out star performances. It placed director
Mike Nichols into the front rank of directors. He went on to direct
other intelligent films, usually where the central character resists
sensibilities to do their own thing. The soundtrack by Simon and
Garfunkel was beautifully integrated into the film's direction, adding
much to its energy. No longer were youth-oriented films dependent
on beaches, fast cars, or hot chicks.

Though the message is topical, it is not dated. It speaks of youth
alienation. It's a young man's fight and flight from the establishment.
It is the plastic world his parents have formed that he despises. A
world he cannot be happy in, at least for the moment.

This conformity was in line with what was going on during the
turbulent 60s when **The Graduate** was being formed in someone's
head. Young people were demonstrating on campus, smoking pot on

the lawn, campaigning violently against Nixon and Vietnam or whatever the "silent" majority represented. The country was being torn apart and turned on. There were love-ins and sit-ins, and something called flower power. This is not the ideal time for Benjamin, a sensitive young man who has just graduated from college. He sees his parents' world as empty swimming pools and mindless chit chat. Nichols frequently places some type of glass around Benjamin, as if it is some kind of invisible barrier or clear ceiling. There are phone booths, windshields, a snorkel mask, and an aquarium. Poor Benjamin seems to relate to the fish in the tank. They swim around and around and arrive nowhere. To find some measure of happiness, he decides he must leave this claustrophobic existence.

But he is young, a virgin in many ways. He doesn't know how to do it. No one has taught him how to live in his parents' world. He has a lot of fear. It doesn't help that his parents constantly tell him he has all of the necessary advantages in front of him…You just graduated from college. You are a track star. You have the world at your feet in our world.

Then comes the seduction. Mrs. Robinson represents the dark side of the world he is both terrified of and confused about. She picks up on his weakness. Women of her age and experience have developed skill at detecting weaknesses. Trying to both encourage and thwart her advances, he tells her "I think you're one of the most attractive of all of my parents' friends." However, the line that clinches his fate has become the often-repeated party joke that asks "Are you trying to seduce me, Mrs. Robinson?"

This is a very funny seduction, but his problems really begin when he meets Mrs. Robinson's pretty daughter, Katherine Ross, and falls in love with her. This is a natural occurrence of events since he isn't ready or wanted in the Robinson world. He is idealistic, not materialistic. Naturally he connects with someone else who shares his same conviction (and naiveté).

Furious at this overt rejection, arrogant and not really stable, Mrs. Robinson reveals her claws. She wants him for herself but something better for her daughter. Like the generation the young people

Chapter 29

protested against, she is selfish and would deny her own daughter a chance at happiness. By escaping from Mrs. Robinson, he is escaping from the world he doesn't really want to be a part of…yet. Naturally, with these ideas, he meets a lot of resistance.

The highlight, of course, is the seduction scene. As Mrs. Robinson, Anne Bancroft is cool, shrewd and calculating. When crossed, she is about as friendly as a buzz saw. Her scenes are the funniest in the film. She treats him as a boy toy, but then expects him to be worldly. She likes to shock. Early on, without warning, she asks Ben "did you know I was an alcoholic?" Bancroft's performance approaches legendary status. "Are you going to Mrs. Robinson me" became a buzzword for a young man being seduced by an older, more experienced woman. She would be pleased to know young men everywhere are grateful for the role this particular type of woman plays in their sexual education.

As good as Bancroft is, it's interesting to note that she didn't make it in films until she was middle-aged. Her early failure in Hollywood drove her to Broadway. Before leaving, she said she was going to a place that didn't require a big bust (this was around the time of Jayne Mansfield). It was a long haul to some sort of industry recognition. Producers didn't view her as an asset to their movie until she repeated her stage success in **The Miracle Worker** (1962). That brought her a Best Actress Oscar.

In contrast to her struggle, Hoffman was a true overnight success. His film experience was in Volkswagen commercials, one line in **The Tiger Makes Out** (1967), and a featured role in a low budget European gangster film. Then Mike Nichols saw him in an off-Broadway production of *Eh?* and the rest was cinematic history. Hoffman became the role model for every repressed youth trapped into a grown-up world.

While his career took off, Bancroft's performance didn't have any positive effect on her fortunes. It was ten years later when she co-starred with Shirley MacLaine in the popular but dull **The Turning Point** (1977). Actresses of her generation are seldom able to find regular employment in film. Bancroft was fortunate. She was able to carve out a long and rewarding career in theatre and film up to her death in 2005.

The Graduate was based on the book by Charles Webb, and the screenplay is by Calden Willingham and Buck Henry. Henry has a small and funny role as the super-efficient hotel desk clerk. When a 25th anniversary edition of the home video was released in 1992, Henry said that Bancroft, Hoffman, and Ross were not the original choices for the roles. The producers had wanted Doris Day, Robert Redford, and Candice Bergen. They had also hoped for Ronald Reagan as Ben's father. Redford said no, explaining that nobody would believe he was that naïve. Day said she could not imagine herself rolling around in the sheets with someone half her age. Bergen was unavailable, and Reagan, as Governor of California, had officially retired from films. Instead, William Daniels won the father role.

In retrospect, Bancroft was the perfect Mrs. Robinson. At 36, she was actually about 10 years younger than the character she portrayed—and only 5 years older in real life than Hoffman! Apart from Doris Day, there were a number of higher profile actresses considered for the role. The list included Ava Gardner (but they thought she was too sexy) and Jeanne Moreau (she was too European), Susan Hayward and Audrey Hepburn. Henry satirized his role as screenwriter of this film in Robert Altman's **The Player** (1992). In this black comedy on the Hollywood game, Henry played himself and pitched an idea for a sequel to a producer. With complete sincerity, he said the plot would have Ben and Elaine, who were now middle-aged, caring for an invalid Mrs. Robinson at their home.

The film's impact continued in other forms of mass marketing, something its premise did not endorse. Alfa Romeo, who manufactured the roadster Ben received as a graduation present, christened an entry level version of the car as the *Graduate*. This version continued in production until 1994.

Look closely for actor Richard Dreyfess as one of the boarding house students, and actor Ben Murphy as one of the fraternity brothers. Another soon-to-be famous person associated with the film is Linda Gray, who went on to star in TV's blockbuster *Dallas* as J.R.'s wife.

Chapter 29

Then a model, it is her luscious leg that's pictured in the famous promotional poster. When the film was adapted into a play for Broadway, she accepted the role of Mrs. Robinson for the 2001 London version.

During the 1992 Academy Award's telecast, Bancroft and Hoffman were reunited as presenters, providing one of the brighter moments of the evening. Hoffman (then 56) asked Bancroft (then 62) if she was trying to seduce him. Her reply "not anymore" was distinctly Mrs. Robinson for a brief moment and literally brought the house down.

Cast

Anne Bancroft	*Mrs. Robinson*
Dustin Hoffman	*Benjamin Braddock*
Katharine Ross	*Elaine Robinson*
William Daniels	*Mr. Braddock*
Murray Hamilton	*Mr. Robinson*
Elizabeth Wilson	*Mrs. Braddock*
Norman Fell	*Mr. McCleery*
Alice Ghostley	*Mrs. Singleton*
Buck Henry Hotel	*Hotel Desk Clerk*
Marion Lorne	*Miss De Witt*
Richard Dreyfuss	*Boarding House Resident*
Mike Farrell	*Bit part in hotel lobby*
Ben Murphy	*Bit part in fraternity house*

Production

Mike Nichols	*Director*
Charles Webb (novel), Buck Henry, Calder Willingham	*Writers*
Joseph E. Levine, Lawrence Turman	*Producers*
Robert Surtees	*Cinematographer*
Dave Grusin, Paul Simon	*Original Music*
Patricia Zipprodt	*Costumes*
Embassy Pictures/Lawrence Turman	*Production Company*
USA/105/1967	*Country/Runtime/Year Released*

Chapter 30

The Haunting

"Psychic phenomena is subject to certain laws."
—Dr. John Markway

The Haunting (1963) is based on Shirley Jackson's 1959 novel, *The Haunting of Hill House*. Writer Jackson was a specialist in the macabre. Her superb ghost story has since become a classic must read. Since **The Haunting** retains the flavor of her brilliant work, it is one *very* scary movie. It's not for the squeamish, people with a heart condition, or young and impressionable children. Instead, it's of interest to the mature, intelligent adult who enjoys a good jolt—one that's created from suspense and tension. Unlike the slash and gore type films that tend to populate this genre, this outing is a bit more upscale. Even those who ordinarily avoid horror movies will enjoy this dark tale.

You can trace its film roots to the horror classics of early Hollywood when creative, low budget films initiated the careers of Boris Karloff and Bela Lugosi. It also has a similar relationship to the Roger Corman films that used the poetry of Edgar Allen Poe. Still, it offers a highly original approach toward scaring the living daylights out of anyone who decides to view it.

The singular attraction to **The Haunting** is in its presentation: there are no central ghosts or ghouls to see or mistrust. The horror is the omnipresence of evil. It seems to be an invisible force all around, putting everybody at risk. As opposed to viewing evil face-to-face, we experience it with our senses. It is refreshing that **The Haunting** doesn't rely on traditional shock visuals to keep you on the edge of your seat. Thankfully, it's far removed from attractive young people out trying to have a good time on Halloween or Elm Street.

Like the viewer, the players in this horror-drama have individual perceptions of the strange things going on at Hill House. They don't

Chapter 30   165

know what lurks underneath their bed, behind the couch, or at the top of the stairs. Director Robert Wise uses the terror of the unknown to excellent effect. As the story progresses, he carefully constructs visual manipulations for the cast and the viewers so that imaginations run wild. Viewers may find themselves checking to see what evil lurks in their closet! While the execution is remarkable, the story is rather straightforward.

For various reasons, four people are chosen to visit 90-year-old Hill House to research the supernatural. The house is a gothic mansion with a history of coaxing residents to die before their time. The characters also have a peculiar set of traits, strength, and weaknesses. Early on, the ghost(s) seems to zero in on each perceived weakness.

The lead is Julie Harris. Of the four, she is sensitive with an air of fragility. She's lived in an isolated state all of her life, very much like the poor, dead descendants of Hill House. A spinster pushing 40, she is about to embark on middle-age without developing into her own person. Quite childlike, she even has trouble driving around the block without getting nervous. There is a strong implication that she receives consistent care and attention from relatives— and probably doctors. She doubles as narrator so we are privy to her innermost thoughts. Her lack of experience has made her fragile and vulnerable and her shortcomings serve to heighten the tension in the movie.

We know she's weak and has no defenses. She has a superb mind, though, and her thoughts do make sense. Peculiar as it may seem, she relies on her instinct to get her through. Not a bad way to react, unless you have a limited range of experiences and you find yourself resting in a haunted house. Some circles say that Clair Bloom's character is lesbian. The acting talent of Ms. Bloom places the character's sexual choice as an open question— probably to appease censors in the early 60s, but also to avoid stereotypes. Apart from grappling with her sexual orientation, Bloom has Extra Sensory Perception (ESP) and appears to be privy to everyone's thoughts and inclinations. She also has the ability to see things one step ahead of the other. Thus, the audience is coaxed to feel a great deal of tension when she gets in one of her uptight moods.

Richard Johnson is the anthropologist who arranged the expedition. Tall, academic, and angular, he appears to be all wise and knowing. His weakness is in his choices. His work takes precedence over his life. His handicap, all book and no feeling, ends the film with a shriek. It's a terrifying realization to the audience that his job is to protect the investigation from evil—and he doesn't have the ability to do so.

Russ Tamblyn rounds out this cast of flesh and blood. Except for his slight and youthful build, he appears to be the average man about town. He speaks in clever lines and walks with a sure step. Boasting confidence and disbelief in the paranormal at the same time, he says he's next in line to inherit Hill House and the only reason he's there is to protect his investment. When that transaction does occur, you can be sure Mr. Tamblyn will be much older and wiser.

Though **The Haunting** is supposed to take place in Boston, the movie was filmed entirely in England (note the car Ms. Harris drives—that particular model was not imported to the United States in any great numbers). Real locations, though, were not a necessity in this case. With few exterior shots, this claustrophobic atmosphere enhances the tension.

As proof of the effectiveness of the film's approach to create terror, the most recent (and extremely profitable) **The Blair Witch Project** (1999) borrowed a page from **The Haunting**. In this example, the folks that tangle with the Blair witch never see the evil that lurks out there. However, they know something is out there in the dark, waiting to strike—but only after enjoying a bit of torture. Not knowing what "it" looks like or when it is going to attack only serves to heighten the tension and suspense. This approach guarantees individual viewer interpretations of the events that take place. Since two individuals will offer different views of what is behind the breathing door, shaking the staircase, or is causing the cold zone, the overall suspense reaches a high note. It is recommended that you watch it with someone else and discuss these individual perceptions. Companionship heightens the fun, but also adds a much-needed sense of security.

Another film from this period, **The Innocents** (1961), with

Chapter 30   *167*

Deborah Kerr, is also worth seeking out. Kerr's cerebral character, a headstrong governess, offers a unique comparison to the role played by Julie Harris. Because of the emotional wall they have built around themselves, both women are their own worst enemy.

In a long and productive career, Director Robert Wise had an eclectic list of films to his credit. He moved with apparent ease from one genre to another. A few examples of his outstanding catalog of work include **The Day the Earth Stood Still** (1951), a science fiction film with an important message for world peace; **Executive Suite** (1954) was about corporate politics, greed and labor, while **I Want to Live!** (1958) offers a searing portrait of a woman accused of a crime and her route to the gas chamber. **West Side Story** (1961) and **The Sound of Music** (1965) are the two definitive musicals of the 60s. He was also at the helm of Star Trek: The Motion Picture in 1979.

Under the same title, another version of Jackson's ghost story was released in 1999. Even with expensive special effects and a good cast (Liam Neeson, Catherine Zeta-Jones) the dimension of suspense isn't as deep or frightening as what one experiences in this version.

Cast

Julie Harris	*Eleanor Lance*
Claire Bloom	*Theodora*
Richard Johnson	*Dr. John Markway*
Russ Tamblyn	*Luke Sanderson*
Fay Compton	*Mrs. Sanderson*
Rosalie Crutchley	*Mrs. Dudley*
Lois Maxwell	*Grace Markway*
Valentine Dyall	*Mr. Dudley*
Diane Clare	*Carrie Fredericks*

Production

Robert Wise	*Director*
Shirley Jackson (novel), Nelson Gidding	*Writers*
Denis Johnson, Robert Wise	*Producers*
Davis Boulton	*Cinematographer*

Humphrey Searle	*Original Music*
Mary Quant	*Costumes*
Metro-Goldwyn-Mayer/Argyle Enterprises	*Production Company*
UK/112/1963	*Country/Runtime/Year Released*

Chapter 31

It's a Mad, Mad, Mad, Mad World

*"We're the ones with the Imperial
and we're running last?"*

—*Mrs. Marcus*

There is something distinctly American about **It's a Mad, Mad, Mad, Mad World**. First, we have the obvious. The automobiles are big and flashy. The clothing, hairstyles, and furnishings look like something from a 1963 stateside magazine. And the filming locations in the desert are in the great state of California, that special place in America where cultural trends begin before infecting other parts of the country.

Then there is the less obvious to the uninformed. The not-so-subtle attitude of the main characters moves the story forward. They are aggressive, capitalistic, independent, competitive, supremely confident—they have open prejudices toward those different from themselves. Americans certainly do not hold all of these traits—but a composite of these values does create something peculiar to the people who live in this country.

For example, you may notice that British Terry-Thomas is the only foreigner in the film (with star billing). Quite frequently the others mock his English manners. They also refer to him as a blimey, a rough slang for the British. At one point in the film, he comes to blows with Milton Berle after a heated discussion on cultural values or lack thereof. In this long duel, being a proud American, including music accompaniment, comes up more than once. This gung-ho attitude pushes the forces into play. It's the way the characters think, interact, and treat one another.

Running close to three hours, the film is essentially one long chase. There are pratfalls, obnoxious behavior, slapstick with people and cars, and zingy one-liners. It's a rather mindless good time with a great cast that includes many, many fun people who find themselves caught in defective airplanes, locked in hardware stores, or driving too fast for the conditions. This film makes a statement about what is important to these Americans. In this case, it is spelled M-O-N-E-Y.

It all begins when a lone driver (Jimmy Durante) crashes his car off the side of a cliff. Some passersby (Milton Berle, Sid Caesar, Buddy Hackett, Mickey Rooney, and Jonathan Winters) stop their cars to offer assistance. Boy, do they get an earful from the dying man. Before everyone's had their coffee, Durante tells these five strangers there is $350,000 in hidden loot buried under a Big "W" at a state park in California—and they believe him! Thus, they begin their respective journeys to get there first and claim the money. Since none of them trust each other, it soon turns into a free-for-all. When the detective obsessed with the case, Spencer Tracy, learns that these innocent bystanders can lead him to the money, he begins their surveillance.

Familiar faces from television, circa early 60s, appear throughout the movie, along with a few surprises. They include some of the world's funniest men and women. Interestingly, Zasu Pitts is the one cast member from the Keystone Kops era, the time and place in which this movie definitely has roots. She had played drama in silent movies (including the lead in Stroheim's 1924 **Greed**). But her birdlike quality forced her into comedy when sound arrived. She is the switchboard operator at the police station who cheerfully replies "you're through to homicide" in an overly happy, fluttering, and hilariously inappropriate voice.

Tracy is in his next-to-last role and looks weary, but there are moments of enthusiasm and vigor. His telephone conversations with his family are a highlight. As the only character grounded in reality, his comedic timing is perfect when he finds himself surrounded by wacky people. His necessary performance is the stuff that glues the movie together.

The husband and wife writing team, William and Tania Rose, seldom allow the characters to go beyond two dimensions. In some

Chapter 31

movies this leads to terminal boredom and is the kiss of death. However, this personally works to the movie's advantage. You want it to be light and airy, to have that caricature effect you see in a cartoon.

The humor comes mainly from the conflicts the characters experience during their run to the money. But they also bring issues with them to block their progress. For example, Berle is recovering from a nervous breakdown, precipitated by his mother-in-law Ethel Merman. She barks: "Yeah, you were working real hard, trying to keep costs down the day that you ran out of the office and stood screaming in the street." The costs she is referring to are from the Edible Seaweed Company, Berle's brainchild into which Merman has dropped $15,000 of her own money. She concludes "and not only does nobody like it, it cost over $4 a can."

There is nothing normal about Dick Shawn. Check out the décor in his bachelor pad. He lives within minutes of the Big "W" but he is having a fling with luscious Barrie Chase. In bathing attire, they shimmy, grind, and twist to a tune by the Shirelles, and ignore the phone calls from raging mama Merman.

Perhaps the funniest sequence occurs when Merman finally reaches Shawn on the phone and attempts to draw his attention to the money. It's a mother calling her son at the wrong time, a classic example of somebody wanting to be boss with someone who wants to enjoy the intimate moments after making whoopee. Merman is the definitive control freak. She's brassy, fearless, and loud. Her performance leaves us with a permanent record of her non-singing comedy achievements. A variation of the Merman role was originally offered to Groucho Marx, but his salary demands could not be achieved.

The exceptional cast of players meant that opportunities were ripe for ego trips. To can any attempts at scene stealing, Stanley Kramer, the director and producer, insisted on no script changes, adlibbing, and unscheduled performances. If someone did deviate from the script, he said the shot would not be printed. They all accepted his terms and by all accounts, each one has an equal share of the laughs.

Credits were also a sticky concern. In Hollywood, there is a saying, don't shack up with anyone lower in billing than yourself. To prevent anyone from going lower, all are listed alphabetically (except for Tracy). Then they are rotated to give each starring cast member top billing, if only for a moment.

According to Merman's biography, the cast members were always playing practical jokes on the set. In retaliation for one against her, she got on the phone and pretended to be speaking to her agent. She thanked him for the special billing arranged just for her, and she made sure other cast egos were listening. On cue, the others ran to the phones to call their agents to arrange the same thing. To their embarrassment, they could see Merman laughing hysterically over the successful ruse she had perpetrated.

Perhaps the fiercest competitor for large ego was Milton Berle. Not only did he steal jokes, he routinely tried to steal scenes from the other players by lagging a few steps behind whenever the camera was filming a crowd shot. He did this with the intent to have more screen time than his peers.

Ernie Kovacs was supposed to be in Sid Caesar's role, but he died in a car accident before filming started. His widow Edie Adams still appears, but Sid Caesar plays her screen husband.

Kramer said many television performers were asked to be in the movie. They included Bob Hope, Red Skelton, Lucille Ball, Martha Raye, Dick Van Dyke. Even Lee Marvin, who had received his first leading role from Kramer in 1952s **Eight Iron Men**, was approached. But these might-have- beens were unavailable. In retrospect, Charlton Heston said he wished he had been asked. It is also interesting that Lucille Ball, under the *Lucy-Desi Comedy Hour*, took a similar trek across the desert with *Lucy Digs Uranium* in 1957, which could have sparked this idea.

The cast remains a once-in-a-lifetime list of greats. Sad but inevitable is the fact that many are gone now. In a 1990 **Bob Newhart Show**, handyman Tom Poston said he was going to watch this movie to get out of the doldrums. When he realized how many cast members are no longer with us, it made things worse. It is satisfying to know the performers were at the height of their powers, and their antics do make you feel better. At least the world-weary public had

Chapter 31

something to occupy their thoughts in the fall of 1963 in the aftermath of the John F. Kennedy assassination, the time this movie was released. The public opted to go see this simplistic comedy to escape the grim political realities of the day, and it offered a big box office to its producers during the holiday season.

After 50 years, the movie still holds major interests for diehard fans. The original version ran 192 minutes (excluding overture). This long version was later re-edited to 162 minutes, then cut further to 154 minutes, which eventually found its way onto VHS/DVD. In the 90s, additional footage was used to create a new "video restoration" that runs approximately 186 minutes. Around this same time, a non-profit organization, *Mad World Campaign*, had regular newsletters and a bumper sticker, but no clout to achieve its goal of restoring all edited out material through an act of Congress. This particular drive was the brainchild of Eric K. Federing (his media release said he was mad, mad, mad, mad). Federing's research about the film characters is revealing.

He said Buster Keaton was cast as Tracy's only friend and confidant in the movie, but his role was diminished to a long shot and three words for the final print. He was to originally talk to Tracy about escaping with a boat. (Kramer said that one of his regrets was reducing Keaton's role to practically nothing). Bikini-clad Barrie Chase was supposed to be married to another man and, thus, having an adulterous affair with Shawn. The red Dodge convertible he is seen driving was stolen from her husband. Jonathan Winters was actually a more sympathetic character in the film. His cut monologues revealed that he planned to share some of the loot with his invalid landlady. There were also periodic news broadcasts with journalists reporting to the audience the whereabouts of this band of merry makers. Federing's bold move actually prompted a Congressional debate with one member asking constituents if they really wanted to hear additional yelling from Ethel Merman.

When one thought there would be no more new footage, a DVD was introduced in 2014 that added entirely new scenes, expanded dialogue of others, and included commentary from three experts that added up to 197 minutes.

The Shirelles in collaboration with Ernest Gold were to provide a more expansive soundtrack, but only "Thirty-One Flavors" was prominently used. The entire soundtrack is now available and includes the title track and "Everybody's goin' Mad." The movie was released in a process called Cinerama, one of the handful of films to use this technique. Cinerama originally used three cameras against a curved screen. It was an expensive marketing concept designed to lure viewers away from television. It worked for this film, but was too expensive a gamble to try for the long run.

After **Mad World**'s success, there were a number of similar pieces that came about. Two years later Blake Edwards tried with **The Great Race**. In the 70s, there was the **Gumball Rally** (1976), and the 80s had Burt Reynolds with **Cannonball Run** (1981). In 2001, there was something called **The Rat Race**, which was as close a take-off as one could get without upsetting the original producers. All of these lacked the substance and polish of their original.

Director Kramer, Tracy, and William Rose were reunited in 1967 for **Guess Who's Coming to Dinner**. The dinner guest was Sidney Poitier, a black man engaged to a white woman with the hope of achieving both parents' blessings. Apart from being Tracy's last performance, the concerted effort garnered Academy Awards for co-star Katharine Hepburn and writer Rose.

The internet has revealed a loyal and obsessive fan base. There are web sites that compare and contrast 1963 filming locations with the exact site as it appears today after five decades of time. This offers a unique visual perspective. While the rock formations in the desert have not changed, State Highway 74 (AKA Roy Wilson Memorial Highway in Palm Desert) looks the same, but what was once undeveloped Los Angeles may now be acres of condos. A single leaning palm tree, supposedly from the group that formed a "Big W" survives and can be located with a good search engine.

Chapter 31

Cast

Spencer Tracy	*Captain T.G. Culpepper*
Milton Berle	*J. Russell Finch*
Sid Caesar	*Melville Crump*
Buddy Hackett	*Benjy Benjamin*
Ethel Merman	*Mrs. Marcus*
Mickey Rooney	*Ding "Dingy" Bell*
Dick Shawn	*Sylvester Marcus*
Phil Silvers	*Otto Meyer*
Terry-Thomas	*J. Algernon Hawthorne*
Jonathan Winters	*Lennie Pike*
Edie Adams	*Monica Crump*
Dorothy Provine	*Emeline Marcus-Finch*
Eddie Rochester Anderson	*Second cab driver*
Jim Backus	*Tyler Fitzgerald*
Ben Blue	*Airplane Pilot*
Edward Everett Horton	*Mr. Dinckler*
Marvin Kaplan	*Irwin*
Buster Keaton	*Jimmy the Crook*
Don Knotts	*Nervous Man*
Charles Lane	*Airport Manager*
Mike Mazurki	*Miner*
Charles McGraw	*Lieutenant Matthews*
Cliff Norton	*Reporter*
Zasu Pitts	*Switchboard operator Gertie*
Carl Reiner	*Air Traffic Controller at Rancho Conejo*
Madlyn Rhue	*Schwartz*
Roy Roberts	*Policeman outside garage*
Arnold Stand	*Ray*
Nick Stewart	*Truck Driver*
Joe DeRita (Three Stooges)	*Fireman*
Larry Fine (Three Stooges)	*Fireman*
Moe Howard (Three Stooges)	*Fireman*
Sammee Tong	*Chinese Laundryman*
Jesse White	*Radio Tower Operator at Rancho Conejo*

Jimmy Durante	*Smiler Grogan*
Jack Benny	*Man in Car Who Offers Help to Mrs. Marcus*
Jerry Lewis	*Man in Car Who Runs over Culpepper's Hat*
Joe E. Brown	*Union Official*
Alan Carney	*Police Sergeant*
Chick Chandler	*Detective Outside Laundry*
Barrie Chase	*Sylvester's Girlfriend*
Lloyd Corrigan	*Mayor*
William Demarest	*Police Chief Aloysius*
Andy Devine	*Sheriff of Crockett County*
Selma Diamond	*Mrs. Culpeper (voice)*
Peter Falk	*Third Cab Driver*
Nicholas Georgiade	*Detective at Grogan's Crash Site*
Norman Fell	*Detective at Grogan's Crash Site*
Paul Ford	*Colonel Wilberforce*
Stan Freberg	*Deputy Sheriff*
Louise Glenn	*Billie Sue Culpeper (voice)*
Leo Gorcey	*First Cab Driver*
Sterling Holloway	*Fire Chief*

Production

Stanley Kramer	*Director*
William and Tania Rose	*Writers*
Stanley Kramer	*Producer*
Ernest Laszlo	*Cinematographer*
Ernest Gold	*Original Music*
Bill Thomas	*Costumes*
United Artists	*Production Company*
USA/188/1963	*Country/Original Runtime/Year Release*

Chapter 31

Chapter 32

It Should Happen to You

"Would you come out and look at one sign?"
—Gladys Glover

The comic delights of Judy Holliday are happily on full display in **It Should Happen to You** (1954). This was Holliday's third starring role in what is probably her best film. Her career was short, but the films she made left a solid gold legacy that we can all enjoy. This film, perhaps a bit more than the others, showcased her rather unique talent as one of the screen's most gifted comediennes. Holliday could make even the most neutral line funny. Her natural gift was due, in part, to the tone and texture of her voice, coupled with a pair of innocent eyes, and a somewhat black and white view of the world. The overall effect was an unlikely but winning combination for a major star. Her thick New York accent would have been a liability for many actresses, but not in her case. She tweaks it much to our delight.

As an actress, Holliday reveals a wide range of dramatic ability, moving easily from comedy to drama. She also has incredible warmth that leaps off the screen. For example, during an intimate moment with her costar, Jack Lemmon, she sings to him and the affect is rather hypnotic—to him and to the audience.

Her abilities were framed by a strong intellect—something not really apparent in her characterizations. Her superior intelligence remains hidden until called upon, and then she lets those who question her ability or motive have it with full impact. To the untrained, she looks void of any analytical ability. But later you begin to slowly realize that she couldn't command your attention so well if there wasn't something going on behind those orbs. She appears to be focused on a different subject or playing a different game. At times she is very childlike, setting herself up with naive observations made to the so-called sophisticated and worldly adults. We feel some sort of glee when she eventually deflates them. She is like a snake just aiming to strike. This distinctive touch, which hasn't been equaled, usually wipes the other actors off the screen. Only an actor of high intelligence could pull this off—and Holliday's IQ was reported to be at the genius level.

Jean Hagen's character in **Singin' in the Rain** (1950), and the performances of Gracie Allen and Carol Channing are all related to Holliday's style. They are fine actresses, but there is a difference. Holliday has a unique way of seeing things in life. While the other ladies appear to be missing something or to be just plain dense, Holliday is going fast forward. She often leaves off the first sentence to her paragraph or thought. It's not done to intentionally confuse the other characters; she just sees the picture very clearly and leaves out introductory details. In other words, she's on to something else before the others are ready.

It Should Happen to You is a comment on celebrities and why our culture is fascinated with them. Those that study human behavior admit that some people crave attention and admiration from strangers. These people lean toward show business, or the business of showing. To be successful, or to hold the attention of an audience, you usually need breathtaking good looks or the ability to do something special. But if you cannot sing, dance, act, write, or paint, you can be famous for being famous. This happens to Gladys Glover, our main character and heroine. Gladys is actually in very good company. Others famous for being famous personalities include the likes of Charo, Zsa Zsa Gabor and Paris Hilton.

Gladys lives in the Big Apple with the dream of becoming famous. But things aren't going well. She gets fired from her modeling job because she's put on a few pounds. She tries to sulk in Central Park but only gets involved in an embarrassing situation. In final desperation, she puts her name (and nothing else) on a rented billboard on Columbus Circle.

Suddenly her life becomes very exciting, but also complicated. She no longer has any privacy. The media pursues her, as well as other

Chapter 32

people hoping to cash in on her temporary fame. One such suitor, playboy Peter Lawford, even tries to make her into a star for a soap commercial.

Placing your name on a sign to become famous is an intriguing idea. In recent years at least one millionaire has tried the idea to promote his busty, much younger wife. Her figure has been prominently displayed on billboards in Hollywood for over a decade, but job offers of substance haven't come her way.

Jack Lemmon co-stars and it is significant that he is the only cast member that liked the main character before she became famous. It is actually his first film (his second film **Phfft!** was also with Holliday, later in the year). It's early Jack Lemmon, just developing his screen persona, as the average, well-meaning, decent man confronted by the naked truths in the world. We also get to see what became his trademark show of exasperation when confronted by something that just isn't fair. He is at first surprised that someone can even think of such a thing. A temporary numbness persists for a few moments, followed by a look of horror and disbelief. Then we see and hear his anger. He serves Holliday well as a soundboard, since being famous can get complicated.

There's a moral to this story. Director George Cukor seems to say the trappings of celebrity may not outweigh the disadvantages. While you may get the best seats in the theatre, you also lose your privacy. That means you have to listen to the truth from strangers.

There are many fun Holliday moments in this film. Her reading of the idiot cards is hilarious. She is pure Judy on a talk show surrounded by the politically correct (old Hollywood is represented by Constance Bennett, Elka Chase, and Wendy Barrie). These women offer a neat inside joke, since they were now middle-aged, out of movies and had become famous for being famous.

Holliday made eleven films in ten years. Of these, six were in starring roles. Five of her films were directed by famed woman's director George Cukor. Her first star part (and film role) was Billie Dawn, the junk dealer's girl intellectualized in **Born Yesterday** (1950). It was a repeat of her stage success. The film version was originally planned as a Rita Hayworth vehicle, but the producers finally settled on Holliday—but not before some friends and luck helped her land the role. Before Billie Dawn, she had just done a turn as a wife on trial for attempted murder in the very funny Katharine Hepburn-Spencer Tracy film **Adam's Rib**. Hepburn told the right people (Columbia's Harry Cohn) that Holliday was stealing the whole picture. This was Kate's campaign to secure the star making role in **Born Yesterday** for Judy. Fortunately for Judy, Rita had just gotten married and wasn't interested in movies at the time. Thus, Holliday repeated her Broadway triumph and earned raves for the film. She went on to win the Best Actress Oscar against the stiffest competition in history: Gloria Swanson (**Sunset Blvd.**) and Bette Davis (**All About Eve**).

The Solid Gold Cadillac (1956) was another peak in Holliday's short career. In this film, her questions to a corporate board during a stockholder's meeting are embarrassing—for them. There is one scene that is especially funny for Holliday fans. She is being cross-examined on the witness stand by a nasty prosecutor. After making her look foolish, he ends his interrogation with "I rest my case." Her response is priceless: "Now he quits." Her last film was the musical **Bells are Ringing** (1960). In this one her knowledge of classic records fouls up everybody's plans. This had been a second Broadway triumph for her.

Holliday's life was bittersweet and short. She was one of the few actors respected by Columbia Chief Harry Cohn for her talent and intellect. Cohn, though he had a gift for making movies, was one of the most hated and feared studio chiefs in Hollywood. Their initial meeting is a well-known anecdote in Hollywood folklore. The wardrobe department exquisitely dressed the actress to meet Mr. Cohn. When she walked into the room, he made his move. In the confusion, out popped a falsie. Without hesitation, she said "don't worry, Mr. Cohn, they're yours."

Her close friend was a suspected communist and this brought Holliday much grief when the government investigated Hollywood in the early 50s. During Holliday's testimony, she cleverly projected innocence—similar to her movie characters—and survived the ordeal. There was also a weight problem. A heavy smoker, she succumbed to throat cancer in 1965 at age 43. Gone was a lady whose unique talents have not been equaled.

Cast

Judy Holliday	*Gladys Glover*
Peter Lawford	*Evan Adams III*
Jack Lemmon	*Pete Sheppard*
Michael O'Shea	*Brod Clinton*
Vaughn Taylor	*Entrikin*
Connie Gilchrist	*Mrs. Riker*
Walter Klavun	*Bert Piazza*
Whit Bissell	*Robert Grau*
Constance Bennett	*Herself*
Ilka Chase	*Herself*
Wendy Barrie	*Herself*
John Saxon	*Boy in Park*

Production

George Cukor	*Director*
Garson Kanin	*Writer*
Fred Kohlmar	*Producers*
Charles Lang	*Cinematographer*
Jean Louis	*Costumes*
Frederick Hollander	*Original Music*
Columbia	*Production Company*
USA/86/1954	*Country/Runtime/Year Released*

Chapter 33
Kiss Me, Stupid

"If you've got what it takes, sooner or later somebody will take what you've got."

—*Dino*

Kiss Me, Stupid was Billy Wilder's loud satire on sex, values, and mores. His idea of a good time was considered hot, heavy, and vulgar when first released in 1964. It was promptly condemned by many and admired by few. In retrospect, when placed in context with other studio offerings produced around the same time, **Kiss Me, Stupid** was essentially a pioneer in reversing puritan attitudes toward S-E-X on the screen. If you compare this film against some of its contemporaries, like **Pillow Talk** (1960), **Goodbye Charlie** (1964), or **Under the Yum Yum Tree** (1963)—three major studio efforts with similar aspirations—**Kiss Me, Stupid** is the one that continues to fascinate. Its off-color humor holds up better than its peers under today's more permissive times.

Wilder, of course, is now regarded as one of the best directors of the golden era. He was directly responsible for many classics spanning the generations, including **Double Indemnity** (1944), **Stalag 17** (1953), and **Witness for the Prosecution** (1957). In this effort, Wilder assumed the role of producer, director, and co-screenwriter (with partner I.A.L. Diamond). However, as producer, it was Wilder who bowed to pressures of conformity. In fact, he ran a public apology in the trade papers for bringing this work to fruition. Time has been on his side, though, since there is a growing consensus that his blush was a bit premature.

Today, you might wonder what the fuss was about. **Kiss Me, Stupid** involves wife-swapping, adultery, and prostitution among leading players Dean Martin, Kim Novak, and Ray Walston, to an extent never seen before in a major production. Wilder does not stop with the dialogue and situations. Even the desert flora contain sexual shapes, as though the whole idea was lifted from Hugh Hefner's landscape. Wilder's touches are both blatant and subtle. Upon repeated viewing, audiences can recognize even more sex symbolism with repeated viewings.

Martin plays an egocentric crooner named Dino, a name the actor sometimes used in real life. Martin's off-screen persona placed a lot of emphasis on the act of boozing. Perhaps he exaggerated his antics for comedic effect—we hope. Still, Dino borrows heavily from his public personality. His most notable addiction, apart from the booze, is that he needs to have sex every night in order to prevent a migraine.

The film opens with Dino finishing his nightclub act in Las Vegas and traveling to Hollywood to make a picture. During his drive through the desert, he finds himself detoured through some small towns. His first response to the State Trooper at the roadblock is whether "that Sinatra kid is lost again," which was in reference to a real and unfunny kidnapping of Frank, Jr. that actually happened around this time. (After much fanfare, Frank, Jr. was returned to his worried papa, shaken but unharmed). The State Trooper offers Dino a helpful and provocative detour route: "you come out Firestone by way of Warm Springs, Paradise Valley, and Climax."

Once Dino does reach Climax (Nevada) he meets two amateur songwriters, Ray Walston and Cliff Osmond. They recognize he's a celebrity and try to sell him their songs. He turns down their offer, but they secretly sabotage his car so that he will have to listen to their work. Now stranded, he is coaxed to spend the night at Walston's house. Since Martin has a problem with migraines, they hire Polly the Pistol (Kim Novak), a popular waitress at a local dive called *The Belly Button*, to pose as Walston' s wife—and Dino's aspirin cure. The idea is to use the wife as bait, as a way of being friendly to the guest. Walston approves the ruse since the lady put forward is not his real wife.

Since Walston's real wife (Felicia Farr—Mrs. Jack Lemmon) has to be removed from the house for this exchange of favors, there is a nice bust-up scene (it was a pink Rambler…NO!, it was a Volkswagen!) and she runs home to her parents.

The resulting charade among Dino, Novak, and Walston forms the sexual triangle, which ultimately reaches a peak in misunderstanding manipulation. The dialogue, of course, is full of double meanings. For example, Novak doesn't know Walston is describing his home when informing her that "it's not big, but it's clean." Or when Novak says "I see you in church every Sunday, playing your organ." Perhaps the most telling remark occurs when Walston pours Chianti for Martin and Novak and exclaims his part of the bargain: "White wine with fish, red wine with lamb chop." Lamb chop, being of course, his (real) wife's nickname.

The songs by Walston and Osmond are intentionally funny. The titles suggest playing them at a party when you want the guests to leave. They include the incomprehensible *Gently - Baby, it's Mothers Day*; a quaint number that misses its mark by 400 miles, *I Left My Heart in San Diego*; and the Oedipus inspired *I'm Taking Mom to the Junior Prom Because She's a Better Twister Than Sister*.

Females Novak and Farr turn out to be brains with nice bodies. While the males create the money-making schemes that fail to ignite, it's the two women who manipulate the situation to their advantage. They clearly emerge as winners, if this is a war between the sexes.

Novak's performance is excellent. Her Polly is someone who's been around the block a few times (in a small camper), but still holds an ounce of pride and respect. Though she accepts a meager $25 for a night of games, she still bawls at riding to the destination in a dingy tow truck.

Novak had been in films for 10 years by the time she accepted the role of Polly, and it was clearly something that audiences had never seen her do. She was one of the last manufactured stars of the old studio system, so her roles had always been chosen. Polly was not the kind that befits a big star, but of an actress taking a risk. Her fame came when she had been placed under contract just as Columbia's reigning goddess, Rita Hayworth, was either getting remarried or losing her box-office. However, the pressures of this system did not agree with Novak and she frequently clashed with studio chief Harry Cohn. One of those clashes, curiously, was when she dated fellow Rat Packer Sammy Davis, Jr. Her earlier work cast her in interesting if self-conscious roles. Now gently past 30 and ripe, she's more flesh and blood than before—and offered real proof that she could play comedy with another member of the Rat Pack, and with some degree of flair.

At the time, Novak needed good reviews in a popular film to retain her box office appeal. Unfortunately, this wasn't the film for the job. Regrettably, her output dwindled to nearly nothing by the end of the 60s, followed by brief stints in television. Her most recent and watchable movie performance was in **The Mirror Crack'd** in 1980. Looking particularly stunning in middle age, she played a rival movie diva to Elizabeth Taylor. The cutting remarks they hurled at each made the film a lot of fun.

A major casting switch occurred once this film was underway. Peter Sellers, riding a wave of success from **The Pink Panther** (1963) and **A Shot in the Dark** (1964) where he essayed the role of bumbling Inspector Clouseau, was first cast as the jealous husband. Shortly after production began, he suffered a severe heart attack. Instead of shutting down the production to wait for him to recover, Wilder assigned TV star Ray Walston (*My Favorite Martian*) the role after considering Tony Randall, Bob Hope, Danny Kaye, and Tom Ewell. Sellers was incensed and subsequently placed ads in the trades depicting Wilder as a cruel despot. It's difficult to see what Sellers' creative genius would have done with this opportunity. However, Walston offers neurotic energy to the role of a doltish man not secure in his abilities as a husband. His jealous scenes with Farr are splendid.

Martin, appearing half corked throughout most of the film, gets laughs by doing an extended version of his nightclub act. Since the Rat Pack is mentioned in the proceedings—a celebrity click including Martin, Frank Sinatra, Joey Bishop, Peter Lawford, and Sammy Davis Jr.—his role further pokes fun at his own lifestyle. It was an unprofessional image he honed, one he became increasingly comfortable with and especially evident when he appeared on talk shows with drink in hand. Like most of his films during this period, he constantly ribs his pal Frank. When asked to croon like Sinatra, he says "I'm trying all the time."

The expensive Italian car that Martin drives was a Dual-Ghia. Custom built in Italy and the U.S. during the late 50s, it was an appropriate phallic symbol for Hollywood personalities of that time. Apparently members of the Rat Pack competed fiercely to own one of the only 117 built.

Someone with Wilder's stature was able to attract the best character players in the business. Though opting for a small amount of screen time, familiar faces (or voice) of Mel Blanc, John Fiedler, Barbara Pepper, and Alice Pearce all have brief but memorable moments.

Fearing the worst, United Artists removed its name from this film and released it through a subsidiary, Lopert Pictures. This didn't matter. It played to empty cinemas around the same time that **Mary Poppins** and **Goldfinger** were pushing all the right buttons during the 1964 holiday season. Audiences preferred Julie Andrews, James Bond, and Pussy Galore.

Cast

Dean Martin	*Dino*
Kim Novak	*Polly the Pistol*
Ray Walston	*Orville*
Felicia Farr	*Zelda*
Cliff Osmond	*Barney*
Barbara Pepper	*Big Bertha*
Skip Ward	*Milkman*
Doro Merande	*Mrs. Pettibone*
Bobo Lewis	*Waitress*
Tommy Nolan	*Johnnie Mulligan*
Alice Pearce	*Mrs. Mulligan*
John Fiedler	*Reverend Carruthers*
Arlene Stuart	*Rosalie Schultz*

Chapter 33

Howard McNear	*Mr. Pettibone*
Cliff Norton	*Mack Gray*
Mel Blanc	*Dr. Sheldrake*

Production

Billy Wilder	*Director*
Anna Bonacci (play), I.A.L. Diamond	*Writers*
I.A.L. Diamond, Doane Harrison, Billy Wilder	*Producers*
Joseph LaShelle	*Cinematographer*
André Previn	*Original Music*
Mirisch Company	*Production Company/Distributor*
USA/116/1964	*Country/Runtime/Year Released*

Chapter 34

The King of Comedy

"Is Mr. Langford expecting you?"

—*Receptionist*

The marketing arm of Columbia Pictures must have faced a difficult task in the early 80s in effectively promoting **The King of Comedy**, one of its major investments. The dilemma was due in part to events that had recently shocked and saddened the world. First, ex-Beatle John Lennon was assassinated outside his New York apartment by a crazed fan in December 1980. Just a few months after that, John Hinckley shot and wounded President Ronald Reagan. News reporters savored Hinckley's obsession with actress Jodie Foster. Then Pope Paul John II was shot in May 1981. Both the Pope and Reagan recovered from their physical wounds, but the impact this had on the public increased the awareness of obsessed fans, stalkers, and the politically distraught who pose a threat to national figures.

Timing is everything in advertising and promotion, and it just so happened that **The King of Comedy,** directed by Martin Scorsese and starring Robert DeNiro, was ready for the theatres around the time of these attacks on prominent figures. To echo Murphy's Law, the film involved criminal activity between a crazed fan and a celebrity. In happier times, it was thought to be a hilarious black comedy, but now its contents seemed quite dire to a public who was preoccupied with the safety of beloved celebrities and dignitaries.

In 1983, with a fully recovered Reagan in control (and very popular) after the American hostages held in Iran had returned home, and the recession out of the news, **The King of Comedy** was finally released to the cinemas. It didn't matter what was going on in the world—though it was an excellent movie—few people went to see it. This was unfortunate for the producers and the viewers since it was a perceptive study at how one can become famous, as well as the relationship celebrities have with their sometimes-overzealous fans

Along with Robert DeNiro, it starred Jerry Lewis in a rare serious role, and comedienne Sandra Bernhard, plus a few well-known faces playing themselves. In happier times it could have encouraged a stampede at the box office. Unfortunately, the public wasn't buying a story that was too close to reality at the time.

DeNiro's character is Rupert Pupkin, a failure at 34 by society's standards. Apparently still living at home, single, and unemployed, he dreams of becoming the funniest man on earth, to become **The King of Comedy**. His grand illusion is gloriously portrayed on film, viewed from his vivid imagination. He talks an awful lot to himself. He does his monologue to his mirror and dreams of becoming the best pal of Jerry Langford, a celebrated late night talk show host. Jerry Langford is ultra cool to Pupkin. He looks up to him as a father, mentor, or all knowing guide. The part, played by Lewis, is patterned very much after *Tonight Show* legend Johnny Carson. In fact Carson (plus Dean Martin and Frank Sinatra) was considered for this role.

There are several fine bits when DeNiro imagines Langford pleading with him to take over the show for a few weeks. It's perhaps fitting to his ego that his mentor finally seeks his help. They have a power lunch and make a business decision over a martini. DeNiro's fantasy continues to expand when he imagines getting married on the Jerry Langford show.

As usual, DeNiro is great, providing us with another character in a large catalog of excellent work. He isn't known to take on conventional leading man roles, and Rupert stays true to his form. His character is emotionally immature in many ways, which creates comic tension. He appears to lack the social graces that come with age and experience. In other words, he doesn't interact positively with people. He doesn't know when to praise, keep his mouth shut, leave the room, or score points. Thus, he creates a bad impression with everyone he comes in contact with—which may explain his unemployment. His initial meeting with Langford is a perfect example. After forcing himself into the limousine with the popular host, he talks nonstop to the exhausted man about his wild scheme of becoming as famous as he is. Lewis, not known for subtle movements, beautifully underplays the scene, dropping hint after hint for him to get out of the car and go home.

This movie is about despair, frustration and rejection in a business not known for sensitivity. When Rupert approaches the studio where Langford's program is produced, he doesn't even get past the front desk. For anyone who has looked for a job and faced a glass wall, there is some degree of revenge when Rupert asserts himself. But of course it's all in vain since he's carted off by a group of burly security guards the minute he demands a job. Again, he lacks the learned ability of how to do things properly.

If the movie had been a success, it may have opened up another career for Jerry Lewis—one that would have supplied him with lots of character roles. He is quite good and different from what we have been accustomed to in his movies. There isn't a trace of his mugging or overplaying, which generally annoyed mainstream audiences. His part generously reveals the trappings of stardom. There's no privacy and one must deal with a love/hate relationship with the audience. Simply walking down the street, he has to generously signs autographs for his fans. When politely refusing a request to speak on the pay phone with a lady's husband, she screams "I hope you get cancer." He should have been nominated for an academy award, but the film wasn't popular enough to gather the momentum needed for such an honor.

If Langford's worst nightmare is Rupert, his major hell is Sandra Bernhard. She's delightfully wacky in possibly the only role to fully utilize her unique look and talent. Her background is very dark. She drives around in a new Mercedes, wears preppie clothes, and lives in an expensively furnished townhouse. She apparently hates her parents, who generously provide her with security, but have failed to love her. Also emotionally ignorant, she's only attracted to someone she can see on TV. She seeks what the ultimate fan desires: To touch and play with Langford. When she gets her wish, her monologue is tense, somewhat spontaneous, and very, very funny. Incidentally, the

Chapter 34   *191*

rough men on the street with which she trades insults were several members of the rock group *The Clash*.

Looking inward to the industry he pokes fun at, Scorcese finds plenty of opportunities. Tony Randall, a regular fixture on talk shows during this period, is a delight, right down to how fast one should turn the cue cards. As Jerry's announcer and second banana, Ed Herlihy spoofs Ed McMahon, down to his well-placed guffaws. And with concern about DeNiro's fantasy of marrying on the program, the marriage of Tiny Tim to Miss Vicki on *The Tonight Show starring Johnny Carson* is affectionately recalled. In DeNiro's fantasy, the bridesmaid is Dr. Joyce Brothers, and Victor Borge plays the music. The blushing bride, played by Diahnne Abbott, was in fact the real Mrs. DeNiro at that time. A closer connection to the Johnny Carson show is realized by engaging Fred De Cordova as Jerry's producer. De Cordova was Carson's real producer from 1971 to 1992 when Carson retired.

Rupert's comedic monologue is very revealing. If the pertinent facts of his life aren't fully developed during the movie, you can read between the jokes to realize that life hasn't been kind to him. But all isn't lost. The ending is truly a surprise and very bizarre. The movie never really goes over the top until the end, and you'll find yourself saying it can only happen in America.

Just a few years before the attempt on President Reagan's life, Jodie Foster had a supporting role in a Martin Scorsese film, **Taxi Driver** (1976). John Hinckley said this film led him to Reagan. **Taxi Driver** presented a rather disturbing view of a psychotic (Robert DeNiro) bent on an assassin in New York City. You can probably derive a number of parallels between DeNiro's **Taxi Driver** character and the actions of Hinckley. Hinckley was released from institutional psychiatric care on September 10, 2016. He now lives full-time at his mother's home.

Lennon's death, Reagan's assassination attempt, the attack on Theresa Saldana (who appeared in Scorsese's **Raging Bull** with DeNiro in 1980), and the murder of actress Rebecca Schaeffer, all created the need for "stalking" legislation. Interestingly enough, the stiffer laws that were enacted were put into good use in early 1995 when a man was arrested for stalking none other than Jerry Lewis.

Cast

Robert De Niro	*Rupert Pupkin*
Jerry Lewis	*Jerry Langford*
Diahnne Abbott	*Rita*
Sandra Bernhard	*Masha*
Frederick De Cordova	*Bert Thomas*
Shelley Hack	*Cathy Long*
Ed Herlihy	*Himself*
Lou Brown	*Band leader*
Tony Randall	*Himself*
Dr. Joyce Brothers	*Herself*
Liza Minelli	*Herself*
Victor Borge	*Himself*

Production

Martin Scorsese	*Director*
Paul D. Zimmermann	*Writer*
Arnon Milchan	*Producer*
Robbie Robertson	*Original Music*
Fred Schuller	*Cinematography*
20th Century Fox/Embassy International Pictures	*Production Company*
USA/101/1982	*Country/Runtime/Year Released*

Chapter 35
Lolita

"How did we produce such a little beast?"
—*Charlotte Haze*

The opening scene in Stanley Kubrick's **Lolita** has a pair of male hands lovingly and tenderly painting the nails of a young girl. If she is of legal age, it is a matter of opinion. Many would guess that she's not, since Vladimir Nabokov's novel of the same name, upon which this film is based, made it clear that middle-aged Hubert Humbert is sexually attracted to young girls. He refers to them as nymphets, and they must be between the ages of 8 and 14. After that, he loses all erotic desire and interest. Both the book and the movie are quite controversial—then and now.

This movie offers a portrait of a pedophile, and all of those fiendish rituals they are known for (apart from psychologically damaging their victim). The practice is still quite shocking today, makes adults very uncomfortable, and it is not uncommon for those convicted of such crimes to receive life sentences. Nabokov's work created quite a sensation in 1955 when his novel was first published because it offered a portrait of a tortured man attracted to children. Despite qualms about the subject, you won't be able to put the book down, nor will you find one ounce of boredom in the movie, which plays over two hours.

The film closely resembles the book in style and substance. The narrative doesn't compromise what literary circles call one of the best novels of the century. However, Hollywood doesn't listen to literary circles; they respond to censors. As is, the novel could not be filmed until some adjustments were made. To present the idea to the masses, Lolita's age was moved up to a more respectable 16. Casting Sue Lyon's well-developed curves make her a very mature 16.

The story is a love foursome, one of the strangest on film. One fourth of this square is Humbert, who is obsessed with bedding dear sweet Lolita. He is quite mad, hiding behind an air of respectability and English manners. James Mason plays the duality of the character as close to perfection as one could hope. He has the grace, diction, and style of his character, complete with a tiny squint in his eyes. When that happens, you know Humbert's sexual wheels are turning.

Mason never achieved the lofty status of other English actors of his generation like Laurence Olivier or Rex Harrison. In contrast, their images prevented them from playing this type of role when they were middle-aged. David Niven was one such actor who turned the role down, fearing it would upset his fans. Though not in the same league as Olivier or Harrison, Mason's career lasted an incredibly long time. From 1935 to his death at 75 in 1984, he appeared in a prolific number of star roles. It didn't seem to matter if the movie was good or bad, he always had an air of class about him. Any production could be elevated up a few notches with his participation.

Then there is Peter Sellers who juggles multiple roles as the eccentric playwright Quilty. As the second player, he plays games with Humbert in the most peculiar manner. He teases and tortures the man (and the class he represents) for whom he has contempt. Sellers unique characterizations in three roles was so convincing that he was asked to repeat another set of characterizations for Kubrick's next film, **Dr. Strangelove** (1964). A gifted mimic, Sellers prolonged his checkered career as the bumbling Inspector Clouseau in Blake Edward's **Pink Panther** series. One of his last films was a personal and critical success—**Being There** (1979). He died the following year after a massive heart attack.

The object of these two contrasting fellows' attention is, of course, Lolita. At 16, this was Sue Lyon's movie debut. Critics sniped at her platinum hair, since it was suppose to be chestnut, but it was an otherwise auspicious film debut of a young hopeful in the industry. Perhaps Kubrick was responding to America's fascination with blondes. Carroll Baker had just made a big splash with her portrayal of a child bride named **Baby Doll** a few years back in 1956.

Chapter 35   *195*

Like Mason, Lyon was not the first choice for the role. Tuesday Weld turned it down to study at the Actor's Studio, citing a desire to graduate to more mature roles. Maybe it was a good career move for Tuesday. Unlike Weld, Lyon's film career abruptly ended by the early 70s due in part to poor roles and personal problems.

The fourth square involved in this tug of war is Shelley Winters, as Lolita's vulgar and love starved mom. It is one of her best performances, garnering her a best supporting actress nomination. (She won two supporting Oscars during her long career). In the early 60s, when Ms. Winters was, by movie star standards, middle-aged and stout, her forte was portraying slightly overripe broads prone to disaster. Her skill at this was remarkable. Many of her best roles, **A Double Life** (1947), **The Night of the Hunter** (1955), **The Big Knife** (1955) and **The Poseidon Adventure** (1972) are variations of women making a fatal mistake. For daughter Lolita, she again sets herself up to be the ultimate loser. The scene in which she realizes her competitor is her own flesh and blood is touching and sad. Thankfully, Kubrick didn't allow her to go over the top and become funny, which she had a tendency to do. This is one of her most affecting performances. Winters' career went against the norm. Arriving in Hollywood in the early 40s, she started out as a glamour girl (she was roommate to Marilyn Monroe). She was soon content to work nonstop in subsidiary roles if she was going to survive in a town full of beautiful women. Perhaps in contrast to her work here, she ditched Michael Caine in **Alfie** (1966) for a male version of **Lolita**. Her last high profile role was the grandma to *Roseanne*, in the popular TV sitcom.

Director Kubrick wrote the screenplay and he leaves most of the novel's narrative intact, though it becomes subtle under his guidance. You have to imagine that Mason dreams of marrying Lolita, settling down, and having Lolita satisfy his desires. You also have to guess that Miss Lolita has a few skeletons in her closet.

New York Bronx-born Kubrick did not film as regularly as other directors of his generation, even as an independent. Audiences and critics always greatly anticipated the release of his work. Often he spent years on individual projects, obsessing over the details until he was remotely satisfied. This perfection does show in the final product, and his work as a unit is frequently thought-provoking, often macabre. He reached a critical and audience peak in the 60s with **Dr. Strangelove** (1964), where he fashioned a black comedy on the destruction of the world, and with **2001: A Space Odyssey** (1968), a visual feast into the outer limits. Kubrick filmed **Lolita** in England, where he lived, even though the setting is supposed to be United States. The limited sets and exterior shots provide the film with a stark, surreal effect, adding to the mystery and quality of the film.

Kubrick was a taskmaster at heart and despised studio interference. He controlled his work with a compulsive iron fist. He re-edited **The Shining** (1980) after its release date by shipping new reels with a revised ending to the theatres. This attitude eventually earned him enormous respect from the industry, and actors clamored to be in his films. Benchmarks in filmmaking typically accompany the accolades bestowed on his work, including **Clockwork Orange** (1971) and **Full Metal Jacket** (1987). His last film, **Eyes Wide Shut** (1999) was released shortly after his death. Though one wished it had been a home run, by any other measurement it had the interest of the world for a moment.

Director Steven Spielberg finished what would have been Kubrick's next feature, **Artificial Intelligence: AI** (2001). Kubrick fans claim they can see where Kubrick left off and Spielberg began. Its release, also, caused much excitement within the industry.

Another version of Nabokov's work was filmed in 1997 under the same title. This version cast Jeremy Irons in the role of the Professor. It had difficulty finding a distributor since its interpretation was closer to the novel. This even more controversial version also has its admirers. The name Lolita has since become an adjective in the dictionary meaning a precocious young girl seductively attracting an older man.

Cast

James Mason	*Professor Humbert Humbert*
Shelley Winters	*Charlotte Haze*
Sue Lyon	*Dolores "Lolita" Haze*

Chapter 35

Peter Sellers	*Clare Quilty*
Gary Cockrell	*Dick Schiller*
Jerry Stovin	*John Farlow*
Diana Decker	*Jean Farlow*
Lois Maxwell	*Nurse Mary Lore*
Vivain Darkbloom	*Marianne Stone*

Production

Stanley Kubrick	*Director*
Vladimir Nabokov (novel), Stanley Kubrick	*Writers*
James B. Harris, Eliot Hyman	*Producers*
Oswald Morris	*Cinematographer*
Bob Harris, Nelson Riddle	*Original Music*
Harris-Kubrick Productions	*Production Company*
Gene Coffin	*Costumes*
USA-UK/152/1962	*Country/Runtime/Year Released*

Chapter 36

The Long, Long Trailer

"Think of it as a train, 40' of train!"
—*Service Garage Attendant*

As with any individual who becomes a national institution while still living, there's an interesting story behind the reason why everyone loves Lucy. The viewing public had many opportunities to love Lucille Ball, but for twenty or so years, chose to ignore her talents. She entered films in bit parts in 1933, and gradually worked her way up to supporting comic relief roles. But she was never in the big league, in the A product line. By the end of the 40s it was obvious she was not going to be a big star in movies. Like many of her contemporaries who toiled in the same yards and were approaching middle age (Joan Blondell, Ann Sothern, Eve Arden), she realistically turned to television.

This move worked for Lucy on several different levels. It was an opportunity to be with her husband, Cuban bandleader Desi Arnaz. They met on the set of **Too Many Girls** in 1940 when he asked if she liked to Rumba. She said yes. Though they liked to Rumba, they were still childless after 10 years of marriage. She later admitted they were always apart—he on the road with his band and she in Los Angeles making films. This put the marriage at risk.

She was doing a program entitled **My Favorite Wife** on radio when CBS approached her to do a situation comedy under the same premise. To save her marriage she insisted on Desi as her TV husband. CBS initially balked, but as everyone knows, it became one of the most successful programs in that medium's history. It was so successful that Desilu became a production company, eventually purchasing RKO Studios, the couple's former employer.

It was a bold, risky move on their part. The movie industry was

Chapter 36   *199*

in turmoil, having lost their distribution arm, so they could not pick and choose theatres for their product. At the same time, television was in its infancy and promised to lure people from theatres to living rooms. In the eyes of a nervous studio head, any performer venturing into these enemy waters was akin to Benedict Arnold. They reasoned the public wouldn't put on their coats and pay to see Lucy and Ricky when they could watch them for free on Monday nights. This was the same line of questioning MGM directed at Lucy and Desi in negotiations for **The Long, Long Trailer**. To add insurance that people would pay to see them, they asked that it be filmed in color—their television fans could only view them in black and white. Vincente Minnelli (Liza's father) was hired to direct the movie between two MGM musical assignments, **The Band Wagon** and **Brigadoon**. The movie was one of the brightest comedies of 1954 and a qualified success. By opting for a percentage of the profits, television's favorite couple received a windfall.

For the movie, they played it safe by not straying too far from their established public personas. Lucy and Ricky become a pair of newlyweds named Tacy and Nicky. Nicky is an engineer and his job takes him all over Western United States (The breathtaking views are found at Yosemite National Park). Tacy wants to be with her husband while he works (shades of Lucille Ball), so she envisions pulling a trailer, their home, through the western United States.

All of the famous Lucyisms are on display in glossy MGM color. Her sense of wide-eyed fun creates one slapstick situation after another. She tries to prepare a meal in a moving trailer, has her own special way of driving, reading maps, and collecting unusual memorabilia like rocks and jam.

She is in especially top form when they visit Tacy's Aunt Anastasia (Madge Blake). The aunt lives in a nice large home with a well-manicured lawn. Strapped for cash on all of the unseen expenses associated with a trailer, they expect to receive a large monetary gift from this sunny, outgoing woman. Unfortunately, the task of backing the 40' train into the driveway is too much for Nicky. With Tacy's assistance, there is the inevitable disaster. The hysteria peaks when

Auntie comes unglued and screams "you ran over my rose bush with your dirty, stinking trailer."

Another bright moment occurs when they attempt to pass a mountain range upward of 8,000 feet. They put on a brave act as the car's engine strains up the long, steep grade. They try to play it cool, creating a ridiculous conversation, amid the strain of the engine. At one point they talk about a brunette actress married to Michael Wilding who likes squirrels. The subject in question must be Elizabeth Taylor!

The movie is full of 50s stuff, when appliances and cars were brightly colored, full of push buttons and supposed to make our lives easier. The trailer and 1953 Mercury Monterey convertible are bright yellow (though a 1953 Lincoln with a larger engine can be seen in some shots). The mobile home is full of period wares including a Sunbeam Mixmaster, Skotch Thermos and Pyrex multicolored bowls. Redman, a multi-divisional corporation based in Dallas that is now the second largest manufacturer of mobile homes, manufactured Lucy and Desi's trailer, a 28 foot model called New Moon. In sales promotions that coincided with the release of this movie, Redman heavily promoted their units as mobile homes—not trailers. If Redman had their way, the title to this film may have been **The Long, Long Mobile Home**.

Physical intimacy is only implied, of course. Like the bedroom in their television program, they have double beds with enough middle ground to park a chaperone in between. There is a touching moment when Tacy says she was originally attracted to Desi because he needed a button sewn on his shirt. But we really know what their attraction was—they could Rumba—and how!

Keenan Wynn and Lucy were teamed in several films in the 40s. Most notable was the Spencer Tracy-Katharine Hepburn film **Without Love** (1945) where they played the second leads. Wynn puts in a cameo appearance as a tempered traffic cop directing the long trailer through a busy intersection.

Lucy and Desi made one more theatrical film together, **Forever Darling** (1956). It involved a guardian angel, a troubled marriage,

Chapter 36   201

and no slapstick. James Mason played Lucy's G.A. and he admitted, after a long career in films, that it was his least favorite movie. Though filmed in color, it was not a success.

Lucy and Desi divorced in 1960. He sold his interest in Desilu to her, then virtually retired from show business, resting on his well-earned success. He died in 1986.

As head of a major television studio, Lucy was one of the few female production moguls, until selling her concern to Gulf & Western in 1967. This in no way curtailed her activities or popularity. She kept a busy pace in film, TV, specials, and personal appearances until her death in 1989.

Cast

Lucille Ball	*Tacy Collini*
Desi Arnaz	*"Nicky" Carlos Collini*
Keenan Wynn	*Policeman*
Majorie Main	*Mrs. Hittaway*
Moroni Olsen	*Mr. Tewitt*
Bert Freed	*Foreman*
Madge Blake	*Aunt Anastacia*
Walter Baldwin	*Uncle Edgar*
Oliver Blake	*Mr. Ludlow*
Howard McNear	*Mr. Hittway*

Production

Vincente Minnelli	*Director*
Clinton Twiss, Albert Hackett, Frances Goodrich	*Writers*
Pandro S. Berman	*Producers*
Robert Surtees	*Cinematographer*
Adolph Deutsch, Richard A. Whiting	*Original Music*
Helen Rose	*Costumes*
Metro-Goldwyn-Mayer	*Production Company*
USA/103/1954	*Country/Runtime/Year Released*

Chapter 37
Lonely are the Brave

"Believe you me, if it didn't take men to make babies, I wouldn't have anything to do with any of you!"

—Jerri Bondi

In 1990, when 74-year-old Kirk Douglas was on the talk show circuit promoting his first novel, *Dance With The Devil*, it provided an opportunity to reflect on his long and successful career in Hollywood. During this promotional tour, he was naturally asked to name his favorite film. He said, without missing a beat, **Lonely Are the Brave**. He admitted that it was a small film, didn't do well commercially, but that he's rather proud of it. Mr. Douglas has every good reason to be.

In a long career by any standards, **Lonely Are the Brave** stands out among Douglas' portrayals of executives, heels, and tough guys. Perhaps the film didn't do well when released because his portrait of a modern cowboy doesn't fit the public's image of either a cowboy or Douglas' typical roles.

Lonely Are the Brave is different from his usual lot of men who take more than they receive. He's the opposite of selfish by being without a self. The undying passion to help others propels the story along to a chilling, dramatic climax.

The movie opens in a New Mexico desert. Douglas is sprawled out by the campfire and his trusty horse is in the distance. He looks like a piece of whipped leather, resting on his laurels after a big cattle haul. You can almost imagine this to be the 1860s, not 1960s, until the obtrusive sound of a jet is first heard and then seen streaming overhead. This is one of the main themes throughout the film, the jarring sounds of modern man. The noise may be trucker Carroll

Chapter 37

203

O'Connor hauling bathroom fixtures across the interstates. It may be Police Chief Walter Matthau's jeep tearing across the rugged terrain, or pilot Bill Bixby scoping out the mountains in his helicopter.

On one level, the movie pits Douglas against the confines of modern man. He's against anything that can tie him down. He cuts fences and refuses to get a social security number or identification card, telling those in charge "I know who I am." In an exercise against the usual Douglas character, he lands himself in jail on purpose, simply to talk to his friend. It's an incredible degree of giving. This bold move almost backfires because he is so personable at the police station that he has to slug one of them to ensure incarceration.

As the story unfolds, we learn more nice things about this middle-aged cowboy and his code of honor. Despite the obstacles he's faced along his life, he still has a happy swagger. Douglas' mastery of this character tells us things haven't gone his way, without offering any accountability or anger. His acting is so good that one wonders if he had been miscast all of these years. Certainly his range is wider than one would first think. Douglas clashes with responsibility. The adult citizens who are responsible, specifically Gena Rowlands, tell him he has to abide by the rules or else. Ms. Rowlands seems to understand boys in grown-up bodies. Her line, "If it didn't take men to make babies, I wouldn't have anything to do with you" implies that she would rather have the stability of a machine to keep her company, rather than an immature adult male. But Douglas knows the chemistry between two people can't be manufactured. His scenes with Rowland are short, but telling. Though she is his best friend's wife, there's the obvious attraction. Unlike one of his other movie's characters, he side steps her advances and continues on his way.

Matthau also admires this code of honor. Douglas is probably the first criminal he's chased that has too much integrity. When Douglas does break from jail, it becomes man against modern power. Though sworn to uphold the law, Matthau does come through with some flexibility and warmth. His skill as a lawman offers dimension when you're led to believe that he wouldn't be disappointed if cowboy Douglas makes it to freedom. The battle between muscles and metal doesn't end in victory, though. Douglas wins the race, but loses the match because he uses his heart over his head. He does what anyone would do if in his situation. The end result is both a surprise and shock.

Despite the serious issues this movie tackles, there is a small aspect of sentiment about it. It explores the intimate bond between a cowboy and his horse. The horse almost becomes his sweetheart. "Whiskey" is often referred to as if she were his wife. Whiskey has a mind of her own though, and as her name implies, you don't do anything fast once you're on her back. There are ominous warnings to come, along the way of this relationship. These scenes are juxtaposed by the 60s modern version of the contemporary cowboy—tractor-trailer drivers. The rigs pulled are nothing more than modern saddlebags.

The film offers first-rate character actors for the minor roles. Most of these actors became stars in their own right within several years. George Kennedy bares his teeth as a sadistic prison guard. A couple of years later he was in prison to support Paul Newman in **Cool Hand Luke** (1967). His performance as foe-then-friend to Newman won him a best supporting Oscar. Bill Bixby's role is unbilled. It would be several years before he found his niche on TV. The same goes for Carroll O' Connor, who found widespread popularity on TV's *All in the Family*. Walter Matthau's presence is very strong in this movie. His potential was realized a short time later when he appeared on Broadway as one of *The Odd Couple*, and won the Best Supporting Oscar for his role as a conniving lawyer in **The Fortune Cookie** (1965).

The excellent scripting is by Dalton Trumbo. Trumbo was a writer who found himself in exile during the Hollywood blacklist in the late 40s. The experience of being victimized by "the system," no doubt was a major influence in how this film flows. In a courageous move, Douglas (along with Otto Preminger) broke the blacklist by hiring and promoting Trumbo as the screenwriter for **Exodus** in 1960. This film was their second collaboration. Though considered a small film in 1962, (the more mainstream **Two Weeks in Another**

Town was Douglas' other film that year, a belated sequel to **The Bad and Beautiful**), it holds up better than most of Douglas' other offerings. It's slightly ahead of its time. Man's dependence on technology is probably more relevant today than it was in 1962.

The title of Douglas' novel, *Dance With The Devil*, is revealing. It was "fire" that propelled Douglas to stardom in the 1940s, after growing up in poverty. He pulled himself up by the bootstraps, so to speak, and literally shoved his way to stardom. His first role was a showy one in a good film: **The Strange Love of Martha Ivers** (1946). He was part of the strange love of Barbara Stanwyck and in the end he took the noble way out. Full stardom came with **Champion** (1949) three years later, as a boxer who didn't pull any punches in and out of the ring.

Once a star, Douglas' drive and intensity propelled his career. Actors with long careers usually have very forceful personalities. According to his peers, he has more than his share of stuff that makes men aggressive. He's been described as self-centered, with elements of arrogance and insecurity. On screen, this approach appeals to both sexes—he's successfully intimate with women and has the respect and camaraderie of males. Perhaps the definitive role for Douglas was **The Bad and the Beautiful** (1952) when he played a crude movie producer. He manipulated the people around him like pieces of furniture. The final product made them all look good, but he got the credit in the end.

Cast

Kirk Douglas	*Jack Burns/John W. Burns*
Gena Rowlands	*Jerri Bondi*
Walter Matthau	*Sheriff Morey Johnson*
Michael Kane	*Paul Bondi*
Carroll O'Connor	*Hinton*
William Schallert	*Radio Operator (Harry)*
George Kennedy	*Deputy Sheriff Gutierrez*
Karl Swenson	*Reverend Hoskins*
William Mims	*First Deputy in Bar*
Bill Bixby	*Helicopter Pilot*

Production

David Miller	*Director*
Edward Abbey (novel), Dalton Trumbo	*Writers*
Edward Lewis	*Producers*
Jerry Goldsmith	*Original Music*
Philip H. Lathrop	*Cinematographer*
Joel Productions	*Production Company*
USA/107/1962	*Country/Runtime/Year Released*

Chapter 38
Lord Love a Duck

"Don't you realize these things are supposed to be dirty?"

—*Miss Schwartz*

Lord Love a Duck was one of the first movies to satirize the Southern California lifestyle. Unfortunately it came out at a time when nobody really knew Southern California needed satirizing. When released in 1966, Director and Writer George Axelrod believed that California's slightly different approach to life deserved closer examination and a few pokes in the ribs. Today, we can view the film with nostalgic pleasure to glimpse at the kookiness that was going on at a time when the golden state was experiencing a massive population, economic, and cultural expansion.

Lord Love a Duck came about in an era when another movie genre was gently starting to wane: The beach party scene. Whereas the beach films were specifically targeted to teenagers, **Lord Love a Duck** is not a juvenile film with simple dialogue and innocence about kids wanting to have some fun on the beach. Though extremely funny at times, there is one particularly sad moment that stops the flow of laughs. This abrupt change is disconcerting but does provide a serious undertone to the crazy goings on. Overall, those with an interest in the absurd will find the film enjoyable.

Surprisingly, many of the issues Axelrod pokes fun at are contemporary, thus providing the film with some degree of vision. It lampoons the problems that continue to ail our society—a struggling education system, the separation of church and state, single parents trying to scratch out a living, peer pressure, and a growing (and probably) unhealthy obsession with celebrities. Despite a current relevance, you will be required to turn your time clock back to 1966 to fully accept this period piece.

The satire takes place at a high school called Consolidated. It sounds more like a factory than a source of learning and inspiration. The curriculum at Consolidated offers such things as Plant Skills (for botany), Adolescent Ethics, and Commercial Relationships. To get an idea of how effective its methods are, in one example a teacher instructs her students where to place beauty marks. By the next day, one of her students is wearing the fake mole on the outside of her blouse!

The details are subtle and easy to miss, but these priceless tidbits are worth seeking out. Some obvious care went into the writing, though at times you will need repeated viewings to fully grasp the intended situation. You might miss the sand pouring out of the leading man's jacket when he picks it up during the beach scene, or the echoes in the "conversation pit" of Ruth Gordon's ultra-modern home. In a long shot at the graduation scene, a pregnant girl in cap and gown can be seen smoking. A bit more obvious is the topless beach dancer who isn't what you think she is. The distortion in Lola Albright's mirror during her Cary Grant exercise routine to prevent the onslaught of middle age pokes at our obsession for youth.

Though the film has a fairly high level of sophistication, it lacks the technical quality of a first class production. For example, a boom with a microphone can be clearly seen in the early scene when the police chase Roddy McDowell to the top of the school building.

Despite these limitations, the performances of the actors are first rate. Tuesday Weld is Barbara Ann Green, the high school senior who has fantasy aspirations ("everybody has got to love me"), but lacks the maturity, knowledge, and patience to achieve her desires. Enter Roddy McDowell, a gifted peer who isn't afraid to provide her with everything she wants and goes to great lengths to grant her wishes because he secretly loves her. First come cashmere sweaters, then bigger and better things like a handsome, rich husband.

Roddy McDowell's character is very strange. At one time, he does a goofy imitation of a duck. Worldly, wise and with a genius IQ, his Alan is not able to relate intimately to Barbara. If he looks a bit old in

Chapter 38   209

the role (McDowell was well into his 30s), it doesn't matter, because he may not be a real person, so to speak. He has no home of his own and is a companion to anyone as long as it works to his advantage. There's a telling scene when the school's frustrated social worker tells Alan the inkblot pictures are supposed to be dirty. Perhaps ambivalent toward sex, he also shows very little emotion and empathy. What feelings he has, if any, are only directed to Barbara. But it's no use since his duck will never turn into a swan. He also understands that Weld, already a beautiful swan, will never be intimate with someone outside her pond. Thus, to remain close to the fetching swan, he must be her servant.

Ruth Gordon plays mom and she's the mother-in-law everyone has nightmares about. Her forte is psychology—probably learned from her late husband. He was a psychiatrist whose idea to validate his patients parking tickets made the family very wealthy. She must have listened in to his conversations with patients since she offers his simplistic evaluations to problems. Her lack of depth in the subject is apparent and frequently hilarious. When nothing adds up, she simply says the entire episode is a "death wish, pure and simple."

One of the more embarrassing conversations occurs between Lola Albright and Ruth Gordon when Albright is decked out in her bunny outfit. It's a howl, but sets up the sadness in the next couple of scenes. This is a turning point in the film. The audience now understands that all is not going to be fun and games with these people. That is somewhat unsettling to the viewer and not what we were expecting or had hoped for. This action takes the film to another level.

The other members of the cast are equally strong. Max Showalter seems to play word games with his daughter—first at the hamburger stand, and then at the dress shop. Martin West plays the hapless bridegroom who becomes an anchor to Miss Weld's bid for stardom in a bikini beach picture. Notice he has to ring the bell to go into his own house! And Harvey Korman is fun as the incompetent principal. Each phrase Korman speaks is a well worn cliché and this excessive use of tired language becomes ridiculously amusing. He says "time heals all wounds," speaks of "democracy in action," and "one day we will have a good laugh about all of this." His opening shot is revealing. He's anxiously chewing on the Venetian blind cord. The beauty on the yacht is Jo Collins, a *Playboy* Playmate in the August 1965 issue. Lovely Miss Collins frequently tells her mentor, movie producer Martin Gabel, that everything is "such a drag."

In a long and interesting career, Tuesday Weld has never given a bad performance. Unfortunately, her choice of roles prevented her from becoming a star of the same box office might of Faye Dunaway or Jane Fonda. In fact, she turned down the role of Bonnie Parker (so did Natalie Wood) in **Bonnie and Clyde**. Apart from being breathtakingly beautiful, her fans seek out her work since she projects a natural honesty about her. There are moments when she reveals great sensitivity. In this film, you see her progress from a rather innocent girl to someone who becomes cynical and headstrong, with an overwhelming feeling of entitlement. Her role with McDowell changes somewhat during the course of the film. He becomes a weak parent and his gifts make her a spoiled and bratty beauty. In contrast to this role, she had one her best parts of the 60s in **Pretty Poison** (1968) as a manipulative sociopath. Like all strong players with determination, she continues to find work today in small, specialized roles. **Falling Down** (1993) offers one of her most recent performances in a mainstream film.

Ruth Gordon (1896-1985) had three periods of activity in film. While still a teenager, she was an extra in silent pictures filmed in New Jersey before the movie industry moved to Hollywood. After a long hiatus, she reappeared in character roles in the 40s, most notably in **Abe Lincoln in Illinois** as Mary Todd and **Two-Faced Woman** (1941), which was Greta Garbo's last film. After another long period of film inactivity, she surfaced in the mid 60s. In 1968, at the age of 72, she won the Best Supporting Actress Oscar for her role in **Rosemary's Baby**. This accolade made her a movie star. She had another juicy part in **Harold and Maude** (1971). As Maude, she played an elderly woman dating a man some 60 years her junior. In between these three distinct careers in film, she wrote books, Academy Award winning screenplays (often in collaboration with her husband Garson Kanin),

Chapter 38

and appeared on stage. A rather remarkable woman, she wrote the screenplay for **The Actress** (1953), with Jean Simmons in the title role, from her autobiographical play, *Years Ago*.

Muscleman Dave Draper, who takes a pounding from scrawny McDowell, followed this with a featured role in the Tony Curtis vehicle **Don't Make Waves** (1967). Today, he remains an icon of fitness by sending out a witty and interesting email newsletter to his many legions of followers. It touts good health and muscle mass, two items he has faithfully retained well into middle age.

Director and writer George Axelrod, who wrote the screenplay for Marilyn Monroe's **The Seven Year Itch** in 1956, had worked his way up to writing and directing by the mid 60s. He did this between the very funny **How to Murder your Wife** (1965) and the unfunny **The Secret Life of An American Wife** (1967). He could also be serious, as seen in **The Manchurian Candidate** (1962).

Cast

Roddy McDowall	*Alan "Mollymauk" Musgrave*
Tuesday Weld	*Barbara Ann Greene*
Lola Albright	*Marie Green*
Martin West	*Bob Bernard*
Ruth Gordon	*Stella Bernard*
Harvey Korman	*Weldon Emmett*
Sarah Marshall	*Miss Schwartz*
Lynn Carey	*Sally Grace*
Max Showalter	*Howard Green*
Donald Murphy	*Phil Neuhauser*
Joseph Mell	*Dr. Milton Lippman*
Dan Frazer	*Honest Joe*
Jo Collins	*Kitten*
David Draper	*Billy Gibbons*
Donald Foster	*Mr. Beverly*
Martin Gabel	*T. Harrison Belmont*

Production

George Axelrod	*Director*
George Axelrod, Al Hine, Larry H. Johnson	*Writers*
George Axelrod	*Producer*
Neal Hefti, Ernie Shelton	*Original Music*
Daniel L. Fapp	*Cinematographer*
Paula Giokaris	*Costumes*
United Artists	*Production Company*
USA/105 minutes/1966	*Country/Runtime/Year Released*

Chapter 39
The Loved One

"Whispering Glades is a way of life."
— *Aimee Thanatogunos*

The advertising used to promote **The Loved One** claimed the movie was guaranteed to offend everyone. The copywriter who came up with that clever, cryptic line really hit the bullseye. It's very true that there's something in the film to push everybody's sensitive button. This shock or surprise, though, does not turn off people who have values completely. On the contrary, you stay glued until the end, wondering what director Tony Richardson (and writers Evelyn Waugh, Terry Southern, Christopher Isherwood) are going to come up with next. It's a very black comedy, though not bleak. Totally unique in content, style, and presentation, it offers candid and refreshing perspectives on a funeral, a ceremony we eventually attend, either as a guest, relative, or as the honored person.

The Loved One (1965) is based on Evelyn Waugh's 1948 novel of the same name. Waugh's writings are generally sophisticated in wit and black humor, and essentially a series of ideas uniquely relating to each other. Screenwriters Southern and Isherwood lift these devices from the book, downplay the British Colony angle, and add a few of their own dynamics, including the subject of space travel. Waugh was born in London, and this is his only book set in the United States. Apparently he dreamed up the idea after spending a few weeks visiting Hollywood. Ironically, he died (1903-1966) shortly after this film was released.

The Loved One, of course, is another name for the dearly departed. It begins with the song, *America, The Beautiful* as poet Robert Morse lands in Los Angeles from Great Britain and calls on his uncle (John Gielgud), who works at a Hollywood movie studio. Shortly after he arrives, though, there is a shake-up at the studio and Gielgud is fired.

Morose and despondent, the elderly man commits suicide. This leaves the nephew to take care of the funeral arrangements. In doing so, we discover a complete lack of sensitivity on his part and the people who have made a profession of burying the departed, in terms of acceptable social behavior in specific cultures. The subjects revolve around death (pets and humans), sex (alternative and in coffins), religion (or lack of), and food (the morgue icebox doubles for other things too). The writers' conclusion? Well, they imply that anything pure cannot survive in our society.

Morse's first interaction on U.S. soil is with an obnoxious customs agent (James Coburn), who does not like anything being imported to the United States. This sets the stage for the clash of cultures. There is a colony of English actors (including a very funny Robert Morley) who find work in Hollywood movies as butlers and chauffeurs, but look down their noses at their employers. The movie studio's administration (including Roddy McDowell) is also about as callous as they come. He fires Gielgud after 31 years of service after he fails to teach an American actor, Dusty Acres, proper English usage so that he can become an American James "Jim" Bond. Dusty Acres is actually Robert Easton, an actor known for his many voices and one who has routinely coached other actors in this trade. Even closer to home, Gielgud finds out he has been terminated by walking into his office, only to find it inhabited by another fellow (who happens to be real-life producer Martin Ransohoff!).

Though distributed by MGM, this scenario was probably not too far from reality for many of the major studios around this time were experiencing financial problems. Their fortunes were in a decline and they were ready to enter crisis mode. In fact, MGM started selling off its memorabilia to pay the bills a few years later, after several expensive flops depleted its cash reserves.

Other segments fragment the landmark. Funeral staffers Rod Steiger and Anjanette Comer do a dance around the dead folks. Liberace is a coffin salesman who would be just as comfortable selling automobiles. Jonathan Winters has a dual role as the unscrupulous proprietor of Whispering Glades and as the terrified movie executive who will do anything to save his position.

Chapter 39

Attention must be paid to Rod Steiger, as Mr. Joyboy and his mother (Ayllene Gibbons), who is as big as an elephant. Effeminate Steiger prisses around and courts (surprisingly) Comer, meanwhile catering to his mother's constant demand for nourishment. Gibbons, as Mrs. Joyboy is a standout in an already strong cast. She watches TV food commercials instead of the programs they sponsor. Her orgasmic scene with lobsters offers a field day for psychologists. And when she wrestles with the refrigerator, the outcome is, well, a sight to see.

There is also a nice bit by Milton Berle and Margaret Leighton. Again, it is a British actress facing off with someone distinctly American. They argue (and it goes beyond caustic words) while their departed loved one, a dog, is draped across the banana bar in the kitchen.

Other notables include Oscar-winning songwriter Paul Williams (then 25) playing the 13-year old boy genius. It is his first film. Barbara Nichols plays the deceased soldier's wife, now stripping, which is something she did early on in her career. Tab Hunter has a nice bit as a graveyard tour guide. Ruth Gordon and Jayne Mansfield were hired for cameo appearances. However, their scenes were not included in the final cut.

This was Richardson's follow-up to the overwhelming international success of **Tom Jones** (1963), for which he won the best director Oscar (it also won the best picture Oscar), thus providing him with an enormous amount of clout. He may have wielded this power to hire veteran comic actor Lionel Stander, as a rough newspaper columnist who hides behind a façade of manners. This was Stander's first major Hollywood film after being blacklisted by the House Un-American Activities Committee in the early 50s.

Since no funeral home would understandably allow Richardson to film on its property, the famed Harold Lloyd Estate was used for Whispering Glades exterior shots.

Cast

Robert Morse	*Dennis Barlow*
Jonathan Winters	*Henry/Wilbur Glenworthy*

Anjanette Comer	*Aimee Thanatogunos*
Dana Andrews	*General Buck Brinkman*
Milton Berle	*Mr. Kenton*
James Coburn	*Immigration Officer*
John Gielgud	*Sir Francis Hinsley*
Tab Hunter	*Guide*
Margaret Leighton	*Mrs. Kenton*
Liberace	*Mr. Starker*
Roddy McDowall	*D.J. Jr.*
Robert Morley	*Sir Ambrose Ambercrombie*
Barbara Nichols	*Sadie Blodgett*
Lionel Stander	*The Guru Brahmin*
Claire Kelly	*Receptionist*
Bernie Kopell	*Assistant to the Guru Brahmin*
Reta Shaw	*Strip Club Worker*
Paul Williams	*Gunther Fry*
Rod Steiger	*Mr. Joyboy*
Ayllene Gibbons	*Mrs. Joyboy*
Robert Easton	*Dusty Acres*
Martin Ransohoff	*Lorenzo Medici*
Jamie Farr	*Waiter at English Club*

Production

Tony Richardson	*Director*
Evelyn Waugh (novel), Terry Southern, Christopher Isherwood	*Writers*
John Calley, Neil Hartley, Haskell Wexler, Martin Ransohoff	*Producers*
John Addison	*Music*
Haskell Wexler	*Cinematographer*
Rouben Ter-Arutunian	*Costumes*
Metro-Goldwyn-Mayer/Filmways Pictures	*Production Company*
USA/122 minutes/1965	*Country/Runtime/Year Released*

Chapter 39

Chapter 40

The Love Bug

"Without a real car, I'm only half a man."
—Jim Douglas

Entrepreneur and creative genius Walt Disney (1901-1966) built an empire on family and youth entertainment. Possessing an incredible imagination, his accomplishments and contributions to the industry with movies, television, and theme parks are well known to millions of parents and children. What is remarkable is that his movie studio, under his guidance for nearly four decades, was one of the most consistent and profitable concerns in the industry, riding the crest of a wave, without the ups and downs the rest of the industry suffered. Perhaps the formula to this achievement can be found in his quote "I don't make pictures just to make money. I make money to make more pictures." Today, the company he pioneered is one of the most powerful media conglomerates in the world.

Walt's early success can be directly attributed to those lovable characters he created or popularized from novels and history. Mickey, Cinderella, and even Daniel Boone concurrently worked on several dimensions of intellect and interests. First, their appeal to young people was ageless and universal: The characters were clean-cut, sensitive, and nice. They had a childlike perception that children could relate to. But they also succeeded when forced to operate in adult situations. They had high standards of right and wrong, and morals of which even the strictest maiden aunt would approve. Parents wouldn't be overly concerned if their children wanted to watch something from Disney. They know Uncle Walt would provide a safe harbor for their children.

Although released three years after Walt's death, **The Love Bug** repeats the "safe harbor" formula and became one of the most successful Disney films of the late 60s. The title character, **The Love Bug**, was a 1963 Volkswagen Beetle, affectionately named Herbie. He's smarter than the average car and quite like a warm puppy, easily winning the hearts of children and adults.

Herbie isn't an ordinary Volkswagen. He thinks, acts, feels, and he gets drunk, tired and jealous of other cars. In other words, he offers a full range of emotions. He even tries to commit suicide by jumping off the Golden Gate Bridge. As co-star Buddy Hackett puts it, Herbie's secret is his "heart." That's all that needs to be said about this special car. Apart from scene stealing Hackett, the other real people involved with this thinking and feeling machine include Dean Jones, Michelle Lee, David Tomlinson, and Joe Flynn.

Jones plays a down-on-his-luck race car driver who's reduced to competing in demolition derbies. Through fate he acquires Herbie. Together, they take those 40 horses and compete successfully against Lamborginis and Maseratis. He then tries to convince himself that it's solely his driving. Boy, does he have a lot to learn!

It's also significant that he has trouble with women. Lee is Dean's potential love interest but their courtship is a bumpy ride. Again, Herbie intervenes and brings these two together, perhaps to explain the title of the movie. According to a short documentary Disney produced for the DVD release, the film is based on a story entitled *Car-Boy-Girl*. This would have clearly brought the triangle into a sharper focus. Also of note in the DVD: gorgeous Yvette Mimieux was first in line to play Carole.

Along with this supernatural premise, the dialogue sparkles and moves along at a quick pace. Although Dean and Lee are pretending to talk about machinery, adults can read between the tread marks. When Lee asks "have you had any experience with cars" it is perhaps the most subtle pick-up line in any Walt Disney production. Ultimately, Jones gains confidence with cars and girls, thanks to Herbie. Borrowing from Shakespeare, the movie ends with a marriage, though adults may wonder if he married the car or the girl.

Herbie also has to contend with David Tomlinson. Just a few years before, Tomlinson was the kindly and self-centered Mr. Banks,

Chapter 40

employer of **Mary Poppins** (1964). Now Tomlinson is Herbie's antagonist in the classic tradition of evil villains. Delightfully arrogant, Tomlinson runs a ritzy dealership that caters only to high-priced precision machinery. The people's car is not on his social register. But he senses that Herbie is no ordinary car and is determined (or obsessed) to find out how an economy machine can be so quick and agile, easily outdistancing his exotic flock. When a final race and wager put Herbie's ownership (and life) at stake, Tomlinson pulls out all stops to win. In a delightful show of frustration and anger, he exclaims "Now I've finished being generous George!" His banter with his weak assistant, Joe Flynn, is frequently hilarious. His narcissistic schemes are foiled one by one, but not without some real belly laughs. It's quite similar to the game played between the coyote and the roadrunner (not a Disney cartoon) but who says one shouldn't borrow from the best.

Buddy Hackett answers to Tennessee, but his diction is anything but southern. He's the definitive product of San Francisco, circa 1969, which was then experiencing the full-blown effects of the hippie movement. He explains Herbie's existence like any other mind-altered guy who likes wearing a Nehru jacket. He also names the car. His Uncle Herbie was bulbous and reminded him of a Volkswagen. Amusing and off center, children will find his anecdotes harmless and delightful. On another level, adults realize fairly quickly that he's got some powerful (and mind altering) contacts in the Haight-Ashbury district. It's significant to the story that he is off center, as the official liaison between Herbie and the humans.

One of the nice things about Disney films during this period is the opportunity to see veteran actors in small but memorable roles. One of special note is Iris Adrian. Then 57, her small part in **The Love Bug** as the brassy carhop adds to the film's fun. In films since the 30s as a dime-store blonde, she played bits, saloon broads, and best friends. She even appeared in a Laurel & Hardy short as one of the "girls." Her career of small but interesting roles was prolonged to good advantage in a handful of Disney films during the 60s and 70s. Also of special note in her scene: that's unrecognizable Dean Jones playing the "chickie baby" hippie.

The Love Bug was the most profitable film of 1969, even beating **Midnight Cowboy** and **Butch Cassidy and the Sundance Kid** to the finish line. Its overwhelming success spurned three movie sequels. Unfortunately, they were all mediocre in content and execution—the creative inertia after Disney's passing was apparently gone. **Herbie Rides Again** (1974) found the lovable bug retired from racing and owned by Helen Hayes. His ride this time was to battle crooks, which was quite a yawn. To liven things up a bit, Jones was brought back in 1977 to race again in **Herbie Goes to Monte Carlo**. Don Knotts and Julie Sommars filled in the Buddy Hackett and Michelle Lee roles. In 1980, our favorite car was racing in South America with **Herbie Goes Bananas**. However, by this time, quality control at Disney was down (the 70s were creatively unkind to Disney). When children and adults failed to show up to this one, a TV show with Jones was aired in 1982. It also ran out of gas fairly quickly. Jones put in a neat cameo in a slight reworking of **The Love Bug** in 1997 for television. And still another variation was released in 2005. Most striking difference: Herbie's owner was now a young female.

The German Volkswagen was an obvious choice for the role of Herbie. Then at the height of popularity (sales of the Beetle peaked in 1970), the car transcended time. For example, the Ford Pinto, and Chevrolet Vega, which were introduced shortly after this film was released to compete with the Beetle, looked out of date after a few years. However, the Beetle didn't age. It created a style of its own. While other cars offered more room, power and a better heater, few could compete with the workmanship, charm or the envied reliability of a Beetle.

This appeal doesn't work for all cars. For example, Stephen King's **Christine** (1983), a 1958 Plymouth Fury wasn't as memorable since the main character was a rather vulgar looking car from another styling era. What ever happened to the original Herbie? From a total of 16 cars, at least four are still in existence. Each one was equipped with special unique qualities such as the ability to pop a wheelie, open doors automatically, or squirt automotive fluid on an unsuspecting shoe. A private collector, a fireworks manufacturer, owned and displayed one of the originals in his museum in South Carolina for a number of years. By coincidence, his first name was also Herbie. After his death, his collection was liquidated in 1995 and the car was sold for $18,900, which surprised everyone, except those who knew the kind of emotions **The Love Bug** was capable of inspiring.

There is a version of Herbie called the "Porsche Herbie," since it's equipped with a modified Porsche engine capable of powering the bug to 120 miles per hour! This particular Herbie was built from a 1960 and 1963 Beetle and can be identified in the movie by a distinctive roll bar. Its last whereabouts was in the hands of a Florida collector.

Another original Herbie can be found on display at the Swigart Antique Auto Museum in Huntington, Pennsylvania. Like most real and wannabe love bugs, he's wearing red, white, and blue racing strips, and the number 53. Dean Jones also owns a Herbie, perhaps as a keepsake from what surprisingly turned out to be a very special film.

To coincide with the film's release, Volkswagen of America ran a series of clever advertisements (there's one showing hundreds of "Herbies" watching the actual movie at a drive-in). Volkswagen dealers also offered a racing strip and number kit to turn any Beetle into a pseudo love bug. Volkswagen pulled the Beetle from the United States market in 1977. The rear, air cooled engine could not meet pollution standards and sales were doomed. A more modern body (with front engine and drive) brought it back to the states in early 2000 to much applause from car buyers looking for something nostalgic and different. Volkswagen of Mexico produced the last original concept Volkswagen—number 21,529,464—on July 30, 2003. The historic occasion was marked with a broad display of VW shaped memorabilia, including a replica of Herbie. Mr. Jens Neumann, president of Volkswagen's North American region, said the Herbie movies made the bug one of the only cars to ever become a star on the silver screen. He added "the real stars know when to retire, and the public knows that very well."

Cast

Dean Jones	*Jim Douglas*
Michele Lee	*Carole Bennett*
David Tomlinson	*Peter Thorndyke*
Buddy Hackett	*Tennessee Steinmetz*
Joe Flynn	*Havershaw*
Benson Fong	*Mr. Tang Wu*
Andy Granatelli	*Association President*
Joe E. Ross	*Detective*
Iris Adrian	*Carhop*
Ned Glass	*Toll Booth Attendant*

Production

Robert Stevenson	*Director*
Gordon Buford (story), Don DaGradi, Bill Walsh	*Writers*
Bill Walsh	*Producer*
George Bruns	*Original Music*
Edward Colman	*Cinematographer*
Walt Disney Pictures	*Production Company*
USA/107/1968	*Country/Runtime/Year Released*

Chapter 40

Chapter 41
The Manchurian Candidate

"Raymond Shaw is the kindest, bravest, warmest, most wonderful human being I've ever known in my life."

—*Bennett Marco*

The Manchurian Candidate doesn't easily fit into a specific category or subject matter, which only adds to its appeal as a great film. Released in 1962 at the height of the Cold War, most would typify it as a political thriller because the individuals pitted against each other represent hostile nations. But on another level, it's a horror film. There is definitely a monster under the bed. But then again, it is a terrific black comedy. The film does have some tense and thrilling situations, but there are some very funny moments as well. The beauty of the film is that it operates well on any of these levels. And thanks to its re-release to theatres in 1987, after a long absence from public view, its popularity has eclipsed an early and difficult showing in 1962. If you'll recall, the early 60s were problematic times for the U.S. The Cold War was in full season and President Kennedy had scheduled an engagement in Dallas for November 22, 1963.

This film is also very interesting because the people involved in the production were well connected and very powerful. Frank Sinatra, who in 1960 campaigned for JFK, had become his friend. Sinatra, being politically correct at the time, informed Kennedy he was planning to make **The Manchurian Candidate**, based on the best-selling 1958 novel by Richard Condon. When Kennedy asked Sinatra who was going to play the mother, Sinatra took this question as permission to film the book. In retrospect, Sinatra's caution was guided by the fact that Kennedy had his hands full at the time.

There was the Bay of Pigs debacle, the Cuban Missile Crisis, Francis Gary Powers and a spy plane, and Soviet leader Nikita Kruschev telling the free world "we will bury you."

Condon's novel is, of course, about what was on everyone's minds in the late 50s and early 60s: The friction between freedom and communism and the assassination of political leadership.

JFK's question to Sinatra is intriguing. The mother part, as JFK implied, is the one to watch in the film. Sinatra's original choice was Lucille Ball. That casting would have been very interesting. However, Angela Lansbury was eventually settled on. Director John Frankenheimer had just worked with Lansbury the previous year in **All Fall Down** (1962) and knew how good she was. In that film, Lansbury survived the horror of her life by pretending that her son was really a nice boy who just hadn't really found himself. It was a very different mother from Mrs. Iselin.

Though only three years older than star Laurence Harvey who plays her son Raymond Shaw (she's 37, he's 34), she is the center of the film. She naturally projects evil in what is one of her most interesting roles in a long and distinguished career. Without her technical expertise, the nightmarish aspects of brainwashing, mother love and hidden agendas in the plot would not be as potent. It's rather curious that Lansbury received supporting status in the credits, though her role is much larger and more important than that of Janet Leigh, who received above the title star billing, after Sinatra and Harvey.

Lansbury's mothering skills and clothing are clinical, much to our delight. She controls her dimwitted husband's thoughts (James Gregory) not as a partner, but as a mother. Rather bold, she tells him not to think, which sounds like what an abusive mother would say to one of her unruly children. Another example of her skill is at the masquerade party. It seems appropriate to have a party like this during the film because the costumes hide true character. Notice that Lansbury wears Little Bo Peep and is looking for her sheep. As for her normal clothes and thoughts, they are equally interesting. The Oriental motif is there in her clothing, and we frequently hear her repeating instructions—a mild form of manipulation and brainwashing.

Chapter 41

Her husband, Raymond's stepfather, appears as Abraham Lincoln at the masquerade party. You may notice there are several portraits of Lincoln shown throughout the film. One can easily recall what happened to him at Ford's theatre. Less obvious are the young lovers: Laurence Harvey looks as though he belongs in a bull ring and poor Leslie Parrish is the queen of hearts. Khigh Dhiegh is particularly memorable as the more obvious villain. His character, Dr. Yen Lo, recites catchphrases from American culture, including "taste good like a cigarette should." It's all very chilling. A few years after this film he guest starred on the TV series **Hawaii Five-0** for a similar study in brainwashing terror.

Henry Silva plays Laurence's Korean valet. During his fight scene with Sinatra, Ole blue eyes broke his finger when doing a karate chop to the table. Apparently Sinatra took the injury in stride. Silva, who was a member of Sinatra's Rat Pack, was seen as a close friend of Sinatra. Some audience members laugh uncomfortably during this sequence as they see Sinatra beating the hell out of Silva while screaming "what was Raymond doing with his hands?"

The most interesting and creative use of film occurs in the dream sequence. The piece that appears in the final cut was actually a rough presentation of what was supposed to be something more elaborate. But Frankenheimer thought it was good and decided to keep it in as is. Audiences gasped at something they really hadn't been privy to in cinema. A seemingly harmless group of ladies are at a garden club in New Jersey. In truth, it reveals the most inner thoughts of some-one's memory of a trauma. Laurence Harvey, who had a long career in film despite few favorable reviews by critics, approached his role like a log floating downstream. In this case, it works out very well. Critics who warned audiences of his limited abilities said it was his most convincing performance. For most of the film he appears to be dazed and confused. If his acting range is poor, it works this time around for what the role demands. For once, he creates an excellent characterization.

Other elements offer interesting contrasts. For example, Sinatra and Leigh are orphans, so there is no parental element. They are free to do whatever they want—including marriage. Leigh's name is Rosie and coincidentally rhymes with Josie (Leslie Parrish), who becomes Harvey's love interest.

The other roles are also meaty. John McGiver becomes Harvey's father-in- law. For the first time in Harvey's life, he feels loved by a strong father figure. On the other side, James Gregory is Harvey's step dad. His McCarthy- like exchanges echo a dark time in American history when being labeled communist was the worst thing you could say about anyone. The bartender in the "jump into a lake" scene was Jilly Rizzo. Apart from being known as a party animal and Sinatra's best friend, he has the distinction of being buried beside Mr. Sinatra, (along with Sinatra's parents).

The film was released, unfortunately, around the time of Kennedy's assassination. Thus, it was pulled from public view and considered a flop. Sinatra was one of the most powerful players in Hollywood and pretty much called the shots in managing his career. He must have felt like a tortured soul at this moment and effectively prevented **The Manchurian Candidate** from again being shown to the public for 25 years. He also pulled the plug on another film released in 1954. In **Suddenly**, he played a presidential assassin. JFK's alleged assassin, Lee Harvey Oswald, claimed he had watched **Suddenly** shortly before the JFK tragedy.

Sinatra had also suffered some personal setbacks during this time. His son, Frank Jr., had been kidnapped. Fortunately young Sinatra was returned unharmed, his kidnappers caught and sent to prison. After the kidnapping and after Dallas, Jacqueline Kennedy sent Sinatra a personal note and said 1963 was a very difficult year for both of them, but there was some comfort for her to know that his ordeal had a happy ending. Despite what was going on in the world at large, this by far is Sinatra's best film of the 60s.

In 1987 **The Manchurian Candidate** was re-released to theatres. Audiences could still gasp at a really good film. After that, of course, the Berlin wall fell and the Soviet Union dissolved. Though the U.S. is the world's only remaining superpower, the film still packs a pow-erful wallop when you think about brainwashing. For example, the

Chapter 41

pilots who slammed passenger planes into the World Trade Center on September 11, 2001, are thought to have received some type of brainwashing.

Director Frankenheimer had a troubled personal life. In 1968 he drove Bobby Kennedy to the Ambassador Hotel for a personal appearance, which, of course, ended in tragedy. He later fell into alcoholism. Apparently recovered late in life, some of his last work, **Ronin** (1998) revealed that he hadn't lost the intelligent touch he had with audiences. How things have changed since 1962. In 1999, Sergei Khrushchev, the son of the Soviet Union's leader during the Cold War, became an American citizen. In an interview after he passed his citizenship test, he politely said he liked to shop at Home Depot. An updated version of **The Manchurian Candidate** appeared in 2004 in time for the presidential election. Frank Sinatra's daughter Tina was credited as one of the executive producers and Merle Streep played the mother role with star billing in what was a very good, if predictable film.

Cast

Frank Sinatra	*Bennett Marco*
Laurence Harvey	*Raymond Shaw*
Janet Leigh	*Rosie Chaney*
Angela Lansbury	*Mrs. Iselin*
Henry Silva	*Chunjin*
James Gregory	*Senator John Iselin*
Leslie Parrish	*Jocie Jordon*
John McGiver	*Senator Thomas Jordon*
Khigh Dhiegh	*Dr. Yen Lo*
James Edwards	*Corporal Alvin Melvin*
Douglas Henderson	*Colonel*
Albert Paulsen	*Zilkov*
Barry Kelley	*Secretary of Defense*
Lloyd Corrigan	*Holborn Gaines*
Madame Spivy	*Female Berezovo*
Tom Lowell	*Private Bobby Lembeck*
Jilly Rizzo	*Bartender*

Production

John Frankenheimer	*Director*
Richard Condon (novel), George Axelrod	*Writers*
George Axelrod, John Frankenheimer, Howard W. Koch	*Producers*
David Amram	*Original Music*
Lionel Lindon	*Cinematography*
Moss Mabry	*Costumes*
M.C. Productions	*Production Company*
USA/126 minutes/1962	*Country/Runtime/Year Released*

Chapter 42

Midnight Run

*"I already know you all of two minutes
and already I don't like you!"*

—*Jack Walsh*

Through the years, the buddy-buddy movie has offered many variations of two adult males who bond and eventually experience a life-change. The two characters are almost always males with opposing views of the world. They may be forced into a situation of togetherness to stay alive as in **Butch Cassidy and the Sundance Kid** (1969). They may be together because they share the same occupation, such as crime fighting in **Lethal Weapon** (1987). Or the relationship may happen by sheer chance, bad luck, and misfortune, as in the appropriately titled **Buddy, Buddy** (1981).

Male camaraderie revolves around the act of doing activities with each other, such as playing sports or having a beer and watching television. When the activity is over, they go home to their respective mates. Friendship is more implied than explicit. These characters will echo this pattern, and their brief friendship will be deeply valued, if only in memory. The best of friends confront, support, and educate each other. That is what happens in **Midnight Run**.

This genre sprung from Laurel and Hardy shorts, progressed into law and order on TV with programs that included **I Spy** in the 60s and **Starsky and Hutch** in the 70s. In film, it probably reached a zenith when Paul Newman was Butch and Robert Redford was Sundance. They were the nicest pair of outlaws you'd ever come across. The popular appeal of **Butch Cassidy and the Sundance Kid** prompted a reunion with director George Roy Hill for another profitable bonding, **The Sting** (1973). Theirs was an unspoken friendship.

Newman was the older and more experienced confidence man. He nurtured the talent of the up-and-coming Redford.

One of the best male-bonding films to come along since the Newman- Redford outings is **Midnight Run**. It has comedy, action, and fireworks between the two leads. The fireworks come from being opposites. They are from different classes. One lives in a supposedly safe white-collar environment—counting widgets and wearing button-down shirts. The other is tough, street smart, and a loner. Both are survivors in a mean, unjust world. Both genders (but especially males) can identify with their frustrations. More significant, one is instantly drawn to them with the hope they get through the mess and find some degree of happiness. The performances are excellent. Both the leads are personable and offer great chemistry. Robert DeNiro plays the tough guy. He's the burned out ex-cop, turned bounty hunter. Apparently he was an honest cop who worked with dishonest cops, and it cost him his career. Now he takes contracts just to survive. Suddenly, he gets a job offer he can't refuse. For $100,000, all he has to do is find an embezzler (Charles Grodin) who jumped bail. "It's a **Midnight Run**," says the nervous bondsman to DeNiro, "a piece of cake."

But the job is not a piece of cake. There are more complications. The FBI is after Grodin since he has the goods on a top Las Vegas mobster. The mobster will stop at nothing to retrieve the $15 million Grodin stole and donated to charity. There is still more in this circle of junkyard dogs: The bondsman is worried, so he hires DeNiro's rival to make sure Grodin is delivered before the deadline.

DeNiro locates Grodin quickly and then spends nearly the entire movie trying to complete the **Midnight Run**. Grodin, who constantly lectures on smoking, eating lower fat foods, and the importance of good communications skills, often distracts him. "You have two forms of emotion, rage and silence." Of course he's correct, but DeNiro isn't ready to listen, which only adds to his rage. They naturally drive each other batty, and their debates are high points in between the action.

Though they appear to be quite different, some shared values slowly bring them together. Both have faced corruption, had previous

Chapter 42

opportunities to sell out, and refused. The personal choice brought adverse consequences to their lives. Both have strong convictions. Like all good friendships, partnerships, or marriages, each member of the two-man team substitutes for the others' weakness as the movie progresses.

Grodin, in his much-admired biography *It Would Be So Nice if You Weren't Here* (1989) said major stars more famous than him screen tested for his role. Consistently in films from the 1960s and later host of a talk show, this movie is his best film. It's a clever variation of his typical part: the neurotic man in an emotional vise. In this case, as a strategy to get what he wants, he feigns neurotic behavior to manipulate DeNiro. DeNiro adds a comedy portrait to his glowing gallery of mobsters and psychotics. It's a welcome alternative to the repertoire of a star many critics believe is the best actor of his generation.

The two stars are aided by plenty of interruptions from actors in small but interesting roles. Joe Pantoliano is the desperate bondsman. John Ashton is DeNiro's unlucky competitor. Chief underworld low life is Dennis Farina, who has some great zingers involving food. In a rage, he tells one of his associates: "Sidney, sit down, relax, have a sandwich, drink a glass of milk, do something!" Yaphet Kotto also scores as the slow thinking FBI man who seems to be one step behind in the game.

Cast

Robert De Niro	*Jack Walsh*
Charles Grodin	*Jonathan Mardukas*
Yaphet Kotto	*Alonzo Mosely*
John Ashton	*Marvin Dorfler*
Dennis Farina	*Jimmy Serrano*
Joe Pantoliano	*Eddie Moscone*
Richard Foronjy	*Tony Darvo*
Robert Miranda	*Joey*
Jack Kehoe	*Jerry Geisler*
Wendy Phillips	*Gail*
Danielle DuClos	*Denise*
Philip Baker Hall	*Sidney*

Production

Martin Brest	*Director*
George Gallo	*Writer*
Martin Brest	*Producer*
Danny Elfman	*Original Music*
Donald E. Thorin	*Cinematography*
USA/126/1988	*Country/Runtime/Year Released*

Chapter 43

Mogambo

"Can't you get me a canoe, a truck or a pair of roller skates, anything to get me out of here?"
—Honey Bear Kelly

A museum devoted entirely to Ava Gardner is located in the heart of downtown Smithfield, North Carolina, a pleasant community about 30 minutes from the state capitol of Raleigh. Smithfield is close to the tobacco farm where Ms. Gardner was born and lived until becoming one of the world's most popular movie stars. She reached dizzying heights of celebrity fame, stayed on the "A" list longer than most and made both headlines and many friends along the way. A hometown museum honoring her life and career seems entirely appropriate.

Museums like the one devoted to Ms. Gardner are a curious trend. As the last generation of Hollywood legends die, star worshippers flock to the hometowns of their heroes and heroines to pay homage. For example, busloads of people from all over the world travel to Memphis and experience Elvis Presley's home Graceland. Some fans return for multiple visits to these unexpected tourist sites: Cadiz, Ohio hails as the birthplace of Clark Gable; Stuebenville, Ohio salutes Dean Martin; and Kingman, Arizona proudly displays an impressive collection of Andy Devine memorabilia.

Smithfield native Diedre Kraft helped to spearhead the growth of *The Ava Gardner Museum* after the actress died, first as a volunteer, then as chairman of the board of directors for ten years. "Ava never forgot her humble beginnings in the rural community of Brogden, near Smithfield," Kraft said. "Even after she achieved stardom and instant recognition around the world, Ava always came back to Smithfield to be with her family and friends. And no matter where she was living, either in the States or abroad, she always welcomed visitors from home."

The Ava Gardner Museum displays the costumes she wore in movies, correspondence to and from fans, movie posters of her films and personal items like books and jewelry. Entering the theatre area of the museum, one is greeted with a monologue from her autobiography *Ava: My Story*. Gardner (1922-1990) had been working on her life story for more than two years at the time of her death, and it was then completed by Alan Burgess and Kenneth Turan. The audio played in the museum features Ava's words spoken by actress Kathleen Noone whose sensual, distinctive, almost hypnotic performance is a dead ringer for the real thing. One immediately feels welcome to celebrate an old friend's life and career.

AvaFest traditionally falls on the last Saturday of September in downtown Smithfield. This annual celebration includes music, food, souvenirs and a tour of Gardner's birthplace and gravesite. A festival highlight includes the screening of selected Ava Gardner films in the small town's old fashioned theatre. The annual celebration of everything Ava wouldn't be complete without screening **Mogambo** (1953). Ava's co-stars were also "A" list actors: Clark Gable and Grace Kelly.

Gardner's performance in **Mogambo** is said to be the role that most closely resembles her off-screen personality. If this contains the slightest bit of truth, the lady born Ava Lavinia Gardner was simply irresistible.

Her **Mogambo** character answers to Honey Bear Kelly, a New York party girl who takes a trip to Africa to meet a lover. Arriving without money or a return ticket, she finds her ride has gone and her only choice is to bunk up with Clark Gable. Gable is Victor Marswell, a man's man who captures wild animals for the circus and it is significant that Ava's character answers to Honey Bear. All is fine between the two love birds until Grace Kelly arrives with her husband. This guy is an extremely dull and sickly scientist and she naturally succumbs to Gable's charms. Honey Bear finds herself on the sidelines but she has a few tricks of her own.

Directed by John Ford, **Mogambo** is a remake of Director Victor

Chapter 43

Fleming's **Red Dust** (1932). The earlier film took place on a rubber plantation and starred Gable, Jean Harlow and Mary Astor. Gable reprises his same role from **Red Dust**, Gardner takes the Harlow part and Grace Kelly plays the ladylike Astor role.

Twenty years later, Gable's character is middle-aged and the screenplay is updated to ask why a man as handsome and virile as Gable's Victor has never married. Victor is asked the question several times. Ava wonders if Gable likes women and Kelly's unsuspecting husband is also perplexed. At first Victor appears to have no use for women. However, Victor's attitude changes fairly quickly after discovering Honey Bear taking a shower at his place. A kiss leads to a passionate embrace and we imagine that an intimate encounter has occurred when Gardner appears refreshed the next morning, banging the keys of an organ and singing "when a body meet a body comin' thro the rye." Communicating sex had to be subtle and imaginative in old Hollywood. This was an era when stating or showing the obvious increased the risk of censorship.

Gardner was the reigning sex goddess in 1953, accepting the honor from Rita Hayworth and then passing the title on to Marilyn Monroe. Unlike many other beautiful women stars of the era, Gardner received favorable reviews beginning with her first major appearance in **The Killers** (1946). Gardner's interpretation of Kelly nicely dominates the entire movie. She is a fun girl with no pretenses. Kelly carries her own luggage (matching, of course), hops on the back of a truck heading for a Giraffe hunt with a cheerful "wait for me" and doesn't complain about mud on her high heels. She knows the score, how the game is played. She is quick with a clever line and voices her objections with cheerfulness. She admits when she is wrong and doesn't sulk. One of her many admirers says she has scars; they just don't show.

Perhaps Ava's magnetism reaches a peak during the dinner scene. Everyone is on edge attempting to keep passions hidden and out of the husband's awareness. Gable and Kelly have star quality, but it is Ava's show all the way. She makes everything fascinating: sitting in a chair, holding a cigarette or loving her man.

That she has depth to her acting comes across strong when she's seen standing on the deck of a slow moving flat boat. The camera stays on her a bit and there is no dialogue. We only hear the sound of the engine as the boat slowly moves away from the shore (and Gable). She projects frustration, loss and anger at the same time and it all rings true.

Gable at 52 is noticeably mature, in shape and one can believe that two beautiful women are competing for his affection. Still, the studio that nurtured his career (he was one of MGM's longest running contract players) wasn't renewing his contract when it expired the following year. He began to freelance and his movies were more variable. However, there was renewed interest in his work each time **Gone with the Wind** (1939) was released theatrically. His last movie is one of his best. He died shortly after filming was completed on **The Misfits** (1961), never getting to enjoy the outstanding praise of his performance.

Gardner was married to Frank Sinatra, her third and last husband, during the filming of **Mogambo**. Her career was flourishing at the time but his prospects were dim. The story goes that she used her connections (and expense account) to secure what became his academy award winning role, playing the sad and doomed Maggio in **From Here to Eternity** (1953). Gardner received her sole academy award nomination for **Mogambo** but lost to Audrey Hepburn's work in **Roman Holiday** (1953).

Gardner matured gracefully on the screen and remained employed well into middle age. Her Maxine in **Night of the Iguana** (1964) offers another standout performance, but like the character of *Honey Bear*, the real Ava was self-depreciative in interviews. David Shipman's *The Great Movie Stars, The International Years* reported that Ava asked film critic Rex Reed in 1966: "What did I ever do worth talking about? Every time I tried to act they stepped on me. That's why it's such a goddam shame. I've been a movie star for twenty-five years and I've got nothing, nothing to show for it...But I never brought anything to this business and I have no respect for acting. Maybe if I had learned something it would be different. But

Chapter 43 237

I never did anything to be proud of. Out of all those movies, what can I claim to have done?" Reed suggested two titles. 'Hell, baby, after twenty-five years in this business, if all you've got to show for it is **Mogambo** and **The Hucksters** (1947), you might as well give up."

Director John Ford (1895-1973) ranks as one of the great film directors of all time. His personal style is very evident in **Mogambo** with his usual trademarks. The characters are loners in an isolated setting and they reveal themselves by action instead of dialogue.

Cast

Clark Gable	*Victor Marswell*
Ava Gardner	*Honey Bear Kelly*
Grace Kelly	*Linda Nordley*
Donald Sinden	*Donald Nordley*
Philip Stainton	*John Brown-Pryce*
Eric Pohlmann	*Leon Boltchak*
Lawrence Naismith	*Skipper*
Denis O'Dea	*Father Joseph*

Production

John Ford	*Director*
Wilson Collinson (play), John Lee Mahin	*Writers*
Sam Zimbalist	*Producer*
Robert Surtees, Freddie Young	*Cinematographers*
Helen Rose	*Costumes*
Metro-Goldwyn-Mayor	*Production Company*
USA/115/1953	*Country/Runtime/Year Released*

The Ava Gardner Museum
325 E. Market Street
Smithfield, NC 27577

(919) 934-5830
www.avagardner.org

Chapter 44

Murder at the Gallop

"I shall have to investigate this myself."

—Miss Jane Marple

During the winter of her life, actress Margaret Rutherford enjoyed an unprecedented surge in popularity. It was remarkable that she had star parts so moviegoers could enjoy her full time. For most of her career she was usually seen in small, supportive comic relief roles that were not always crucial to the plot. Her late-blooming star power was due in part to her portrayal of Miss Jane Marple in four theatrical films based on Agatha Christie novels. The best of these four movies, all produced in the early-to mid 60s, was **Murder at the Gallop** (1963).

Rutherford's late blooming popularity wasn't really a fluke. It was deserved. She had her share of good and bad movies, but even in the darkest circumstances, coupled with the most dreadful lines, she could rise to the occasion. Her charm was unlimited. She was everybody's favorite grandmum, spinster aunt, or town eccentric. The appearance, style, intelligence, and behavior she brought to each characterization made it very easy to win the admiration of the most hard-pressed member of the audience. Rutherford was never a pretty woman, even in her youth. But that face, with just the slightest protrusion of her jaw, could suggest wisdom, contempt, and good nature all in one. Her figure moved with the agility of a barge. Despite hip and back problems that later plagued her, she moved with a sureness of step. She knew exactly where she was going and what had to be done to get there.

Her appeal was universal. She was comfortable with the upper crust of English society, often exposing their arrogant ignorance. But when necessary, she could mop the floor with the guttersnipes.

Chapter 44

Audiences couldn't get enough of her warmth, wit, and generosity. Toward the end of her life, critics didn't review her performances. They wrote her love letters.

Rutherford's character was the same person—Miss Marple—in all the films. They had the same sets, the same chief of police and the same companion, Mr. Stringer. Much to our delight, the quartet provided an outlet for 80ish Miss Marple to do things and play games that most people would never do at half her age. Holding a set of iron-clad values, she was constantly in search of dangerous situations as if drawn to controversy. When things didn't go her way (she was routinely ignored by the police) she planted traps to smoke out a murderer, often using herself as bait along the way. She also flirted and tamed the men folk. Watching her snoop around the crime area with a large flashlight in the middle of the night was a pleasure. She even made that look funny.

These films were very popular at the time, especially in Europe. The first was **Murder, She Said** in 1962, based on Christie's *4:50 From Paddington*. In this one, she witnessed a murder but the dense yet pleasant Lt. Detective Craddock doesn't believe her. Affably played by Charles Tingwell in all four films, he received constant lessons in sleuthing from Miss Marple, yet he never gave her credit for her ability until the final reel. Since the police routinely ignore her clear and logical thinking, she takes matters into her own hand. Infiltrating the murderer's den, she tames a dysfunctional family and entraps the fiend. Who cared if the plot was full of holes—all eyes were on Rutherford.

This film was successful enough to prompt **Murder at the Gallop,** based on Christie's *After the Funeral*. This is the best of the quartet, by a narrow margin, because it co-starred Robert Morley and Flora Robson, two more varieties of English bacon and very tasty indeed. Again, she broke into the circle that housed the murderer and solved the crime—but not before performing the twist in a thin-strapped black evening dress.

Murder Ahoy (1964) was the only film of the batch that wasn't based on a Christie story. Still, there was a particular joy in watching our heroine do battle in a sword fight with the villain. The last film, alas, was **Murder Most Foul** (1965). It returned to the Christie format, basing the screenplay on *Mrs. McGinty's Dead*. Here she was the lone juror determined to prove a man's innocence. Again, it was the same successful formula. The opening scene is particularly funny with an obstinate Miss Marple doing her thing in the staid courtroom. George Pollock directed all four films with some verve and skill. (He also directed one of the most famous Christie novels, **Ten Little Indians** (1966). Their minimal budget meant they were filmed on the same set, with the same furnishings and props. With all of this sameness came a certain degree of continuity. The music is particularly whimsical (by Ron Goodwin). In fact, each time the familiar notes begin to play, it is a clear signal to us that Miss Marple is going to be reaching into her bag of tricks, much to our amusement.

In 1966, Frank Tashlin directed **The Alphabet Murders**, basing the project on Agatha Christie's *The ABC Murders*. It starred Tony Randall as Hercule Poirot and offered Margaret Rutherford as Miss Marple as a gag walk-on. That same year, Rutherford was made Dame of the British Empire. Such was her popularity that Agatha Christie herself dedicated her 1963 novel *The Mirror Crack'd From Side To Side* to Rutherford in admiration.

Born in 1892 in London, Rutherford started out as an elocution and piano teacher, but she craved acting. Her stage debut came in 1925. By 1938, she was landing steady work. Her first peak came from her work in **Blithe Spirit** (1945). The role of the eccentric medium had been a Rutherford success on stage. Other notable films include **The Importance of Being Earnest** (1952) as Miss Prism (which was also a repeat of stage success), and as one of **The VIP's** (1963) for which she won the best supporting actress Oscar. A rare serious role in Orson Welle's **Chimes at Midnight** (1966) was another high mark, at least personally, since the film received limited exposure.

When she passed on in 1972, there wasn't anyone to replace her. An icon was gone in the movies and theatre, and the world was a sadder place for it. Margaret Rutherford and Stringer Davis were married in real life. During their long marriage they adopted four children. One of their sons, writer Gordon Langley Hall, became their daughter in 1968, after a sex change operation. In 1972, this daughter wrote a biography of Rutherford under the name of Dawn Langley Hall. Davis died in 1973, 15 months after Rutherford.

Cast

Margaret Rutherford	*Miss Jane Marple*
Stringer Davis	*Mr. Stringer*
Robert Morley	*Hector Enderby*
Flora Robson	*Miss Milchrest*
Charles "Bud" Tingwell	*Inspector Craddock*
Gordon Harris	*Sergeant Bacon*
Robert Urquhart	*George Crossfield*
Katya Douglas	*Rosamund Shane*
James Villiers	*Michael Shane*
Noel Howlett	*Mr. Trundell*
Finlay Currie	*Old Enderby*
Duncan Lamont	*Hillman*

Production

George Pollock	*Director*
Agatha Christie (novel), James P. Cavanagh	*Writers*
Lawrence P. Brachmann, George H. Brown	*Producers*
Ron Goodwin	*Original Music*
Arthur Ibbetson	*Cinematographer*
Metro-Goldwyn-Mayor	*Production Company*
UK/81/1963	*Country/Runtime/Year Released*

Chapter 45
Nashville

"This isn't Dallas. This is Nashville!"

—Haven Hamilton

A maverick among American directors, Robert Altman's movies are unconventional by Hollywood's established cinema rules. To use a well worn cliché, he thinks outside the box. By doing so, he often achieves greatness. If the approach does misfire, it still remains an interesting departure from the mainstream.

For example, he routinely breaks tradition by often hiring unknowns. Actress Shelley Duvall was not pursuing a career in films when she met Altman at a party in Houston. Singer Lyle Lovett, also with no acting experience, has received work in his pictures. And baseball's Jim Bouton once found himself in a role in an Altman film. What did these people say to him when he told them he wanted them? "I have never acted before. Should I get some instruction?" His reply: "no, that would ruin everything." Another element of Altman's work includes extra dialogue in group settings, not to confuse the audience, but to add layers to the situation. He encourages his actors to improvise, often letting their ideas appear in the final print. In group settings, he puts a microphone on all members of the cast, no matter how large the number, and lets them go at it. In the editing room he listens and then picks what he wants to be in the final print. By doing this and more, he consistently succeeds with fresh, offbeat, and witty observations on our culture.

When Altman is good, he is one of the best directors in the business of movie making. He pulls unusual elements together and captures the sad and wonderful human condition. He records characters actions, moods, and responses when they think nobody is watching them. He focuses less on glamour than on style and situations. More than most, he can reach in and tug at your heart, soul, and funny bone, usually within minutes of each other.

One of his peaks in a long career is **Nashville**. His creative juices were especially strong and evident in this 1975 film. **Nashville** offers a five-day view in the lives of over two-dozen characters. They represent a large segment of Tennessee life, people from all walks of life. The overall picture, after seeing bits and pieces of how their days go by, paints a rather superb and engrossing portrait of a city known for its country and western music. The fifth day ends at a political rally, complete with upcoming bicentennial trimmings. As the viewer gathers information on these characters, the tension mounts. When the final curtain goes up on this motley group of people, there is a big wow at the end.

Since the movie takes place in the heart of country music, southern folks thought it was a put down of the region, exposing their culture as phony, insincere, and rather backward. But if you remove the southern accents, the moderate temperatures, and cornbread, you realize the human condition is rather universal. Altman simply uses the southern culture as a backdrop to focus on the self-absorbed, which live everywhere. Joan Tewksberry's script also uses national politics as a backdrop, as we learn more and more about these people. It's 1975, one year before the Presidential election and directly after Watergate. Most of the country is fed up with the two choices so a Replacement Party candidate gains some momentum in the primaries. We never actually see the man with the ideas, but we learn his platform includes abolishing lawyers from Congress, making churches pay taxes, and changing the national anthem. For the upcoming Tennessee primary, the Replacement Party's slick promoter (Michael Murphy) ingratiates himself in the community. The story weaves through the characters he contacts to sing at a rally. The assortment includes singing stars, various relatives, business partners, fans, and other hangers-on.

Actors playing singing stars include Henry Gibson, Karen Black, Ronee Blakely, and Keith Carradine. It is remarkable that all wrote and performed their own songs. Gibson's and Black's tunes are hilarious sendups. It's rather spooky that they found the right degree of mediocrity to keep us interested as well as entertained. Ronee Blakely is electrifying; perhaps it was her previous experience as a country and western singer and songwriter that enhanced her appeal. Her performance as a troubled singer with a selfish manager-husband earned an Academy Award nomination. She reminds one of the various troubled female singers who became too dependent on families for support and direction. The film conversation with her manipulative husband while she is in the hospital is uncomfortably funny. At one point during their discussion of her career, he boldly tells her "Don't tell me how to run your life, I been doing pretty good with it."

Keith Carradine won the Academy Award for his song, *I'm Easy*. Also worth mentioning is Barbara Harris, who with the unlikely name Albuquerque, spends her time on the screen searching for a star-making gig. One can hope and believe that she finds it at the end of the movie. Geraldine Chaplin is the odd fish in the bunch. She portrays a journalist from the BBC, hopelessly out of touch with the culture and customs of this dog-eat-dog bunch. Her priceless exit line translates into missing the scoop of the decade.

Despite the complexity and number of characters, Altman offers fine definition, even if we only see visuals of what they're doing. Scott Glenn is a Vietnam veteran still in uniform and has virtually no lines. When he finally does speak, it is at the most inappropriate moment. Other priceless moments courtesy of Altman include pencil-thin Shelley Duvall being told her diet is going to kill her, Jeff Goldblum's appearance and magic tricks pulling fans away from the stars, even for a moment, and Barbara Baxley speaking of her love for the Kennedy boys and why JFK lost the state's electoral vote in 1960. Her thoughts offer a hint at the evil that exists in the community.

Lily Tomlin (in a role inspired by and originally announced for Louise Fletcher) is parent to two deaf children, an especially poignant idea. She is also one of several women having an affair with Carradine. Her silly husband, Ned Beatty, is a sloppy attorney to the stars who also has roving eyes. Another Altman moment occurs when the car he's driving, a tacky yellow Cadillac Eldorado, scrapes

Chapter 45

its huge door on the curb when he gets out. The film's editing is superb. The movie unfolds through a series of quick cuts, some lasting only seconds. Eventually they form an in-depth study of many characters and interactions. In total, the entire project becomes a revealing insight into their drives, aspirations, and imperfections. Often the people are photographed and recorded saying mindless phrases that sting. They're like a group of children who never matured into adults. Their lines are sly, cutting, and in real life, socially inappropriate. They reveal weakness, insecurity, and anger. For example, when Henry Gibson introduces rival star Karen Black, he tells the audience she's a substitute for the real star, and that she's just come direct from the dentist chair where she was having root canal work. Then, spoken like an afterthought, he slashes her with: "she is a wonderful singer in her own way." One of the cultural exchanges that appear with great frequency is the traditional southern courtesy of greeting everyone with "how are you." It's still a habit very much alive in the South. Altman uses this custom to the point of overkill. By the time Tomlin utters it at a barbecue, its insincerity is complete.

There is much drama beyond the satire on southern customs. A chilling example occurs when Ronee Blakely has a "nervous breakdown" on stage, just before she is supposed to perform. It reportedly was based on a similar incident with country singing legend Loretta Lynn. Elliott Gould, having appeared in Altman's first major success, **M*A*S*H** in 1970, and Julie Christie, from **McCabe and Mrs. Miller** (1971), appear as themselves at a party. The reactions from make-believe celebrities toward the real thing are additionally amusing.

Nashville was a popular film with critics and moviegoers. ABC records even put out an album of music from the film to cash in on the popularity. There is definitely a misplaced feeling of pleasure listening to the satirical songs, especially *Tapedeck in a Tractor*. Altman tried the montage effect again with **A Wedding** in 1978 and **H.E.A.L.T.H.** in 1979. However, both marked a decline from the bite that can be found in **Nashville.** In fact, **H.E.A.L.T.H.** was so bad that it had trouble finding a distributor.

Altman rebounded nicely with **The Player** in 1992 and **Short Cuts** (1993). If **Nashville** offered a hilarious satire on southern culture, then **Short Cuts** dug the same hole on its approach to Southern California lifestyles. Though he continued to tell a good story with great interest—**Cookie's Fortune** (1999) and **The Gingerbread Man** (1998)—**Prêt-à-Porter** in 1994 was a send-up of the garment industry and failed to spark. But **Gosford Park** in 2001 was a rebound, even if the English accents at times were unintelligible.

With the freedom he provided to his actors, it's not surprising that Altman had a fiercely loyal following. Often big stars worked for scale just to be in his movies. In 1992, his satire on the Hollywood community, **The Player**, offered scores of names like Cher, Julia Roberts, Bruce Willis, and others who had worked for him in the past. Some of Hollywood's largest egos were all too happy to adjust their schedules and reduce their fee just to be involved in his productions.

Toward the very end of his life, Altman received the lifetime achievement academy award. Though he had been nominated multiple times, he had never won. Accepting this honor at the 2006 Academy Awards, he admitted health problems in the past that he kept private in order to receive financing for his work. His last film was **A Prairie Home Companion** (2006).

Cast

David Arkin	*Norman*
Barbara Baxley	*Lady Pearl*
Ned Beatty	*Delbert Reese*
Karen Black	*Connie White*
Ronee Blakley	*Barbara Jean*
Timothy Brown	*Tommy Brown*
Keith Carradine	*Tom Frank*
Geraldine Chaplin	*Opal*
Robert DoQui	*Wade Cooley*
Shelley Duvall	*L.A. Joan*
Allen Garfield	*Barnett*
Henry Gibson	*Haven Hamilton*

Chapter 45

Scott Glenn	*Private First Class Glen Kelly*
Jeff Goldblum	*Tricycle Man*
Barbara Harris	*Albuquerque*
David Hayward	*Kenny Fraiser*
Michael Murphy	*John Triplette*
Allan F. Nicholls	*Bill*
Dave Peel	*Bud Hamilton*
Cristina Raines	*Mary*
Bert Remsen	*Star*
Lily Tomlin	*Linnea Reese*
Gwen Welles	*Sueleen Gay*
Keenan Wynn	*Mr. Green*
James Dan Calvert	*Jimmy Reese*
Donna Denton	*Donna Reese*
Merle Kilgore	*Trout*
Carol McGinnis	*Jewel*
Richard Baskin	*Frog*
Elliott Gould	*Himself*
Julie Christie	*Herself*
Howard K. Smith	*Himself*

Production

Robert Altman	*Director*
Joan Tewkesbury	*Writer*
Robert Altman, Scott Bushnell, Robert Eggenweiler, Martin Starger, Jerry Weintraub	*Producers*
Arlene Barnett, Jonnie Barnett, Karen Black, Ronee Blakley, Gary Busey, Keith Carradine, Juan Grizzle, Allan F. Nichols, Dave Peel, Joe Raposo	*Original Music*
Paul Lohmann	*Cinematography*
ABC/Paramount Pictures	*Production Company*
USA/159/1975	*Country/Runtime/Year Released*

Chapter 46

Network

"I want you to go to the window, open it, stick your head out and yell: 'I'm as mad as hell, and I'm not going to take this anymore!'"

—*Howard Beale*

Rarely does a movie becomes more topical, more pertinent and current as it gets older. Superb movies can be scintillating entertainment, but even after a few years, what was being said might not be as new as it once was. Ideas, styles, and opinions are subject to change as time marches on.

Network is an outstanding exception to this rule. It gets better with age. We could even say that it is closer to reality than when first released in 1976. It has vision. Paddy Chayefsky's original and brilliant screenplay has incredibly transcended time and space. Those who first saw **Network** in the nation's bicentennial year essentially previewed a series of coming attractions for society. It's all happening right now. The themes they plot are today's issues, give or take a change in fashion. Today, with interactive and reality television, we may learn about a world mess faster than we did in 1976. This, by itself, can be quite alarming if you stop and think about it.

Chayefsky's forward thinking analysis examines the business side of network television. UBS is fourth in the ratings (behind ABC, CBS, and NBC), and decides to take drastic action to gain a rating point or share of the audience. It's important because each share means additional millions of revenue for the station since advertisers pay according to audience reach. To get out of the ratings cellar, UBS initiates something called counter programming, a concept very much alive today. It places the controversial against the traditional, or the conservative against the liberal.

UBS station executives don't care what the public sees. They only want the public to be enthralled and purchase the sponsors' products. It doesn't matter if the presentation of information is part of an overall agenda that is uniform and avoids balance. This practice is becoming quite common today. It even has a clever name: Alternative facts. Due to corporate acquisition of news and entertainment organizations, there is increased concentration of companies that control the national media. As consumers of information, we can guess that what is or is not being reported represents biased interests.

Network also points a sharp fingernail at the TV generation. Faye Dunaway plays Diana, a program director for UBS. She represents the first generation to go from child to adult while watching television. William Holden, in contrast, represents the older generation (the Edward Murrow school of journalistic integrity). He eventually concludes "I'm not sure she is capable of any real feeling. She's television generation. She learned life from Bugs Bunny." This offers rather chilling implications for those who learned to walk while watching television.

Dunaway has all the ill symptoms of this visual medium. She's manic. Each thought she emits must be attention getting, as if all of her audience is competing for a rating point. If not, she searches until she finds the proper lever, even if it brings pain to her audience. She will do anything for a rating point, for example, programming real acts of terrorism. She even thinks about airing a show called *The Dikes*, a drama about a relationship between a lesbian and her husband's mistress. This, of course, was rather shocking in 1976, but "confessional" shows are happening right on today's television.

Frustrated Holden tells her "You're television incarnate, Diana, indifferent to suffering, insensitive to joy. All of life is reduced to the common rubble of banality. War, murder, death—all the same to you as bottles of beer, and the daily business of life is a corrupt comedy. You even shatter the sensations of time and space into split seconds and instant replays. You're madness, Diana."

Holden plays reality, as the news director riding out his last years. We hate to see him go. He's the one we're comfortable with and the one we trust. He is the stalwart of integrity. It makes perfect sense that Diana would go after him, gain his love, and then try to destroy him.

The center of the storm belongs to Peter Finch. It is his show all the way. He's the newscaster who becomes the "Mad Prophet of Doom." His life and ratings are in a steep decline, so he tells his TV audience that he's going to blow out his brains in the next broadcast. He gets high ratings for the first time and, unexpectedly, permission from the bean counters to continue in this line of commentary. Now with a purpose in life, he forgets suicide and tells viewers that everything is bullshit and that TV isn't real. However, when he starts to gain a strong power base, those in charge are frightened and decide to take action.

Finch speaks his dialogue as if he's reading poetry. There is a delicious rhythm to it all. His now famous line "I'm mad as hell, and I'm not going to take it anymore," became a national phrase, if only too briefly that year. In 1978, when **Network** premiered on network TV, college students and others near a window did what he asked. Now that's power. The rest of the cast is also first rate. Robert Duvall excels as the company hatchet man. With an air of resignation, he says "I'm an executive without a country."

Ned Beatty, chairman of the board, tells a frightening story in his few minutes of screen time. He delivers his visionary statement with the arrogance of a proper narcissist. Dunaway, Straight, Chayefsky, and Finch (posthumously) all won academy awards for their work. Critics were alarmed at Straight's win, since she only had one major scene. The criticism wasn't aimed directly at her. This was a tough time for women in the movies, with substantial roles virtually drying up. Dunaway was singularly lucky during this period. To find work, most actresses were either cast as monsters, had to be naked in bed, or shot into outer space. In this role, Dunaway combined all three. Holden was originally offered the Finch part (so was Henry Fonda), but decided to be Max, the conscientious maverick. The role maintained his overall screen image, and is similar to his role in **Stalag 13** in 1953, which won him the Academy Award.

Chapter 46   *251*

Finch died of a massive heart attack during a promotional tour in early 1977, before the Academy Awards. He was 61. His widow accepted his Oscar. A posthumous academy award has only happened one other time: Heath Ledger's supporting actor Oscar for **The Dark Knight** (2008).

The assassin is none other than actor Tim Robbins. He appears uncredited in what was his first film role.

At the time this film was released in 1976, the U.S. economy was reeling from a recession, prompted mainly by the Arab oil embargo. The major oil suppliers in the Middle East doubled oil prices, which in turn pushed inflation to double digits and sent the world economy into shock. Since most Americans were cruising around in large American cars that got 12 miles to a gallon, our freedom to move around became more expensive. This also filled the coffers of those who controlled oil. The petrodollar profits the Arabs accumulated were reinvested in U.S. businesses. The American public viewed this investment with some suspicion. Chayefsky's script reveals a hidden agenda behind this investment. When a silent group of investors arrange to buy control of UBS, a medium that can influence U.S. public sentiment, the alarm goes off. Today, we have many alarms going off, but no one is listening. Gasoline doubled in price during 2007-2008. We now have a handful of major corporations owning all three networks (along with cable companies). This creates a very fuzzy path to the people who can determine what goes on the air.

In retrospect, many of the Arab investments lacked focus. Still, the theme of foreign investment and loans persists, if only under a different guise. It was being asked in 2017 if the Russians hacked into the internet and influenced the U.S. Presidential election outcome.

The framing of this unwelcome influence is another example of Chayefsky's brilliance. Take special note of the rather ghoulish boardroom conversations.

Another noteworthy film written by Chayefsky is **The Hospital** (1971). Like **Network**, it was written as satire and one could draw parallels between television and medicine. The film starred George C. Scott as a physician directing a large New York City teaching hospital.

His personal issues (suicide ideation, impotence) are suddenly interrupted by a series of inexplicable deaths in the hospital. He also gets involved with helpful Diana Rigg, whose father is a patient. It is no coincidence that Dunaway's character has Diana as her first name. Chayefsky was fond of Rigg and his private joke was done with affection and honor.

Cast

Faye Dunaway	*Diana Christensen*
William Holden	*Max Schumacher*
Peter Finch	*Howard Beal*
Robert Duvall	*Frank Hackett*
Wesley Addy	*Nelson Chaney*
Ned Beatty	*Arthur Jensen*
Conchata Ferrell	*Barbara Schlesinger*
Darryl Hickman	*Bill Herron*
Beatrice Straight	*Louise Schumacher*
Tim Robbins	*Assassin*

Production

Sidney Lumet	*Director*
Paddy Chayefsky	*Writer*
Howard Gottfried	*Producer*
Elliot Lawrence	*Original Music*
Owen Roizman	*Cinematography*
Metro-Goldwyn-Mayer/United Artists	*Production Company*
USA/120/1976	*Country/Runtime/Year Released*

Chapter 47
One, Two, Three

"Is everybody in this world corrupt?"
—*Otto Ludwig Piffl*

One, Two, Three remains a fascinating curio now that the Cold War has past, Germany is once again united (in 1989), and pieces of the Berlin Wall are being sold as souvenirs to tourists. But looking back, when this movie was released in 1961, the two superpowers—the U.S. and Soviet Union—were in a strategic face off. Each nation had enough ammunition to annihilate the world several times. Despite their respective might, they were paranoid that one would become overtly stronger than the other and able to exert some degree of dominance. This difference of opinion created enormous tension in certain areas of the world. Postwar Germany was one of these hot spots. **One, Two, Three** gamely pokes fun at a serious subject. By doing so, humor is used therapeutically to gently release some of the pressure from this boiler.

If today's younger audiences may wonder what the fuss was all about, a short history lesson might help one to fully understand Director Billy Wilder's comic approach to the situation. After World War II, Germany was divided into two halves, East and West. Occupying the free Western sector were the Allied forces—the U.S., Great Britain, and France. The Eastern Sector became a satellite country to Communist Soviet Union. Since Berlin was the capital of Germany, it was also divided into a West and East sector. And since West Berlin was surrounded by all of East Germany, the city became a notorious free zone within a Communist country. The Communists fiercely protested Allied occupation of territory inside the Iron Curtain. They correctly assumed it could be used as a propaganda tool. In an unsuccessful attempt to drive the Allies out, transport roads to the city were cut off. The Allies reacted with the Berlin Airlift. Every 15 seconds or so, a plane landed at West Berlin's airport with supplies.

Meanwhile the free world spared no expense to revitalize a city that had once rivaled Paris as the cultural Mecca of Europe. Consequently, to the world, Berlin became a symbol of freedom.

By 1960, thousands of East Germany's skilled labor force had pulled up stakes and walked across the border to a place resembling a Christmas tree. To stop this drain of manpower, the East German government severed communication lines and constructed a huge wall around the city. One would think it would be easier to change policy than to build a retaining structure, but that is what the Communists did.

There were only two exits in the Berlin Wall. One could walk through the Brandenburg Gate or drive through Checkpoint Charlie. To access either exit required a special visa. It was easier to buy a winning lottery ticket than to get one of these permission slips. Thus, tragically, families were divided, and those that trespassed were shot on sight. Amid all this chaos, Billy Wilder fashioned **One, Two, Three**. In light of the tension the world felt in 1961, Hollywood's solution was a fast-paced comedy that pitted Western ideology against the East, trashing icons on both sides.

Inspired by a one-act play from the 30s by Ferenc Molnar, Wilder and I.A.L Diamond plant a capitalistic landmark, Coca-Cola, in West Berlin. A slick executive and self-promoter, James Cagney, manages this familiar company. Desiring upward mobility and to earn points, he agrees to take care of the boss' hot-blooded and very southern daughter (Pamela Tiffin) while in Europe. Her parents had in fact sent her away from the United States to avoid a marriage. In defiance to adults (remember she's a teenager), she crosses the wall and marries a Communist subversive (Horst Bucholz). Cagney realizes that mom and pop are not going to be happy about having a communist son-in-law. Seeing that his soft drink career is placed in jeopardy, Cagney turns on the heat, charm, and finesse to solve the problem. He is a joy to watch in what was thought would be his final film.

Chapter 47

Very contemporary for the era, the name-dropping jokes read like a who's who in 1961. There are references to West German Chancellor Willy Brandt, Secretary of State Dean Rusk, newscasters Chet Huntley and David Brinkley, Soviet Premier Khrushchev, and Attorney General Robert Kennedy.

Current events are also ribbed. The world map in Cagney's office detailing Coca Cola plants looks surprisingly like a war plan. The meandering process used to phone East Germany after the lines were cut is actually true. It was nearly impossible to get through. Other tidbits include the Algerian situation (The French, to their embarrassment, were told to get out), and germ warfare in Laos (the United States should have gotten out). Cuba is also included: "They send us cigars, we send them missiles." There is also a fitting tribute to Khrushchev and his now infamous shoe pounding on the table incident.

Wilder points his finger at two of our national pastimes: pop music and our search for material wealth. The Communist equivalents to our lifestyle appear very foolish. Instead of copying the best-selling car in the United States—a Chevy—they copy the Nash, which disappeared in 1957 due to lack of public interest. To extract a confession from a supposed spy, they play one of our pop tunes at the wrong RPM. Note that the elderly bandleader at the Grand Hotel is singing "We Have No Bananas Today," an American novelty song from the depression. As for background music, Andre Previn's version of Khachaturian's *Sabre Dance* adds much to the frenzied pace of the film.

Cagney is perfect as the American businessman trying to do what he does best: achieve power and make money. At 62, (and standing at 5'6) he's full of energy and pizzazz and not at all afraid to poke fun at past successes. He's a symbol for the United States. You'll catch him whistling *Yankee Doodle Dandy*, the title song of the movie that won him an Academy Award in 1942, and he isn't afraid to poke fun at his well known film trademarks. He threatens Horst Bucholz with a grapefruit, but the breakfast is less formal than in **The Public Enemy** (1931) when he dusted Mae Clarke's cheek with the same item. Red Buttons, in an uncredited cameo, offers a "dirty little rat" imitation.

Cagney even takes aim at rival gangster Edward G. Robinson. When he learns that Scarlett is pregnant, he moans "A mother of mercy, is this the end of Rico?" This was Robinson's famous line from **Little Caesar** (1930).

Berlin born (1932-2003) Horst Bucholz plays the card-carrying Communist with intensity. His character is a little bit naive about the world, but is soon straightened out by the more experienced Cagney. In reality, Bucholz had to grow up quite fast. As a young boy during World War II, he experienced first hand the harsh realities of conflict. He survived being target practice for soldiers, allied bombings, and starvation as the world squeezed the trigger on Germany. Handsome as an adult actor, he scored an international hit with **Confessions of Felix Krull** (1957). There were several important American movies to the mid 60s, but his subsequent films in Europe weren't shown outside the country of origin. However, a view of his contemporary work, seen by many Americans, was as the uncaring doctor in **Life is Beautiful** (1997). This was an unsympathetic part that he almost turned down. It's no surprise that the aging Cagney didn't get on with handsome Bucholz during the filming. Perhaps feeling threatened by a young buck, he accused him of showy scene stealing. In retrospect, Cagney had little to be concerned about. Like all strong players, he had kept his hold.

Arlene Francis made a rare film appearance as Cagney's longsuffering wife. She achieved widespread popularity on TV as a regular panelist on *What's My Line*, from 1950 to 1975. Wilder hired her again for a small part in **Fedora** (1978), which would become her last big screen appearance. Alzheimer's robbed audiences of the ever affable Francis in 2001.

Pamela Tiffin hits all the right notes as the dizzy bride. At 19, and only in her second film, she suggested something intelligent behind that gorgeous southern facade. She worked steadily in youthful leads during the 60s in fairly good films. When things began to dry up later in the decade, she revealed all in *Playboy* and then trekked off to Europe to finish her brief career in film.

Like Bucholz, Lilo Pulver was a familiar name in Germany. Like many beautiful and blonde actresses around this time, her appearance clearly mimics Marilyn Monroe. In fact, Wilder had filmed Monroe two years previously in **Some Like it Hot**. The producers from Mirisch Corporation, in true Coca Cola capitalism style, hoped the participation of Bucholz and Pulver would be a boost to the European box office.

One, Two, Three was only partially filmed in Berlin since real Cold War tensions forced the cast and crew to retreat and finish the production in Munich.

Actress Joan Crawford, then an ambassador for arch rival Pepsi-Cola, claims responsibility for the final joke.

This was Cagney's final film during his golden period and in true style he went out with a bang. Concerning his departure from the game, he said he had lost enthusiasm for acting and preferred gardening and reading. The "retirement" lasted 20 years. Apparently to fend off boredom and on the advice of his doctor, he returned in 1981 for **Ragtime**. It turned out to be a good role in a good film. Perhaps this success prompted him to do a made-for-television movie, **Terrible Joe Moran** (1984), shortly before his death. He consistently ranks on lists of the world's greatest actors. For another definitive Cagney performance, and in contrast to this one, catch **White Heat** (1949). It ranks as one of the best gangster with-an-issue films of all time.

Cast

James Cagney	*C.R. MacNamara*
Horst Buchholz	*Otto Ludwig Piffl*
Pamela Tiffin	*Scarlett Hazeltine*
Arlene Francis	*Phyllis MacNamara*
Howard St. John	*John Hazeltine*
Hanns Lothar	*Schlemmer*
Leon Askin	*Peripetchikoff*
Ralf Wolter	*Borodenko*
Karl Lieffen	*Fritz*
Lilo Pulver	*Ingeborg*
Hubert von Meyerinck	*Count von Droste Schattenburg*

Lois Bolton	*Melanie Hazeltine*
Peter Capell	*Mishkin*
Til Kiwe	*Reporter*
Henning Schluter	*Doctor Bauer*
Karl Ludwig Lindt	*Zeidlitz*

Production

Billy Wilder	*Director*
Ferenc Molnar (play), Billy Wilder, I.A.L. Diamond	*Writers*
I.A.L. Diamond, Doane Harrison, Billy Wilder	*Producers*
Andre Previn	*Original Music*
Khachaturyan's *Sabre Dance*, Richard Wagner's opera *Die Walkure*	*Non-Original Music*
Daniel L. Flapp	*Cinematography*
Mirisch Company/Pyramid Production / United Artists	*Production Company*
USA/115/1961	*Country/Runtime/Year Released*

Chapter 47

Chapter 48

On Her Majesty's Secret Service

"This never happened to the other fella."
—*James Bond*

Somewhere around 1968, the people responsible for the James Bond series of movies were faced with a challenge. Their star performer, Sean Connery, an actor who created the persona and early success of Ian Fleming's super spy, had announced that he would not play Bond again. Connery feared the curse of typecasting and had decided to branch out as an actor. Despite international popularity and the ability to command a king's ransom in salary, he was determined to convince the world that he could play a variety of other roles. Thus, he left the field open to another contender. This was a formidable challenge, one that probably caused much consternation between producers Harry Saltzman and Albert Broccoli. They literally owned a gold mine. The first Bond film, 1963's **Dr. No** was a major hit in Britain and a modest one in the United States. **From Russia With Love** and **Goldfinger** were international hits in 1964. At one time, the fourth Bond film, **Thunderball** (1965) was on the list of all-time box office champs. The return receipts for **You Only Live Twice** (1967) were less, but only when compared to its predecessors. (Also, in 1967, **Casino Royale**, the sole Ian Fleming novel with film rights not owned by Saltzman and Broccoli, was very popular when released, and probably absorbed business from **You Only Live Twice**.)

This being the case, the producers picked from their book shelf what is regarded as the most interesting of all Ian Fleming novels, **On Her Majesty's Secret Service**, and gamely brought in a newcomer to fill in for departing Connery. His name was George Lazenby, an Australian exmodel with little acting experience. For box-office insurance, his leading lady was Diana Rigg, a very popular star on television at the time.

As before, the film's emphasis was on action, international locations, beautiful women, gadgets, and a psychopath villain. In addition, though, and this is what set the story apart from other Bond outings before and after, was the love story with Bond getting married. Bond affectionados believe this entry is one of the best in the genre, and for good reason. However, because Connery was so identified with the role, audiences and critics were cautious or downright hostile toward Lazenby. Today, his performance isn't seen as detraction, and the movie's virtues far outnumber the complaints lodged against it in 1969.

Typical of the series, we have all the familiar faces: Bond's boss "M" as played by Bernard Lee; his flirtatious secretary Miss Moneypenny (Lois Maxwell), and "Q" or Desmond Llewelyn, the clever man in Research and Development responsible for the high-tech gadgetry. The one American in the cast, Telly Savalas, played the evil genius Blofeld. As most fans know, the Blofeld character appeared in the series from time to time, usually with a feline in his lap. This time, he schemes to blackmail the world with germ warfare.

No Bond outing is complete without a clever opening sequence to set the stage. This time our hero is sporting along the coast in his Aston Martin when he spots a beautiful woman in distress (Rigg). He saves her from harm by giving several karate chops to some thugs assaulting her. To his amazement, after saving her, he watches her drive off in his car. In exasperation, and to poke fun at what he is up against, he turns to the audience (the impregnable fourth wall) and exclaims, "this never happened to the other fella." It's a clever icebreaker to a movie that offers many rewards.

There is still more in the memory banks. Later, when Bond is in his office, he goes through some mementos of his previous escapades (told in a brief flashback), and we see another dimension not usually allowed in Connery's character: sentiment. When his bride is killed (this should not be a surprise to any enlightened Bond fan), his

Chapter 48

denial further branches out to emotional sides of Bond that audiences weren't privy to before or after this movie.

Rigg was the perfect choice as Tracy, the Italian-British Contessa Bond falls in love with and marries. Unlike the other leading ladies for Bond—cold Pussy Galore (Honor Blackman), spacey Tiffany Case (Jill St. John), or vague Octopussy (Maud Adams)—Rigg can take care of herself. She drives a car as well as he can, skis like an Olympic medalist, and handles some of Blofeld's boys without hysterics. Her character is a variation of the skilled Mrs. Peel, the lady she played in the popular British TV show, *The Avengers*, the series she quit to accept the part in this film. Despite her light action roles, it's interesting to note that Rigg was professionally trained in Shakespeare. She doesn't leave it entirely behind when reacting to Telly Savalas' request for love. This was the second time Rigg had to contend with villain Savalas. They had co-starred together the previous year in **The Assassination Bureau**. In 1994, because of her contributions to stage and screen, she became Dame Diana Rigg.

Director Peter R. Hunt adds fun details to the film. Lazenby and Rigg's courtship ritual plays against the backdrop of a bullfight. As they spar, the metaphor cuts to the action in the ring. Later, the ice melts to the tune of Louie Armstrong's *We Have All the Time in the World*. The visual montage is touching, but the song is sadly untrue for these two lovers. As in most James Bond outings, the international intrigue takes us to some beautiful scenic locations. These include Great Britain, Portugal, and Switzerland. Blofeld's hideout is actually Mount Schilthorn, a ski resort in Switzerland. This particular area is one of the best ski slopes in Switzerland, and a popular tourist attraction. The winter climate also offered an opportunity for a nifty stock car race on ice and a mind-boggling toboggan chase. The movie takes place during the winter holidays (and was released during the 1969 holiday season), so Christmas festivals were nicely integrated into the storyline. There is also the obligatory bevy of international beauties. They represent a dozen countries as Blofeld's Angels of Death. The foreign exchange of double entendre is provocative to Bond viewers—especially when he tells one playmate that he feels a stiffness coming on.

However, despite all of this, this outing was not strong enough for Lazenby to get hired for the job again. Besides carping critics, it was rumored that he had difficulty getting along with others on the set. This was, of course, not very sporting behavior for an untried performer. Lazenby said he refused to be saddled with the role every time it came up. As a result of his boldness, and the fact that the film did less business than any of the other Bond films, he hasn't worked steadily since. When he does appear, it's usually a jokey part on the one role for which he will forever be remembered.

While all this was going on, Connery was trying his hand at other contrasting roles, notably without toupee. They didn't exactly set the box office on fire, so he was anxious to return to the fold. In accepting **Diamonds are Forever** in 1971, the producers guaranteed a huge salary (which he donated to charity) and two additional movies of his choice. The return film was set in Las Vegas and broke all former Bond box-office records and restored Connery to his previous lofty position in the industry. After that, British actor Roger Moore stepped in and played the hero.

If Moore appeared to have less testosterone than Connery, he created a more elegant and smooth characterization. He portrayed Bond in seven popular films, retaining and collecting many admirers. Interestingly enough, in the opening sequence to **For Your Eyes Only** (1981), Moore's Bond is paying his respects to Tracy at her graveside when interrupted by a visit from an old nemesis, Blofeld. Despite his abilities, the years went by and he eventually retired from the part. Bond continues but without distinction. Since there are no more Ian Fleming books to base the movies on, another edge has disappeared from the film. Purists of the series were especially alarmed when Bond started driving a German BMW in a recent Bond film.

Connery was Bond again, with some fanfare in 1983, in the appropriately titled **Never Say Never Again**, a loose remake of **Thunderball**. Connery said the title was an idea from his wife, and is a play on his own words. It was certainly something he could now laugh about. Despite being strongly identified as 007, he has proven himself a gifted actor for the long term. He eventually received a

Chapter 48

supporting actor Oscar for his role as mentor to Elliott Ness in **The Untouchables** in 1987.

The elderly lady seen for a brief moment sitting at the card table is silent screen actress Bessie Love. Born in Texas in 1898, she began her career under the direction of D.W. Griffith in 1916 in one of the first important films in cinema: **The Birth of a Nation**.

The Bond franchise remains one of the longest running characters in film. The actors, plots and locations may change over time (he became rugged and blond in 2006) but it doesn't seem to matter. The series can run indefinitely with clever marketing.

Cast

George Lazenby	*Commander James Bond*
Diana Rigg	*Contessa Teresa "Tracy" di Vincenzo*
Telly Savalas	*Ernst Stavro Blofeld*
Gabriele Ferzetti	*Marc-Ange Draco*
Ilse Steppat	*Irma Bunt*
Lois Maxwell	*Miss Moneypenny*
George Baker	*Sir Hilary Bray*
Bernard Lee	*M*
Desmond Llewelyn	*Q*
Bessie Love	*American Guest*

Production

Peter R. Hunt	*Director*
Ian Fleming (novel), Richard Maibaum,	*Writers*
Albert R. Broccoli, Harry Saltzman,	*Producers*
Stanley Sopel	
John Barry	*Original Music*
Michael Reed	*Cinematography*
Danjaq Productions & Eon Productions, Ltd.	*Production Company*
UK/140 minutes/1969	*Country/Runtime/Year Released*

Chapter 49

Ordinary People

"I would like to be in more control."

–Conrad Jarrett

Beginning in the late 70s and continuing for nearly half a decade, a group of "therapy" movies hit the big screen. Therapy movie was a term coined by the late, great film critic Pauline Kael. She used the phrase to describe a plot that had the main characters experience an extreme personal crisis—something far beyond forgetting to buy that carton of milk at the store. During this crisis, we witness on a grand scale the emotional upheavals, self-realizations, private thoughts, and dialogues with their therapist. If the "therapy" is good, the film totally absorbs us into their problems. We actually can feel their pain, as well as their joy. Always, in the final moments before the film ends, we feel there is a faint ray of hope for these troubled folks, and things will get better for them. We better receive some optimism. Otherwise, we all will need to go on some type of anti-depressant.

Without coincidence, this period of time was also the era when men were asked to be more sensitive and open with their feelings. It would make for better relationships, females and sociologists argued. Consequently, Alan Alda was fashionably in while he-man John Wayne was riding into the sunset. By far the most compelling therapy movie by a mile was Robert Redford's **Ordinary People** (1980). It's remarkable that in his directorial debut, Redford created a superbly crafted film concerning the tragic sequence of events of a well-to-do family that suffers the loss of the older son in a boating accident. All elements of a good therapy movie are on display. Redford unfolds them with great detail and care, much like when a very proper lady unfolds her linen napkin.

Individuals from dysfunctional families understand how painful

Chapter 49

265

the holidays are since that's the time when family is supposed to come together and affirm connections. If something isn't working, these connections fail to materialize. These family gatherings can cause great stress and depression because normal expectations are never fulfilled. Taking this cue, **Ordinary People** uses holidays as an outline of action. It neatly lays out Halloween, Thanksgiving, and Christmas, as well as vacations to sunny places. This progression of seasons is also utilized as a metaphor. The fall motif of something dying or resting, and then coming alive again in the spring may sound like an oversimplification, but the movie is complex, and richly rewarding. While the characters are distinctly WASP, their problems are ordinary and quite common in our society. They just have the money or health insurance to pay for expensive therapy.

Ordinary People marked young Timothy Hutton's (he was 20) film debut. He plays the younger son who lived in the older brother's shadow. Since he didn't drown, his survival guilt is a part of his therapy. As was fashionable at the time, he's the tender and sensitive one, the one who doesn't get into trouble. But any self-respecting psychiatrist understands that being too perfect is not a sign of good mental health. The older brother is more manly and macho. Hutton's more interested in the arts than swimming, though his parents insist he stay on the team in the sport in which his older brother excelled. He also isn't the favorite son, in the eyes of mother Mary Tyler Moore, so the story isn't just about sibling rivalry. She feels her disappointments through her surviving son, with devastating results.

Moore's casting is inspired. She's nothing at all like the perky Laura Petrie or the warm and sexy Mary Richards who can turn everybody on with her smile. As Beth, she's cold, brittle and afraid of intimacy. Therapists would have a field day analyzing her personality disorder. She comes off as selfish and arrogant, punctuated by a lack of empathy. This, of course, creates major damage in this three-person family. There are some brilliant collisions between the survivors as they try to grow and develop into sensible and mature adults. When the mother and son collide, the emotional fireworks the actors create make them perfect candidates for an Academy Award.

Donald Sutherland is father and husband. It's his nature to stabilize the family, something he's failing at. It's more than coincidental that his son's name begins with C, for Conrad, while his is C for Calvin. They eventually form something like NATO, with the opposing forces belonging to Beth and dead son Buck. It's CC against BB.

Like other out of whack families, for whatever reason, they aren't operating in coordination and support like ordinary families. In this case, especially along the upper crust North Shore circuit, there are appearances to be made. There is plenty of posturing to show everybody else on the block in this affluent suburb of Chicago that all is well.

Redford skillfully sums up the subject with a quick series of takes and information. The party scene is the perfect example. Each cut is short and telling. In the end, most of these people try to look happy, act delighted to see each other, and pretend to be interested in everybody else's story. Not really, says Redford with his camera observations. He turns up the volume on appearances to a level that everyone can understand. They do really sound like ordinary people.

Moore's Beth is the master of appearances. While Christmas shopping, she sees a friend on an adjoining escalator and exclaims, "Isn't this madness?" When you view her next scene, it really is madness.

The secondary characters are also terrific. Dinah Manoff (Actress Lee Grant's daughter) is Conrad's ill-fated Jewish friend and the one he falls for. Sweet Elizabeth McGovern is the one that gets him through the crisis, though the going gets rough. It's interesting to note that all female characters aren't sensitive, warm, and caring. Even Conrad's macho swimming buddy, Fredric Lehne, offers a tender side when nobody is looking. The movie offers one of the most realistic portrayals of a working psychiatrist. Judd Hirsh appears to co-star because his role is so pivotal, but actually it's a featured part. Taking time out from his light comedic role on TV's *Taxi*, he's a surprisingly powerful presence in the film. He wasn't the first choice and came in at the last minute. He filmed the role in a matter of days to coincide with the *Taxi* shooting schedule. First choice Gene Hackman bowed

Chapter 49

out. It's not clear why, but in interviews, Hackman admits that the script and money are the two deciding factors in accepting a role. In this instance, it must have the money since the psychiatrist role was very dynamic.

The opening dialogue showcasing Conrad meeting his psychiatrist faithfully examines the control issues between therapist and patient. By mid-movie, the bond is set between these two characters and the results are riveting. One scene between Hutton and Hirsch, in which Hutton understands a crucial point of his depression, was good enough to win him the Academy Award prize for best supporting actor.

The screenplay by Alvin Sergeant was based on Judith Guest's book. Sergeant tightens the narration to Guest's story, but is very sensitive to the original idea. Realizing many films change directions once adapted, Guest said she was happy and lucky with the results. Her ideas for the dialogue (which rings true) were lifted from her very own personal files: she had teenagers of her own.

It took courage for Moore to tackle the role of Beth. She explained how she got the plum part in her biography *After All* (1995). Redford was her beachfront neighbor in Malibu. He saw her strolling on the beach and wondered what darkness lurked below her smile. In an interview with Larry King, she said her film character took shape from using her father as a model. She added that she and her father get along great, and she understands his behavior was simply passed down from generation to generation. Her surprising performance makes the movie that more interesting. The contrast to her previous work offers a glimpse of her range. Her brittle and cold nature is not entirely unsympathetic, which is a credit to her subtlety. She is more pathetic than destructive. You can actually feel her tension. For example, watch what she does with a dishtowel when Sutherland questions her about Buck's funeral.

Sadly, her real son Richard had a history of trouble at school and drugs. He shot himself at 24, just as this film was being released—a very sad coincidence. Moore was an especially beloved TV star. When she died at the age of 80 in early 2017, the media spoke very highly of her accomplishments in TV, film and stage, and for her work for charitable causes.

Hutton is the look-a-like son of actor Jim Hutton. The elder Hutton died the year before Timothy won his prize and they were very close. It was especially poignant when the younger Hutton told the Academy audience he wished his dad could have been there to share the prize. The elder Hutton's specialty was light leading roles in comedy and drama. An accomplished comedian, his performance in **Who's Minding the Mint** (1967) made it one of the best comedies of the late 60s.

Young Hutton said he had no desire for comedy, though, and proceeded to tackle heavy subjects. In hindsight, it was probably a poor career move. Another highlight of his film career is **Daniel** (1983) where he was a son investigating the lives of his father and mother, who had been executed for treason. Since that time, nothing that he's done has had staying power. In an interview he said he had approached his career with the finesse of a serial killer. He turned down the lead in **Risky Business** (1983). In middle-age, his career received a boost by playing the younger sidekick to *Nero Wolfe* on cable television and more importantly, *Leverage* (2008), where he played the leader to a group of folks who commit crimes to make the world a better place.

Therapy movies were very popular, but like everything that comes in groups, their quality varies tremendously. Some of the better offerings included **The Great Santini** (1979). This one had Robert Duvall as an ex-marine sergeant in conflict with his son (and himself). **On Golden Pond** (1982) had Jane Fonda working on her relationship with her father Henry, in what may have been based on fact. It's notable for winning Katharine Hepburn her unprecedented fourth Academy Award. **An Unmarried Woman** (1978) was the blow-up of a bitter divorce from start to finish. **Kramer vs. Kramer** (1979) was another variation of a terminal marriage, only this one added the complexity of child custody. And **Terms of Endearment** (1983) featured Shirley MacLaine and Debra Winger as a sparring mother and daughter, until the daughter gets a fatal illness. This batch of movies were quite popular in their time, especially at the Academy Awards.

Chapter 49

In addition to Hutton's win, **Ordinary People** won the Academy Award for best screenplay, picture, and director. Moore, Sutherland, and Hirsch were nominated for best actress, actor, and supporting actor, respectively.

Cast

Donald Sutherland	*Calvin "Cal" Jarrett*
Mary Tyler Moore	*Beth Jarrett*
Judd Hirsch	*Dr. Berger*
Timothy Hutton	*"Con" Jarrett*
M. Emmet Walsh	*Coach Salan*
Elizabeth McGovern	*Jeannine*
Dinah Manoff	*Karen*
Fredric Lehne	*Lazenby*
James Sikking	*Ray Hanley*
Basil Hoffman	*Sloan*
Scott Doebler	*Jordan "Buck" Jarrett*
Quinn K. Redeker	*Ward*
Mariclare Costello	*Audrey*
Meg Mundy	*Grandmother*
Richard Whiting	*Grandfather*

Production

Robert Redford	*Director*
Judith Guest (novel), Nancy Dowd, Alvin Sargent	*Writers*
Ronald L. Schwary	*Producer*
Marvin Hamlisch	*Original Music*
John Bailey	*Cinematography*
Paramount Pictures/Wildwood	*Production Company*
USA/124/1980	*Country/Runtime/Year Released*

Chapter 50
The Pajama Game

"My, but you're an impetuous girl."

—*Sid Sorokin*

Those familiar with the career of Doris Day conjure up the image of a bright, optimistic, and peppy girl. In most of her early films, she was someone you would want to take home to meet your mother. Later, she played the career girl guarding her virginity with the same ferocity of a porcupine guarding her brood. Day was vivacious with a liquid voice, yellow ice cream hair, trim hips, and an ample bosom. Despite that sexy figure, Hollywood muted her sensuality. Still, we all liked what we saw and heard. It's a compliment to her enduring appeal that she's referenced in two popular songs in the 80s—Billy Joel's *We Didn't Start the Fire*, and George Michael's *Wake Me Up Before you Go-Go*. This minor accolade arrived nearly twenty years after her last film.

George Michael's specific lyric, "You make the sun shine brighter than Doris Day," perhaps was inspired by **The Pajama Game**, Day's best screen musical and best film if you discount her pairings with Rock Hudson which made her one of the most bankable stars of her generation.

The Pajama Game has distinction when measured against other musicals of the period. If not careful, one tends to concentrate on Gene Kelly, Fred Astaire, and those Technicolor wonders at MGM. Also very popular were a strong of musicals with leggy film star Betty Grable at 20th Century Fox. However, **The Pajama Game**, under the guidance of Stanley Donen and George Abbott at Warner Brothers, deserves a special place on the same mantle.

The original Broadway cast (1,063 consecutive performances) is intact, except for Day, who replaced Janis Paige, and the choreography is by Bob Fosse. It's some of his first work in film, when he was learning all facets of production and changing the way we looked at and admired dance.

The story takes place in the middle of the country—America's heartland— at a labor-troubled pajama factory. The new plant superintendent (John Raitt) arrives and immediately bumps heads with the chair of the grievance committee (Day). The sparring eventually becomes a mutual attraction and love, but not before they contend with the problems of being on opposing sides. It becomes labor versus management, all over a 7.5 cent raise demanded by the workers. In relative terms, this seemingly minor amount works out to be a .65 cents of buying power today, after adjusted for inflation. songs integrate the story and paint the picture. *Racing With the Clock* details day-to-day pressures at the factory and the growing cracks between labor and management. Day and Raitt sing of love from their respective gender's point of view. Day remains aloof with *I'm Not at All in Love* and Raitt takes on the male aggressor stance with *Hey There*. Reading between the lyrics, audiences realize their relationship is consummated between *Small Talk* and *There Once was a Man*.

Day's co-star John Raitt had his only starring role in this film. He offered a remarkable performance, such that one would have liked to see him in other roles. But it was not to be. His daughter, Bonnie, seems to have inherited much of his talent. She won a clutch of Grammys for her work in popular music in 1990. After her win, the spotlight once again focused on the elder Raitt. In 1992, white-haired and barrel-chested, father Raitt enthusiastically performed *Hey There* in a duet with daughter Bonnie. Their performance together pleased multiple generations of admirers. If the film's fine vocals belong to Day and Raitt, the pizzazz quotient goes to Carol Haney with the spirited *Steam Heat* and the very clever *Hernando's Hideaway*. The latter cleverly contrasts dark and light through striking matches, creating a very good and sensual effect.

The hint of theatrical greasepaint among the cast members doesn't detract from the performances. Each actor has a well-developed sense of character. Often you can see them make quiet talk in broad theatrical gestures when removed from the camera's central focus. Several members of the original cast are worth singling out. Reta Shaw, a familiar and imposing face to TV and film in the 60s, has a good chance to strut her stuff. Eddie Foy, Jr. is the resident knife thrower. His lack of compassion seems a bit removed from the proceedings (especially at the picnic), and creates some tension for the rest. Barbara Nichols, a former stripper who arrived in Hollywood to compete with the likes of Jayne Mansfield for Marilyn Monroe leftovers, is nasal-voiced, peroxide, and cynical. Her supporting bits in films during this generation were consistent and slightly naughty fun.

This film marked Day's return to musicals after completing some highly dramatic roles in **Love Me or Leave Me** (1955) and in Alfred Hitchcock's **The Man who Knew Too Much** (1956). She would do one more musical, **Jumbo,** in 1962. When it flopped, she resigned herself to comedies.

Day began her career at Warner Brothers in a supporting role in, ironically, a Janis Paige vehicle, **Romance on the High Seas** (1948). Ms. Paige's career would weave in an out of Day's career for the next decade. By 1960, she was in a supporting role (albeit a good one) in the Day vehicle **Please Don't Eat the Daisies**.

Pillow Talk in 1960 teamed Day with Rock Hudson. Together they turned on the movie-going public for several more outings. Since her character's virginity was usually discussed in her 60s comedies, the films she made haven't worn well with today's more sexually sophisticated audiences. Curiously, Ms. Day stifled her career when she turned down Mrs. Robinson in **The Graduate**. "I couldn't see myself rolling around the sheets with a man half my age," she said. Television was much kinder to Day, and she had a popular sitcom until 1973.

In 1975, she desensitized her fans with a tell-all biography. Beneath the illusion of happiness and warmth was a woman who had lived a fairly tough life. As a teen, she was hospitalized for a year. Her first husband was a psychotic who tried to abort her child. (He did not and her son Terry grew up to become a record producer). After her third husband's death (Martin Melcher), she discovered she was broke. Melcher had apparently mismanaged her lifetime of earnings. She fought back and was eventually awarded $22 million in damages from her late husband's lawyer-partner.

Chapter 50

In 2011, 89 year old Day released her first album in 17 years. *My Heart* included material recorded earlier but never heard by the public. It immediately charted on Billboard's Top 200 and become Day's first ranking in 47 years.

Today, Day devotes her time to a grandson, animal rights, and a motel in Carmel, California (which allows guests to bring their pets). She still gets film offers and said no thanks to the title role in **Mother** (1996). Debbie Reynolds later accepted it.

Shirley MacLaine was Carol Haney's understudy in the Broadway production of **The Pajama Game**. When Ms. Haney broke her leg before a performance, MacLaine went on with the show. Movie Producer Hal Wallis happened to be in the audience at that time and the rest is history.

Cast

Doris Day	*Katie "Babe" Williams*
John Raitt	*Sid Sorokin*
Carol Haney	*Gladys Hotchkiss*
Eddie Foy, Jr.	*Vernon Hines*
Reta Shaw	*Mabel*
Barbara Nichols	*Poopsie*
Thelma Pelish	*Mae*
Jack Straw	*Prez*
Ralph Dunn	*Hasler*
Owen Martin	*Max*

Production

George Abbott, Stanley Donen	*Directors*
George Abbott (also play), Richard Bissell	*Writers*
George Abbott, Frederick Brisson, Stanley Donen	*Producers*
Richard Adler, Buddy Bregman, Jerry Ross	*Original Music*
Harry Stradling Sr.	*Cinematography*
Warner Brothers	*Production Company*
USA/101/1957	*Country/Runtime/Year Released*

Chapter 51

The Pink Panther Strikes Again

"I thought you said your dog did not bite!"
—Chief Inspector Jacques Clouseau

Movie stars with long careers generally have a larger than life screen presence, something that's often closely aligned to their own personality. For example, it's hard to believe that Cary Grant wasn't charming and suave off the screen, or that Jimmy Stewart wasn't likeable when he was having dinner with friends. The portrait and image they carefully nurture on the screen usually remains constant throughout their screen career. It is what the public expects and wants. Peter Sellers' star power uniquely contrasts with this standard approach. His screen persona wasn't his real personality. He created a vast assortment of characters, and most of them would have a difficult time surviving in the real world. His greatest triumph was his interpretation of Inspector Clouseau in five Pink Panther movies he made with director and producer Blake Edwards. He was able to create a lovable but terminally stupid police inspector attempting to solve highprofile crimes. His caricature was outrageously funny and immediately popular with audiences. Sellers' Clouseau delighted two generations of moviegoers, first in the early 60s and after an interval, again in the mid 70s.

Early on in his variable career, Sellers' established himself as a supreme mimic. When his fortunes soared, he had the opportunity to play several characters in a single film. Singularly, they weren't a great acting feat, but in total they were always interesting and frequently entertaining. His career was at its first peak when he elected to do **The Pink Panther** (1964) for Blake Edwards. He had just finished multiple performances of great force for Stanley Kubrick in **Lolita** (1962) and **Dr. Strangelove** (1964). To consolidate his international stardom, he

Chapter 51   275

decided to take this co-starring role with David Niven. Niven was the elegant, self-assured jewel thief that Inspector Clouseau would be up against.

The ensemble cast offered an international mix of actors. There was Capucine for the French, Robert Wagner for the Americans, and Claudia Cardinale for the Italian markets. Taking a page from the currently popular James Bond films, numerous European locations were included for eye appeal.

As perfect as he seemed in the part, Sellers wasn't the first choice. Peter Ustinov was offered the role but turned it down, not wanting to play a supporting role to David Niven. Ustinov had reason to feel confident at the time. He had just won a supporting actor Academy Award for his role as a bumbling thief in **Topkapi** (1964) and believed he was ready for star parts.

The Sellers character is introduced as a bumbling French detective who solves his cases through mistakes and stupidity. He's an odd fellow of sorts. His French accent is forced and he hopelessly mispronounces key words. This creates lots of confusion in his profession. He also destroys ordinary objects he contacts. They are simple things like doors, furniture, and telephones. He also has a lofty ego. He must somehow give a tidy explanation when something goes wrong. He does not like being accountable, which reveals a rather fragile ego— and a high degree of immaturity. Thanks to clever screenwriting, his unique method works to his advantage, as all his other faults do. He always solves the crime in the end and is heralded a hero.

Almost all of his bumbling causes some type of body pain. The injury isn't something that would land one at death's door. At its worst, there's the possibility of a slipped disc, torn ligament or minor concussion. These "accidents" are Edwards' equivalent of a pie in the face, It's usually broad and intrusive, so we are aware that this slapstick would seriously injure a real person.

Due mainly to Sellers superlative work, and a standout performance among a strong ensemble cast, **The Pink Panther** was an international success. Thus, **A Shot in the Dark** (1964) immediately followed it. This continued the successful formula: international beauties and locations, but the central character was now Clouseau. Subsidiary roles were built around his character. Herbert Lom was introduced as his perplexed boss, a smart administrator who can't understand how Clouseau succeeds. During one fit of rage he says, "The atom bomb isn't needed, that ten Clouseaus could destroy the world." Burt Kwouk became Clouseau's manservant and trainer. Kwouk keeps the Inspector on his toes by surprise kamikaze attacks when he walks into his flat. And Graham Stark plays his "able" assistant. If possible, this character may be a bit dimmer than Inspector Clouseau.

This second film was a fast paced series of pratfalls and insanity. It also included a lengthy scene within a nudist colony, which was pretty racey stuff at the time. It was extremely popular and cemented Sellers rise to the top. There were bumps in Sellers' road, though. He had started work on Billy Wilder's **Kiss Me, Stupid** (1964) but suffered a massive heart attack and had to abandoned the film. He took time off, recovered, and went on to appear in a string of successful films for the next few years. By the early 70s, though, his star was burning less bright. Around this time he sought financing for a pet project, a film based on Jerzy Kosinki's novel, **Being There**. It was the story of a childlike man raised entirely on TV who becomes the darling of the video world. Sellers couldn't find a backer since his box-office appeal had weakened.

Director Blake Edwards was having similar difficulties. He had a love/hate relationship with Sellers and had vowed to never work with him again after **A Shot in the Dark**. Since he hadn't had a major success since the last Pink Panther film the star and director mended fences, pooled their resources and revived the character with **The Return of the Pink Panther** (1975). Middling reviews didn't stop the stampede at the box office, and the Pink Panther was on another of its nine lives.

The Pink Panther Strikes Again in 1976 was yet another success and much better than its predecessor. The Clouseau character was established, so audiences could be heard laughing from start to finish. It turned out to be the zenith of the series. In the film, his former boss,

Chapter 51   277

Herbert Lom, goes off the top and is placed in a mental institution. However, Lom escapes and decides to conquer the world. Clouseau is responsible for his madness and becomes one of his many targets. The long opening scene sets the stage for the lunacy. Lom appears totally in control with his emotions in check when Clouseau comes to visit him at the hospital. You can imagine what happens next when Sellers' starts his funny business. As before, Clouseau comes in contact with people or objects who end up wishing they had never seen the man. The situations include interrogating a group of bewildered house staff, visiting a gay bar, crossing a drawbridge, and frolicking in the bedroom with beautiful Lesley-Anne Down. One highlight (and it puts Clouseau into one of his many disguises) has him as a dentist inhaling laughing gas together with patient Lom. Lom is simply superb as he reaches the end of a long frustrated rope. Laughing hysterically, he says, "kill him."

Edwards difficulties with Sellers during production deserves closer examination. To devise the comedy, Sellers was put in a given situation with little or nothing to go on. He then spent all day improvising and building the scene until the genius jelled. In some instances only one scene was shot in a day. This created long and agonizing delays for both director and co-stars. Apparently Sellers was more complex than the characters he could play to perfection. For some reason, he refused to do any scenes with Orson Welles in **Casino Royale** (1967). On the set, he remained aloof with cast and crew during production. His method was to stay in character 24 hours a day, no matter how bizarre the personality. This unique behavior didn't really matter. The ravings of a comic genius are overlooked when the returns are good.

The Pink Panther Strikes Again was followed by **Revenge of the Pink Panther** (1978). It was a waning effort but still had some bright moments with costar Dyan Cannon. It made money for its backers, though, and three hits in a row enabled Sellers to undertake his pet project: **Being There**. His zombie performance in **Being There** (1979) was different from anything else he had done. His very subdued performance achieved personal raves and an Oscar nomination.

This professional happiness, though, was short for Sellers. This time he suffered a fatal heart attack during the summer of 1980. He was only 54.

The Pink Panther series should have ended there, but Edwards didn't give up. Outtakes were combined from previous films for **Trail of the Pink Panther** (1982). It was more interesting than successful. Another effort, **Curse of the Pink Panther** (1983), offered TV star Ted Wass trying to fill Clouseau's shoes. He was placed into routines like a marionette and the results were embarrassing. Edward's last and failed attempt to generate interest in the series was **Son of the Pink Panther** (1993). At least it gave some of the old stars (Herbert Lom, Claudia Cardinale, Burt Kwouk, Graham Stark) work.

In between the Pink Panther series, Edward's superlative work included romantic comedy (**Breakfast at Tiffany's** in 1961), drama (**Days of Wine and Roses** in 1962), comedy (**10** in 1979) and musical comedy (**Victor/Victoria** in 1982). **10** and **Victor/Victoria** also starred his wife (since 1969) Julie Andrews. In 2004 he received an honorary Academy Award for his contributions to the industry.

Next to Santa Claus, Ronald McDonald, and Fred Flintstone, the Pink Panther is one of the most instantly recognizable cartoon characters. The 70s films all open with the rose cat outfoxing the cartoon man in the trench coat. A piece of brilliance is the opening sequence in **The Pink Panther Strikes Again**. It's a send-up of old and current movies. The score is also instantly recognizable. Henry Mancini said it was the easiest thing he ever composed because you develop the first bars and then repeat on another lower key to finish.

Cast

Peter Sellers	*Chief Inspector Jacques Clouseau*
Herbert Lom	*Former Chief Inspector Charles Dreyfus*
Lesley-Anne Down	*Olga*
Burt Kwouk	*Cato*
Colin Blakely	*Alec Drummond*
Leonard Rossiter	*Inspector Quinlan*
André Maranne	*Francois*

Chapter 51

Bryon Kane	*Secretary of State*
Dick Crockett	*The President*
Omar Sharif	*Egyptian Assassin*

Production

Blake Edwards	*Director*
Blake Edwards, Frank Waldman	*Writers*
Blake Edwards	*Producer*
Henry Mancini	*Original Music*
Harry Waxman	*Cinematography*
United Artists	*Production Company*
UK/103/1976	*Country/Runtime/Year Released*

Chapter 52
Point Blank

"We blew it."

—Walker

An intense and dark movie, **Point Blank** exists almost entirely in a dying man's mind, which makes it a very enriching and absorbing viewing experience. As his private audience, we are privy to his thoughts, fantasies and wishful thinking. This unusual point of view provides the film with an amount of intellectual tension not usually found in a heist movie. Furthermore, since he isn't really all-together, his thoughts are free from social rules and laws. He conducts himself as he wishes. Though he isn't physically capable, his fantasy is to seek revenge and redemption from those who wronged him. He goes through the motions of someone dealing with a life-threatening trauma. First there is denial, then some deal making, and finally acceptance.

The movie opens at long deserted Alcatraz Island with two buddies (John Vernon and Lee Marvin) preparing to hijack money from a mob organization. Marvin's wife is also present. They steal the money from the gang members, but Vernon later double-crosses Marvin and shoots him "point blank" in one of the cells. As Marvin collapses on the cell floor, he overhears a conversation between his wife and Vernon, revealing their affair, as well as her involvement in the double-cross.

Caught in a web of deceit and terror, Marvin tries to cope with the shock and trauma in the last few minutes of his life. He questions his judgment. "How did I ever get into this mess?" The answer is revealed in a series of flashbacks. The tale twists somewhat when Marvin imagines what he would do if he were to survive the double-cross.

The first hint we have that he is living a fantasy is when he leaves

Chapter 52

Alcatraz by swimming away. No one in the history of confinement at Alcatraz has ever escaped by swimming toward the Bay, especially with a bullet wound. Continuing, Marvin ends his swim on a tour boat, sitting comfortably, appearing fit and healthy, talking to a mysterious man in black. This man (Keenan Wynn) conveniently provides him with the necessary information to avenge his partner and wife. He is perhaps the Angel of Death and his appearances throughout the movie offer Marvin inside information and encouragement, which fully realizes the fantasy.

Based on the novel *The Hunter* by Richard Stark, the film follows Marvin as he plots to even the score with the man that double-crossed him (and slept with his wife). During the hunt, there are casual remarks concerning his death. One of the hoods he comes in contact comments "I thought he was dead!" A cocktail waitress, surprised to see him after a long interval, asks "you still alive?" When his wife's sister (Angie Dickinson) fails to get a rise out of his death mask, she says "how good it must be being dead." Later on she tells him prophetically "why don't you just lie down and die." Taking revenge on his own terms allows him to penetrate four levels of criminal activity. Each layer is progressively more clever and complex. But since he's imaging the eventual showdown, he is unstoppable. He is free to provide himself with magical powers. For example, he's clairvoyant, able to predict what his foe is going to do. He's invisible, able to enter a top security mob complex with uncanny ease. And, he is impervious to pain and injury. For example, he rams a car into a concrete barrier and escapes without a scratch. Even a frenetic beating from Dickinson doesn't seem to bother him.

British director John Boorman weaves a taut, hard-hitting film, one that was criticized for violence, nudity, and use of drugs at the time of its release.

Contemporary audiences will find the texture and feel of the film very up to date. However, images of 1967 are everywhere. Take note of the mod décor in a strip joint, just before the brawl. This isn't a detraction since there's a certain nostalgic interest in the colorful backdrop of San Francisco when the Haight-Ashbury period of hippy culture was in full bloom. The location shooting at the Alcatraz Island Prison Complex adds another seamy element to the movie. This maximum-security prison was no longer active when it closed in the early 60s, and it was deemed too expensive to maintain. The facility later was turned over to the National Park System and is now a very popular tourist attraction. The mob organization boasts cast members Lloyd Bochner and Carroll O'Connor, who run the organization as efficiently as a Fortune 500 company. The major difference is that when they need to get rid of bad employees, they fire them with a gun.

Bochner, a familiar face to the big and small screen, later achieved brief notoriety for one particular scene in the TV nighttime soap opera, *Dynasty*. His unfortunate character suffered a heart attack during some overzealous love making to vixen Alexis, fittingly portrayed by Joan Collins. His exhaustion was more fun than potently dramatic. His luck didn't hold out in **Point Blank**, either. After sporadic movie appearances, Carroll O'Connor achieved worldwide fame on television. First, he was the bigoted but lovable Archie Bunker in 1971, in the ground breaking *All in the Family*. He later worked in another successful series, *In the Heat of the Night*, as the crusty southern sheriff.

Dickinson had last appeared with Marvin in **The Killers** in 1964, as a psychopathic party girl. **The Killers** also cast Ronald Reagan as a heel (his last film role before moving to politics). It was also Marvin's last venture as a screen villain, and what a loss it was to fans of the genre. Dickinson is perhaps one of the most underrated actresses of her generation. She has worked steady on television (she was a gorgeous *Police Woman*) or the big screen for over 40 years without any career upheaval. In this outing, she offers delicious sensuality to role that could have been merely played as decoration by a lesser actress. She played the title character in Roger Corman's **Big Bad Mama** in 1974, a film worth viewing if you really admire her body of work.

By the late 60s, Marvin was in his honeymoon period of super-stardom. After spending the 50s as a heavy, he graduated to leading roles and won an Academy Award for his dual performance in **Cat Ballou** (1965). Several action-oriented films, including **The**

Chapter 52

Professionals (1966); a follow- up with Boorman, **Hell in the Pacific** (1968); and the group leader to **The Dirty Dozen**, (1968) solidified his ranking as a box office superstar. He worked as a star for another 20 years, always with solid performances in films not always of superior quality.

A high profile case involving palimony and common law marriage brought him to the forefront again in the late 70s, if only briefly, to prove that publicity can at times be very good for a career when you are a movie actor. He died in 1987.

In 1999, Mel Gibson reworked **Point Blank** into a package called **Payback**. Mel & Company chose to update it as a story, rather than as subtle psychological fantasy. It took place outside Mel's head, losing most of the appeal of the original.

Cast

Lee Marvin	*Walker*
Angie Dickinson	*Chris*
Keenan Wynn	*Yost*
Carroll O'Connor	*Brewster*
Lloyd Bochner	*Frederick Carter*
Michael Strong	*Big John Stegman*
John Vernon	*Mal Reese*
Sharon Acker	*Lynne Walker*
James Sikking	*Hired Gun*
Kathleen Freeman	*First Citizen*

Production

John Boorman	*Director*
Donald E. Westlake (novel), Alexander Jacobs, David Newhouse, Rafe Newhouse	*Writers*
Judd Bernard, Robert Chartoff	*Producers*
Stu Gardner, Johnny Mandel	*Original Music*
Philip H. Lathrop	*Cinematography*
MGM	*Production Company*
USA/92/1967	*Country/Runtime/Year Released*

Chapter 53

The Rainmaker

"Can a woman take lessons in being a woman?"
—Lizzie Curry

The Rainmaker stands as one of the more interesting films of the mid 50s because it discusses the sexual differences between men and women. It takes the discussion further than just physical attractiveness. Since this film is a product of the repressive 50s, it tackles the subject with a clever metaphor. Shortly into the film, one soon realizes the plot has nothing to do with weather, rain, thunderstorms, or a drought. It's all about Lizzie Curry's ability to attract and keep a man. Metaphorically speaking, her well is running dry. She is approaching spinisterhood, a role that both Lizzie and her family believe is a fate worse than death.

Sometime ago, an unwise researcher said a woman of 40 was more likely to be shot by a terrorist than to find a man who would marry her. The principal reason cited was that available men of the same age can attract and marry someone younger and society isn't really concerned over the disparity. Mature women, on the other hand, rarely marry someone much younger than themselves.

Katharine Hepburn plays drought stricken Lizzie, a woman slightly past her prime. She is of a certain age, not too young and not too old. This lonely woman has probably never been kissed, never been courted, nor loved in a sexual way—at least for any length of time. Like all living organisms, she needs moisture in the form of passion to keep from drying up. She feels increased pressure from within and from her family to find and hold a man. Then along comes a handsome man who calls himself a rainmaker. Played by Burt Lancaster, he is a perfect male specimen who struts, smiles, and charms the petticoats off the ladies. When they meet, Lizzie does

Chapter 53   285

what she always does to drive sexual predators away: She shows them just how smart and clever she is. She shrugs off their accomplishments, deflects their charm, and recites what they actually mean to say. This courtship ritual between boys and girls is a game that Lizzie doesn't understand. This component of her personality offers proof that intelligent people don't always successfully relate to others. Since no man wants their ego bruised, they quickly retreat. That is until Burt Lancaster shows up.

His challenge is to teach her the concept and more, and he's up for the challenge. She isn't ready to hear what he has to say on the subject. She dishes out reality and logic, something that doesn't interest him. Still, he is a successful con artist, one that's able to detect and exploit human weakness. He can size up a town or woman with just a glance. Lizzie represents the ultimate challenge. Besides, he has nothing else to do while the police are looking for him.

Both characters are complex. When they do meet, they have many things to share, learn, and discuss. Each has a firewall around their soul that has the opportunity to wash away in a spring shower. All they have to do is process the new information.

The use of the rain metaphor keeps viewer interest at a high level. It even affects featured roles. For example, Wendell Corey, says he doesn't want a dog because they run away. We later learn his wife has also run away. He, too, is experiencing a dry spell in relationships.

In a long and varied career, Katharine Hepburn, then 48, is at one of her peaks of perfection in this film. She magnificently creates a woman on the verge of desperation. She plays it with underlying passion and warmth, and a small degree of fear. Her Lizzie believes she speaks the truth and that's a very important thing to do. She is vigilant about what is real and what is make-believe. This logic contrasts sharply Lancaster's glib nature. Despite their differences, they create a strong chemistry. Hepburn is actually more beautiful and physically striking than ever.

The family dynamics are very interesting. Hepburn's father, Cameron Prud'Homme, is loving but weak. Her oldest brother, Lloyd Bridges, is in charge because of the father's lack of leadership. Bridges uses his position of power to sabotage potential relationship opportunities of his two younger siblings. One can hear it in the discussions he has with Hepburn and younger brother Earl Holliman on the subject of intimacy. Perhaps Bridges is responsible for Hepburn's drought and Holliman's low self esteem. Holliman lacks confidence with women. When he does succumb to the charms of a girl, it's through the use of symbols. She wears red and drives a red roadster. The unusual scene that has them molded as one in the car and going around in circles emerges as another creative metaphor. As surrogate father, Bridges is really the loneliest character. Unless he changes his focus, he will become what Hepburn fears she is moving towards. He may never find a soul mate.

All characters are allowed to fully develop into recognizable people. The dialogue offers insights into their weaknesses and strengths, and eventual acceptance of themselves. Ultimately, **The Rainmaker** is a nice, thoughtful, and intelligent film.

Katharine Hepburn (1907-2003) said she lasted longer than any of her contemporaries because they had all died. It's a witty and clever thing to say, but she had to have something extra to amass her incredible body of work. She was actually more popular at the box office in the 1960s than in the 1930s, something unheard of from the generation of performers she started with. Her last big screen appearance was in 1994, when she was 87 years old, as Warren Beatty's crusty old aunt in **Love Affair**. Father Time, professional or personal setbacks failed to stop her from being one of the superstars of the cinema. At the time of her death, she held the record for Academy Award nominations for best actress—12.* Hepburn has also won more Academy Awards than any other actor or actress. Her fourth and final win was in 1981 for **On Golden Pond**. She was nominated for her performance in **The Rainmaker**.

Some 30 years after this film was released, Earl Holliman said in an interview that Hepburn would feed him lines off stage, as opposed to the typical process of engaging an extra, since she wouldn't be on camera and wouldn't be heard. She cared that much about her craft, and it added much to his performance. Her generosity and professionalism was something he never forgot.

Chapter 53

A few years after this film, Burt Lancaster would become **Elmer Gantry,** one of his most celebrated portrayals. He won the Academy Award for his performance as an unscrupulous evangelist. The roots of Mr. Gantry were planted in Starbuck. **Elmer Gantry** willfully uses people to his advantage, whether it hurts them or not. In this outing as Starbuck, you get the sense that he disappoints people because that's what he does to survive. Lizzie is the flower he waters and through the process he learns another survival skill.

It's interesting that Lancaster started out as a circus performer before turning to acting. His very physical nature in **The Rainmaker** betrays that former occupation. Watch him jump from a wagon or simply sit down in a chair. He moves with the smoothness and balance of a cat walking atop a fence.

Like Hepburn, Lancaster's long, illustrious career remains unassailable in the Hollywood hierarchy.

Cast

Burt Lancaster	*Bill Starbuck*
Katharine Hepburn	*Lizzie Curry*
Wendell Corey	*Sheriff File*
Lloyd Bridges	*Noah Curry*
Earl Holliman	*Jim Curry*
Cameron Prud'Homme	*H.C. Curry*
Wallace Ford	*Sheriff Thomas*
Yvonne Lime	*Snookie*

Production

Joseph Anthony	*Director*
N. Richard Nash (also play)	*Writer*
Paul Nathan, Hal B. Wallis	*Producers*
Alex North	*Original Music*
Charles Lang	*Cinematography*
Edith Head	*Costumes*
Paramount	*Production Company*
USA/121 minutes/1956	*Country/Runtime/Year Released*

*Meryl Streep currently holds the record for most Academy Award nominations of any actor. She has been nominated 20 times since 1979. Jack Nicholson and Katherine Hepburn are tied in second place with 12. Both Streep and Nicholson have each won three academy awards. Hepburn is the only performer who has won four academy awards as of 2017.

Chapter 53

Chapter 54

Raising Arizona

"You go right back up there and get me a toddler."
—Edwina "Ed" McDonnough

The ten-minute prologue to **Raising Arizona** effectively introduces two flaky but lovable main characters that go by the name of Hi and Ed (short for Edwina). In a matter of minutes, through some sophisticated editing and whimsical music we are privy to how they first meet, fall in love, and get married in circumstances that would usually repel rather than attract two people to one another.

This rather bizarre pairing, though, is tame compared to what happens during the rest of the movie. As we move towards the climactic finish, the entire project becomes surreal. It isn't really true—or is it? Like Hi and Ed and all of the other unique characters that come out of the woodwork, you feel like you're having a crazy dream, one that doesn't make sense in an ordered world. If you can connect with these people and enjoy their bumpy ride, you're going to cherish this film experience. If you think rationally like an accountant during tax season, you're not going to have as much fun.

Hi (Nicolas Cage) and Ed (Holly Hunter) prove that opposites attract, although they have more in common after further analysis. He's a convicted felon (he specializes in robbing convenience stores) and she's the policewoman coordinating his fingerprinting and mug shots. The two opposing worlds they live in doesn't derail their mutual attraction for one another. Cage is a repeat offender and sees Hunter several times at the police station. Thus, each mug shot becomes a date with Ed. He eventually catches her at an emotional low ("my fee-an-say left me") and she promptly succumbs to his charms.

This marriage, conceived in unique circumstances, is put to the test after boredom and frustration enters work and home. At first,

290   Chapter 54

our engaging couple attempt to make a normal, if bland, life together. They plant their mobile home in Tempe, Arizona in what appears to be the middle of the desert. Hi gets a monotonous job in a shop drilling holes in sheet metal while Ed resigns from the force to devote her time to homemaking. Only they have trouble making a home. The marriage goes into a tailspin when they find out that Ed can't conceive. Due to the added stress of a very structured and low paying job, Hi finds himself driving by convenience stores. However, he doesn't want to return to his old lifestyle. Both husband and wife realize they must take desperate measures to save their marriage and retain any sense of a normal life.

It just happens that a local merchant, Nathan Arizona, makes news with the birth of quintuplets. Nathan's a local tycoon who owns and operates the successful "Unpainted Arizona," a retail line of unpainted furniture and bathroom fixtures. Hi and Ed figure Mr. and Mrs. Arizona have more children than they can handle, so they decide to steal one of the infants. From a choice of Larry, Harry, Barry, Garry, and Nathan, Jr., they pick Nathan. "I think I got the best one," says proud father to mother as he presents her with the abducted infant.

With the family unit in place, they attempt to live as a couple with child. Soon afterwards they have some people over. However, inviting Hi's boss, his talkative wife, and their awful kids leads to disaster. On the subject of their awful kids, the letters OPE and POE that are painted on the trailer wall are the same acronyms director Stanley Kubrick used in **Dr. Strangelove: or How I Learned to Stop Worrying and Love the Bomb**. The letters formed the secret code necessary to prevent a nuclear attack on the Soviet Union by the United States. Used in this context, one can only imagine the destruction these brats are capable of doing.

More trouble occurs when two of Cage's former cellmates (brothers John Goodman and William Forsythe) escape from prison and run to their friends' mobile home for cover. "We released ourselves on our own recognizance" they explain to Hi and Ed.

Meanwhile, Nathan Arizona gets to the airwaves and offers a

Chapter 54

reward for the return of his missing son. This attracts the attention of a professional bounty hunter, Leonard B. Smalls (played by former professional boxer Randal "Tex" Cobb). He is later described appropriately as a warthog from hell.

Cobb appears in Cage's surreal nightmare. This sequence and others suggests that Cobb is Cage's dark side, an evil mask in the image of his father. He must ultimately deal with this father figure to gain control of his life.

A surreal quality also exists when Goodman and Forsythe escape from prison. Their escape from a muddy hole in the ground appears to be a birth. Goodman arrives head first; while brother Forsythe, the dumber of the two, lands on his feet upside down. They immediately steal a car at a gas station, breaking it away from a gas filler nozzle, perhaps symbolizing the severing of an umbilical cord.

Scriptwriters Ethan and Joel Coen alternate terse, grammatically incorrect dialogue against polished, almost intellectual language. This contrast between sophisticated critical thinking and simplistic thoughts maintain the element of surprise and are a source of frequent humor. One neat example occurs when one of the rugged prison escapees inexplicably says, "As per usual, the source of marital friction is financial." Whereas Hunter, the only character with a professional degree who should be articulate, says "You get out or I kick you out." Another source of humor comes from situational chaos. The characters demand a sense of order and control but their lack of insight and vision only derails their efforts. In one particular standout scene, during a bank robbery, customers and employees are ordered to freeze and drop to the ground. The entire group remains motionless for a few seconds until an aging farmer defiantly asks "Now which is it young fella? Do you want I should freeze or get down to the ground? I mean to say if I freeze, I can't rightly drop. And if I drop I'm going to be in motion."

The writers have also devised a clever reversal of behavior between adults and newborns. The infants, despite what is happening all around them, are content, happy, and relaxed. However, it is the adults that send out primal screams when things get out of hand.

The chase scenes are wild and creative. Only the big Detroit gas guzzlers from the 1970s are used—and to great effect. Plus, the unusual insertion of cattle calling harmonies during action times adds much to the overall enjoyment of the film.

The striking photography comes with a stamp of individuality. Photographer Barry Sonnenfeld created the same, almost cartoonish affect for **Throw Mamma Off The Train** (1987).

Cage and Hunter, virtual unknowns at the time of filming, appeared in other pictures the same year that garnered world-wide acclaim. Cage, a relative of Francis Ford Coppola, is the flaky younger brother in the very popular **Moonstruck** (1987) who falls hard for Cher. At the same time, Hunter was nominated for best actress for her work in **Broadcast News** (1987), but lost. However, she did win the same prize for the much admired **The Piano** in 1993. This role was specifically written with her in mind. In 1995, Cage took the Oscar for best actor in the decidedly downbeat **Leaving Las Vegas**.

Trey Wilson, as Nathan Arizona, had a solid career ahead of him, including character rolls in **Bull Durham** (1988) and **Miss Firecracker** (1988) but was felled by a fatal heart attack in 1989. The tubby and affable Goodman was co-starring in the hit TV series *Rosanne* (1988-1997) during this period. Since that time, he has become one of Hollywood's busiest actors, finding work in featured or starring roles including **Sea of Love** (1989), **Arachnophobia** (1990), **Barton Fink** (1992), **The Big Lebowski** (1988), **The Flintstones** (1994), **O Brother, Where Art Thou?** (2000) and **Inside Llewyn Davis** (2013).

Frances McDormand, (Joel Coen's wife) has a brief bit as Dot. Coen later directed his wife in **Fargo**, one of the most praised movies from 1996. She won the Academy Award for best actress for her performance. When asked how she got the part, she said "The fact that I'm sleeping with the director may have had something to do with it." Her witty observation could have been lifted from a scene in **Raising Arizona**. Another professional highpoint for the Coen Brothers directing writing team was **No Country for Old Men** (2007). The dark and intense film won Academy Awards for best picture, screenplay and direction. **A Serious Man** (2009) was a low budget film based on the Coen Brothers childhood experiences growing up in Minnesota. It was nominated for two Oscars, best picture and screenplay. **True Grit** (2010) was based on Charles Portis 1968 novel. It had been filmed before in 1969 with John Wayne and Glen Campbell. When **True Grit** earned 10 academy nominations, the brothers' response was a lame attempt to hide their genius: "Ten seems like an awful lot. We don't want to take anyone else's."

Cast

Nicolas Cage	*"Hi" McDonnough*
Holly Hunter	*Edwinia "Ed" McDonnough*
Trey Wilson	*Nathan Arizona Huffines Sr.*
John Goodmon	*Gale Snopes*
William Forsythe	*Evelle Snopes*
Sam McMurray	*Glen*
Frances McDormand	*Dot*
Randall "Tex" Cobb	*Leonard Smalls*
T.J. Kuhn	*Nathan Junior*
Lynne Dumin Kitei	*Florence Arizona*
M. Emmet Walsh	*Machine Shop Ear-Bender*
Ruben Young	*"Trapped" convict*

Production

Ethan Coen, Joel Coen	*Directors*
Ethan Coen, Joel Coen	*Writers*
Ethan Coen, James Jacks, Deborah Reinisch, Mark Silverman	*Producers*
Carter Burwell	*Original Music*
Barry Sonnenfeld	*Cinematography*
Circle Films	*Production Company*
USA/94/1987	*Country/Runtime/Year Released*

Chapter 55

Rear Window

"What people ought to do is get outside their own house and look in for a change."

—*Stella*

Much has been written on the art and genius of Alfred Hitchcock. Perhaps the definitive book on his work is Donald Spoto's *The Art of Alfred Hitchcock*, (1976). In his careful analysis, Spoto individually explores each Hitchcock movie in great depth, exposing the layers of his genius. It's a must read for any admirer of Hitchcock.

Hitchcock found his suspense niche early on in his career, starting in silent movies in Great Britain and arriving in the United States in 1940. His long career of consistently colorful and entertaining movies has not been equaled by another director. The overall theme of his work exposes the dark side of human tension. His rare gift for both high art and commercial success at the box office rates him as one of the top audience and critic pleasers of all time. His name above the title consistently meant first rate excitement to moviegoers from the 1930s to the 70s.

There are plenty of good reasons why scholars study and write about Hitchcock. There is always more there than meets the eye in his movies, as one can vividly experience with **Rear Window**. In this particular outing, the "master of suspense" was at the height of his creative powers. Hitchcock frequently spoke of something he called the Macguffin in interviews. This was the term he devised for the element that propels the story along, but is not the central theme. If you concentrate on the Macguffin, which is usually the murder or plot, you'll miss the whole point. His ability to create several themes around a "Macguffin" is a favorite topic in film circles because of the suspense it carefully nurtures and maximizes.

In 1954's **Rear Window**, the audience is led to believe that the movie concerns a supposed murder. A lame photographer (James Stewart) with a vivid imagination and lots of free time believes one of his neighbors (Raymond Burr) has murdered his wife. He slowly pulls his beautiful girlfriend (Grace Kelly) and nurse (Thelma Ritter) into the cat-and-mouse suspense game. That's the Macguffin. While it propels the story, the real meat concerns the relationship between Stewart and Kelly. They are like Romeo and Juliet, two people in love with opposite backgrounds. She is chic, all Park Avenue, and quite the ornament. In fact, she was the archetypal cool blonde Hitchcock spent a lifetime searching for. Stewart, on the other hand, is earthy, resilient, and somewhat of an intellectual adventurer. He isn't afraid to get his hands dirty (or to break a leg) to capture incredible moments on film. The progression of the Stewart/Kelly relationship is interrupted by the Macguffin.

While recuperating from his most recent accident, Stewart spends his idle time watching the relationships evolve among his neighbors. His observations add to his anxiety, his inability to make a commitment to the woman he loves. He somehow believes that he may wind up like one of these poor unfortunate souls he views all day. These neighbors include a childless couple with a little dog, a frustrated songwriter, a nearly nude ballet dancer, an eccentric sculptress, Miss Lonelyhearts, and some hotblooded newlyweds.

But one couple in particular has caught his attention: the bickering pair (Burr and Irene Winston) directly across the courtyard. They represent the dark side of Stewart and Kelly. Winston is wealthy and Burr is a struggling salesman. They too appear to be a mismatch and their arrangement is awfully similar to what Stewart and Kelly are considering. Consequently, the idea of marrying someone on another social rung may be life threatening. Stewart is actually looking at his rear window—the window to his own private world.

The film's cast is superb. Stewart is the boyish, slightly asexual photojournalist (Hitchcock opted for Cary Grant when he needed someone with a bit of dash). His camera is his weapon and his prey is a car crash, fiery explosion, or murder. His profession searches for controversy. He even uses the flash attachment to ward off evil.

Kelly is breathtakingly beautiful and Stewart doesn't expect guts and determination could exist in the expensive attire. She demands term limits to their relationship, finally asking him "you don't think either one of us could change?" He says no, his lifestyle is not for her. But she turns out to be game and willing to risk her life just to gain his affection. Kelly is especially sexy when she pulls out a negligee from her *Mark Cross* overnight case and says "preview of coming attractions."

Ritter was classified as a supporting character actress, but her presence and style elevates her to an equal basis in the trio, at least in the audience's eyes. She tells it like it is or like it should be. Her views on relationships are rational, saying couples make things too complicated before considering a commitment. She also has some of the wittiest lines, especially her observations on the suspect's strange behavior. Noting his expression, she says his grimace isn't going to get him a quick loan at the bank.

Rear Window was sandwiched in between two of Hitchcock's lighter efforts—**Dial M For Murder** (1953) and **To Catch a Thief** (1955). All three starred Ms. Kelly, with the latter being filmed in Monaco, where she was introduced to Prince Rainier. A fairy tale marriage resulted and she retired from the industry, much to the chagrin of Hitchcock. He tried coaxing her back for **Marnie** in 1964, and she was interested, but the higher-up Monaco authorities frowned on the idea. Thus, she relinquished the role which went to Tippi Hedren. Kelly and her celebrity family were a favorite of star watchers and fan magazines for years. Tragically, her life ended in a stroke-induced car accident in 1982.

Stewart appeared in three Hitchcock movies: **The Man Who Knew Too Much** (1956) and what film purists believe to be Hitchcock's masterpiece, **Vertigo** (1958). Though he campaigned for the lead in **North By Northwest** (1959), Hitchcock instead chose Cary Grant. Hitchcock didn't try his hand at other genres, with one exception. A

Chapter 55

romantic comedy, **Mr. and Mrs. Smith** (1941) was made as a promise to another remarkable blonde, Carole Lombard. More versatile directors have offered imitations of his style. The best of the best copies have been John Huston's **The List of Adrian Messenger** (1963) and Stanley Donen's **Charade** (1963). When director Brian DePalma developed a series of successful low-budget suspense thrillers, it was hoped he would inherit Hitchcock's mantel. Unfortunately, he borrowed heavily from the master instead of bringing new ideas to the table.

Hitchcock's casting of Raymond Burr as the villain was said to be an inside joke: the actor greatly resembles David O. Selznik. Selznik had imported Hitchcock from England in 1940 and signed him to a seven year contract. His first assignment in Hollywood was to direct **Rebecca** (1940). Both producer and director were headstrong and frequently clashed over control. Hitchcock's last film in association with Selznick should have been **Notorious** (1946), but financially strapped Selznick sold the film, stars and director as a package to RKO Radio Pictures.

In 1998, a remake of **Rear Window** appeared as a television film. It marked a notable return to acting by Christopher Reeve, who hadn't been in front of a camera since a tragic riding accident in 1995 had left him in a wheelchair. This update had the main character paralyzed and living in a high-tech home filled with tools designed to assist the quadriplegic. He would rely on this equipment when the villain of the story came to his apartment for an unfriendly visit.

Several of Hitchcock's best efforts (including all of the Stewart films) were pulled from distribution and unavailable for public view while royalty provisions were deliberated in court. This issue was thankfully resolved after Hitchcock died in 1980. His art, especially **Rear Window**, has since been rediscovered by new generations of appreciative fans.

Cast

James Stewart	*L.B. "Jeff" Jeffries*
Grace Kelly	*Lisa Carol Fremont*

Wendell Corey	*Lieutenant Thomas J. Doyle*
Thelma Ritter	*Stella*
Raymond Burr	*Lars Thorwald*
Judith Evelyn	*Miss Lonelyheart*
Ross Bagdasarian	*Songwriter*
Georgine Darcy	*Miss Torso, the Ballet Dancer*
Sara Berner	*Woman on Fire Escape*
Frank Cady	*Man on Fire Escape*
Jesslyn Fax	*Miss Hearing Aid*
Rand Harper	*Newlywed Man*
Irene Winston	*Mrs. Anna Thorwald*
Havis Davenport	*Newlywed Woman*
Man in music room	*Alfred Hitchcock*

Production

Alfred Hitchcock	*Director*
John Michael Hayes, Cornell Woolrich (story)	*Writers*
Alfred Hitchcock	*Producer*
Robert Burks	*Cinematographer*
Franz Waxman	*Original Music*
Edith Head	*Costumes*
Paramount Pictures/Patron Inc.	*Production Company*
USA/112/1954	*Country/Runtime/Year Released*

Chapter 56
Reservoir Dogs

"All right ramblers, let's get rambling!"

—Joe Cabot

If movie fans want to be riveted to their seats, they should settle on the four controversial films released between 1992 and 1995 created in one way or another by Quentin Tarantino. They are seductive, hypnotic, intense, and offer new heights for tawdry violence and sex. For many, what appears on the screen may be uncomfortable to watch. But just try to look away. The core market pushing Tarantino into the forefront of popular movies during this time were males under 35. Many a young man could be found reciting Tarantino dialogue at local hangouts with their buddies. Soon, word of mouth eventually spread to girlfriends, sisters, and wives. This was enough activity to make Tarantino a household name—a hot commodity in Hollywood.

Tarantino's auspicious directing, writing, and co-starring debut was **Reservoir Dogs** (1992). He faithfully recreated in great detail the bitter aftertaste of a robbery gone wrong. His second film, the one that put the Cannes prize in his pocket, was the phenomenally successful **Pulp Fiction** (1995). Besides resurrecting John Travolta's career, it was another strong exercise in underworld nastiness.

Tarantino provided only the story for the other two movies: Tony Scott's **True Romance** (1993) featured young lovers on the run from dope dealers and Oliver Stone's **Natural Born Killers** (1995), a nightmare dream sequence on serial killers. With any of these films, the audience left the theatre numb and exhausted from over stimulation. In less than two hours, one experiences a lot of living.

Tarantino's living world includes people who talk stylishly vulgar, commit violent crimes among themselves, and involve innocent bystanders. Collectively, in all four excursions, you witness gut

300   *Chapter 56*

wrenching violence in great detail. From this quartet, there are at least two tortures that include burning the skin and slashing. There is a perverse male rape. A beautiful girl gets her face bashed in by a brutal thug in one of the most graphic David and Goliath conflicts on record. Another female snorts the wrong thing up her nose and has a terrible reaction. In yet another incredible situation, a thug is called in for his special service: To houseclean a murder scene.

While the plots are from the old shelf, these shocking events add a new luster to the underworld tales. The other half of the interest is the scintillating conversations we hear among these crooks. The dialogue offers layers and layers of characterization. One begins to wonder where they're going to take the conversation, what they plan to say next. When it gets real juicy, you expect the director to cut to the next scene because some things are supposed to be private. But that doesn't happen. They keep going, we are there, and our senses are burning.

Of the four mentioned movies, the most quotable dialogue comes from **Reservoir Dogs** by a paw. The movie's roots can be traced back to such classics as **The Asphalt Jungle** (1950), **The Killers** (1946), **Kansas City Confidential** (1952) and **The Anderson Tapes** (1972). It's the story of a bungled bank job in which a group of crooks, all with their specialties and dependence on each other, screw up. Then, all run for cover to recover from the fiasco. Of course they don't get very far, with the police at the doorstep and the conflicts among themselves. While **The Asphalt Jungle** and the other films mentioned place some emphasis on the plot, to obtain loot, escape, or settle a score, **Reservoir Dogs** doesn't even show the heist or the miscalculation. It's unique in that it rests squarely on the characterizations.

With this point of reference, the audience can truly experience the seedy side of life. They are introduced to humans who place no value on life. We are privy to their innermost thoughts and feelings. It's an unsafe place that we want to quickly visit and leave. The most interesting thread in the characterizations is loyalty and honor among thieves. Tim Roth and Harvey Keitel play informant cop and closet gay tough-guy, respectively. Their relationship is subtle,

Chapter 56

but when Keitel combs Roth's hair, you know there's more than just a friendship going on. Keitel can't see through the veneer because he's in love with Roth—an infatuation that principally unravels the project.

Roth's character is a variation of the gangster moll, the kept male companion who eventually goes to the police and squeals. Curiously, this update has no principal female roles. Loyalty also creates a snag for the gang boss. Big cheese Lawrence Tierney hires Michael Madsen because he kept his mouth shut and went to the slammer for him. This isn't a very good business decision since Madsen is slightly more wacky than the rest of the recruits. Tierney also hires his son (Chris Penn) and makes him vice-president of the operation. Again, hiring someone stupid because of a bloodline is not a good business decision. The loyalty among psychopaths lasts to the end until some vicious self-disclosures in a clever standoff. Then it's too late and all become victims of their own actions.

Tarantino's style is very tight. Characterizations and acting are excellent and each scene is crucial and pertinent. For example, there is a minor segment in which Tierney is speaking on the telephone to a peer. The thug on the other end is complaining that crime doesn't pay. If you didn't know they were crooks, one could almost imagine Tierney as a Chief Executive Officer mentoring one of his colleagues. There's also a touch of irony. If Tierney transferred his energy to something legitimate, he would probably be very successful. He knows how to create a marketing plan, how to research, and how to distribute. He's a little weak on personnel, but nobody's perfect. It's nice to see veteran Tierney in a good role. At 73, he had been in films since 1943, playing tough and ruthless characters in mainly grade Z fare.

Steve Buscemi is the obstinate troublemaker of the bunch. He asks the questions and makes the stupid remarks that start all of the arguments. He doesn't want to be Mr. Pink because the color isn't manly. He also doesn't tip waitresses. His remark in the diner sparks a very funny conversation about tipping. It's especially hilarious that these thieves tell each other in great detail to be honest with the people who make a living on tips. Buscemi also gets laughs when he constantly repeats how professional he is in a business not known for its professionalism.

There are other remarkable conversations that keep things exciting. Aging baby boomers will recognize old TV names like Honey West and Christie Love and Vicki Lawrence (yes, she was the one that shot Andy in *The Night The Lights Went Out in Georgia*). The sacred name of Lee Marvin is also raised. Marvin, at his bad guy peak, would have been delighted to give this bunch some lessons in destruction.

Other original touches Tarantino brought to the table include a soundtrack full of 70s hits with a narrative voice over by Steven Wright. Perhaps riding the resurgence in 70s music in the mid- 90s, Tarantino used it for humor and familiarity. The catchy tune *Little Green Bag* (it's not a bag of money) is a perfect credit opener.

The sequencing of events calls attention to itself. The frequent flashbacks may be jarring and confusing at first, but it all gels toward the midpoint of the film. The script doesn't alter time and distance like **Pulp Fiction**, but all the same, this distinct non-chronological approach makes an old story very fresh and exciting.

Tarantino cast himself in a minor role as one of the ill-fated thugs. Flexing his muscles, he also played a larger role in **Pulp Fiction**. However, by surrounding himself with strong talent and perfect characterizations, his limited acting experience becomes a bit obvious. His most prominent handicap is a lack of presence.

Tarantino was in his early thirties when he hit success with this quartet. In an interview he said his two favorite directors were Brian De Palma and Howard Hawks. They're interesting choices since Hawk's sequencing and editing rarely called attention to itself, while De Palma's is visually dazzling.

Tim Roth was not the first choice to play Mr. Orange. The part was originally offered to James Woods, but apparently his representation never brought him the offer. Woods said that omission prompted him to change agents.

The most eloquent compliment an artist can receive is when he

Chapter 56

or she becomes a benchmark of quality. During the O.J. Simpson murder trial in the summer of '95, screenwriter Laura Hart McKinny was subpoenaed with great fanfare to offer testimony for the defense on her work titled *Men Against Women.* She was an important witness for the defense because her technical source for the screenplay was Mark Fuhrman, the detective who found much of the damaging evidence against Simpson. *Newsweek* reviewed the product of their collaboration. Their fair judgment: Ms. McKinny was no Quentin Tarantino.

Tarantino's genius continues to keep audiences on the edge of their seat. **Kill Bill Vol. 1** (2003) explored a terribly wrong marriage between two partners skilled in martial arts. **Kill Bill Vol.2** (2004) was eagerly anticipated to see how they worked out their differences without an attorney.

Death Proof (2007) offered high-octane stimulation. It featured Kurt Russell as a serial killer who uses his beefed-up car to murder his victims. His black Dodge Charger purposely resembled the car Steve McQueen chased through the streets of San Francisco with his Mustang in **Bullitt** (1968)—the granddaddy of all great car chase films.

Inglourious Basterds (2008) was a very popular fictional story set in Nazi Germany during World War II about political assassinations. **Django Unchained** (2012) was a revisionist Western set in 1858 Mississippi. Actor Christopher Waltz had featured roles in both films and his performances won the best supporting actor academy award. **Django Unchained** received raves and became Tarantino's top moneymaker of his career, thus far.

Cast

Harvey Keitel	*Mr. White/Larry*
Tim Roth	*Mr. Orange/Freddy*
Michael Madsen	*Mr. Blonde/Vic*
Chris Penn	*Nice Guy Eddie*
Steve Buscemi	*Mr. Pink*
Lawrence Tierney	*Joe Cabot*

Randy Brooks	*Holdaway*
Kirk Baltz	*Marvin Nash*
Edward Bunker	*Mr. Blue*
Quentin Tarantino	*Mr. Brown*
Rich Turner	*Sheriff #1*
David Steen	*Sheriff #2*
Tony Cosmo	*Sheriff #3*
Stevo Polyi	*Sheriff #4*
Michael Sottile	*Teddy*

Production

Quentin Tarantino	*Director*
Quentin Tarantino, Roger Avary (radio dialogue)	*Writers*
Lawrence Bender	*Producer*
Andrzej Sekula	*Cinematographer*
Dog Eat Dog Productions/Live Entertainment	*Production Company*
USA/99/1992	*Country/Runtime/Year Released*

Chapter 57

Robinson Crusoe on Mars

"A-Okay."

—Kit Draper

Robinson Crusoe on Mars initially took the same bumpy road usually reserved for awful movies. It arrived with little fanfare, parked in empty drive-ins, and then quietly disappeared. A failure for the studio in 1964, many people, including star Paul Mantee, agree that its title killed audience interest. They may have a good point. Perhaps the adults stayed away because they thought it was a film for children. And the kids who saw it were either bored by the adult circumstances, giggling when Mr. Mantee jumped nude into a small pond, or too young to understand man's aversion to loneliness. It was too bad the film died a fast death. It deserved more attention than it got.

Mantee, in his first starring role, revealed in bits and pieces that he had the acting gift. Perhaps its lack of success doomed Mantee's star aspirations. However, unlike truly horribly movies, the film continues to live on television and home video through a small, loyal, and appreciative audience.

When the film's VHS/DVD/Laserdisc was on moratorium, admirers of the film could pay up to $200 for a bootleg copy. Apparently a small faction of baby boomers and science fiction aficionados were willing to pay a premium to view a film that probably only returned a minute portion of its costs when first released.

As the title implies, the film reworks Robinson Crusoe, and came about while the United States was exploring space. These were exciting times for the American public, especially when President John F. Kennedy declared that a man would be walking on the moon by the end of the decade. It seemed natural to update Daniel Defoe's classic story into something current.

Apart from the title, Crusoe's name comes up as the story progresses, especially when a sidekick for the hero, Kit Draper, comes along and is named Friday, in honor of Mr. Crusoe. Like the Dafoe novel, it is all about surviving, meeting one's basic needs for food, shelter, and air. As for the latter need, since the film takes place on Mars, oxygen is the greatest physical challenge for our hero. More importantly the film deals with man's need for companionship. An aspect of loneliness is deeply explored here. For example, when Draper comes upon his crashed spaceship, he runs across the desert patch thinking his Captain (Adam West) may have survived the impact. When he finds the worst, you can feel his pain and great disappointment. Small solace exists in Mona the Wooley Monkey, but that is a poor substitute for human warmth. Later there is a glimmer of hope when he meets one of the slave natives. Still, the man he calls Friday is only a mirror of himself since he doesn't communicate on the same level as Kit.

This frustration of being unable to communicate with another human being is set appropriately against some of the most beautiful and stark examples of solitude in the United States. The background was Death Valley and the camera shots are breathtakingly glorious. Visitors to this national park will recognize the volcano pit and other formations that offer no haven for life, but become remarkable landscapes. In this case, they offer a good substitution for what one may imagine Mars to look like—and without the benefit of what we presently see for real on the planet today through our space exploration program. The special effects are creative for 1964 standards, but of course cannot hold a candle to what is available now with computer assisted graphics.

The script further gets away from the children's motif by discussing religion and having spiritual overtones. The rings around the wrists are symbolic of a union, and once they are removed, one becomes liberated. It's also interesting that Kit's real name is Christopher, thus alluding to the Christopher Columbus aspect of discovering a new world.

Paul Mantee said he was picked for the role because of his physical

Chapter 57   *307*

resemblance to astronaut Alan Shepard, one of the most famous men in America at the time. He said the producers instinctively liked him and getting the part was his lucky break.

You can see several things emerge as you watch his 'Kit' Draper. His buff appearance and accent does not betray his fiery Italian heritage. At times he is explosive and angry, one who wants it his way. While he is tough, he is not without compassion. During this particular part of his journey, he is forced to learn to trust and help others in his desperation for companionship. He also performs this difficult task with someone who comes into his life from an entirely difficult planet. As the movie progresses, his original boldness softens as he develops a friendship. It's unfortunate that Mantee didn't find a solid place in the Hollywood hierarchy. He shows a certain degree of skill and aptitude in a complex part. But it wasn't enough. Mantee's only other starring role in a theatrical film was a low budget spy film, **A Man Called Dagger** (1968). His character's full name was Dick Dagger. The project had been filmed in 1966. It struggled to find a distributor and died the death of all bad films.

When offers did not come his way, Mantee started to teach acting in the mid-60s. He also carved out his niche in small roles and on TV. He was a member of the Police Department with the hit television series *Cagney and Lacey* (1983-1988). He played Poppy on *Seinfeld* (1989-1998) in the episode entitled *The Pie* (1994). He was Poppy the fiery Italian pizza maker who failed to wash his hands before preparing Jerry's meal. It was one of the more memorable performances in this very popular and long-running series.

Mantee also became a successful author in the 1980s—penning *In Search of the Perfect Raviloi* and *Bruno in Hollywood*. Both books reveal his sharp wit and intelligence. It was also interesting to find him cast (with only one line) in Ron Howard's **Apollo 13** (1995), another movie focusing on the hazards of space travel.

In contrast to Mantee, Victor Lundin approaches his role as if Friday just came out of a coma, adding little to the energy of the film. Lundin later wrote and performed songs about his stint in this film.

Like the movie, the applause was limited to those who find this film fascinating.

Adam West auditioned for the lead role in this film, and had very little to do, apart from the opening and dream sequence. However, he went on to another piece of make-believe a year later that would make him world renowned (and very popular with children) on television as *Batman.*

The producers were optimistic and assumed their unique and creative film would find an audience. A sequel entitled **Robinson Crusoe in the Invisible Galaxy** had been planned but wasn't launched due to poor box office returns.

A few years after this film disappeared from memory, Dick Van Dyke appeared in another reworking of the Defoe classic, appropriately entitled **Lt. Robin Crusoe, U.S.N.** (1966). It was in direct contrast to **Robinson Crusoe on Mars**. Van Dyke played a Navy man stranded on a paradise island after a plane crash. Since there were women on the island, the problems he had were very pleasant, funny, and in direct contrast to Kit Draper.

Cast

Paul Mantee	*Cmdr. Christopher 'Kit' Draper*
Victor Lundin	*Friday*
Adam West	*Col. Dan McReady*
Mona	*The Wooley Monkey*

Production

Byron Haskin	*Director*
Daniel Defoe (novel), John C. Higgins,	*Writers*
Ib Melchior	
Aubrey Schenck, Edwin F. Zabel	*Producers*
Van Cleave	*Original Music*
Winton C. Hoch	*Cinematography*
Devonshire/Paramount Pictures	*Production Company*
USA/110/1964	*Country/Runtime/Year Released*

Chapter 57

Chapter 58

Roger & Me

"Well, the million tourists never came to Flint."
—Michael Moore

The effects of World War II left the entire industrialized world devastated, except for the United States. The U.S. was one of the few countries involved in the conflict that wasn't bombed or invaded on its own turf. Thus, in the post-war climate, the United States was in position to produce in great quantities what was needed during this transition to peace.

It performed this task because it was the right thing to do and because it restored a sense of order to the world.

There was a drawback to this generosity. By offering funding to rebuild the bombed out factories of war torn Europe, these factories became more modern and more efficient than United States facilities, which had no infusion of cash to move towards greater efficiency. By the end of the 50s the world had recovered from the horrors of war, at least physically. In fact, Western Germany and Japan were doing quite well and were building some of the best products available in the world. Many of these products found their way to the garages of the American consumer. This created several alarming situations for the American automobile industry. Up until that time, almost everything on the American road was sold by the big three U.S. automakers—General Motors, Ford, and Chrysler.

The 1973 and 1979 oil crisis and recessions played havoc on the American automobile industry. Almost overnight, there was a demand for small, fuel efficient automobiles, a product not readily found in American car dealer showrooms. Japanese cars like Toyota, Honda, and Datsun, and the German Volkswagen, offered quality and fuel efficiency and gained a significant foothold in the U.S.

market. In 2008 there were three United States automotive manufacturers. In contrast, just after World War II, there had been over a dozen U.S. makes to choose from.

This slow erosion of market share sent pink slips to thousands of American workers who couldn't easily transfer their work skills into a comparable paying job. This illusion of a secure job was entirely in their heads, as producer, writer, and director Michael Moore captures in his **Roger & Me**. His documentary blends dark humor and tragedy against the backdrop of harsh economic realities.

Moore's work specifically documents GM's economic problems in the late 70s. Changing marketplace conditions forced the world's largest industrial facility to close eleven of its auto manufacturing plants and lay off 40,000 workers in Flint, Michigan. Poor Flint became one of the most economically depressed communities in the nation. The aftershocks of a major employee layoff to this blue-collar community were devastating. Moore offers personal details and the ripple effect this massive job loss had on the people living in a once thriving Midwest City.

Roger in the title is Roger Smith, the Chairman of GM from 1981 to 1990. He was the man in charge during the closings and the one Moore goes fishing for.

Moore is fairly straightforward with what he wants to accomplish with his documentary. His desire is to get a personal statement from someone in the executive suite whose decisions have adversely affected the entire community. To nobody's surprise, Roger Smith proves very elusive. We never hear his thoughts on the increased crime, suicide, depression, bankruptcies and other social ailments that occur when people lose their jobs and paychecks.

Moore has an interesting perspective on the situation. He paints the despair to the bleakest point and then stands back, as if to let us take it all in and absorb the horror. Then we get another education in human relations. We are privy to the local reactions and solutions to the despair. These reports range from ill advice to bizarre.

We see families evicted from their homes. These visuals would break anyone's heart. You see the up close face of a confused child

Chapter 58   *311*

when the partially decorated Christmas tree is hastily thrown into the open bed of a pickup truck. Perhaps the equivalent to the masked executioner, a big guy in a trench coat named Rick does this dirty work and he doesn't have a shortage of clients. Employed by the Sheriff's department, he has the most secure job in Flint, and one of the hardest.

Apart from not paying the mortgage or rent, people also stop eating out, shopping, and bowling. Moore manipulates these situations. He plays with our emotions. We witness lots of gloom and doom, but he knows when to back off. He includes carefully spaced hilarious bits giving off a strange mix of black humor and irony. You feel the pain of these people, and the pain is alleviated by a batch of personalities bussed in and paid to provide advice to the demoralized citizens.

There is an unflattering portrait of Pat Boone, who calls Roger Smith a "can do kind of guy." Yet the actor or singer, once a spokesman for Chevrolet, cannot ever remember meeting Smith. TV's *Newlywed Game* host Bob Eubanks doesn't fare any better when his ethnic slurs are videotaped. He later said his remarks were supposed to be off the record. Then there's Anita Bryant, who knows what it's like to be in the middle of controversy. She tries to be sunny and optimistic but finally throws in the towel after talking a few minutes of corn. She candidly admits to the world "I don't know," admitting frankly that there are no easy answers to this problem. Moore paints a colorful portrait of the people who live in Flint. He interviews the well-to-do retired folks who are sipping champagne on the lawn or freely swinging golf clubs at their exclusive Country Club. They fail to understand that good jobs are hard to come by for those without the benefits of education, old money, family connections, and favors.

One of the most telling interviews occurs with Kay Lani Rae Rafko, then Miss Michigan. She parades down a dirty main street in downtown Flint in a convertible, on her way to the 1988 Miss America Pageant. Moore asks her if there is anything cheerful she could say to these folks. Without flinching, she smoothly tells them to keep their fingers crossed and wish that she wins the crown in the upcoming competition.

Other insights from Moore reveal a town in the middle of a meltdown. To survive, people are willing to try anything, from selling rabbits (as meat or pets), performing color analysis, or promoting Amway products. Others become prison guards or sandwich artists at fast food restaurants. Of course, none of these ideas point to a sustaining career or profession. The most incredible idea to revive the economy comes from local government. They decide to promote the city as a tourism hotspot. The campaign fails, of course, but not before encouraging both laughter and tears.

Moore is frequently on camera. Heavy set and imposing, he wears a cap that announces on the front "I'm out for a big trout." It's a great metaphor for what he really wants to do. While trying to interview the big boss, he browbeats public relations folks and security guards on GM grounds and in the executive hideout. You can see the staff's fear when he approaches them. Even the most routine question makes them very nervous. The answers they provide are shocking and an embarrassment to the profession of public relations.

Moore has a personal connection to the story. His father and other close relatives worked for GM in Flint during the heady years. Ironically, the city happened to be the birthplace of the United Auto Workers. Moore said he grew up with many of the autoworkers who lost their jobs and livelihoods. His story reveals the importance he attaches to their lives. To finance this very personal project, he sold his house and most of his belongings. He even resorted to Tuesday night bingo parties to raise the capital necessary to complete the film.

Roger & Me became a widespread commercial success and won a clutch of awards. Critics and audiences loved its fresh, original, and unflinching view of the state of things in Flint. Its release during a recession year was also a plus. Audiences across the nation, fearing for the worst, felt a kinship with the people in Flint. Stay tuned for the closing credits. Moore's final observation is a real zinger.

The film's success encouraged Moore to film a short sequel in 1992: **Pets or Meat: The Return to Flint**. It zeroed in on one of the film's most notorious characters, the woman who incredulously sold rabbits as either friend or food. He also developed a similar style of

Chapter 58

journalism for the small screen with *TV Nation*, a summer replacement series in 1994.

More importantly, in 2002, **Bowling for Columbine** was another Moore triumph. The title refers to the 1999 tragedy at Columbine High School when two students shot and killed 12 classmates, a teacher, and themselves. Once again his unique skill and style brought depth to the subject of gun control. This film brought him an academy award for best documentary. In accepting the Oscar, he used the podium to criticize U.S. aggression in Iraq. His piercing remarks continue to spark both controversy and admiration. They were especially evident in **Fahrenheit 9/11** (2004), a film heavily critical of the Bush Administration's response to the September 11, 2001 disaster, and **Sicko** (2007) an exposé on medical insurance practices not healthy for those fortunate to have some type of health insurance.

Roger Smith left GM with a multi-million dollar golden parachute, much to the chagrin of the stockholders. Under new leadership and during the go-go 90s, GM's profits once again swelled. However, the 2001- 2002 recession reversed this trend. In 2009, GM (along with Chrysler) went into bankrupcy protection and began receiving government assistance to survive in what was the deepest economic downturn since the Great Depression. The Pontiac, Hummer, Oldsmobile and Saturn Divisions were jettisoned. GM's new leadership apologized for market miscalculations and shoddy products, and promised to deliver a new kind of corporation.

GM did return to profitability in late 2010 as a much leaner version of its former self. It remains to be seen if a resurgence of Detroit based automobile manufacturers can lift the city from economic crisis. In 2013, Motor City became the largest municipal bankruptcy filing in U.S. history by debt, estimated at $18-$20 billion.

Cast

James Bond	*Himself*
Pat Boone	*Himself*
Rhonda Britton	*Herself (Pets or Meat)*
Anita Bryant	*Herself*

Karen Edgely	*Herself*
Bob Eubanks	*Himself*
Ben Hamper	*Himself*
Dinona Jackson	*Herself*
Timothy Jackson	*Himself*
Tom Kay	*Himself*
Michael Moore	*Himself*
Kaye Lani Rae Rafko	*Herself (Miss America)*
Ronald Reagan	*Himself*
Fred Ross	*Himself (Eviction Deputy)*
Richard Earl	*Himself (Spot Welder)*
Robert Schuller	*Himself*
George Sells	*Local TV news anchor*
Roger B. Smith	*Himself*
Steve Wilson	*Himself*

Production

Michael Moore	*Director*
Michael Moore	*Writer*
Michael Moore, Wendy Stanzler	*Producer*
Chris Beaver, John Prusak, Kevin Rafferty, Bruce Schermer	*Cinematographers*
Dog Eat Dog Films/Warner Brothers	*Production Company*
USA/91/1989	*Country/Runtime/Year Released*

Chapter 59

Ruthless People

"I've been kidnapped by Kmart."

—Barbara Stone

Bette Midler is loud, brassy, and has big boobs. With good material, she can make one believe she is a beautiful diva. One of her early career successes was as a recording star, unearthing old chestnuts like The Andrew Sisters' *Boogie Woogie Bugle Boy* before reviving a musical past became fashionable. Later, on award and talk shows, she revealed an intelligent gift for witty, provocative observations. It was only a matter of time before her unique personality carried her to success in the movies.

Her first effort was tailor made. **The Rose** (1979) detailed the rise and fall of a Janis Joplin like singer. The fictional character she created had withering lows and high highs, plus some delicious self-disclosures. Though the movie has not aged well, the performance brought her recognition, popularity, and an Academy Award nomination. She didn't win the Oscar, and in 1980, as a presenter, she trashed the Academy for laughs. It was the wittiest remark of the evening.

Then her flame went out after some major conflicts with stars and directors. After a couple of losers, the producers at Disney's new Touchstone Studios hired her and softened the edges a bit. She was no longer slightly trashy or tarnished. She was mature, sensible, with a wacky sense of fun.

Her brightest effort for Disney was **Ruthless People** (1986). This film had an ensemble cast of talented people—all with equal screen time. However, she dominates the activities just by entering the room. It's a very funny film for two reasons: 1) she's in it and 2) she's allowed to do her thing. Jim Abrahams, David Zucker and Jerry Zucker were the brains behind this movie. It contained a variation of their special blend of comedy, as evidenced by their earlier successes, **Airplane** (1980) and **Naked Gun: From the Files of Police Squad!** (1985). Unlike these, however, **Ruthless People** wasn't unreal or incongruous. Its premise centers around people who lie, cheat, steal, attempt murder, blackmail, double-cross, kidnap, and all the other unsavory things ruthless people can conjure up. There's a broad atmosphere of silliness, though, and nobody really gets hurt unless they truly deserve it.

Midler plays wife to Danny DeVito. On the surface, they appear to be a perfect match. They are two angry people who have found each other. He married for her parents' money, but her folks didn't die until 15 years into their marriage. He's been with her for 15 years and she's a prima donna with an attitude.

The two nice people DeVito stomped on during his journey to riches were Judge Reinhold and Helen Shaver. Reinhold and Shaver are Ken and Sandy and they are about as nice as their names. They aren't doing well financially and blame DeVito for their misfortune. Seeking revenge, they kidnap Midler and demand a ransom from DeVito. However, in a variation of the classic story *Ranson of Red Chief,* DeVito is delighted to hear that his wife has been kidnapped.

This fun gains momentum when DeVito refuses to pay the ransom. He wants her murdered so he can shack up with his honey, the delectable Anita Morris. However, Morris has her own set of ideas. She and her dumb-blond boyfriend (a clever gender reversal) plan to double cross DeVito. Through sheer bad luck and coincidence, their plan involves the Police Chief—which keeps the game rolling. The direction and writing provide layers and layers of surprises. For example, take time to view the landmarks around Los Angeles used as backdrops. Pay particular attention to the hot dog stand where Reinhold makes a ransom phone call to DeVito. That hot dog is what you think it is. Later on in the movie, watch the background shot at Devito's mansion. You will see a policeman playing tennis on the grounds.

DeVito is perfect as the unscrupulous weasel. He's obnoxious and

Chapter 59   *317*

vulgar. It's obvious what's necessary for him to keep a girlfriend's interest: buy her expensive gifts. His short, tubby frame is used to good comic effect; even down to sitting in one of those horrible looking chairs in his outrageous Bel Air home. He also has some of the nastiest lines. "I love wrong numbers" will never be the same. He also sets the comic tone in the opening sequence, admitting that he "married his wife befause she was very, very rich and her wealthy father was very, very sick."

Reinhold and Slater are more like Ken and Barbie than Ken and Sandy. Likable and sensitive, Slater worries whether Midler will like them. Reinhold's aptitude as a kidnapper is very weak, especially when up against De Vito, who is used to calling the shots. The pleading calls and misguided chloroform are highlights from this pair.

Despite everyone's extreme competence in creating a funny situation, it's Midler's show all the way. She has more than her share of golden moments. The unloved look on her face when she realizes her husband has refused to pay the ransom is a real hoot. Let's not forget the failed escape from her kidnappers when she uses a hand-held kitchen mixer as a weapon. Finally, her devilish conversation with Ken and Sandy when they revise their demands is worth the price of popcorn.

Midler's character grows in this film. In publicity surrounding the movie, Midler said she could relate to her character, who loses 20 pounds during her captivity, gets a new wardrobe, and a new outlook on life. It's not unlike what this film did for Midler's career. Today, Midler's mid-career thrives on TV and in movies. As befits a big star, her vulgar lounge act has been long been diluted for the family. While she has lost some of the zing that made her well known, her appeal to mainstream audiences is unassailable. Her rendition of *One for My Baby* to Johnny Carson on his final *Tonight Show* (1962-1992) was especially poignant.

Anita Morris was probably more famous on Broadway in *Cats* for her acrobatic animal dance than in movies. She decorated a handful of films, mostly forgettable. She also turned down an offer from *Playboy* to pose nude. Fortunately, she was allowed a brief opportunity to shine in this class film. A native of Durham, North Carolina, her voice, gentle manner, and beauty would have placed her in the category "most desirable older woman you'd like to be stuck with on a deserted island." Sadly, she died of cancer at 50 in 1993.

The soundtrack adds to the spirited proceedings. Mick Jagger breathes the title track, and Billy Joel's *Modern Woman* is an inspiration for someone desiring to reinvent their life.

Writer Dale Launer said he was more inspired by the kidnapping of heiress Patricia Hearst than *The Ransom of Red Chief*.

Cast

Danny DeVito	*Sam Stone*
Bette Midler	*Barbara Stone*
Judge Reinhold	*Ken Kessler*
Helen Slater	*Sandy Kessler*
Anita Morris	*Carol Dodsworth*
Bill Pullman	*Earl Mott*
William G. Schilling	*Police Commissioner Benton*

Production

Jim Abrahams, David Zucker, Jerry Zucker	*Directors*
O. Henry (The Ranson of Red Chief), Dale Launer	*Writers*
Michael Peyser	*Producer*
Michel Colombier	*Original Music*
Jan de Bont	*Cinematography*
Touchstone Pictures	*Production Company*
USA/93/1986	*Country/Runtime/Year Released*

Chapter 59

Chapter 60
The Silencers

"Why am I here? A guy could get killed doing this."
—Matt Helm

The overwhelming success of **Austin Powers** (1997), a wacky series of films starring a British hipster who dabbles in the spy business, renews interest in the four theatrical films made in the swinging 60s that starred Dean Martin as secret agent Matt Helm. Both Austin and Matt spoof James Bond but with major differences in approach. Mr. Helm really turned on the girls, and he was extremely competent in the field of espionage. Mr. Powers has a 21st century point of view and looks back fondly to the good old days. His egocentric attitude has him believing that he's attractive to women, and that he's the world's greatest spy. We know he's not. He's just very lucky, and that's why we're laughing.

Produced during the height of the spy movie craze (thanks to James Bond), the films with Dean Martin are mainly of interest to males since they represent the ultimate male fantasy. Mr. Helm is what young males aspire to be when they grow up. He is the super cool dude with great looks and style. That means he has access to an endless supply of gorgeous girls. His profession affords him excitement, the excuse to carry a weapon, trips to exotic locations, and a generous paycheck. And when he does work, it's independent of any supervision (he frequently tells his boss "I ain't going."). He's also supplied with the best wheels of the day, and these big, masculine machines are often fully equipped with a bed and wet bar. His pad has all the creature comforts needed by a hot blooded bachelor, and more if you like a round bed that can plop you into a pool. And by the last reel, he has become a national hero, having saved the world from some crazed maniac. This is the perfect male fantasy. Fortunately most males outgrow this dream fairly quickly. They get an 8 to 5 job, marry, have kids, and hope all turns out well. This sexual fantasy may return briefly with the onset of middle age, but that's beyond the scope of this book.

Perhaps the most appealing aspect of Matt Helm's persona to men is the absence of responsibilities. He has nobody to look after except himself. He doesn't even have a dog. Most young males avoid commitment like the plague. Only maturity allows them to experience the joy of family and a permanent union with someone that can be counted on. But to a young man not far from puberty, Helm lives the perfect life. Alas, it's one that could only be written in a book or screenplay.

The Helm movies were made from 1966 to 1969. They came in when the spy craze was in full bloom and ended when the fad was coming to a close. There's more appeal to these films, though, than creating a male utopia. They are consistently fun with a harmless tongue-in-cheek style, look, and texture. Martin's professional image as a mass consumer of wine, women and song supplies most of the fun. If **The Spy Who Came in From the Cold** (1966) is a stark and realistic version of espionage, then Matt Helm is at the opposite end of the playing field. Even James Bond has to be serious at some point between his witty appraisals of the situation. But not Matt Helm. He always looks surprised, a bit tipsy, and angry that he's involved in a mess that distracts him from his enjoyable pursuits. He would rather be taking pictures of pretty girls for his calendar than fighting a villain. Thanks to the easy going charm of Martin, the results are always watchable.

The first film in the series, **The Silencers**, is the best, by a couple of inches. It's popularity placed Martin, for the first time, in the magic boxoffice ten in 1966. Its success ensured the series would continue: **Murderer's Row** (1967), **The Ambushers** (1968), and **The Wrecking Crew** (1969) were the other three entries.

While Martin was listed by exhibitors for his box-office might, voluptuous Stella Stevens should also receive some of the credit for the film's large-scale success. Besides being great to look at, the two of

Chapter 60

321

them—Martin and Stevens—offer great sexual chemistry. Their fight scenes are a comic highlight: At one point, Martin gets her intoxicated in an attempt to obtain top-secret information. She eventually tells him sarcastically: "I can't tell you anything because I signed my name in blood."

Victor Buono is splendid as the prissy villain. When things don't go his way, his psychopathic hissy fit is fun. Like most good villains, his pompous manner has everyone angry in just a few moments. We're all delighted to see him get it rather bluntly in the end.

The rest of the cast is first rate. James Gregory is Mac—Helm's boss. He's able to handle Helm's boyish tantrums with the right amount of benign authority. His approach to his ace spy is always straight. When he argues with Helm that he must "off" himself if caught by the enemy, he simply says "they can brainwash a vacuum cleaner." Also worth seeing is Beverly Adams. Like Stevens, she's a must for bosom watchers. It is interesting to note that she later became rich and famous as Beverly Sasoon.

Many of her fine hair care products are runner up gifts to losing contestants on game shows. Her movie career was brief and almost solely confined to these films. In this series, she goes by the name of Lovey Kravesit, the "more than a secretary" to Mr. Helm. Along the lines of Bond's Miss Moneypenny, she is a bit obvious in her willingness to please her favorite spy. Gregory and Adams appeared with Martin in three of the four films. Gregory said he declined to appear in **The Wrecking Crew** when producers refused to pay him his usual fee.

Cyd Charisse is the most pleasant surprise in the film. At 45 and long retired from MGM's fabulous musicals, she does two bits of dance and nothing else. This is all too brief an appearance, but her entrance does make an impact. Her first number is a slow sexy tease during the opening credits. The second has her wearing something that makes her appear nude. It's a skin colored leotard, punctuated with dots in strategic locations. Charisse and choreographer Robert Sidney appear to have lifted the latter dance from their MGM past: It's very similar to the routine in **Party Girl** (1958), the film which concluded Charisse's MGM contract. In style and appeal, she really has no dancing peer.

Similarities exist in all four films, and what they have in common can be found in almost all spy flicks from this era. Each movie has a villain intent on dominating the world. There is always an American girl involved, usually competing with an import for Mr. Helm's affections. Naturally, the American girls have their way in the end. The title tunes are catchy, and the weapon gadgets are ridiculously clever.

Frank Sinatra, one of Martin's pals, gets some friendly ribbing in each outing. Martin may take a swipe at Sinatra's singing or a bomb may blow up Ole Blue Eyes on a billboard. Sinatra returned a few jests at Martin in some of his films around the same time. The spars are more interesting than funny.

With the death of Sinatra and Martin, and with several made-for-cable films on The Rat Pack, interest returned to this group of revelers who turned on Las Vegas for a couple of years with their antics. If one isn't familiar with the popularity these fellows commanded at the time, then their fun seems forced and dated.

Sex also gets a work-out, almost to the point of exhaustion. Again, it will appeal to male fantasies. The most interesting example is the name of the spy network Helm faces in each film. They call themselves Big O. One does not need three guesses to determine what Big O stands for.

On a related subject, all four films provided jobs for some of the most beautiful and sexy women in 60s films. Senta Berger, Ann-Margret, Janice Rule, Elke Sommer, Nancy Kwan, Dahliah Lavi, Camilla Sparv, Tina Louise, and Sharon Tate were some of the names involved. Other females on hand simply went under a category titled "slaygirls," much to the chagrin of feminists, who were just beginning to come into their own.

The female critics do have some justification. Perhaps correcting this disparity when James Bond got a new generation of younger actors to continue the series, head boss "M" was portrayed by British actress Dame Judi Dench. Senta Berger, who played a sensuous spy in **The Ambushers,** spoke on women's roles in movies in 1987. Berger,

Chapter 60

then under contract at Universal, said she burst into tears when told by her employer that she had the role of Francesca. Berger said she was serious about her career and didn't want to portray another sexy spy. When she made her goals pretty clear to her employer (Universal), they said she was ungrateful. After that, she uprooted herself and pursued her career in Europe, where it continues today. The other three Matt Helm films with Martin offer additional fun in the same mold. **Murderer's Row** featured a kaleidoscopic dance sequence by Ann-Margret, a chrome dome villain, and Karl Malden. The pop singing group *Dino, Desi, and Billy* also sang a couple of songs. Dino was Dean's son and he gets to poke fun at his old man in the disco.

Besides Ms. Berger, **The Ambushers** boasted Janice Rule, an arty fight scene inside a beer factory, Oleg Cassini fashions, an insanely funny firing squad, and a device that could unzip clothing.

If **The Wrecking Crew** was an attempt to return to earlier form (Director Phil Karlson was brought back), seeing Sharon Tate in her final film appearance before her brutal and senseless murder puts a downer on the entire project. Also of interest in this last entry: technical supervisor for the karate scenes was Bruce Lee.

The closing credits for **Wrecking Crew** announced that a fifth Matt Helm film, The **Ravagers** was in the works. The project was cancelled due to Martin's disinterest and the declining box office.

The Matt Helm character was created from a series of books by Donald Hamilton. In the 70s, when private eyes were in demand on television (*The Rockford Files, Barnaby Jones, Cannon*, etc.), Mr. Helm was resurrected as a TV movie and series with Tony Franciosa. It was more true to the books, but Tony could not erase the earlier image created by Dino. Lack of viewer interest cancelled the project very quickly.

Curiously, around this same time, Stella Stevens appeared with Martin's ex-partner Jerry Lewis in what Lewis fans consider to be his masterpiece, **The Nutty Professor** (1964). Martin and Lewis had split some ten years before and their parting was not an amicable one. **The Nutty Professor** has Lewis play two types: a slick womanizer and a nerd. The slick half may be based on Martin's actual personality. Martin and Stevens were reunited in 1968 for the agreeable **How to Save Your Marriage (and Ruin Your Life)**.

Stevens' has been content to work in subsidiary roles in a career that spans five decades. Sam Peckinpah's **The Ballad of Cable Hogue** (1970) offered her a rare opportunity to work with a quality director in a good film. Her most commercially profitable film was **The Poseidan Adventure** (1972). In both films she played prostitutes.

Cast

Dean Martin	*Matt Helm*
Stella Stevens	*Gail Hendrix*
Daliah Lavi	*Tina*
Victor Buono	*Tung-Tze*
Arthur O'Connell	*Joe Wigman*
Robert Webber	*Sam Gunther*
James Gregory	*MacDonald*
Nancy Kovack	*Barbara*
Roger C. Carmel	*Andreyev*
Cyd Charisse	*Sarita*
Beverly Adams	*Lovey Kravezit*

Production

Phil Karlson	*Director*
Donald Hamilton (novel), Oscar Saul	*Writers*
Irwin Allen, James Schmerer	*Producers*
Burnett Guffey	*Cinematographer*
Elmer Bernstein	*Music*
Moss Mabry	*Costumes*
Claude Productions/Meadway	*Production Company*
USA/102/1966	*Country/Runtime/Year Released*

Chapter 60

Chapter 61
Slap Shot

"I got a good deal on those boys. The scout said they showed a lot of promise."
—*Joe McGrath*

When first released in 1977, many critics evaluated **Slap Shot** as a voyeuristic look at a struggling fifth rate hockey team. The buzz created by the film wasn't centered on the story, star, or direction. It was on the dialogue. Traditional moviegoers and hardcore Paul Newman fans found it rather shocking to hear some of the bluest language found in an "A" budget production, by a star consistently on the "A" list. Many thought Mr. Newman had pushed the wrong button.

Going beyond the vulgarity, **Slap Shot** is a compelling character study of male athletes (and their wives) whose lives are centered around their occupation. It is also a perceptive outline of industrial decline, specifically the post oil embargo recession and the devastating effect the economic downturn had on working class America. Though less true today, hockey once had a strong appeal to men who earn a living with their muscles and hands. Consequently, when there is an economic downturn for employment in the trades and other blue-collar occupations, the same decline occurs in the sport they can no longer support.

In this film, we are offered a picture of the rust belt, that area of the country that witnessed the expiration of industries relating to the production of automobiles. This sent shock waves through various communities as the employment sector increasingly tilted toward a service industry in the mid 70s. In this example, the town's main employer, a steel mill, is closing its doors. Hundreds of people are being thrown out of work. This upheaval threatens the lifeblood of the community, which includes this beloved hockey team.

326   *Chapter 61*

Slap Shot is also a good examination of sports politics, public relations, and corporate tax write-offs—all of which affect the bottom-line score. We're offered a contrast between the men who play the sport and the people who make a corporation out of it and worry about the profit margin. This isn't really going to surprise us. Like other movies depicting the cruel underbelly of sports, hockey has its share of takers and givers. Our sports heroes, besides talking dirty, are manipulated into violence and outrageous behavior just to keep playing the sport they love. While we may laugh at their antics, there is a serious side to it all. You wonder what happens to them after they pass 35, when their shoulders are dislocated, their knees are shot, and they have no training for other occupations. They also are without health insurance.

Unlike the typical exploitation film that shows violence to titillate, this film makes a serious point. It's morality verses violence. One must decide if it's okay to send someone to the hospital with a cracked skull, but not okay to parade around naked in public.

Newman, who was a trim 52, literally went on the ice to make this film. Never before had such a major star, still in the prime of his career, spewed out such obscenities and profanity. The situations may be slightly dated, but the dialogue still packs a wallop. It's crass, unsophisticated, gutter talk and one would think a man wrote it. However, there is a surprise— the screenplay is by Nancy Dowd. She did her research, like all good writers do by placing tape recorders in male locker rooms. Her diligence rewards us with an accurate portrayal of what men may talk about when women aren't in sight. In fact, she offers a full-scale opera of being male. Weaknesses and strengths are under a magnifying glass. We are privy to recent conquests (real and imagined), penis size, sexual prowess, and anything else males avoid talking about when having tea with Aunt Emma.

Michael Ontkean plays Newman's young antagonist. He doesn't have the experiences and knocks that a hard life brings. Thus, he doesn't fully understand how the system works. Unlike other characters in the movie, he is clean cut, highly educated, and from an upper-middle class family. When things turn sour, he cries foul and

Chapter 61   327

says he's in it for the sport and fun. It's ironic that his ignorance inspires Newman to save the team. Ontkean had his first break on TV's *Police Story*. Once a real hockey player in college (he won a scholarship to play), he was ready to give up on a career in acting when he won this role. His very funny bit at the conclusion of the film should please female members of the audience who've felt cheated by all of the machismo.

Other members of the supporting cast don't have much screen dialogue, but plenty of visual bits and blasts detail their livelihood. Jerry Hauser is theatrical in his performance on ice and brands himself "Killer." There are the usual other playboys and burnouts to watch and enjoy. Perhaps the Hanson Brothers are the most colorful trio. Recruited in midseason, they inject new life into the game because their methods on ice are childlike and crude. Appropriately called goons, they play with toys and appear to be mentally stunted. Most importantly, they have no scruples on the playing field. Thus, the fans fall in love with them.

Strother Martin brings the right attitude as manager for Newman's failing team. He puts his career first and the team last. His philosophy is to not be the captain that goes down with the ship. This philosophy puts him at odds with Newman. He does provide one hilarious pep talk at the end. If his line wasn't so vulgar, it might be as quotable as the one he spoke to Newman in **Cool Hand Luke** (1967) when he said "What we have here is a failure to communicate."

Despite the advantage of a female screenwriter, the film isn't kind to women. But many films during this period left women on the sidelines with nothing to do but look pretty. Lindsey Crouse has a small scene with Newman. Much better was her role and work with Newman in **The Verdict** (1982), for which she received a best supporting actress nomination. Jennifer Warren plays Newman s ex-wife, perhaps to show that he had good taste in women, if nothing else. There's also a brief glimpse of talented actress Swoosie Kurtz, as one of the player's wives. Her heavily made-up face is very unflattering.

This was Director George Roy Hill's third teaming with Newman. The first two were blockbusters: **Butch Cassidy and the Sundance**

Kid (1969) and **The Sting** (1973). While not a blockbuster, this film was very popular when released and did nothing to hurt Newman's standing with his box office. If anything, it kept him in touch with younger moviegoers who were less sensitive to four letter words. Today the film stands up very well against other strong portrayals of sports politics, including **North Dallas Forty** (1979), **Bull Durham** (1988), and **A League of Their Own** (1992). A sequel **Slap Shot 2: Breaking the Ice** was produced for home video in 2002. For those interested—and there were a few—it offered a contemporary view of the Hanson Brothers.

In retrospect, Mr. Newman's risk worked to his advantage. He continued to stay current in roles that required his name above the title. **The Color of Money** (1986) was a belated sequel to **The Hustler** (1961) and it brought him his second Academy Award—he had been honored the previous year for lifetime achievement.

At 77 he starred with Tom Hanks in **The Road to Perdition** (2002), still in the game, and very much a gold-plated movie star. His performance netted him a supporting actor nomination from the Academy and rounded out a first-rate career.

When he succumbed to lung cancer in 2008, his film tributes also highlighted his philanthropy and a long-running marriage (since 1958) to actress Joanne Woodward.

Cast

Paul Newman	*Reggie Dunlop*
Strother Martin	*Joe McGrath*
Michael Ontkean	*Ned Braden*
Jennifer Warren	*Francine Dunlop*
Lindsay Crouse	*Lily Braden*
Jerry Houser	*"Killer" Carlson*
Andrew Duncan	*Jim Carr*
Jeff Carlson	*Jeff Hanson*
Steve Carlson	*Steve Hanson*
David Hanson	*Jack Hanson*
Yvon Barrette	*Denis Lemieux*

Chapter 61

Production

George Roy Hill	*Director*
Nancy Dowd	*Writer*
Stephen J. Friedman, Robert J. Wunsch	*Producers*
Vic Kemper	*Cinematographer*
Pierre Tubbs	*Original Music*
Universal Pictures/Kings Road Entertainment/Pan Arts Productions	*Production Company*
USA/122/1977	*Country/Runtime/Year Released*

Chapter 62

Sunset Blvd.

"I am big. It's the pictures that got small."
—Norma Desmond

During the early part of the last century, when Hollywood was young and without audio, its group of celebrities would later be called silent screen stars. There were dozens of actors and actresses who graced the screen, and they were known for their mannerisms, as opposed to their voice. The long roster included Mary Pickford, Rudolph Valentino, Charlie Chaplin, and others who didn't speak, but could command attention with just a sly grin or sweeping wave of the hand. When sound arrived in the late 20s, the voice became one of the key acting instruments. Those who couldn't make the transition found the going tough. Those who could speak well still had to overcome the label of being from another era even though they may have recently been the darling of the critics and audiences.

Careers dried up fairly quickly if the celebrity failed to embrace this new requirement for the profession. If one had the right connections and talent, the 20s were a great time to be in the profession of filmmaking. You could be young, beautiful, and adored in an industry that seemed to hold no restrictions. You could whoop it up all night at parties because you didn't have to memorize lines for the next day's filming. You could also become fabulously wealthy since income taxes had not come about and Los Angeles property was cheap. Sound, and the stock market crash in 1929, ended the good life of this special colony of people in an industry that was evolving into an era that would make more demands on the technicians and cast. Apart from sound, the films made before the stock market crash were decidedly different than those made after. The mood of the country shifted, as well as income available for entertainment.

Before the crash, popular pieces were epics made on a grand scale. Most of the stories filmed weren't exactly real—they were illusions of extravagance. It was the roaring 20s, after all. That changed after the stock market crashed. Unemployment was high and money was tight. Comedy and music were the big draws because people wanted to escape from these economic woes. If your celebrity image was based on being wealthy, wild and free, the new order of things worked against you. Other liabilities could include a thick foreign accent or the inability to sing.

A degree of flexibility was also required. There had to be an ability to take risks, to learn a new skill, or to change with the current of things. This brings us to fictional silent screen star Norma Desmond, whose palatial home is on **Sunset Blvd.** She may have had talent, but no flexibility. She was not able to make a successful transition to sound. Now 50 in 1949, she still has her fortune, but little else remains from her glory days. She's not a survivor in the sense that she picked up her toys and went on to something else to achieve self-fulfillment. On top of the world at 25, she has steadily eroded into a middle-aged neurotic, still dreaming of reviving her celebrity.

A chance encounter with a young down-on-his-luck Hollywood writer (William Holden) inspires her to try the industry again. She hires him to write a screenplay about Salome. By the time he finishes it, she's seduced him into her demented world and he has become a paid companion. Swallowing his pride and his Midwest values, he empties her ashtray on command and parades around in expensive clothes. One imagines that he also provides comfort to her in her swan-shaped bed.

This odd pairing, probably more common than one would like to think in a glamour industry, is creepy, fascinating, and brilliantly entertaining. Her obsessive behavior and his tiny ounce of self-respect move this film to grand heights of enjoyment for anyone interested in movies about movies. It has no rivals as being one of the first and best film on the dark underbelly of Hollywood.

Billy Wilder who co-wrote the screenplay with Charles Brackett and D.M. Marshmann, Jr. directs the film. Wilder and Brackett provided scripts for Paramount during the 30s and 40s. This was their last collaboration and proved to be their darkest and most cynical view of human decadence. On one level, it's the story of a dramatic fall of someone once held in great esteem. On another level, it's a satirical jab at all the trappings and trimmings of the Hollywood celebrity game.

Numerous Hollywood artifacts are unearthed to give an inside view of a very political industry. At a New Year's gathering, we are privy to a group of aspiring actors and writers hanging out, waiting for that big break. Most are too early in the game to have become discouraged. Holden's friends are these eager folks, including Jack Webb and Nancy Olson. Also at the party and playing themselves and one of their songs, *Buttons and Bows*, are songwriters Jay Livingston and Ray Evans. This tune won best song Oscar in 1948's **The Paleface**. These friends represent hope and reality to Holden, the writer. Olson married Jay Livingston's younger brother, Capitol Record Executive Alan W. Livingston in 1962.

On the other side of the city lives Norma and her faithful servant, Max. They are "sleepwalking" in an industry that has long forgotten them. Their fame has become a curse. They are prisoners in their own success. In between these opposing forces are a slew of carefully chosen cameos to add spice to the cynical surroundings. Famed Director Cecil B. DeMille does a turn as himself and we get to actually see him at work on one of his real films, 1950's **Samson and Delilah**. Hedda Hopper, one of Hollywood's original gossip columnists, turns up to report on the lurid goings on.

Cameos by actual silent screen stars who suffered a career upheaval during Norma's days include Buster Keaton, Anna Q. Nilsson, and H.B. Warner. If one is curious about these people, whom Holden refers to as waxworks, each one has an interesting story of popularity and decline. Keaton's career was hampered by alcoholism. Studio restrictions also killed his creative powers, and his career declined sharply in the mid-30s. However, he was soon to reemerge in popularity once his films were revived on television. Even with only five seconds (and no lines), he smiles, as if olden times. Ms. Nilsson was a Swedish import, very

Chapter 62

popular in silents. But a riding accident and age (she was 40 in 1930) curtailed her activity in the early 30s and she spent the rest of her career in small, unremarkable roles. H.B. Warner had been in films since 1914, and played Christ in C.B. DeMille's **The King of Kings** in 1927. He played many character roles over the years, including **Lost Horizon** (1937) and worked fairly steady to the middle 1940s.

The real interest in the movie is the intertwining life of Gloria Swanson and Norma Desmond. On first glance, it might be believed that Swanson is Desmond, and there are some valid reasons to believe this. Both reached the height of their success in silent movies. Both epitomized glamour, and both were much married. Swanson was even directed by Erich Von Stroheim in **Queen Kelly** (1927). Swanson produced and financed this classic silent, but fired Von Stroheim for artistic differences and the film was never completed. A small clip from this movie is the silent viewed by Swanson and Holden in her personal screening room. Von Stroheim plays Max in **Sunset Blvd.**, Norma's more than faithful servant. Even more similarities persist since much of Swanson's early success was from a series of films directed by Cecil B. DeMille in the early 20s.

However, thankfully, the mental state of both actresses is the contrast. Swanson proved she could talk and sing in the new age, but a series of poor vehicles put her career in the doldrums. To keep active, she started numerous business ventures, including fashion design and painting. She broadened her appeal by appearing on Broadway for the first time in the early 50s and continued into the early 70s, most notably in *Butterflies are Free*.

Most people who know of Swanson only know her from this film, not realizing she was one of the most popular silent screen stars. She was nominated for an Oscar for her portrayal of Norma Desmond, but lost to Judy Holliday. The fact that she made the role seem so real deserved some type of recognition, though that probably didn't come from her peers. Mae Murray, a silent screen star who wasn't successful after sound, was heard to say after the screening of **Sunset Blvd.**, "We were never that crazy."

Swanson received a number of movie offers after this success, but they were variations on her Desmond character, which she didn't want to reprise. In 1952 she filmed **Three for Bedroom C** in the hopes of erasing any illusions the audience may have had about actress Swanson and her close association to Norma. She was once again cast as a movie star. This time she was grounded and able to attract men by being interesting (as opposed to having money). She was also a single parent, a mother who put her family before career. In fact, as the story goes, her character keeps turning down roles offered by a film producer played by Fred Clark. Clark, incidentally, was cast in **Sunset Blvd.** as a harried producer who turns William Holden down. This film, because it was her follow-up to Norma Desmond, remains a footnote in its relationship with **Sunset Blvd**. It flopped and did nothing to further her standing in the film industry. After that she appeared only twice in movies (one in 1956, the other in 1974).

However, Swanson was able to retain her popularity through TV. There were notable appearances (which included a spoof of silent films) on *The Beverly Hillbillies* (1962-1971) and *The Carol Burnett Show* (1967-1978). She frequently appeared on TV talk shows, promoting the virtues of health food. She married for the sixth time at 77 and wrote her autobiography at 82, writing frankly about her love affair with Joseph Kennedy, the Kennedy family patriarch. She died at 84 in 1983, a true survivor of fame and celebrity, unlike the character for which she is most famous.

Despite playing their roles perfectly, Holden and Swanson were not the first choices to play Norma and Joe. Montgomery Clift originally accepted the role, but pulled back when his lover, famed torch singer Libby Holman, pressured him to do so. Holman was 30 years older than Clift and thought script similarities were too close for comfort. Wilder then approached Fred MacMurray, who politely turned it down because he didn't want to play a "male prostitute." Holden was asked third. He accepted the part on the condition that it would become the focus of the movie. Since Holden was under contract to Paramount, Wilder went to his bosses. They demanded that he play the role as written. It turned out to his advantage. The film put him in the big league of stars, a place he maintained for 30 years.

Chapter 62

Mae West was the first actress asked to play Norma Desmond. She had never been in silent pictures and her career in films was on temporary hold. However, her nightclub with a select group of body-builders was thriving at the time. Also West, then 57, was furious that anyone would ask her to play someone past her prime. Mary Pickford wanted too much control over the project so she was nixed. Silent screen star Pola Negri also felt insulted when asked. Once a rival to Swanson, Negri's career died the day talkies arrived because of her thick Polish accent. Director George Cukor recommended Swanson to Wilder and it was another example of being in the right place at the right time.

The film won three Academy Awards for screenplay, art direction, and score. It was very popular with critics and found an audience, but not without some difficulty. Wilder hid the intended screenplay, code named *A Can of Beans*, from Paramount executives until pre-production was complete, fearing the controversial content could bomb the project early on. Completed in 1949, the original test screening in Evanston, Illinois found audiences howling in the worst way at the opening scene. This scene was later cut and replaced with squad cars racing down **Sunset Blvd**.

The cut scene would have been fascinating. It had William Holden lying in a morgue on a slab. He gets up in a ghostlike form and begins his narration. The other corpses in the same room then get up and respond accordingly. This bizarre opening didn't set the proper mood for the film in 1949 so a frantic Wilder called the actors back for some additional scenes. This delayed the film's release to 1950.

The film's long popularity really belongs to TV, where it always finds a fascinated audience when televised. It also has become something of a pop icon, influencing a number of artists. Andy Warhol's **Heat** (1972) was a variation of this Hollywood tale. Bette Davis played in another variation in **The Star** (1952), though the content was more melodramatic.

Salome, the film Norma hires Joe to write, was actually filmed in 1923 with Nazimova in the title role. This Russian silent screen actress was known for her bold and haunting acting style, perhaps a distant relative to Norma Desmond's thespian abilities. A straighter version of this biblical heroine appeared in 1953 with Rita Hayworth. Wilder and Holden tried to recreate some additional magic in 1978's **Fedora**. Holden played a movie director trying to coax an ancient movie queen out of seclusion. They had wanted Marlene Dietrich for the aging movie queen, but she wouldn't do it. This film failed commercially and artistically.

Sunset Blvd. later became a musical fixture on Broadway and won seven Tony awards in 1994. The idea of converting this piece to music was inspired by Swanson herself, who sought backing in the mid-50s for a Broadway musical on the role she made famous. However, the deal eventually fell through. Swanson, so it seems, was ahead of her time.

The real thoroughfare named Sunset Blvd. runs through the middle of Hollywood, through Beverly Hills and extends into Brentwood. However, the actual mansion used in the movie was not on this very famous and busy street. The "Norma Desmond mansion" was built in 1922 several streets over from Sunset Blvd. By 1950 it was owned by Getty Oil Company and home to Mrs. J. Paul Getty. She rented it to Paramount on the unusual condition that a swimming pool be built on the grounds. However, for reasons best known to her, Mrs. Getty changed her mind and had the infamous prop filled in after filming was complete.

Like many of the impractical palaces constructed during Norma's heyday, the Getty mansion proved uncomfortable to live in and expensive to maintain. So in 1957 the mansion was torn down and replaced by an office building to house all of Getty's business concerns. It stands there today on the northwest corner of Wilshire and Irving.

Cast

William Holden	*Joe Gillis*
Gloria Swanson	*Norma Desmond*
Erich von Stroheim	*Max Von Mayerling*
Nancy Olson	*Betty Schaefer*
Fred Clark	*Sheldrake*

Chapter 62

Lloyd Gough	*Morino*
Jack Webb	*Artie Green*
Franklyn Farnum	*Undertaker*
Larry J. Blake	*First Finance Man*
Charles Dayton	*Second Finance Man*
Cecil B. DeMille	*Himself*
Hedda Hopper	*Herself*
Buster Keaton	*Himself*
Anna Q. Nilsson	*Herself*
H.B. Warner	*Himself*

Production

Billy Wilder	*Director*
Charles Brackett, D.M. Marshmann, Jr.,	*Writers*
Billy Wilder	
Charles Brackett	*Producer*
Jay Livingston, Franz Waxman	*Cinematography*
Edith Head	*Costumes*
Paramount Pictures	*Production Company*
USA/110/1950	*Country/Runtime/Year Released*

Chapter 63

Superman: The Movie

"We all have our little faults. Mine happens to be in California."

—*Lex Luthor*

When DC Comics introduced the character of Superman in 1938, a completely new generation of comic book heroes was inspired. Before Superman hit the stands, comic books were usually an expansion of the strips found in the Sunday newspapers. But Superman was an original idea, not attached to any newspaper. Creators Jerry Siegel and Joel Shuster tried peddling it to the newspapers, but there were no takers.

After Superman snowballed into a golden egg for DC, other larger than- life superheroes emerged for fun and profit. Batman arrived in 1939, Robin in 1940, Wonder Woman in 1942, plus the memorable Sandman, Amazing Man, and Human Torch. This was a special time for comics and young readers. Television wasn't available and radio couldn't offer the really cool artwork. Superman's co-creator Siegel explained how the character came about: "All of a sudden, it hits me—I conceived a character like Samson, Hercules, and all the strong men I ever heard of rolled into one, only more so." Perhaps it was a fantasy all Americans at that time could embrace. Though the economy was encouraging, Europe was in chaos, thanks to Hitler and his war machine. Americans were isolated from the trouble overseas by choice and geography, but the informed knew the U.S. couldn't stay out of the conflict forever. Still, it may have been in Siegel and Shuster's unconscious mind that a superhuman could descend down from the skies to solve these problems without the cost to Americans of family disruption and lives lost.

When television arrived, the special period for comic books came to a close. But for Superman, another world opened up. A low budget feature in 1951, **Superman and the Mole Men,** prompted a TV series from 1951 to 1957 starring George Reeves in the title role. After that, there was a long run of cartoons throughout the 60s.

The concept of a grand scale movie looked good to producers in the 70s because the youth who bought the original comic books were still interested in going to movies. Now middle-aged, they were certain to bring their family in tow.

The producers who turned out this awesome extravaganza, **Superman: The Movie** (1978), were the father and son team of Alexander and Ilya Salkind. Correctly determining that the Superman saga must be larger than life, they spared no expense to continue the myth that began in comic books. The best cast and special effects that money could buy prompted the marketing campaign that proclaimed "you will believe a man can fly." From the opening credits and score by John Barry, and the powerful (but brief) presence of Marlon Brando, **Superman: The Movie** becomes entertainment on a grand scale. It's awesome to say the least, and certainly inspirational. For 173 minutes you watch a movie faithful to 1938 ideals but with the sensibility of the 70s. No one was disappointed when this spectacle hit the big screens during the holiday season in December, 1978.

The Superman biography is familiar to most. He is the only survivor of a dying planet called Krypton. Krypton was an extremely advanced society and when Superman entered the earth's atmosphere, he was given extraordinary strength and other powers like X-ray vision. All that can undo him is kryptonite, a green crystal found on Krypton. Since he is everything "good and right," many a crook used the crystal as leverage in an attempt to weaken and defeat the superhero.

Superman's escape rocket was found by a middle-aged childless couple in Smalltown, USA, a small, quaint community in the Midwest with strong values and integrity. Growing up, our hero restrained himself from using his powers in an attempt to avoid unwanted attention. Isolated and lonely, he was 30 when he learned of his background and purpose on earth: to promote truth, justice and the American way of life. To achieve these lofty ideas, he adopts a disguise as mild-mannered Clark Kent, a reporter in the big town of Metropolis. This occupation affords him the opportunity to encounter the untruths and injustices that undermine the American way of life.

His co-workers at the paper are Lois Lane, Perry White, and Jimmy Olson. Lane also searches for truth as a news reporter, but is rather bold and heedless in her approach. As a result, she frequently gets into trouble. Perry White is the paper's editor and Clark's boss. He is a strong, assertive man who wishes Kent could be more aggressive. If he only knew! Boyish Olson is a roving news journalist who, like Lois, often gets too close to the edge for the perfect shot.

Christopher Reeve was chosen from 200 applicants for the title role. Sylvestor Stallone lobbied hard for the role but his Italian good looks was considered a handicap. Paul Newman, Robert Redford, Charles Bronson, Kris Kristofferson, and Arnold Schwarzenegger, tested for the role of the year, but the prize went to a virtual unknown. The 26-year-old, 6'4, and 225-pound Reeve had only previously been employed in a daytime soap opera (as a heel), and on Broadway as Katherine Hepburn's grandson in *A Matter of Gravity*. Apart from physical similarities, Reeve is perfect for the role. He has the necessary level of authority that sends fear to the crooks, yet can offer a reassuring hand to victims. He plays the part straight, as he should, so there is a comic flair to his lines, which are delivered flat but with confidence. Standing straight and broad shouldered, he appears to be a tower of strength and integrity. However, despite his physical presence, he still can feign the bland and weak nature of horn-rimmed Clark Kent.

Those who come in contact with Superman are shocked at his helpfulness. They are not used to such a giving stranger—with no strings attached. Perhaps they are members of the "me" generation, individuals all self-absorbed and self-centered. When the grateful crowd offers an endless stream of thanks to Superman, he corrects their attitude. He says this is what everybody should be doing. The

Chapter 63

dialogue reeks with 30s simplicity and sincerity: "is that man okay?" he asks, after saving an entire community from drowning. However, the whole affect cleverly offers a level of sophistication to keep modern audiences glued to the screen.

Since an unknown played the lead role, the Salkinds chose as box office insurance, a name that could still gain attention. Marlon Brando (as Superman's father) was paid $3 million for just 12 days of work. With his percentage of the profits—the movie was a blockbuster—he is believed to have earned over $16 million. Other cast members were carefully chosen: Glenn Ford is Superman's adopted father. His screen persona as an easygoing nice guy with middle class values made the offer of the role an obvious choice. For his adopted mother, Phyllis Thaxter had her first role in 15 years. In films since the 40s, she masterfully recreates a warm and caring mother. Thaxter was producer Ilya Salkind's mother-in-law at the time of filming.

Susannah York plays Superman's biological mother. If one looked back at her screen roles, there's a touch of independence and unconventionality that's very appealing. Teaming Brando with York offers good chemistry. Superman is wise and knowing like his father, but still thinks on his own terms like his mom.

Gene Hackman's villainy shows off his incredible acting range. Not usually noted for comedic roles, he typically plays everyday types, often getting down to the flesh and blood basics of a middle-aged man. In this case, he does an about face as a sociopath of unknown origin. His idea in crime is to own most of California and his methods to dominate the West Coast are amusing. Hackman accepted the role because he wanted more than anything to work with Brando. It's not certain if they did work together since they share no actual screen time in the movie.

Ned Beatty and Valerie Perrine are Hackman's gofer and girlfriend, respectively. Beatty's character is named Otis, and he is not unlike the same named character on TV's *The Andy Griffith Show*, only he's completely sober. Perrine is quite the showpiece. Just hearing her name—"Miss Teschsmacher"— brings on a frenzy of delight. Perrine was a Las Vegas showgirl before entering films. Naturally, we have eye-popping shots of her assets. Margot Kidder does a good turn as Lois Lane for the 70s and feminism. Other notable actresses considered for Miss Lane included Lesley-Anne Down, Stockard Channing, and Anne Archer. Like Reeve, she is perfect for the role of the slightly scattered career woman, one who forgets to fill the tank with gas, but still is able to finish the story before deadline. Not unlike Superman's biological mother, she's courageous, independent and feminine.

The sexual chemistry between the Man of Steel and Miss Lane is rather obvious in the comic book sense. A carefully chosen song sums up their attraction. Though only a few bars are heard, *Give a Little Bit* by rock group *Supertramp* perfectly summarizes their special relationship.

There are other big names in minute roles, mainly there for the sequel. Terence Stamp and his group of thugs appear in the prologue, but their involvement really introduces the more violent sequel to this film. That sequel had a hard time finding its way to the movie theatres. Brando, co-screenwriter Mario Puzo, and director Richard Donner filed a lawsuit against the Salkinds, saying they were being cheated out of royalties. Nothing was proven in court, and the talent of all three was edited from the sequel for reasons that were never publicly explained. The sequel was planned for the summer of '79, but didn't find its way to theatres until 1981. After that, the stories and mood changed with each passing project, due to different writers and directors. Eventually a total of four films were made. The first with Director Richard Donner is up, up and away the best.

Richard Lester directed **Superman II** (1981) and **Superman III** (1983) with visual flair. Donner's technical skills differentiate these two in look and feel from the original. It only alarmed the purists, though, since both were quite successful.

Perhaps Reeves' clout brought **Superman IV: The Quest for Peace** (1987) to the screen. Reeve, the actor/star, was also involved in the script and direction. It was a sincere effort but the public's lukewarm reception clearly proved this particular series had run its course.

The Salkind father and son team produced **Supergirl** in 1984,

Chapter 63   *343*

but it was a misfire. Faye Dunaway as a campy supervillain and Peter O'Toole remain its main point of interest. The Salkind's last picture together as producers was **Christopher Columbus: The Discovery** (1992), released in time for the 500th anniversary. Filming conditions were tense, Brando also participated, but there was, alas, no stampede at the box office. It received negative reviews and Brando's performance was unfairly cited as one of his worst.

The elder Salkind died in 1997. Today, Ilya appears at film conventions all over the world to discuss the Superman film series with appreciative audiences.

Sadly, in the last few years, Margot Kidder and Christopher Reeve suffered serious personal injuries that prevented them from appearing in front of the camera. Kidder took several years to recover from her injuries on a Canadian movie set. After a long period of absence from film, there were news reports of strange public behavior. Kidder later said she suffered from manic depression, but that her mental state was now under control. During the summer of 1995 Reeve suffered a broken neck in a horse riding accident and became a quadriplegic. In post-accident interviews he voiced confidence that he would walk again and became a leading advocate for biological research, the area that offered the most hope for spinal chord injuries. Despite his handicap, he returned in a big way to the small screen in 1998 playing the victim in **Rear Window**, a made-for-TV remake of the classic Alfred Hitchcock film, indicating that his determination was as strong as the character he became most identified with. He died in late 2004, leaving a legacy of hope for thousands of others who are paralyzed.

The popularity of **Superman** initiated a large batch of films based on comic book heroes. **Flash Gordon** (1980) was one of the first to arrive. It boasted clever optics, but nothing else in terms of character. It was especially embarrassing to the producers when they found out that Sam Jones had posed nude for *Playgirl* magazine sometime earlier. More successful was **Batman** in 1989. In contrast to the Superman films, the main point of interest in **Batman** was the villain. In this outing, Jack Nicholson as the Joker stole all the reviews from

Bruce Wayne, as played by Michael Keaton. In 2002, the big budgeted **Spiderman** was released. A few sharp-eye observers remarked that it bore a strong resemblance in story and texture to 1978's **Superman: The Movie**. If one must take, take from the best. In 1980 a video version of **Superman: The Movie** was released. It offered additional footage not shown in the theatrical release concerning the destruction of Krypton, the town of Smallville, and earthquake scenes. The success of this franchise ensures future Superman movies for mass consumption.

Jerry Siegel and Joe Shuster were compensated for their creation, but bitter lawsuits went on for years over ownership and control. Eventually both Siegel and Shuster were awarded a small yearly stipend. The most interesting aspect of **Superman Returns** (2006) was the casting of Eva Marie Saint as Clark Kent's mother. Rumors were flying that Ms. Saint would have a scene with Marlon Brando—superimposed from their work together **On The Waterfront** (1954). The finished product didn't confirm the rumor and the film didn't excite the audiences at the same level as in 1978.

Cast

Marlon Brando	*Jor-El*
Gene Hackman	*Lex Luther*
Christopher Reeves	*Clark Kent/Superman*
Ned Beatty	*Otis*
Jackie Cooper	*Perry White*
Glenn Ford	*Jonathan Kent*
Trevor Howard	*First Elder*
Margot Kidder	*Lois Lane*
Jack O'Halloran	*Non*
Valerie Perrine	*Eve Teschmacher*
Maria Schell	*Vond-Ah*
Terence Stamp	*General Zod*
Phyllis Thaxter	*Ma Kent*
Susannah York	*Lara*
Jeff East	*Young Clark Kent*

Chapter 63

Marc McClure	*Jimmy Olsen*
Sarah Douglas	*Ursa*
Rex Reed	*Himself*
Larry Hagman	*Major*

Production

Richard Donner	*Director*
Jerry Siegel & Joe Shuster (comic),	*Writers*
Mario Puzo (also story), David Newman,	
Leslie Newman, Robert Benton, Tom Mankiewicz	
Alexander Salkin, Pierre Spengler,	*Producers*
Richard Lester	
Geoffrey Unsworth	*Cinematography*
Alexander Salkin/Dovemead Films/	*Production Companies*
Film Export A.G./International Film Production	
UK/127/1978	*Country/Runtime/Year Released*

Chapter 64

Sweet Charity

"I want very much to change my life."

—*Charity Hope Valentine*

Shirley MacLaine revived her nightclub act from time to time when she was between film projects. She performed with vigor to appreciative audiences in Las Vegas and on the road. Her act borrowed heavily from her movies. One highlight of her show from 1990 was what she referred to as the "hooker-victim-medley." It was performed as a joke since Ms. MacLaine has a large file of these ladies in her movie resume. Throwing her head back and kicking her legs higher than most 56-year old movie stars, audiences were mesmerized by her rendition of *If My Friends Could See Me Now*. The song, of course, is from the movie that best showcases her versatility: **Sweet Charity**.

Most of her contemporaries have retired but Ms. MacLaine continues to interest us, whether in movies, TV, or on the Internet. Her Website offers the philosophical statement "life is a bowl of cherries, so never mind the pits." It, also, is borrowed from **Sweet Charity**. By Hollywood standards, MacLaine was different when she came on the scene in the mid-50s. She was kooky, offbeat and intelligent. By the length of her career, she isn't at all like the victim she brought to life in **Some Came Running** (1958), the movie that first ignited her stardom. She received her first Academy Award nomination for that performance but had to wait until 1983 to win for **Terms of Endearment**. In middle age, she vocalized her support for metaphysics and reincarnation. She also braced an onslaught of press and industry jokes with sincerity and conviction. Her career continued in colorful character roles, notably **Steel Magnolias** (1989) and **Postcards from the Edge** (1990). That she was going to be around for a while longer was confirmed with star roles in **Guarding Tess** (1994)

Chapter 64

347

and **The Evening Star** (1996), a welcome if unremarkable follow-up to **Terms of Endearment**.

In the current phase of her career, she accepts film roles someone past 80 can make interesting: **Elsa & Fred** (2014) and **The Last Words** (2017).

The roots of **Sweet Charity** go back to Federico Fellini's film **Le Notti di Cabiria** or the US title **Nights of Cabiria** (1957) starring Fellini's wife (since 1943) Guilietta Masina. It continually ranks on lists compiling great films and won the Academy Award for Best Foreign Language Film. A decade later, this bittersweet story of a prostitute who only wants to be loved was developed into a musical. Bob Fosse directed his (then) wife Gwen Verndon in the title role in 1966 to much acclaim and success. When it was time to transpose this piece to the big screen, he was entrusted the film assignment, which also became his Hollywood directorial debut. Instead of Verdon, movie star MacLaine was given the title role. Though MacLaine's films of the 60s were checkered with success, MGM reasoned she was still strong enough to carry an expensive musical. Verdon reportedly acted as mentor, coach, and silent partner of her husband to MacLaine, proving she was as much a team player as anyone. What turned out was a good film, but one that didn't return its cost to the producers. Its failure virtually ended the era of expensive screen musicals— and sent Ms. MacLaine to a temporary lull in her career.

MacLaine's Charity Valentine is the proverbial hooker with the heart of gold. Her friend (Chita Rivera, in a rare film appearance) tells her "you're an open, honest, and extremely stupid girl." It's an accurate statement. Charity never learns from her mistakes. Unlike the other prostitutes that become hardened over the occupational hazards of their services, Charity still believes nice people wear nice faces. She retains this innocence, despite the large roster of men with whom she has been intimate. Totally unselfish, a chronic doormat, she frequently sets herself up for heartbreak. In the opening sequence, she's rescued from a pond in Central Park after her "married" fiancé shoves her off a bridge and runs off with her life savings—about $400. Explaining the situation to the police, she says her occupation is social consultant in a dance hall. Once this is announced, they retract any offers of help out of fear or ignorance. After that, the tunes narrate the plotting. *There's Gotta Be Something Better Than This* reveals the hopelessness of her occupation in life.

Then she meets a "normal" guy, an insurance man (John McMartin), and her hopes are sparked with *Baby Dream your Dream*. When he initially accepts her, warts and all, it's the rousing *I'm a Brass Band*. Bob Fosse takes the medium of film to new creative and artistic heights. The curse of transposing a hit play to the screen is usually dull and lethargic staging. However, he avoids any sign of greasepaint and the results are a clever cinematic movie. He incorporates still life, stop-action black and white, handheld movements, slow motion, and fade-ins. It's all done for a reason: the montage of images sharpens the full impact of emotions. The Fosse choreography is sensual, intense, and full of his highly revered trademarks. The dancers are often angular, with complex movements. It appears that each movement to the fingernail is choreographed. It offers no symmetry, in comparison to a number by Fred Astaire or Gene Kelly. Still, a definite rhythm exists. The results are visually stimulating and hoists the screen musical to another level of sophistication. It's unfortunate the audience didn't applaud this groundbreaking effort.

The most rewarding dance occurs in three labeled sequences, *Rich Man's Frug*. The trilogy ends in a love frenzy, suggesting a courtship ritual. There's a nice bit by Sammy Davis Jr. as Big Daddy. He shines with the *Rhythm of Life*, using the San Francisco psychedelic style as a backdrop. He's the cool cat, the hippest of the new religion preachers.

John McMartin repeats his stage performance as the troubled man Charity pins all of her hopes and dreams on. It's a thoughtful performance in a role few actors like having on their resume. It didn't do anything for McMartin's career, except to get more of the same. In **All the President's Men** (1976), he appeared briefly as a colleague of *The Washington Post*'s Ben Bradlee. We're thankful Bradlee dismissed his cautionary advice. His weakness was also used to great comic affect in a segment on the *Mary Tyler Moor Show*. He was a lawyer hired to defend perky Moore in a freedom of press charge. He

Chapter 64   349

showed up at the hearing intoxicated and poor Mary had to defend herself.

Sweet Charity was praised by critics, but audiences stayed away from this pessimistic fairy tale. Perhaps in 1969 it was too painful to experience the frustrations of a childlike woman. You want to believe Charity finds lasting happiness. But realizing how complicated social rules are, there's a chance she won't. Borrowing a claim from Ms. MacLaine, perhaps Charity will be happier in another life.

The failure of the film wasn't a setback for Fosse. It was just the beginning. He met critical and commercial aspirations with his next effort, **Cabaret**, in 1972. He won an Oscar for Directing, adding it to a clutch of Tony awards, and an Emmy all in the same year—the only director to have done this. One of his last efforts was the autobiographical **All That Jazz** (1979). It owned up to a very intense personal lifestyle. He died of a heart attack in 1987 at 60, a huge loss to the modern stage and screen musical.

Verdon divorced Fosse in 1971. Despite their differences, they remained friends. In fact, she was a technical advisor to *FOSSE,* a Broadway dance tribute that showcased his style and innovation in dance. During its successful run and tour, she died from natural causes at 75 in 2001.

Cast

Shirley MacLaine	*Charity Hope Valentine*
John McMartin	*Oscar*
Chita Rivera	*Nickie*
Paula Kelly	*Helene*
Stubby Kaye	*Herman*
Barbara Bouchet	*Ursula*
Ricardo Montalban	*Vittorio Vidal*
Sammy Davis Jr.	*Big Daddy*
Alan Hewitt	*Nicholsby*
Dante DiPaolo	*Charlie*
Bud Vest, Ben Vereen, Lee Roy Reams	*Frug Dancers*
Toni Basil	*Dancer in "Rhythm of Life"*

Production

Bob Fosse	*Director*
Federico Fellini, Ennio Flaiano, Tullio Pinelli (all, screenplay Le Notti di Cabiria), Neil Simon (play), Peter Stone	*Writers*
Robert Arthur	*Producer*
Robert Surtees	*Cinematography*
Cy Coleman, Dorothy Fields (lyrics)	*Original music*
Universal Pictures	*Production Company*
USA/149/1969	*Country/Runtime/Year Released*

Chapter 65

That Man From Rio

"Whoa. Wait till Lebel hears about this."
—Adrien Dufourquet

That Man From Rio or **Homme De Rio, L'** as it's known in its native country of France, reminds you of an encounter with a tasty French dessert. Imagine yourself walking down a Paris street experiencing the sights, sounds, and smells of one of the most culturally rich cities in the world. From a clear glass window, one of those rich pastries catches your senses. Surrounded with white linen and mirrors, the filling oozes out from the side, creating a delightful mouth watering sensation. You can't resist the temptation. You must have it so you immediately seat yourself at a sidewalk table and signal the waiter. It's served, slightly warm with café au lait.. Ah this is one of the distinct pleasures of life.

This French film does the same thing for you, but with less calories. Like a good dish, it has an abundance of rich flavors that satisfy. It's a celebration of the joy of living. Our hero and heroine are chased halfway around the world. It's a combination of cat and mouse and spider and fly. Tireless and fearless, they seem to be saying in their youthful exuberance, that it's better to live than to stop by being caught. You even urge them on, to keep going, even though everyone is out of breath.

Another feature of the picture is the postcard scenery of Rio, Brazil and Paris. This is an armchair vacation for the audience and everyone can be pleased that the chase takes on a particular personality in each respective place. Director and screenwriter Philip de Broca offers many unforgettable moments and colorful characters during the course of action.

Jean-Paul Belmondo and Francois Dorleac are the youthful leads and, together with de Broca, are at the height of their appeal. Because of its fresh approach and attitude, this film was an international hit in 1964 and subsequently influenced the romantic adventure genre. Originally released in the United States with English dubbing, for the purists, **That Man From Rio** is now available with English subtitles.

This new version is a notch above the English dubbing. The dialogue is much closer to the original intent. Plus, the acting is so good that the subtitles aren't distracting. You feel the experience of two young lovers without ever having known a word of French. The exuberance you feel may literally lift you out of your seat.

The anchor of the film is young Belmondo. Just a few years before making this film, he was established as an "overnight" sensation in **Breathless** (1959). It was his good fortune to be around in the early 60s and riding on the crest of The New French Wave. This movement was concocted by a group of young French directors who sought to raise the artistry within the industry and restore French Cinema to its prewar creative powers. There was diverse selection of ideas presented to the public. The first and most widely admired film from this new order was **Breathless** and it became an artistic and commercial success. Directed by Jean- Luc Godard, the story was fashioned around the life of a French hood and his involvement with an American girl (Jean Seberg) living in Paris. It was somewhat improvisational and dependent on the energy and spontaneity of the players. In its wake, Belmondo emerged with a screen persona that took bits and pieces from rebellious James Dean and tough Humphrey Bogart. Still, he was his own creation: He represented repressed youth, yet conveyed a sense of optimism and ebullience. He doesn't have the neurosis that James Dean framed. He tends to be sweet or sour, gentle or forceful. There's no in-between his extrovert and introvert personality. Like Bogart, if his character doesn't have all of the integrity you could hope for, he at least is loyal to his cause and friends. These are very admirable qualities for an actor and a good underpinning for his role in **That Man in Rio**.

The opening scene with soldier Belmondo and his buddy sets the stage for the film in one economical motion. They're on leave for

Chapter 65

eight days, en route to Paris. We see Belmondo playing with an egg. We know exactly what he wants for breakfast and lunch and dinner. Unfortunately, this rooster has to wait, and wait a little longer when some Paris thugs mysteriously kidnap his girlfriend.

Land, sea and air are exploited for what becomes one long chase. Our hero simply uses his instinct or intellect to guide him. He is obviously in love and it's his devotion to his girlfriend that keeps him going in a forward motion.

The chase mechanism involves the rich, powerful, and sinister, and their ways and means of acquiring rare and priceless pieces of ancient art. Belmondo and his girlfriend, the beautiful Francoise Dorleac, keep innocently getting in the way of the processes. As they weave in and around the international intrigue, there's always the unexpected. Just when the thrills and chase get tight, there's the element of surprise. It's not a surprise that terrifies or shocks, but one that makes one smile.

Master storyteller Steven Spielberg borrows from this concept and his best work always has a comedic edge, an element of surprise after a brief build-up.

To warn you of the surprises would weaken your enjoyment. But it involves garbage, finding unlikely comrades in the streets, and a pink car with stars. There's also the engaging personality of Belmondo. Despite the load he has on his mind, he doesn't forget to salute a former officer in the strange land of Brazil.

DeBroca uses the opportunity to spoof American icons, long before it was fashionable. There's a hint at **The Maltese Falcon**, and an overripe chanteuse named Lola (with shades of Marlene Dietrich), a John Wayne type barroom brawl, and even Tarzan gets a ribbing.

As for actor Adolfo Celi's movie name, remember this is 1964 and South America was susceptible to influence from Cuba.

The dialogue is revealing. Like **Breathless**, we are allowed to hear intimate bits from the lives of these people. Most appealing is the sequence of events that prevent the lovers from getting together. First he wants to be intimate but her family remains in the room. She doesn't want to be too obvious.

When she is willing, he has too much on his mind, like trying to prevent them from being killed. In one comedic outburst, he sounds off his frustration to a small boy, delightfully named Sir Winston. This street urchin lives in a tree house, apparently by his wits. It's suspected that he has a greater understanding of women than the adult males.

Francoise Dorleac is perfect as the woman being rescued. She was the older sister of Catherine Deneuve. While both sisters are breathtakingly beautiful, Dorleac's style of performing is more warm and accessible than her younger sister. At the time, she was the more popular of the two. Sadly, her career was at an international height when she was tragically killed in a car crash near Nice airport in 1967. Before that, she was involved in several English and American-backed productions, most notably in her last film, **Billion Dollar Brain** (1967).

Catherine Deneuve and Belmondo did work together with Francois Trauffant in the more interesting than excellent **Mississippi Mermaid** (1969).

DeBroca directed Belmondo in a much-anticipated sequel to this film in 1965. The English title was **Up to His Ears**. The female co-star this time around was luscious Ursula Andress. As sequels go, it wasn't up to the standard of the original. Its main excitement occurred off camera, when Belmondo and Andress left their respective spouses and became companions in real life for several years.

The early 60s contain Belmondo's best and most popular work. Since they were mainly French productions, many did not find their way into mainstream American cinema. He did receive American offers; if he had chosen, he could have attempted an international career. However, he said he liked living and making movies in France.

As a favor to Andress, he appeared uncredited in the James Bond spoof **Casino Royale** (1967). His all too brief appearance required him to speak one line of English and his struggle to do so may have been real. It may also offer a hint at why he chose to remain home in his native France. In retrospect, after witnessing Alain Delon's and Gerard Depardieu's brief and unrewarding flings with Hollywood, it was probably a wise career move.

Chapter 65

Belmondo remains a consistent winner in the popularity polls and is justifiably regarded as France's national treasure. One of his last and widely admired performances was in the French production of **Les Misérables** in 1995.

In 2011, he walked with the help of a cane and needed a translator, but his charm was very much in evidence when he appeared at the 2011 Turner Classic Movie Channel Film Festival in Hollywood to celebrate the restoration of **Breathless**.

Early on in his career, Belmondo said he worked nonstop because he didn't think things would last. He certainly underestimated his appeal.

Cast

Jean-Paul Belmondo	*Adrien Dufourquet*
Françoise Dorléac	*Agnès Villermosa*
Jean Servais	*Professeur Catalan*
Simone Renant	*Lola*
Roger Dumas	*Lebel*
Daniel Ceccaldi	*L'inspecteur*
Milton Ribeiro	*Tupac*
Ubiracy De Oliveira	*Sir Winston*
Adolfo Celi	*De Castro*

Production

Philippe de Broca	*Director*
Peter Fernandez	*Writer (English version)*
George Delerue, Almeidinha, Catulo De Paula	*Original music*
Edmond Séchan	*Cinematography*
Dear Film Produzione/Les Films Ariane/	*Production Companies*
Les Productions Artistes Associés (United Artists)	
France/112/1964	*Country/Runtime/Year Released*

Chapter 66

Thelma and Louise

"Let's keep going."

—*Thelma Dickinson*

Hollywood has produced a number of "road" pictures for the past 40 years or so, but especially after the United States became connected by the interstate highway system. Audiences vicariously enjoy an adventure that has characters traveling toward a new destination and achieving a degree of personal growth through camaraderie and friendship. This maturation usually occurs after the individuals face obstacles in their path or when the gas tank becomes empty. The typical road movie involves two or more males. If one fondly recalls TV's *Route 66*, we had two buddies traveling in a Corvette to interesting places in search of adventure. Their whole purpose was to leave behind the security of home; experiment, and see life in a different perspective.

Men have a much easier time on the road than women do, in real life and from Hollywood's point of view. Female road trips are rare, about on par with lady Presidents. When one did appear in 1991, it was an exceptionally good one and it found favor with both men and women. Since it involved women, the heroines faced a different catalyst and set of obstacles. **Thelma and Louise** were two friends who bond in a flight from men—or authority. In contrast, male road trips have the protagonists escaping job or family responsibilities. Thelma and Louise's story is touching and poignant. Their initial plans are to go camping for a weekend, but instead a twist of fate puts them on the run from the police and from themselves.

Feminists rejoiced at this outing and for good reason. It was refreshing to view an intelligent and mainstream movie with two women who take charge of a situation with limited resources. These two women reacted to their experience of male oppression and dominance. The men in their lives failed to respect them. Fortunately not all men are like that. Though the women are quite different from each other, they have the same problem: they were singularly unlucky with men.

Louise (Susan Sarandon) is a waitress at a greasy spoon. Anyone familiar with the food service industry knows that you can make a living dishing it out, but your feet and your pride are going to always hurt. There's also a fine line between being nice and flirting to increase tips. Sarandon's character is, perhaps, the more complex and darker of the two. At first glance, she looks hard, cool, and self- assured. But as the story unfolds, we see she is anything but self-assured behind that very thick cloak of armor she wears. When we learn of her past, we can understand why she buttons her shirt to the collar and keeps her kitchen immaculate. She has a secret waiting to explode.

Thelma (Geena Davis) also lacks job skills to give her economic freedom from a jerk husband. Naive and scared, she's become dependent on a man that nobody with a sense of well being would like being around. Therefore, she must take his abuse. To him, she's only a piece of furniture in a tacky three-bedroom ranch. He's particularly nasty. After an unpleasant breakfast conversation, he tells her he's thankful there are no children being brought up in the household.

Demoralized and oppressed by their lives, these two ladies plan a short vacation to relax, go fishing, and to get away from the stress of living their lives. Unfortunately, the world isn't always a safe place. They find themselves in a situation that neither are equipped to handle. Perhaps learning about escape routes in some bad movie, Thelma and Louise decide to flee to Mexico in a 1966 Thunderbird convertible. Using their limited experiences, they believe running is their only option.

Their story is an incredible one, but very believable. Women will enjoy the growth these two women experience as they rack up the mileage. But there's also much sadness to it. Our two heroines don't know which men to trust. They can't judge who is reliable and who should be discarded. The fine art of sending up a trial balloon or a small test has escaped them. They have become their own worst enemy.

Most of the male characters would be better served in prison. Thelma's husband is an obvious, not-so-bright loser. He channel surfs for football during a telephone call from Thelma when he should have had her undivided attention. Brad Pitt is a good-looking loser, a con who lives by his wits. He's charming, polite, and offers well-defined abdomen muscles to titillate the ladies. Like all of the other men they contact, Pitt pays lip service to Thelma, but he's there to take advantage of an opportunity. The two meet other snakes along the way and in some cases, they're dealt with in a very humorous, yet extremely aggressive method.

Harvey Keitel and Michael Madsen are good guys but women would say that they have trouble communicating. Keitel is an understanding cop who's in touch with their troubles. Michael Madsen offers warmth and companionship, but no commitment. His relationship with Louise is unremarkable, but it's not entirely his fault: he may not understand her fears. It's part of the story that Thelma and Louise fail to recognize the integrity these two men have. There are moments when the audience is manipulated into believing these two ladies can trust a male. But that's just the screenwriter playing with our emotions.

The well-deserved, Oscar winning, original screenplay is by Callie Khouri. Without being maudlin, she touches all of our sensory buttons, providing us with an unforgettable portrayal of two unlucky women. The movie creatively uses water, in the form of rain, irrigation, and street cleaning as a transition. In keeping with the traditional road movie, some of our natural resources are on display, courtesy of the National Park Service. There are breathtaking views of Utah, including beautiful shots of the Arches and Canyonlands.

The soundtrack also pushes our buttons. Fully integrated, this is a nice mix of old tunes with the new. The titles could be chapters to a thesis on women' s issues. Glenn Frey's *Part of Me, Part of You* and Marianne Faithfull's rendition of *The Ballad of Lucy Jordan* are standouts. Both Sarandon and Davis were nominated for academy awards

Chapter 66

and both were strong contenders. However, when two actors from the same movie vie for this top honor, it usually goes to neither since the votes become diluted. Both lost the award to Jodie Foster for **Silence of the Lambs** (1991). However, each won an academy award before or after this film. Sarandon won best actress for **Dead Man Walking** (1995) and Davis won best supporting actress for **The Accidental Tourist** (1989). The movie made young Brad Pitt a full-fledged movie star. His role is brief but memorable, especially when he explains how to rob a convenience store with style, grace, and courtesy. William Baldwin was the first choice for this part, but decided to take the lead in Ron Howard's **Backdraft** (1991). Actor George Clooney was also in the running but it would take several years before he would become a bankable movie star. Goldie Hawn and Merle Streep considered starring in this film, but they opted to do **Death Becomes Her** (1992), a film unflattering to their sex: They played two rivals attempting to maintain their youth and vitality through witchcraft.

Cast

Susan Sarandon	*Louise Sawyer*
Geena Davis	*Thelma Dickinson*
Harvey Keitel	*Hal Slocumb*
Michael Madsen	*Jimmy*
Christopher McDonald	*Darryl*
Stephen Tobolowsky	*Max*
Brad Pitt	*J.D.*
Timothy Carhart	*Harlan*
Lucinda Jenney	*Lena, the Waitress*
Jason Beghe	*State Trooper*
Marco St. John	*Truck Driver*
Sonny Carl Davis	*Albert*
Ken Swofford	*Major*
Shelly Desai	*Motel Clerk*
Carol Mansell	*Waitress*

Production

Ridley Scott	*Director*
Callie Khouri	*Writer*
Mimi Polk, Ridley Scott	*Producer*
Hans Zimmer, B.B.	*Original Music*
Adrian Biddle	*Cinematography*
Metro-Goldwyn-Mayer/Pathé Entertainment	*Production Company*
USA/129/1991	*Country/Runtime/Year Released*

Chapter 67

This is Spinal Tap

"The sights, sounds, and smells of a hard-working rock band."

—*Marty DiBergi*

If you weren't aware that **This is Spinal Tap** is a parody, you might place the rock band in context with any number of musicians who briefly come to the surface, play a few notes, and then sink without a trace. There would be no reason to document these musicians' career, to put it in context with established standards of taste and sophistication. The key to the humor is that these performers aren't worth the expense of a documentary, but someone goes to great lengths to offer an in-depth profile on their art and success. Their success is limited and their art is questionable. Since this whole game is produced with pseudo serious intentions, the end result becomes a very satisfying and funny movie, especially for those who dig hard rock music.

Despite their lack of talent, the imaginary band has energy and bravado, two qualities necessary to keep our interest. The humor works best when the audience is made to feel superior to these slackers, believing they could be better musicians without any preparation or practice. That said, one must realize these boys do hold a certain charm and affability. If their music was slightly better, one could almost understand why this fourth-rate rock band thrived by a half note or two when they were in their prime. Despite the reported fiction, many of the escapades detailed actually happened to real rock bands from the 70s and 80s under the same circumstances. That only serves to make this spoof more meaningful and funny because it's based on a composite of facts. It's another confirmation that art imitates life.

This is Spinal Tap affectionately calls itself a rockumentary. It could also be labeled a mockumentary. The approach remains fresh and appealing, especially with a few surprise guest appearances by real artists who offer their perspectives on the situation. The dialogue is clever, full of political correctness (don't hit them when they are down). Thus, one is allowed to grasp what is really being said and we are not talking about good references. Individuals who abhor rock music will find the story fascinating, if not an affirmation of what they believe about this particular industry.

This film came on the scene shortly after the birth of MTV (Music Television) in the early 80s. This was a confusing time for people in the industry. On radio, one didn't have to look sensual while singing—though it helped when the performer went on personal appearances. When video became an integrated component, it became more of a requirement. One began to wonder if the video inspired the music or the music inspired the video. At least one heavyset (and middle-aged) performer complained that all one needed to land a gig on television was the ability to look good in a pair of jeans. On another level, **This is Spinal Tap** pokes fun at rock industry dysfunctions created by oversized egos who believe that style is far more important than talent. Perhaps the bizarre behavior occurs when they eventually realize talent can last longer than appearance.

Rob Reiner made his auspicious debut as director for this movie. He co-wrote the screenplay with Christopher Guest, Michael McKean and Harry Shearer, who are cast as members of a group that calls itself *Spinal Tap*. This particular band has seen better days and is now attempting a comeback of sorts. Reiner, as real director, plays the hack filmmaker who enthusiastically takes on this project. His fake documentary does, in effect, reveal the sights, sounds, and smells of a hard-working rock band— much to the delight of rock music fans everywhere.

His ability as a historian of important events reveals a group of musicians with hopelessly low abilities. Perhaps their stupidity saves them from embarrassment: They can offer no insights into their waning popularity. Their answers to the most routine questions

Chapter 67

clearly reveal a lack of understanding. Guest, McKean, and Shearer are excellent in their characterizations of the three "surviving" band members. In fact, together with Reiner, all have played privately together in their own band. One hopes their sound is much better than what is created here, but we will never know.

The challenge to portray terminally stupid characters is pulled off with detail, style, and a naturalness that makes the entire production very engaging and lifelike. You begin to anticipate what their next failure will be. This movie is especially funny to anyone familiar with rock band biographies. Like a product, a band has certain unique selling points. If they're good, it can be found in their sound and lyrics. But it typically means that a group of other tangibles are necessary to keep or maintain audience interest, from spandex tights to special effects. When all this fails, one must turn up the volume, so to speak, to keep people from walking out. For example, despite a relatively short career, Jimi Hendrix had a number of trademarks that delighted fans at his concerts. He played the guitar with his teeth. *The Who* also subjected themselves to traditions in that genre, like smashing a guitar at the end of their performance. Mick Jagger of *The Rolling Stones* offers facial contortions and peacock dance moves he admits he stole from Tina Turner. These real flesh and blood gimmicks undoubtedly influenced Reiner and his collaborators during the development of this movie.

The easiest job for Reiner must have been collaborating on the songs for **This is Spinal Tap**. He may have toured men's restrooms for ideas. They are intentionally grade Z material and offer a glimpse of the artistry: *Gimme Some Money, Smell the Glove, Break the Wind*, and the unforgettable *Intravaneous DiMilo*. They even suffer when compared to the notorious bad music from **Ishtar** (1987).

As a rockumentary, we are a shadow to **Spinal Tap**'s many, many embarrassing moments. Apparently, the band had one hit, 15 years before the rockumentary was produced. Not surprisingly, this has been followed by a string of high-profile failures. In fact the review was down to two words on their album *Shark Sandwich*. This flop resulted in a six-year hiatus from touring. Now, in 1984, to everyone's amazement, **Spinal Tap** has signed with another record label. One has three guesses as to what the producer was doing when they were signed.

The humor has roots in their desperation. Since we know their pain isn't real, we're allowed to laugh shamelessly. Do we feel for them? Maybe. They need a hit at this time if they plan to be around for the long-term. However, the strain begins to show behind the scenes. There are numerous backstage brawls or artistic disagreements. The marketing ideas turn sour when major retailers like K-Mart refuse to display their album on the grounds that it is offensive to women. This happened to the artist formerly known as *Prince*, when he appeared nude on his album cover. Undaunted, and in contrast to *The Beatles* white album, our boys decide to put their work in a symbolic black sleeve.

Their personal manager appears to be disorganized and their promotions fail to promote. But in all fairness to these hapless souls, part of their ineffectiveness stems from not having a good product to sell. After 15 years, *Spinal Tap's* legion of fans have grown up, settled down, and listen to the more quaint melodies of *Ratt*, *White Snake* or even *Aerosmith*. When one goes to a Rolling Stones concert, members of the audience span three generations. In frightening contrast, **This is Spinal Tap's** core audience grew up and deserted the band. Their music is so bad that the majority of young people will not listen to their albums. Thus the people who seek out the group are on the fringe of society. They are young men who decorate their rooms with posters and other paraphernalia ordered from comic books. They play their music very loud in an attempt to escape from reality and/ or drive their parents crazy. Predictably, many of them are without jobs or responsibilities—or in prison.

Since their albums have sold poorly, cost cutting crimps their style, much to our amusement. The best moments belong to the props that fail to open or are accidentally designed too small.

Many musicians and groups have disbanded and disappeared from **Spinal Tap's** era and this movie makes it easier to understand. Some bands are realistic about their appeal. For example, Pete

Chapter 67

Townsend, lead guitarist of *The Who* said his band no longer had the impact it did in the 60s, so they called it quits in the mid 80s. Money and fame was not the issue for *The Who*, but satisfying the demands of a fickle young audience was just too much of a hassle. When they returned to touring some fifteen years after their farewell performance, it was for nostalgia. They offered nothing new—just memories to people who enjoyed their music during the golden era of the rock group.

While this seriousness exists in this satire, **This is Spinal Tap** is not a downbeat movie. The band finds temporary salvation at the eleventh hour with an entirely new audience. Not surprisingly, they speak a totally different language and are unable to comprehend the lyrics.

Playing in a band must be a grueling experience professionally and personally. As time goes on, most bands have key personnel changes and internal upheavals. It is generally suspected that *The Beatles* split was spearheaded by Yoko Ono. Members of *Jefferson Airplane* also jockeyed for power by kissing up to lead singer Grace Slick. Like these and other bands with sexual politics, **Spinal Tap** finds itself involved with a dangerous woman who splits them up. But it can't always be blamed on predatory females: they've had 37 personnel changes in their short life—and the details are hilarious.

If one were to recall the San Francisco based group *Jefferson Airplane* from the 60s, they later graduated to *Jefferson Starship* for reasons probably only understood by their lawyers. After some more hits and internal changes, they were renamed *Starship*. One can safely say that the packaged sound of *Starship* in the 80s bore no relation to the pure sound of *Jefferson Airplane* in the 60s, even if Grace Slick sang some of the vocals. **Spinal Tap** has experienced the same changes. They could have been a bit more careful, though, since a spinal tap is a rather intricate (and painful) surgical procedure to the spine using a long needle to withdraw fluid to determine infection.

There is an interesting postscript to this movie. It was very popular with young people, especially on college campuses. Thus, the actors were reunited for some real concerts in the 90s, plus a TV special. Believe it or not, people were willing to purchase expensive tickets to hear their terribly funny music. It was hip to like it. One wonders if the audience was laughing or applauding from their seats.

In 2000, in yet another fake documentary, actor Michael McKean, along with director and actor Christopher Guest, had great success with **Best in Show**, which offered a glimpse of the dog show circuit and the often hilarious human behavior that went along with it. Guest then directed **The Mighty Wind** (2003) an ill-fated attempt at poking some fun at folk music in the same manner as **Spinal Tap**. Despite a strong cast (and an Oscar nominated song) it was a dull thing.

Taking a cue from other rock performers performing for a cause, **Spinal Tap** reunited in 2007 to save the world from global warming. A fictional 15-minute film from Marty DiBergi (Rob Reiner) revealed the surprising depth of their concerns for the environment.

Cast

Rob Reiner	*Marty DiBergi*
Kimberly Stringer	*Fan*
Chazz Domingueza	*Fan*
Shari Hall	*Fan*
R.J. Parnell	*Mike Shrimpton (Drummer)*
David Kaff	*Viv Savage (Keyboards & Vocals)*
Tony Hendra	*Ian Faith*
Michael McKean	*David St. Hubbins (Lead Guitar & Vocals)*
Christopher Guest	*Nigel Tufnel (Lead Guitars & Vocals)*
Harry Shearer	*Derek Smalls (Bass & Vocals)*
Bruno Kirby	*Tommy Pischedda*
Jean Cromie	*Ethereal Fan*
Patrick Maher	*New York M.C.*
Ed Begley, Jr.	*John "Stumpy" Pepys*
Danny Kortchmar	*Ronnie Pudding*
Fran Drescher	*Bobbi Flekman*
Patrick Macnee	*Sir Denis Eaton-Hogg*
Julie Payne	*Mime Waitress*
Dana Carvey	*Mime Waiter*

Chapter 67

Billy Crystal	*Morty the Mime*
Paul Benedict	*Tucker "Smitty" Brown*
Howard Hessman	*Terry Ladd*
Paul Shaffer	*Artie Fufkin*
Anjelica Huston	*Polly Deutsch*
Fred Willard	*Lt. Hookstratten*

Production

Rob Reiner	*Director*
Christopher Guest, Michael McKean, Rob Reiner, Harry Shearer	*Writers*
Karen Murphy	*Producer*
Peter Smokler	*Cinematography*
Christopher Guest, Michael McKean, Rob Reiner, Harry Shearer	*Original Music*
Renee Johnston	*Costumes*
Spinal Tap Productions	*Production Company*
USA/82/1984	*Country/Runtime/Year Released*

Chapter 68

Tiger Bay

"Don't let your emotions run your life."

—Korchinsky

The story is a familiar one in movies: an innocent bystander witnesses a murder and becomes a pawn in the killer's capture, but not before his or her own life is placed in jeopardy. In **Rear Window** (1954), the innocent bystander may only have a vivid imagination. We're manipulated into hoping that he doesn't. In **The Window** (1949), the innocent bystander is a child. Since the small boy has a history of telling fibs, nobody will believe his story. But that doesn't stop the person accused of murder from attempting to permanently silence him.

Borrowing this premise of crying wolf is **Tiger Bay**. Only it creates another angle and then expertly manipulates it to a very satisfying and entirely different outcome. In the olden days, it wasn't difficult to distinguish the good guys from the bad. In simpler times, the bad guys wore black. This story alters this rule. **Tiger Bay** manipulates the audience into siding with the murderer, just as the innocent bystander does. Unlike the other "window" films, the murderer isn't particularly nasty or unattractive. He just has flaws like the whole lot of us. The entire affect is a very absorbing experience since the audience has to choose who is right, and who is wrong and still offer empathy.

Apart from a very good story, the film's success depends on the charisma of the three leads. Hayley Mills is Gillie, a very precocious girl approaching her teen years. She's on the verge of blooming, so there's that awkwardness and isolation from her younger peers. Plus, there is a unique quality about her that distinguishes her from the other youngsters.

She has a tomboyish bent and a gift for weaving tales, which is crucial to the plot. These personality traits have made her very lonely, thus alienating her from her care-taking aunt and her playmates. It's not known where her parents are or what happened to them, but we can easily assume her situation is pretty drab. Her short life has been tough. This boredom and despair engulfs her and sets her up first as a witness and then later, confidant and pal to the murderer.

Horst Bucholz is the villain of this piece, a murderer. These are harsh words and one feels uncomfortable referring to him like this. You see him go into a rage and shoot a woman he thought loved him. This incident distorts our perceptions because she seems to incite his out-of-control temper. We may have done the same thing if given the same set of circumstances. His background is similar to Gillie. He is a Polish sailor, desperate for love and unsuccessful in finding it. The bond he and Gillie develop is created from their common situation.

He's spent much of his time at sea, away from his fiancée, though he's been sending her money with the hope of marrying her. It's probably the sole thing in his life that keeps him going. This fiancée, a Polish woman living in the United Kingdom, is older, more experienced, and has other plans. She's every bit an opportunist and she betrays him. It doesn't matter how Horst got tangled up with this predator of ignorant young men, but again Hollywood stereotypes are thwarted. He appears to be an okay guy with a future. In the opening credits, he's shown slapping the backs of his sailor buddies as he takes leave on shore. Ever smiling, he plays briefly with the children in the street. Tall, affable, and sporting perfect teeth, he doesn't look like the kind of guy who would fire bullets into someone just because she's been taking him to the cleaners. But he does. His most obvious problem is temper. Bordering on rage, it's revealed more than once as the story unfolds. It eventually does him in.

In pursuit of Bucholz is Hayley's real life father, John Mills. As a senior police inspector, the elder Mills has the patience of a saint and the wisdom that only years on the force can offer. He needs it this time since he's up against the likes of clever Hayley and charming Bucholz. Mills is the strongest character of the three, the pillar of strength and integrity. He keeps sleuthing despite the barrage of tricks to derail him down during the cat and mouse games.

The film offers many avenues of adventure and suspense, though the core of the story is about friendship and not murder. At first you wonder if Bucholz will do away with Gillie. He has several clear opportunities to do so and this would certainly ensure his freedom. We also question their friendship. It's an odd match; is it real or opportunistic? There's also the possibility that another luckless man (Anthony Dawson) may get fingered for the crime and the script doesn't allow an ounce of sympathy for him. If Dawson is convicted, Bucholz again has another chance at freedom. The script manipulates and massages these avenues and pulls the audience into a direction it would not have initially chosen.

Unlike most murder stories, we see a fully developed profile of the killer, as opposed to seeing how the law enforcement personnel find their criminal. We actually spend more time with him than we do with the police. The friendship he develops over time with Gillie is very touching and poignant. When they eventually part, he tells Gillie "wherever I am, you're still my friend."

This very unusual film—portraying the murderer as a sympathetic victim—offers several unique scenes. The lovers' quarrel is in Polish in this British-made film, but the acting is so good that you can feel the rage between the actors in increasing waves. Religion is also a frequent backdrop and some vivid scenes take place in and around a church. Unlike most portrayals of criminals and victims, we feel that Bucholz reports to a higher authority and feels a large degree of shame for his act. This was Hayley Mills' auspicious movie debut. Although the part was originally written for a boy, family nepotism (her father is John) intervened. Since father's next film, **Swiss Family Robinson** (1960), was for Disney, Walt was impressed enough to sign young Mills to a five-year contract. Her star was bright for five years as a major money earner for Disney. But like most other child stars, she found the transition to adult roles difficult.

One of her biggest successes for Disney was **The Parent Trap** in 1961. She reprised this role twice in the late 80s for the Disney Channel. Only this time she was cast as the parent with the sassy twins. In 2000 she was the narrator for *Child Stars: Their Story*, a

Chapter 68   371

poignant and earnest made-for-cable documentary tracing the ups and downs of being a young performer in front of a camera.

Tiger Bay was in fact, good for all concerned. John Mills, in films since the 30s, was in career doldrums by the 50s. After this success, things perked up a bit. Papa Mills received a career accolade by winning a best supporting Oscar for his role as a hunchback in **Ryan's Daughter** (1970). He was also knighted in 1976. Sir John Mills (1908-2005) continued to appear sporadically in films, despite blindness and advancing age. John Mills' other daughter is Juliet. It's interesting that she and Hayley both married men much older or younger than themselves. Hayley was once married to director Ray Boulting, 33 years her senior. However, in a change of pace, Juliet is married to actor Maxwell Caulfield, 18 years her junior.

This was Bucholz' first English speaking film. Born in Berlin, in the early 60s he appeared in several large-scale American productions. But his staying power was fleeting. By the end of the decade, he had returned to Europe to pursue his career. American audiences could see him for the first time in years in **A Beautiful Life** (2004) playing an uncaring physician.

Anthony Dawson, the poor chap Gillie tries to railroad as the murderer, played similar hapless type roles in **Dial M For Murder** (1953) and **Midnight Lace** (1960). His taut facial features typecast him as a heavy— which made him perfect for this particular role.

Laurie Johnson provided the music for this production. Several years later he was to provide the classic title track to the popular television show *The Avengers*.

Cast

John Mills	*Superintendent Graham*
Horst Buchholz	*Korchinsky*
Hayley Mills	*Gillie*
Megs Jenkins	*Mrs. Phillips*
Anthony Dawson	*Barclay*
Meredith Edwards	*P.C. George Williams*
Shari	*Christine*

Christopher Rhodes	*Inspector Bridges*
Kenneth Griffith	*Choirmaster*
George Pastell	*Poloma Captain*
Paul Stassino	*Poloma First Officer*
George Selway	*Detective Sergeant Harvey*
Edward Cast	*Detective Constable Thomas*
Eynon Evans	*Mr. Morgan*
David Davies	*Desk Sergeant*

Production

J. Lee Thompson	*Director*
Noel Calef	*Writer*
John Hawkesworth, Leslie Parkyn, Julian Wintle	*Producers*
Eric Cross	*Cinematography*
Laurie Johnson	*Original Music*
Independent Artists	*Production Company*
UK/105/1959	*Country/Runtime/Year Released*

Chapter 69
Till the End of Time

"Are you all in one piece?"

—Scuffy

Just after World War II ended, Hollywood responded with a number of films that detailed the adjustments soldiers had to make as they moved from the armed forces to civilian life. One of the more interesting movies on this subject of peacetime transition was **Till the End of Time**. Today, one can enjoy four things about this neat film: the cast, the title song, its depiction of American values, and its poignant look at individuals suffering from post-traumatic shock syndrome.

Concerning the cast, it's easier for a woman to have a long career in films with beauty as her major asset. In contrast, if a man is handsome, he better have other qualities as well if he's going to have a long run in pictures: confidence, presence, and integrity. This in some ways works off screen too. It generally takes more than striking looks to succeed with women—though it does help.

One male actor who tried the dreamboat route was Guy Madison. This was his second film and it's notable that his physical appearance singularly landed him his first film role. The story goes that Henry Willson (the agent who discovered Tab Hunter and Rock Hudson) spotted the handsome young man in a room full of serviceman on leave during the war. He later saw a truck carrying Dolly Madison donuts. From these two visions, he changed Roger Mosely's name to Guy Madison and convinced producer David Selznick to hire him for 1944's **Since You Went Away**. Madison's bit as the lonely sailor prompted women to write the studio and ask to see more of the handsome face.

Two years later, **Till the End of Time** was his second picture and first starring role. Madison was billed over Robert Mitchum and Bill

Williams, though they were more experienced in front of the camera. They don't have the awkwardness that Madison seems to be afflicted with. His performance is uneven and self-conscious and shows his lack of training. However, Svengali agent Willson was very much part of the production to ensure that nothing would stretch the green talent of his investment.

Madison plays the love interest of widow Dorothy McGuire, who tries to help him adjust to new times. He is angry when he returns home because he's older, without a college degree, and believes he has been cheated out of several years of living. Her advice to Madison is the film's best message: the only people who have a beef about war are those that didn't come back. Still, his emotional problems continue, as do those of the other men who came back with handicaps. Robert Mitchum has a head injury and Bill Williams is without both legs.

McGuire made a deal to do a sequel to **Claudia** (1943), her star-making vehicle of a few years back, in exchange for doing this film. In this outing, for the first (and last) time in her career, McGuire was made to look glamorous. Still, the camera can't hide the fact that she's a bit mature (she was in her early 30s at the time) for Madison. She is also wiser, but at no time does she come across as manipulative. Thus, it's rather incongruous when Madison says he's just a cheap pick-up for her.

McGuire's forte in a long and illustrious career was playing warm, caring mothers or wives who frequently nursed her man or brood back to health, or stood on the sidelines and picked them up when they made an error. One of her last performances was once again in this mold in a TV film with Elizabeth Montgomery called **Between Darkness and Dawn** (1985).

Of the three male leads—Madison, Bill Williams, and Robert Mitchum— it was believed that Mitchum offered the least potential for a long-term career in pictures. In fact, he out-performed most of his contemporaries. He remained in demand for quality productions as long as he wanted to act, which was up to his death in 1997. His role is just as complex as his costars, but there are certain aspects of his performance that add dimension—and contrasts sharply with

Chapter 69

Madison's awkwardness. Mitchum's wink, glance, and walk were all hallmarks of an intelligent leading man. In interviews, Mitchum was always self-deprecating. It was a trait that only added to his appeal. When someone remarked about his particular walk, he said he was just trying to hold his gut in. Not many movie stars would dare to point out their imperfections.

Bill Williams completes the trio. Perhaps he should be the angriest of the lot since he doesn't have anything to stand on and he really doesn't have much to do in the movie either. No one can blame him for not wanting to get out of bed and fight. When he does, it's to help out his friends when they come up against some American-style prejudice.

An army of superb, supporting players contribute to the film's gloss. Jean Porter plays the next door neighbor infatuated with Guy Madison. She was, in fact, married to the film's director Edward Dmytryk. Tom Tully and Ruth Nelson play Madison's parents and their denial of his anguish and concentration on their wants and needs is rather poignant. They can't understand how their son is physically healthy, but is suffering from battle fatigue, or what is now called post traumatic stress disorder.

Nelson had one of her best roles at the end of her life when she played Robert DeNiro's mom in **Awakenings** (1990). Once again she was warm and caring, yet a bit unnerved about changes that were occurring in her son, who has also been traumatized.

Selena Royle plays Williams' mother and though her part is small, you can tell that all isn't well in her home. Her speech about President Roosevelt is rather inspirational. The other characters are distinctly American: Scuffy (Harry von Zell) runs the neighborhood hang-out where one can dance, have a rum and Coke, and find friends. His world was on the good side of town. At the end, our heroes get to tangle with the seamier side of life in a raunchy joint called the Swan Club. It's fitting that they get a taste of prejudice. Just because the war was over didn't mean the world was a safe place. There would be more civil rights work to do during the next two decades.

The movie's title song was a big hit for Perry Como during World

War II. *Till the End of Time* was Como's first record to sell a million and it's based on Chopin's *Polonaise, No. 6 in A-Flat op 53*. Incorporating a popular song within a movie was a novel approach at the time. In this instance, it's used to remind Madison of his infatuation with lovely McGuire.

Though **Till the End of Time** can be classified as very American in taste and content, it's interesting that director Dmytryk was later named as one of the so-called "Hollywood Ten." These ten individuals were members of the Hollywood community who refused to cooperate with the House Un-American Activities Committee. His career went on hiatus and despite renouncing Communism and naming names, his career never regained its momentum. In the 70s (to 1981) he became a respected member of academia by teaching filmmaking. He eventually rose to a chair in filmmaking at the University of Southern California.

A few years after this film, Guy Madison took acting lessons, developed a rugged look and found a home on television by playing Wild Bill Hickok. In the 60s he turned to Italy for gainful employment. Despite limited acting ability, he managed to make a long string of undistinguished but successful movies for the European trade.

One interesting note: Madison may have covered his on-camera acting insecurities with cigarettes. Though smoking was fashionable at the time, he lights tobacco in nearly every scene in this particular film. Sadly, he died from emphysema in 1996 at age 74.

It was also sad when members of Madison's family experienced the horrors of war in October 2008 when Madison's grandson Specialist Spencer T. Karol (from his daughter Bridget) was killed while serving his country in Iraq.

Cast

Dorothy McGuire	*Pat Ruscomb*
Guy Madison	*Cliff Harper*
Robert Mitchum	*William Tabeshaw*
Bill Williams	*Perry Kincheloe*

Chapter 69

Tom Tully	*C.W. Harper*
William Gargan	*Sergeant Gunny Watrous*
Jean Porter	*Helen Ingersoll*
Johnny Sands	*Tommy Hendricks*
Loren Tindall	*Pinky*
Ruth Nelson	*Amy Harper*
Selena Royle	*Mrs. Kincheloe*
Harry von Zell	*Scuffy*

Production

Edward Dmytryk	*Director*
Niven Busch (novel), Allen Rivkin	*Writers*
Dore Schary	*Producer*
Leigh Harline, Buddy Kaye, Ted Mossman	*Original Music*
Harry J. Wild	*Cinematography*
IRKO Radio Pictures/Vanguard Productions	*Production Company*
USA/105 minutes/1946	*Country/Runtime/Year Released*

Chapter 70

Who's Afraid of Virginia Woolf

"You can stand it. You married me for it."

—Martha

For an extended moment in the 60s, Elizabeth Taylor and Richard Burton were the focus of worldwide attention. Curiously, it wasn't for their acting, though both were capable performers. It was their public escapades that seemed to interest the worldwide press. They were rich and beautiful adulterers and their every move was documented for public consumption.

They met on the set of **Cleopatra** (1963), fell in love, ditched their respective spouses and married. Then, despite some consternation from moralists, they stirred the public's fancy wherever they went. They became some of the highest paid performers of the 60s. As if to flaunt their wealth, the couple purchased expensive gifts, traveled all over the world, and made 10 feature films together. Not all of the times were good. There were drunken brawls and embarrassing headlines (*"The night Liz said no to Dick"*). Still, at the height of their popularity, no matter how self-destructive they may have been, the world was at their feet.

Their films were good, too, at least the early ones. Their third partnership was **Who's Afraid of Virginia Woolf** (1966) and it's easily their best film. It was both an artistic and commercial success. It was based entirely on Edward Albee's 1962 socially conscious play about a battling married couple who like to mix and match metaphors. The main characters are George and Martha. Coincidentally, they have the same name of the father of our country and his wife. The other characters are Nick and Honey. Nick is George's antagonist, and it's fitting that one says to the other "We will bury you." The backdrop for all of the action is a tidy New England college where Puritanism and

Chapter 70

379

great minds are supposed to co-habitate. Albee's course of action is to show what's under the veneer of this sacred cow otherwise known as the institution of higher learning. To show the hypocrisy of the upper middle class, Albee "peels the label" because underneath is what you find to be real. Albee seems to be saying that it may not be pleasant, but it's better to know the truth.

The realism ride with George and Martha continues for over two hours and the abuse both couples afflict on each other seldom lets down. The resolution has to come when it does because the four characters are simply too exhausted to carry on.

This film broke new ground for ripe language, at least in the United States. At the time, 1966, it must have been quite a shock to see Liz call Dick "a son of a bitch."

Martha seems to have the most ammunition. She is the daughter of the president of the college and that title provides her with tremendous influence. Offend her and your position with the university is on the line. She's a fat harridan with a foul tongue and temper. She also has eyes for Nick, not because he's young and attractive, but because she can hurt George through him. As one can see, these aren't particularly nice people. But as Albee admits, it's very interesting to see how they live. At times you may laugh, but the undercurrent is one of horror.

Taylor put her public persona on the line to play this role and she was justifiably applauded for this courage. At the time, she was known for her world-class beauty. Then 34, she was in her prime. Actresses who played Martha on stage included Mercedes McCambridge, Kate Reid, and Uta Hagen—actresses not known for world-class glamour. But Taylor was game. She added on the necessary weight, splotched her make-up, and messed up her hair. In what was her first character role, she's very convincing as a vulgar and coarse shrike. There are moments when she is witty, serious, pathetic, and touching. Unfortunately, this characterization is one that Taylor continued, with varying degrees of success, in all her subsequent films.

Taylor had plenty of box-office clout when asked to do this film. She agreed to take the role, as long as husband Burton could play

George. The producers had wanted Arthur Hill, who had played the role on stage and were afraid an English actor would tarnish the proceedings. But Burton's performance as a stuffy history professor matched everyone's degree of intensity. Though Taylor seems to be at the center of things, he has a few tricks of his own. It's a very good fighting match.

George Segal and Sandy Dennis are Nick and Honey. They also have some illusions to peel. Their loss of a child coincides with George and Martha's inability to have a real child. Some theorize the child is a religious symbol. Also, it's interesting to note that both females have rich and prosperous parents, another symbol of the power they brought to the marriage.

Black and white photography was used to cut production costs since Liz, Dick, and Albee received hefty salaries. With a percentage of the profits, Taylor and Burton received upwards of $6 million for their participation. Taylor was in her early 30s during filming. The part called for her to be much older and haggard and it was thought that black and white photography would provide a more realistic age appropriate appearance. Taylor, knowing what her major asset was, was said to have whispered to the cameraman "don't make me look too old."

Playwright Albee received $500,000 for the screen rights to his play, an unheard of sum for a relative unknown to the film industry. More amazing was the hiring of Mike Nichols. Though he had a string of hits on Broadway, this was his first film. He consolidated his lofty position the following year with **The Graduate** (1967).

Segal was not the first choice for Nick— Robert Redford turned the part down.

The film received 13 nominations for Academy Awards. Taylor won best actress, Segal won best supporting actor, and Dennis, in her first film, won best supporting actress. After the awards, Taylor was openly miffed that husband Dick didn't win.

Some question whether Taylor and Burton were really playing themselves in the film. There may be some truth to it. Still, what's up on the screen, illusion or not, is scintillating. Certainly they loved

Chapter 70

each other, but couldn't live with each other. They separated and divorced in the early 70s, remarried and then divorced again in 1976. Both of them had drug and alcohol dependencies. All of their addictions were highly publicized.

After this film, the world's favorite couple tried Shakespeare with the **Taming of the Shrew** (1967). This film received good reviews but they had already reached their pinnacle. Each production afterwards grew increasingly poor. It was as if they were intentionally trying to kill their careers. At least one critic said they were filming home movies. They last worked together professionally in 1983 in the stage production of Noel Coward's *Private Lives*. When Burton died suddenly in 1984 of a cerebral hemorrhage, the world mourned with Liz.

Taylor's movies (without husband) around this time are not without distinction. **X, Y & Z** (1972) found her married to Michael Caine. When Cain takes on a mistress, Susannah York, Liz pulls out all stops to break it up. She shouts, slams doors and packs her suitcase before losing less than her adversaries. Caine later remarked that her performance made him look like an amateur.

Taylor was divorced eight times—counting the two unions with Richard. Perhaps older and wiser, she said she wouldn't marry again after her marriage to construction worker Larry Fortensky ended in 1996. Her film career was also on the back burner, though she did turn up in a substantial role for Steven Spielberg in **The Flintstones** (1994). As Fred's sourpuss mother-in-law, it was yet another variation of Martha.

In her 70s, Taylor devoted much of her energy to business and charitable causes. Her movie icon was resting but she remained one of the most famous women in the world. When she passed away in early 2011, the headlines said the last star was now gone.

Incidentally, the Bette Davis movie in which the immortal line "what a dump" is muttered, is from **Beyond the Forest** (1948). Davis said one of the major disappointments in her life was not playing Martha on film, "but the Burtons were real big at the time."

Cast

Elizabeth Taylor	*Martha*
Richard Burton	*George*
George Segal	*Nick*
Sandy Dennis	*Honey*

Production

Mike Nichols	*Director*
Edward Albee (play), Ernest Lehman	*Writers*
Ernest Lehman	*Producer*
Haskell Wexler	*Cinematographer*
Alex North	*Original Music*
Warner Brothers/Chenault Productions	*Production Company*
USA/134/1966	*Country/Runtime/Year Released*

Epilogue

At some point in time during the history of making movies, film-makers decided to drop the phrase "The End" from what was supposed to be the conclusion of the movie. I think it was a fine idea to stop this practice. When the screen goes blank, the movie magic does not end at that precise moment. We may leave the place where the film was viewed, but our thoughts, questions and excitement of the total experience continues. A compelling movie takes on a life of its own and may stay with us forever.

I hope *Download This Movie For a Reel Good Time* inspires you to seek out and enjoy the movies that can become special to you.

More Downloadable Movies

Since **Download This Movie** was published in 2009, "why stop at 70" is a frequently asked question. The original concept included 100 movies since that figure is a milestone number. The reduction to 70 became necessary when time and space became an obstacle. Subtracting 30 from the original concept was done with regret. Two Barbara Stanwyck films, John Wayne, a silent film from 1926 and many other interesting films were painfully eliminated.

What follows is a list of those 30 films that deserve equal attention. The title, year released, dialogue from a principal character, cast, director and plot synopsis are included to encourage viewing.

71. **A History of Violence** (2005)
    "Jesus, Richie!"
    —Tom Stall

Cast: Viggo Mortensen, Maria Bello, Ed Harris, William Hurt. Intense crime thriller directed by David Cronenberg. Absorbing account of a man who lives quietly in a small town with his family until a violent crime reveals his secret past.

72. **A Star is Born** (1954)
    "The man that got away."
    —Vicki Lester

Cast: Judy Garland, James Mason. Directed by George Cukor. When Garland didn't win the academy award for her performance, most agreed with Groucho Marx's observation: "the biggest robbery since Brink's."

73. **Bad Day at Black Rock** (1955)
   "It's the first time the streamliner's stopped here in four years."
   —Mr. Hastings

Cast: Spencer Tracy, Robert Ryan, Anne Francis, Dean Jagger, Walter Brennan, John Ericson, Ernest Borgnine and Lee Marvin. Western with film noir influences directed by John Sturges. A mysterious one-arm stranger comes to a small town with only 9 inhabitants. They make it very clear that he should leave immediately—he doesn't.

74. **Buena Sera, Mrs. Campbell** (1968)
   "That is the most beautiful story I ever heard."
   —Shirley Newman

Cast: Gina Lollobrigida, Phil Silvers, Peter Lawford, Telly Savalas, Shelley Winters, Lee Grant. Comedy directed by Melvin Frank. Three WWII veterans each believe they fathered a daughter during the war in American occupied Italy. Twenty years later, they are re-united with their former lover, who now goes by "Mrs. Campbell."

75. **Cactus Flower** (1969)
   "Right now, she's surrounded by her husband, her ex-boyfriend, her current boyfriend, and maybe her future boyfriend."
   —Toni Simmons

Cast: Walter Matthau, Ingrid Bergman, Goldie Hawn, Rick Lenz. Comedy directed by Gene Saks. Hawn won an academy award in her first major film role. Matthau and Bergman are equally superb.

76. **Crimes and Misdemeanors** (1989)
   "If you want a happy ending, you should go see a Hollywood movie."
   —Judah Rosenthal

Cast: Alan Alda, Woody Allen, Mia Farrow, Angelica Huston, Martin Landau, Jerry Orbach, Claire Bloom. Compelling comedy-drama written and directed by Woody Allen. Two men (Landau and Allen) have very different moral and philosophical approaches to life.

77. **Double Indemnity** (1944)
"Suppose I have to whack you over the knuckles."
—Phyillis Dietrichson

Cast: Barbara Stanwyck, Fred MacMurray, Edward G. Robinson. Film noir directed by Billy Wilder. Stanwyck and MacMurray dabble in murder and insurance fraud. The plot thickens when Robinson is drawn into the investigation. Three high powered actors at their peak.

78. **Edward Scissorhands** (1990)
"Avon calling."
—Peg Boggs

Cast: Johnny Depp, Winona Ryder, Dianne Wiest, Vincent Price, Alan Arkin. Fantasy directed by Tim Burton. An artificial man who has scissors for hands is invited to live with a suburban family. He is kind and talented but sharp fingers prevent him from being accepted.

79. **Executive Suite** (1954)
"You may think that those who work there are somehow above and beyond the tensions and temptations of the lower floors. This is to say that it isn't so."
—Narrator

Cast: William Holden, Barbara Stanwyck, Fredric March, Walter Pidgeon, June Allyson. Drama directed by Robert Wise. A CEO's unexpected death triggers internal struggles for control of a large corporation.

80. **Five Against the House** (1955)
"I'm a stranger in town. Can you direct me to your house?"
—Brick

Cast: Guy Madison, Kim Novak, Brian Keith. Directed by Phil Karlson. Highly imitated heist film set in Las Vegas. An important film that helped launch Novak's career.

81. **Groundhog Day** (1993)
"Today is tomorrow. It happened."
—Phil

Cast: Bill Murray, Andie MacDowell, Chris Elliott. Comedy directed by Harold Ramis. Hilarious thought provoking film has an obnoxious TV reporter repeat the same day over, and over, and over.

82. **If I Had a Million** (1932)
"There ain't any jail of steel or stone that can hold a body prisoner as tight as one built of old age and lack of money."
—Mrs. Mary Walker

Cast: Gary Cooper, Charles Laughton, George Raft, Jack Oakie, Richard Benett, Charles Ruggles, Alison Skipworth, W.C. Fields, Mary Boland, May Robson, Wynne Gibson, Frances Dee, Gail Patrick, Grant Mitchell, Gene Raymond, Bess Flowers. A dying millionaire decides to give his fortune to seven strangers randomly picked from a phonebook. Entertaining anthology film with all-star cast. W.C. Fields' battle with road hogs is a highlight, but all vignettes are memorable.
Directors: Ernst Lubitsch (*The Clerk*), Norman Taurog (*Prologue and Epilogue*), Stephen Roberts (*Violet & Grandma*), Norman Z. McLeod (*China Shop & Road Hogs*), James Cruze (*Death Cell*), William A. Seiter (*The Three Marines*) and H. Bruce Humberstone (*The Forger*).

388

83. **In the Heat of the Night** (1967)
"I want that officer given a free hand. Otherwise, I will pack up my husband's engineers and leave you to yourselves."
—Mrs. Colbert

Cast: Sidney Poiter, Rod Steiger, Warren Oates, Lee Grant. Drama directed by Norman Jewison. Racial tensions erupt when a wealthy industrialist is murdered. Steiger's performance won academy award. Grant is electrifying in her two brief scenes.

84. **Lifeboat** (1944)
"Like tears, for instance. They're nothing but H2O with a trace of sodium choride."
—Connie Porter

Cast: Tallulah Bankhead, William Bendix, Walter Slezak. Directed by Alfred Hitchcock. British and American civilians occupy a crowded lifeboat after a German submarine sinks their passenger ship. Tensions increase when one of the German's responsible for the sinking is rescued and allowed to board. Perhaps Bankhead's best film. Watch closely for Hitchcock's cameo.

85. **Love Has Many Faces** (1965)
"Nothing illegal, just immoral."
—Hank Walker

Cast: Lana Turner, Cliff Robertson, Hugh O'Brien, Stephanie Powers, Ruth Roman. Drama directed by Alexander Singer.
Entertaining film has wealthy Turner dealing with seamy characters in Acapulco. O'Brien plays a gigolo and the tight, brief swimsuit he wears in several scenes earned him the nickname "no buns" from Turner, during production.

86. **Metropolis** (1927)
   "For her, all seven deadly sins!"
   —Barfly

Cast: Brigitte Helm. German silent film directed by Fritz Lang presents a futuristic city with two distinct classes. The privilege occupy above ground high rises while workers toil in the dark basements with growing dissatisfaction.

87. **Midnight Express** (1978)
   "This place is crazy."
   —Billy Hayes

Cast: Brad Davis, Randy Quaid, John Hurt. Drama directed by Alan Parker. Intense, cautionary film based on a true story. A young American in Turkey receives a harsh prison sentence for drug smuggling.

88. **Mr. Hobbs Takes a Vacation** (1962)
   "No, I just called hey Joe, it's from my experience that there's usually one Joe in a group of fellows."
   —Roger Hobbs

Cast: James Stewart, Maureen O'Hara, Fabian, Marie Wilson. Comedy directed by Henry Koster. Stewart and O'Hara rent a beach home to reunite their adult children and grandchildren for a quiet vacation. Things don't go as planned.

89. **Murder My Sweet** (1944)
   "It's a long story and not pretty."
   —Helen Grayle

Cast: Dick Powell, Claire Trevor, Anne Shirley, Mike Mazurki, Otto Kruger. Film noir directed by Edward Dmytryk and based on Raymond Chandler's 1940 novel *Farewell, My Lovely*. Powell successfully transitioned from lightweight musicals to tough private eye Philip Marlowe.

90. **Penny Serenade** (1941)

"You see, there's so many little things about her that nobody would understand her the way Judy and I do."
—Roger Adams

Cast: Cary Grant, Irene Dunne, Beulah Bondi. George Stevens directed this bittersweet story of young couple trying to start a family.

91. **Raw Deal** (1948)

"The only way you know how to fight is that stupid way with a gun."
—Ann Martin

Cast: Dennis O'Keefe, Claire Trevor, Marsha Hunt, Raymond Burr. Film noir directed by Anthony Mann. An escaped prisoner's relationship with two women complicates his bid for freedom.

92. **Séance on a Wet Afternoon** (1964)

"So bright after a séance. Brightness just seems to fall from the air."
—Myra Savage

Cast: Kim Stanley, Richard Attenborough. Unusual film directed by Bryan Forbes. A psychic wants to demonstrate her abilities by locating a kidnapped child. Stanley preferred the stage and did not work in film for 18 years, until **Frances** (1982). She received Oscar nominations for both films.

93. **The Departed** (2006)

"A lot of guys just want to appear to be cops. Gun, badge, pretend they're on TV."
—Oliver Queenan

391

Cast: Leonardo DiCaprio, Matt Damon, Jack Nicholson, Mark Wahlberg, Martin Sheen. Intense crime drama directed by Martin Scorsese. Two men on opposite sides of the law go undercover to identify each other.

94. The Ghost and Mr. Chicken (1966)
"And they used Bon-Ami!"
—Mrs. Cobb

Cast: Don Knotts, Joan Staley, Dick Sargent, Skip Homeier. Directed by Alan Rafkin. Man aspiring to be a newspaper reporter reluctantly agrees to spend the night in a run-down mansion. Knotts personally contacted Bon-Ami's CEO for permission to use their product name in a running gag. Memorable Vic Mizzy musical score.

95. The Prime of Miss Jean Brodie (1969)
"I am a teacher! I am a teacher, first, last, always!"
—Jean Brodie

Cast: Maggie Smith, Gordon Jackson, Robert Stephens. Drama directed by Ronald Neame. Prep school teacher passes her distorted views of the world onto her young and impressionable female students. Takes place in 1930s Scotland. Smith won best actress academy award for her performance.

96. The Shawshank Redemption (1994)
"Anything you put in my mouth, you're going to lose."
—Andy Dufresne

Cast: Tim Robbins, Morgan Freeman. Intense drama directed by Frank Darabond. An innocent man sentenced to a life term in prison never loses hope, eventually achieving unique status within the penitentiary system. Adapted from the Stephen King novella *Rita Hayworth and the Shawshank Redemption*.

97. **The Shootist** (1976)
"I won't be insulted."
—John Bernard Books

Cast: John Wayne, Lauren Bacall, Hugh O'Brien, James Stewart, Ron Howard. Western directed by Don Siegel. Wayne plays a terminally ill gunfighter looking for a way to die peacefully. The film was Wayne's final film in a career that began during the silent film era in 1926.

98. **Tomorrow is Another Day** (1951)
"Your generation grew up, married, raised families, went to war. But nothing happened to you, Bill. You just got older."
—Prison Warden

Cast: Steve Cochran, Ruth Roman, Lurene Tuttle. Film noir directed by Felix Feist. A man has difficulty adjusting to society after spending his most formidable years in prison.

99. **Touch of Evil** (1958)
"You should lay off those candy bars."
—Tanya

Cast: Charlton Heston, Janet Leigh, Orson Welles, Akim Tamiroff, Marlene Dietrich and Zsa Zsa Gabor. Film noir directed by Orson Wells. Welles was dissatisfied with the final film and wrote a 40 page memo of protest to studio heads. Forty years later, the film was re-edited to match specifications he had outlined in his memo. The re-edited 1998 version is the one to watch.

100. **Witness for the Prosecution** (1957)
Wanna kiss me, ducky?
—Cockney Woman

Cast: Marlene Dietrich, Tyrone Powers, Charles Laughton, Elsa Lancaster, Ruta Lee. Courtroom drama directed by Billy Wilder.

393

Dietrich defends her husband after he is accused of murder. Based on the Agatha Christie play. The final scene packs a wallop. At the end of the film, during the credits, a voiceover suggests the following: *"The management of this theatre suggests that for the greater entertainment of your friends who have not yet seen the picture, you will not divulge, to anyone, the secret ending of Witness for the Prosecution."*

Bibliographical Essay

A&E's *Biography*. Cablevision's award winning program on the Arts and Entertainment network. As they put it: "Meet the real people who make Hollywood happen."

Arnaz, Desi. *A Book*. New York: Morrow, 1976. Desi characterized his biography as "the outspoken memoirs of 'Ricky Ricardo'—the man who loved Lucy."

Benton, Mike. *The Comic Book in America: An Illustrated History*. Dallas: Taylor Publishing, 1989. A colorful history of the comic book from the 1930's to 1980's.

Bergman, Andrew. *James Cagney*. New York: Galahad Books, 1973. Bergman profiles Cagney's film career.

Babyak, Jolene. *Eyewitness on Alcatraz: true stories of families who lived on the rock*. Berkeley, CA: Ariel Vamp Press, 1988. Babyak's father was the last warden at Alcatraz.

Ballard, Robert D. *The Discovery of the Titanic*. Toronto, Ontario: Warner Books, 1987. Ballard successfully located the Titanic wreck in 1985 after an exhaustive 12 year search.

Barbour, Alan G. *Humphrey Bogart*. New York: Pyramid Publications, 1973. Barbour profiles Bogart's film career.

Crist, Judith. *Judith Crist's TV GUIDE to the Movies*. New York: Popular Libary, 1974. Crist offers a compilation of her concise, perceptive reviews, originally published in TV GUIDE.

Dick, Bernard F. *Billy Wilder*. Boston: Twayne Publishers, 1980. Dick profiles Wilder's career in Hollywood.

395

Evans, Robert. *The Kid Stays in the Picture*. New York: Hyperion, 1994. Movie producer Evans' chronicles the personal and professional highs and lows of his Hollywood career.

Everson, William K. *The Art of W.C. Fields*. New York: Bonanza Books, 1967. Everson offers a critical analysis of Fields' remarkable career.

Fleming, Ian. *On Her Majesty's Secret Service*. New York: New American Library, 1963. One of Fleming's 14 novels that featured superspy James Bond.

Grey, Rudolph. *Nightmare of Ecstasy: The Life and Art of Edward D. Wood*, Jr. Los Angeles: Feral House, 1992. Rudolph's biography profiles the interesting life of Wood, a man with more determination than talent.

Grodin, Charles. It would be so nice if you weren't here: my journey through show business. New York: Morrow, 1989. Grodin's humorous autobiography of his acting career.

Guest, Judith. *Ordinary People*. New York: Viking Press, 1976. Guest's fictional bestseller of a sensitive teen and the guilt he assumes when his extroverted brother accidentally drowns.

Haun, Harry. *The Movie Quote Book*. New York: Bonanza Books, 1986. Haun said a prominent Hollywood director has his quote book resting permanently on his nightstand.

Higham, Charles. *Bette: The Life of Bette Davis*. New York: MacMillan, 1981. Higham's profile of Davis' life and career in film.

Holtzman, William. *Judy Holliday, only child*. New York: Putnam, 1982. Holtzman's profile of Holliday's short and sweet career.

396

Hotchner, A.E. *Doris Day: Her Own Story*. New York: Morrow, 1975. Hotchner's intimate look at Day's personal and professional life.

The Internet Movie Database or www.imdb.com. Information on movies and the personalities behind them at your fingertips.

Katz, Ephraim. *The Film Encyclopedia*. New York: HarperCollins, 1994. Ephraim's comprehensive reference on film.

Kelley, Kitty. *His Way: The unauthorized biography of Frank Sinatra*. New York: Bantam, 1986. Kelley offers an absorbing, controversial study of Sinatra's personal and professional life.

Keylin, A. Fleischer, & S. Editors. *Hollywood Album, the lives and deaths of Hollywood stars from the pages of The New York Times*. New York: Arno Press, 1979. Fleischer compiled obituaries of the famous from one of the most respected newspapers in the world.

Kobal, John. *People will talk*. New York: Knopf, 1985. Kobal offers intelligent and thoughtful interviews with many stars from the golden era.

Kramer, Stanley & Thomas M. Coffey. *It's a Mad, Mad, Mad, Mad World; A Life in Hollywood*. Orlando, FL, 1997. A profile of Stanley Kramer's film making career.

Langworth, Richard & Graham Robson. *Complete Book of Collectible Cars 1940-1980*. New York: Beekman House, 1982. A guide to help identify special interest cars seen in the movies.

Lord, Walter. *A Night to Remember*. New York: Holt, 1955. Lord's bestselling account of the Titanic disaster.

Maltin, Leonard. *Leonard Maltin's Movie & Video Guide*. New York: Plume, 1993-. Originally published in 1969, Maltin's annual reference guide to thousands of titles belongs beside every television remote.

Manso, Peter. *Brando: The biography*. New York: Hyperion, 1994. Manso's profile Brando's personal and professional acting and film career.

McClelland, Doug. *The Golden Age of B Movies*. New York: Bonanza Books, 1981. An interesting collection of Hollywood's "less" prestigious product line.

McParland, Stephen J. *It's Party Time: a musical appreciation of the beach party film genre*. Corona Del Mar, California: PTB Production. McParland compiled a wide assortment of documents and memorabilia on 60's style beach music.

Moore, Mary Tyler. *After All*. New York: Putnam, 1995. MTM's frank and intimate autobiography.

Morella, Joe & Edward Epstein. *Forever Lucy: The life of Lucille Ball*. Secaucus, New Jersey: L. Stuart, 1986. Morella and Epstein profile Ball's remarkable life and career.

Nabokov, Vladimir. *Lolita*. New York: Putnam, 1955. Controversial novel admired by literary circles.

Reed, Rex. *Do You Sleep in the Nude?* New York: New American Library, 1968. Reed's compelling interviews with film personalities.

Robertson, Patrick. *Movie Facts & Feats: a Guiness record book*. New York: Guiness Books, 1988. Robertson gathers a comprehensive list of movie facts.

Rutenberg, Michael E. *Edward Albee. Playwright in protest*. New York: DBS Publications, 1969. Rutenberg profiles Albee's work.

Shipman, David. *The Great Movie Stars: The International Years*. New York: Hill & Wang, 1980. Shipman's thoughtful analysis on the careers of stars popular just after World War II. One of the best books written on subject.

Shipman, David. *The Great Movie Stars: The Golden Years*. New York: Hill & Wang, 1979. Companion guide to *The International Years*, Shipman examines the careers of stars who became popular in the very first motion pictures.

Silver, Alain. & E. Ward. *Film Noir: An Encyclopedic Reference to American style*. Woodstock, New York: Overlook Press, 1979. Comprehensive guide to Hollywood crime melodramas from the 1940s and 1950s.

Spoto, Daniel. *The Art of Alfred Hitchcock: Fifty Years of His Motion Pictures*. New York: Hopkinson and Blake, 1977. Spoto's scholarly analysis of the remarkable director's complete body of work.

Spoto, Daniel. *A Passion For Life: The Biography of Elizabeth Taylor*. New York: HarperCollins, 1995. Spoto profiles Taylor's remarkable career and stormy personal life.

Swanson, Gloria. *Swanson on Swanson*. New York: Random House, 1980. Swanson's frank autobiography of her remarkable life and career.

Thomas, Bob. *I Got Rhythm! The Ethel Merman Story*. New York: Putnam's, 1985. Thomas' thoughtful profile of Merman's career on stage, screen and TV.

Thomas, Bob. Joan Crawford, a biography. New York: Simon & Schuster, 1978. Thomas profiles Crawford's long film career.

Tozzi, Romano. *Spencer Tracy*. New York: Galahad Books, 1973. Tozzi's profile of Tracy's life and film career.

Vaughn, Robert. *Only Victims: A Study of Show Business Blacklisting*. New York: Putnam, 1972. *The Man from U.N.C.L.E.* earned his Ph.D. with this research.

Wallace, Irving & Amy Wallace, David Wallechinsky, Sylvia Wallace. *The Intimate Sex Lives of Famous People*. New York: Delacorte Press, 1981. Provocative often fascinating look between the sheets of selected film stars.

Williams, Esther. *The Million Dollar Mermaid*. New York: Simon & Schuster, 1999. MGM Swimming star Williams' life story in and out of the pool.

Winters, Shelley. *Shelley II: The Middle of My Century*. New York: Simon & Schuster, 1989. A continuation of Winters' life and career in film, TV and stage.

Wlaschin, Ken. *The Illustrated Encyclopedia of the World's Great Movie Stars and Their Films*. London: Salamander Books, 1979. Wlaschin offers capsule reviews of stars and their best movies.

Wood, Lana. *Natalie: A Memoir by her Sister*. New York: Putnam's, 1984. A younger sibling offers insights on Nat's life and career.

Zolotow, Maurice. *Billy Wilder in Hollywood*. New York: Putnam, 1977. Zolotow profiles Wilder's directing career.

Glossary of principal actors, actresses, directors, writers and production staff

The number listed after the name refers to the individual movie chapter.

A

Adam West 57
Adolfo Celi 65
Agatha Christie 44
Akim Tamiroff 99
Alan Alda 76
Alan Carney 31
Alan Napier 39
Alan Parker 87
Alan Rafkin 94
Albert Brooks 18
Albert R. Broccoli 48
Alexander Scourby 11
Alexander Singer 85
Alfred Hitchcock 55, 84
Alice Ghostley 29
Alice Pearce 33
Alison Skipworth 82
Allen Garfield 45
Allison Hayes 6
Andie MacDowell 81
Andrea Marcovicci 28
Andrew Robinson 21
Andy Devine 31
Andy Granatelli 40

Angela Lansbury 17, 41
Angelica Huston 76
Angie Dickinson 52
Anita Bryant 58
Anita Morris 59
Anjanette Comer 39
Anjelica Huston 67
Ann Savage 19
Ann Sothern 2
Anna Q. Nilsson 62
Anne Bancroft 29
Anne Baxter 3
Anne Francis 73
Anne Shirley 89
Annette Funicello 9
Ann-Margret 14
Anthony Bushell 4
Aretha Franklin 12
Arlene Francis 47
Arnold Stand 31
Art Carney 1
Arthur O'Connell 60
Audrey Hepburn 15
Ava Gardner 43
Ayllene Gibbons 39

B

Barbara Bates 3
Barbara Baxley 5, 45
Barbara Harris 45
Barbara Lawrence 2
Barbara Nichols 39, 50
Barbara Pepper 33
Barbara Stanwyck 77, 79
Barrie Chase 31
Barry Sonnenfeld 54
Basil Rathbone 17
Beatrice Straight 46
Beaulah Bondi 90
Bernie Kopell 39
Bessie Love 48
Bette Davis 3
Bette Midler 59
Beverly Adams 60
Bill Murray 81
Bill Pullman 59
Bill Williams 69
Billie Burke 20
Billy Crystal 67
Billy Wilder 33, 47, 62, 77, 100
Blake Edwards 51
Bob Eubanks 58
Bob Fosse 50, 64
Bobbi Shaw 9
Bobby Rydell 14
Brad Davis 87
Brad Pitt 66
Brian Keith 80
Brigitte Helm 86
Bruce Lee 25

Bryan Forbes 92
Buck Henry 18, 24, 29
Buddy Hackett 31, 41
Burt Bacharach 13
Burt Kwouk 51
Burt Lancaster 53
Buster Keaton 9, 31, 62
Byron Haskin 57

C

Carroll O'Connor 37, 52
Cary Grant 15, 90
Cecil B. DeMille 62
Cecil Kellaway 27
Celeste Holm 3
Celeste Yarnall 13
Chaka Khan 12
Charles "Bud" Tingwell 44
Charles Brackett 62
Charles Grodin 42
Charles Kimbrough 28
Charles Lane 31
Charles Lang 11, 13, 15, 27, 32, 53
Charles Laughton 82, 100
Charles Napier 12
Charles Ruggles 82
Charlton Heston 99
Chick Chandler 31
Chita Rivera 64
Chris Elliott 81
Chris Penn 56
Christopher Guest 67
Christopher Isherwood 39
Christopher Knopf 26

Christopher McDonald 66
Christopher Reeves 63
Claire Bloom 30, 76
Claire Bloom 76
Claire Kelly 1, 39
Claire Trevor 89, 91
Clark Gable 43
Cliff Osmond 33
Cliff Robertson 85
Clint Eastwood 21
Conchata Ferrell 46
Connie Gilchrist 2, 32
Constance Bennett 32
Cora Witherspoon 8
Cristina Raines 45
Cy Coleman 64
Cyd Charisse 60

D

Daliah Lavi 60
Dalton Trumbo 37
Dan Aykroyd 12
Dana Andrews 39
Dana Carvey 67
Danny Aiello 28
Danny DeVito 59
Danny Kaye 17
Danny Kortchmar 67
Darryl F. Zanuck 3
Darryl Hickman 46
David Arkin 45
David Cronenberg 73
David Draper 38
David McCallum 4
David Miller 37

David O. Selznick 20
David Tomlinson 40
David Zucker 59
Dean Jagger 73
Dean Jones 40
Dean Martin 33, 60
Deborah Walley 9
Dennis Farina 42
Dennis Hopper 16
Dennis O'Keefe 91
Desi Arnaz 36
Desmond Llewelyn 48
Diahnne Abbott 34
Diana Rigg 48
Dianne Wiest 78
Dick Powell 89
Dick Sargent 94
Dick Shawn 31
Dick Van Dyke 14
Dinah Manoff 49
Don Knotts 31, 94
Don Siegel 21, 97
Donald Hamilton 60
Donald Sutherland 49
Donn Pearce 16
Dore Schary 69
Doris Day 50
Dorothy Fields 64
Dorothy McGuire 69
Dorothy Provine 31
Dr. Joyce Brothers 34
Dustin Hoffman 29
Dyan Cannon 13

E

Earl Holliman 53
Earl Wilson 9
Ed Begley, Jr. 24, 67
Ed Fury 27
Ed Harris 71
Ed Herlihy 34
Ed Sullivan 14
Eddie Foy, Jr. 50
Eddie Rochester Anderson 31
Edward Dmytryk 89
Edward G. Robinson 77
Elsa Lancaster 100
Ernest Borgnine 73
Ernest Gold 31
Ernest Laszlo 31
Ernest Lehman 70
Ernst Lubitsch 82
Ethan Coen 54
Ethel Merman 31
Evelyn Varden 7
Evelyn Waugh 39

F

Fabian 88
Fay Compton 30
Faye Dunaway 46
Federico Fellini 64
Felicia Farr 33
Felix Feist 98
Ferenc Molnár 47
Flora Robson 44
Florence Bates 2
Fran Drescher 67

Frances Dee 82
Françoise Dorléac 65
Frank Cady 7, 55
Frank Darabond 96
Frank Pierson 16
Frank Sinatra 41
Frankie Avalon 9
Franklin Pangborn 8
Franz Waxman 62
Fred Clark 62
Fred MacMurray 77
Frederick De Cordova 34
Fredric Lehne 49
Fredric March 79
Fritz Lang 11, 86

G

Gabriele Ferzetti 48
Garson Kanin 32
Gary Cooper 82
Gary Merrill 3
Geena Davis 66
Gena Rowlands 37
Gene Hackman 63
Gene Raymond 82
Gene Saks 75
George Abbott 50
George C. Scott 22
George Cukor 20, 32, 72
George Kennedy 15, 16, 37
George Lazenby 48
George Pollock 44
George Raft 82
George Roy Hill 61
George S. Kaufman 20

George Sanders 3
George Segal 70
George Sidney 14
George Stevens 90
Geraldine Chaplin 45
Gert Fröbe 23
Gina Lollobrigida 10, 74
Glenn Ford 11, 63
Gloria Grahame 11, 62
Glynis Johns 17
Goldie Hawn 23, 74
Gordon Jackson 95
Grace Kelly 43, 55
Grady Sutton 8
Greg Mullavy 13
Gregory Ratoff 3
Guy Madison 69, 80

H

H. Bruce Humberstone 82
H.B. Warner 62
Hal B. Wallis 53
Hal March 1
Harold Ramis 81
Harry Guardino 21
Harry Saltzman 48
Harry Shearer 67
Harvey Keitel 56, 66
Harvey Korman 38
Harvey Lembeck 9
Hedda Hopper 62
Helen Rose 43
Helen Slater 59
Henry Gibson 12, 45
Henry Jones 7

Henry Koster 88
Henry Mancini 15, 51
Henry Silva 41
Herbert Lom 51
Herman J. Mankiewicz 20
Herschel Bernardi 28
Hobart Cavanaugh 2
Holly Hunter 54
Honor Blackman 4
Horst Buchholz 47, 68
Horst Ebersberg 13
Howard Hessman 67
Howard K. Smith 45
Howard McNear 33, 36
Howard St. John 47
Howard W. Koch 41
Hubert de Givenchy 15
Hugh Marlowe 3
Hugh O'Brien 85, 97
Humphrey Bogart 10

I

I.A.L. Diamond 33, 47
Ian Fleming 48
Ilka Chase 32
Ilse Steppat 48
Inger Stevens 1
Ingrid Bergman 74
Irene Dunne 90
Iris Adrian 40

J

J. Lee Thompson 68
Jack Benny 1, 31
Jack Lemmon 32

Jack Nicholson 93
Jack Oakie 82
Jack Webb 62
Jackie Cooper 63
Jackie Joseph 1
James Brown 12
James Cagney 47
James Coburn 15, 39
James Cruze 82
James Dyrenforth 4
James Earl Jones 22
James Gregory 41, 60
James Mason 35, 72
James Stewart 55, 88, 97
Jamie Farr 39
Jan Sterling 27
Jane Downs 4
Janet Leigh 14, 41, 99
Jay Livingston 62
Jayne Mansfield 1
Jean Harlow 20
Jean Hersholt 20
Jean Louise 32
Jean Porter 69
Jeanette Nolan 11
Jeanne Crain 2
Jean-Paul Belmondo 65
Jeff Chandler 27
Jeff East 63
Jeff Goldblum 45
Jeffrey Lynn 2
Jennifer Jones 10
Jennifer Warren 61
Jenny Wright 5
Jerry Houser 61

Jerry Lewis 31, 34
Jerry Orbach 76
Jerry Siegel 63
Jerry Zucker 59
Jesse Pearson 14
Jesse White 7, 31
Jill Dixon 4
Jilly Rizzo 41
Jim Abrahams 59
Jim Backus 31
Jim Kelly 25
Jimmy Durante 31
Jo Collins 38
Jo Van Fleet 16
Joan Crawford 27
Joan Staley 94
Joan Tewkesbury 45
Jocelyn Brando 11
Jody McCrea 9
Joe DeRita 31
Joe E. Brown 31
Joe Flynn 40
Joe Pantoliano 42
Joe Shuster 63
Joel Coen 54
Joey Bishop 1
John Ashley 9
John Ashton 42
John Barrymore 20
John Belushi 12
John Boorman 52
John Cairney 4
John Candy 12
John Carradine 17
John Ericson 73

John Fieldler 33
John Ford 43
John Frankenheimer 41
John Gielgud 39
John Goodmon 54
John Hurt 87
John Huston 10
John Landis 12
John Lee Hooker 12
John McGiver 41
John McMartin 5, 64
John Mills 68
John Raitt 50
John Saxon 25, 32
John Sturges 73
John Vernon 21, 52
John Wayne 97
John Williams 63
Johnny Depp 78
Jonathan Winters 31, 39
Joseph E. Levine 29
Joseph L. Mankiewicz 2, 3
Joseph Pevney 27
Joshua Shelley 28
Judd Hirsch 49
Judge Reinhold 59
Judith Evelyn 27, 55
Judith Guest 49
Judy Garland 72
Judy Holliday 32
Julie Christie 45
Julie Garfield 28
Julie Harris 30
June Allyson 79

K

Karen Black 45
Karen Morley 20
Katharine Hepburn 53
Kim Novak 33, 80
Kim Stanley 92
Kirk Douglas 2, 37

L

Lalo Schifrin 16, 21, 25
Lana Turner 85
Larry Fine 31
Larry Hagman 63
Lauren Bacall 97
Laurence Harvey 41
Laurence Naismith 4, 43
Laurie Johnson 22, 68
Lee Grant 18, 74, 88
Lee Marvin 11, 26, 52, 73
Leo Gorcey 31
Leon Askin 47
Leonardo DiCaprio 93
Lesley-Anne Down 51
Leslie Parrish 41
Liberace 39
Lilo Pulver 47
Lily Tomlin 45
Linda Darnell 2
Linda Evans 9
Linda Harrison 1
Lindsay Crouse 61
Lionel Barrymore 20
Lionel Stander 39
Liza Minelli 34

407

Lloyd Bochner 52
Lloyd Bridges 53
Lloyd Corrigan 31
Lloyd Gough 28
Lois Maxwell 30, 35, 48
Lola Albright 38
Lou Brown 34
Louis Nye 1
Louise Glenn 31
Lucille Ball 1, 36
Lurene Tuttle 98

M

M. Emmet Walsh 49, 54
Madge Blake 36
Madlyn Rhue 31
Maggie Smith 95
Marc McClure 63
Margaret Leighton 39
Margaret Rutherford 44
Margot Kidder 63
Maria Schell 63
Marie Dressler 20
Marie Wilson 88
Marilyn Monroe 3
Mario Puzo 63
Marion Lorne 29
Marjorie Bennett 27
Marjorie Main 36
Mark Wahlberg 93
Marlene Dietrich 99, 100
Marlon Brando 63
Marsha Hunt 91
Martin Brest 42
Martin Goldsmith 19

Martin Landau 76
Martin Ransohoff 39
Martin Ritt 28
Martin Scorsese 34, 93
Martin Sheen 93
Martin West 38
Marvin Hamlisch 49
Marvin Kaplan 31
Mary Boland 82
Mary Tyler Moore 49
Mary Woronov 24
Matt Damon 93
Maureen O'Hara 88
Maureen Stapleton 14
Maxine Elliott Hicks 18
Maxwell Anderson 7
May Robson 82
Mel Blanc 33
Melvin Frank 17, 74
Mervyn LeRoy 7
Meryl Streep 18
Mia Farrow 76
Michael Caine 5
Michael Goodliffe 4
Michael Madsen 56, 66
Michael McKean 67
Michael Moore 58
Michael Murphy 28, 45
Michael Nader 9
Michael Ontkean 61
Michele Lee 40
Mickey Rooney 31
Mike Farrell 29
Mike Mazurki 31, 89
Mike Nichols 29, 70

Mildred Natwick 17
Milton Berle 31, 39
Moe Howard 31
Morgan Freeman 96
Murray Hamilton 29

N

Nancy Dowd 61
Nancy Kelly 7
Nancy Kovack 60
Nancy Olson 62
Natalie Schafer 27
Natalie Wood 13
Nathan Juran 6
Ned Beatty 45, 46, 63
Ned Glass 15, 40
Neil Simon 64
Nicolas Cage 54
Niven Busch 69
Norman Fell 29, 31
Norman Jewison 83
Norman Panama 17
Norman Taurog 82
Norman Z. McLeod 82

O

O. Henry 59
Omar Sharif 51
Orson Welles 99
Otto Kruger 89

P

Paddy Chayefsky 46
Pamela Tiffin 47
Pat Boone 58

Patricia McCormack 7
Patrick Macnee 67
Paul Bartel 24
Paul Benedict 67
Paul Douglas 2
Paul Fix 7
Paul Ford 31
Paul Lynde 9, 14
Paul Mantee 57
Paul Mazursky 13
Paul Newman 16, 61
Paul Reubens 12
Paul Shaffer 67
Paul Williams 39
Paula Kelly 64
Peter Bull 22
Peter Falk 31
Peter Finch 46
Peter Lawford 32, 74
Peter Lorre 10
Peter R. Hunt 48
Peter Riegert 5
Peter Sellers 22, 35, 51
Peter Whitney 11
Phil Karlson 60, 80
Phil Silvers 1, 31, 74
Philippe de Broca 65
Phillips Holmes 20
Phyllis Thaxter 63
Polly Bergen 1

Q

Quentin Tarantino 56
Quincy Jones 13

R

Ralph Waite 16
Randall "Tex" Cobb 54
Randy Quaid 87
Ray Charles 12
Ray Walston 33
Raymond Burr 55, 91
Reni Santoni 21
Reta Shaw 39, 50
Rex Reed 63
Ricardo Montalban 64
Richard Attenborough 92
Richard Bennett 82
Richard Brooks 23
Richard Burton 70
Richard Condon 41
Richard Donner 63
Richard Dreyfuss 29
Richard Johnson 30
Rick Lenz 74
Ridley Scott 66
Rip Torn 18
Rob Reiner 67
Robert Aldrich 26
Robert Altman 45
Robert Ayres 4
Robert Beltran 24
Robert Culp 13
Robert De Niro 34, 42
Robert Duvall 46
Robert Easton 39
Robert Mitchum 69
Robert Morley 10, 39, 44
Robert Morse 1, 39

Robert Redford 49
Robert Ryan 73
Robert Stephens 95
Robert Stevenson 40
Robert Webber 23, 60
Robert Wise 30, 79
Rod Steiger 39, 83
Roddy McDowall 38, 39
Roger C. Carmel 60
Ron Goodwin 44
Ron Howard 97
Ronald Allen 4
Ronald Neame 95
Ronald Reagan 58
Ronee Blakley 45
Russ Tamblyn 30
Ruta Lee 100
Ruth Gordon 38
Ruth Nelson 69
Ruth Roman 85, 98

S

Sandy Dennis 70
Sarah Douglas 63
Scott Brady 23
Scott Glenn 45
Selma Diamond 31
Senta Berger 60
Shelley Duvall 45
Shelley Hack 34
Shelley Winters 35, 74
Shemp Howard 8
Shirley Jackson 30
Shirley MacLaine 64
Sid Caesar 1, 31

Sidney Lumet 46
Sidney Poiter 83
Simon Oakland 26
Skip Homeier 94
Slim Pickens 22
Spencer Tracy 31, 73
Stanley Donen 15, 50
Stanley Kramer 22, 31, 35
Stella Stevens 60
Stephanie Powers 85
Stephen Roberts 82
Sterling Hayden 22
Sterling Holloway 31
Steve Buscemi 56
Steve Cochran 98
Steve Lawrence 12
Steven Spielberg 12
Stringer Davis 44
Strother Martin 16, 61
Stuart Rosenberg 16
Stubby Kaye 64
Sue Ane Langdon 1
Sue Lyon 35
Susan Sarandon 66
Susannah York 63
Swoosie Kurtz 5
Sylvia Fine 17

T

Tab Hunter 39
Tallulah Bankhead 84
Telly Savalas 48, 74
Terence Stamp 63
Terry Southern 39

Terry-Thomas 1, 31
Thelma Ritter 2, 3, 55
Tim Burton 78
Tim Robbins 46, 96
Tim Roth 56
Timothy Carey 9
Timothy Hutton 49
Tina Louise 60
Tom Neal 19
Toni Basil 64
Tony Randall 34
Tony Richardson 39
Tracy Reed 22
Trevor Howard 63
Trey Wilson 54
Truman Capote 10
Tuesday Weld 38
Twiggy Lawson 12
Tyrone Power 100

U

Una Merkel 8

V

Valerie Perrine 63
Vic Tayback 26
Victor Borge 34
Victor Buono 60
Victor Lundin 57
Viggo Mortensen 71
Vincent Price 78
Vincente Minnelli 36
Vladimir Nabokov 35

411

W

W.C. Fields 8, 82
Wallace Beery 20
Wally Cox 1
Walter Bernstein 28
Walter Brennan 73
Walter Lord 4
Walter Matthau 1, 15, 37, 74
Walter Pidgeon 79
Walter Slezak 84
Warren Beatty 23
Warren Oates 83
Wayne Rogers 16
Wendell Corey 53, 55
Wendy Barrie 32
Will Patton 5
William A. Seiter 82
William and Tania Rose 31
William Asher 9
William Bendix 84
William Daniels 29
William Demarest 31
William Holden 46, 62, 79
William Hopper 7
William Hurt 71
William Schallert 37
Winona Ryder 78
Woody Allen 76
Wynne Gibson 82

X, Y

Yaphet Kotto 42
Yvette Vickers 6

Z

Zasu Pitts 31
Zero Mostel 28
Zsa Zsa Gabor 99